The

CIRCUIT RIDER DISMOUNTS

A SOCIAL HISTORY OF
SOUTHERN METHODISM
1865 - 1900

A Da Capo Press Reprint Series

THE AMERICAN SCENE
Comments and Commentators

GENERAL EDITOR: WALLACE D. FARNHAM
University of Illinois

The
CIRCUIT RIDER DISMOUNTS

A SOCIAL HISTORY OF
SOUTHERN METHODISM
1865 - 1900

BY

HUNTER DICKINSON FARISH

DA CAPO PRESS • NEW YORK • 1969

A Da Capo Press Reprint Edition

This Da Capo Press edition of
The Circuit Rider Dismounts
is an unabridged republication of
the first edition published in Richmond,
Virginia, in 1938. It is reprinted from
a copy of that edition in the Oberlin
College Library.

Library of Congress Catalog Card Number 77-87534

Published by Da Capo Press
A Division of Plenum Publishing Corporation
227 West 17th Street
New York, N. Y. 10011

Manufactured in the United States of America

The Circuit Rider Dismounts

Landon Cabell Garland, Chancellor of Vanderbilt University

The

CIRCUIT RIDER DISMOUNTS

A SOCIAL HISTORY OF
SOUTHERN METHODISM
1865 - 1900

BY

HUNTER DICKINSON FARISH

Director, Department of Research and Record,
Colonial Williamsburg, Incorporated,
Sometime Instructor and Tutor in American History,
Harvard University

RICHMOND, VA.:
THE DIETZ PRESS
1938

Printed in the United States of America.

To the Memory

of

An Excellent Methodist
MARY STALLWORTH DICKINSON

PREFACE

THIS book is an account of the influence exerted by one of the great denominations upon social relations in the South during one of the most dramatic periods of Southern history. This period, from 1865 to 1900, was one in which religion played a vital rôle in Southern life. In the lives of a people recently disappointed in their fondest hopes and despairing of the future, a religion that could offer an "experience in grace" which would turn men's thoughts from the trials of this life to the contemplation of a future existence would naturally exert a profound influence. The Methodist Episcopal Church, South, moreover, was thoroughly awake to the unusual opportunities before it. The energy and zeal of the Church made it one of the most potent factors affecting social relations in the section from Lee's surrender to the end of the century.

The book first took form as a thesis written under the direction of Professor Arthur M. Schlesinger of Harvard University. To Professor Schlesinger I owe a profound debt of gratitude for his interest in my undertaking and for his penetrating criticism and advice at all stages of my work. His kindly encouragement was of much assistance. I am not less indebted to Professor Schlesinger's colleague, Professor Frederick Merk, who throughout my career as a graduate student was always ready to advise and encourage me. To these two great teachers I owe my serious interest in the study of American history. In this connection I would acknowledge the debt of gratitude due Professor Schlesinger's wife, Mrs. Elizabeth Bancroft Schlesinger, by myself and a host of other history students for the oases in our work provided by her gracious hospitality.

The investigation of the materials upon which the book is based necessitated extensive travel over a large part of the South. Until recently no systematic attempt was made to assemble the records and literature of Southern Methodism in central repositories. The task of locating such materials was rendered more difficult due to the fact that the central Publishing House at Nashville which for years served as an unofficial place of deposit had twice been destroyed by fire. It was frequently necessary to piece together materials in widely separated cities in order to obtain a continuous record. In the main the materials were found in the editorial offices of the *Advocates* in New Orleans, Nashville and Richmond, and in the libraries of such institutions as Vanderbilt University, Emory University, Wofford College, Gammon Theological School, Duke University, Randolph-Macon College and the Methodist Publishing House in Nashville. Many persons aided me in my search for these materials. Among these should be mentioned Dr. D. B. Raulins, the recent editor of the *New Orleans Christian Advocate,* Miss Bertha Childs, Librarian of the Publishing House at Nashville, Dr. D. D. Wallace of Wofford College, Dr. J. M. Rowland of the *Richmond Christian Advocate,* Dr. Paul Garber of Duke University, and Professor L. M. Thomas II, of Emory University. Dr. A. P. Shaw of New Orleans and Dr. Willis J. King of the Gammon Theological School were kind in making available to me the records of the Northern Church in the South. Numerous individuals who had known outstanding and colorful Methodist leaders of the period gave me interviews in which I gained much interesting information. Among these persons were Dean Wilbur J. Tillet of the Vanderbilt Theological School, Chancellor J. H. Kirkland of Vanderbilt University, Dr. George Beale of Nashville, Mrs. Mollie Shook of the Methodist Publishing House, Bishop Collins Denny of Richmond, Virginia, and President Robert E. Blackwell of Randolph-Macon College. To Professor Paul H. Buck of Harvard University, I am indebted for stimulating conversations regarding conditions in the Southern States during the period covered. I am especially indebted to Mrs. Janie McTyeire Baskervill of Bristol, Virginia, who proved herself a faithful correspondent in providing me with information about her husband, Dr. W. M. Baskervill, and her father, Bishop Holland N. McTyeire, and with many other interesting facts concerning Methodist communicants of the period. I wish to express my thanks also to Miss Margaret Lee Goodwin of the College of William and Mary, who made the index, and to Dr. Earl G. Swem, Librarian of the College of William and Mary who advised me in matters relating to the publication of the book.

H. D. F.

CONTENTS

LIST OF ILLUSTRATIONS

CHAPTER I

THE ORIGINS OF SOUTHERN METHODISM

"IF America is ever ruined," declared a well known lecturer two decades after the Civil War, "the Methodist Church will be to blame. For she is the strongest and most influential Church on the continent of America to-day, and can do more to turn back the tide of ruin than any other Church."[1] While perhaps an exaggerated estimate of the responsibility devolving upon the Methodists, this statement nevertheless serves to emphasize the important rôle played by Methodism in American life during the post-war period, and especially in the South where the Methodists constituted a considerably larger proportion of the church membership than they did in the nation at large and where, as will be seen, conditions were especially favorable to the exercise of Methodist influence.[2] In this book a study is made of the relation of Southern Methodism to social reform during the period from 1865 to 1900.

Until the year 1844 Episcopal Methodism in the South was an integral part of a unified American Methodism. Organically it was a part of the Methodist Episcopal Church in America. In 1844 there occurred a rift in that Church which divided it into two separate and distinct ecclesiastical organizations. Each of these organizations was, by compact, confined in its ecclesiastical jurisdiction to the territory of one of the two great sections of the country. In this way were brought into existence a Northern and a Southern Methodism in the United States. Each of the new ecclesiastical organizations was a coördinate branch of the Methodist Church in the United States, and each equally a co-heir to all

---

[1] The Reverend Joseph Cook of Boston, as reported in the *New Orleans Christian Advocate*, May 3, 1884.

[2] In the nation at large the Methodists in 1890 constituted approximately twenty-two per cent of the entire church membership. In the sixteen States and the District of Columbia which had constituted the late slaveholding territory they constituted approximately thirty-four per cent of the total membership. In the South below the border States the proportion was much larger. In the five States from North Carolina to Alabama it ranged between forty and fifty per cent. *Cf. Statistics of The . . . Eleventh Census*, Vol. XVI, pp. 38-47. *Cf.* also, Table of Statistics, Appendix A, p. i.

its past history and traditions. Thus the origins of Methodism in the South are to be traced in the rise of a unified American Methodism.

Methodism was brought to America when the Wesleyan movement was still in its infancy. The year 1739 is regarded as the date of the birth of the Wesleyan movement and but a few years elapsed after that time before individual members of the English Wesleyan societies emigrated to the American colonies. Among the first arriving in the colonies were several lay preachers who soon displayed zeal in the spreading of the new doctrines.[1] In 1766 Methodist societies were formed almost simultaneously in Maryland and in New York.[2] Three years later, in 1769, the first regularly commissioned ministers were sent out to the colonies by the leaders of the movement in England.[3] Within a few years more, as a result of the exertions of these early laborers in the field, Methodist societies had been established in various parts of the colonies. As yet, however, the system existed only in an inchoate state.

Under the leadership of Francis Asbury and other able men sent from England, the societies began to coalesce and there began a development towards an organic unity. The process was quickened by the outcome of the Revolution, which made desirable a separate leadership for American Methodists.[4] Early in 1784, John Wesley, bowing before the logic of the situation, and desiring to provide for the over-seas groups some form of government "suited to their exigencies," appointed Francis Asbury and Dr. Thomas Coke as joint "superintendents" over them.[5] The latter he ordained with his own hands as a bishop for the new

[1]McTyeire, Holland N., *A History of Methodism* (Nashville, 1884), pp. 236ff; Buckley, James M., *A History of Methodism in the United States* (American Church History Series, Vol. V, New York, 1898), pp. 97ff.

[2]*Idem.*

[3]Buckley, *op. cit.*, p. 121; McTyeire, *op. cit.*, p. 267.

[4]Wesley, himself, had been hostile to the cause of the colonies during the Revolution. His attitude was expressed in his "A Calm Address to our American Colonies", which was published in 1775. Because of Wesley's attitude all Methodists were regarded with suspicion by the colonists during the war. And all of the Methodist preachers except Asbury were driven from the colonies because of their Tory sympathies. *Cf.* Buckley, *op. cit.*, p. 158. *Cf.* also, McTyeire, *op. cit.*, pp. 290-292.

[5]Buckley, *op. cit.*, p. 235.

jurisdiction.[1] Thus while Wesley himself remained in the Established Church of England to his death and always recognized its episcopal jurisdiction, he authorized the formation of the American societies into an ecclesiastical connection entirely independent of that body.

Cut off from the Wesleyan movement in England, the American Methodists soon achieved unity in ecclesiastical organization. In December 1784 over sixty itinerant ministers, meeting in Baltimore at the call of Bishop Coke, formed the first General Conference of the Methodist Episcopal Church in America.[2] Other such conferences followed at intervals, until in 1808 a delegated General Conference adopted a constitution for the Church at large, and specified a regular delegated quadrennial General Conference for the future.[3]

The preservation of organic unity in American Methodism was favored in a number of ways. To a surprising degree, American Methodists have remained in cordial agreement on points of doctrine. But unity was hardly achieved before disintegrating forces were found to be at work. Divisions within the body of American Methodism have usually come, however, not as the result of disagreement over theological matters but rather over matters of ecclesiastical policy.[4]

The solution of these differences hinged on the broader problem of the proper scope and functions of a church of Christ.

---

[1] McTyeire, *op. cit.*, p. 342.

[2] *Ibid.*, p. 348.

[3] Buckley, *op. cit.*, pp. 317-337.

[4] Several divisions in the body of American Methodism that were of lasting importance occurred prior to the great division of the Church in 1844. The first of these took place in 1816 when the colored members of the Methodist societies in Philadelphia, aggrieved at the "unchristian conduct" accorded them by their white brethren and despairing of just treatment in the Church, withdrew from the Methodist Episcopal Church and founded a new ecclesiastical organization, the African Methodist Episcopal Church. Four years later, as a result of similar causes, the Negro Methodists in New York withdrew from the parent Church and established the African Methodist Episcopal Zion Church. *Cf.* McTyeire, *op. cit.*, pp. 563-566. In 1825 the Canadian Conference of the Church, at its own request and because of the difficulties under which it labored due to the foreign character of its bishops, was authorized by the General Conference to form a separate Canadian Church. *Cf.* McTyeire, *op. cit.*, pp. 574-575. In 1828 dissatisfaction with the strong Episcopal government of the Church, which had long been smouldering, led to a secession which resulted in the formation of the Methodist Protestant Church. *Cf.* McTyeire, *op. cit.*, pp. 573-575, 611.

Two theories had gradually developed. One held that the limits of the church's activities were definitely and distinctly defined by the Scriptures. According to this conception, the church and the secular world were separate spheres, and any intermeddling by one in the affairs of the other was to be condemned. Slavery, for instance, being recognized by the Scriptures as an institution subject to temporal authority, was a subject with which the church had nothing to do save to enforce the moral obligations growing out of the relationship. The question of the existence of slavery was a political question, and hence one with which the church must not meddle. The functions of the church, according to this view, were "divinely appointed" and therefore were to be found only in the plain words of the Holy Writ. Similarly it held that moral wrong—which would constitute a sin and therefore demand the interference of the church—was also in all instances specifically defined in the Scriptures.

The second theory, while nominally admitting that the scope of the church and its authority was fixed by the Bible, gave to the Scriptures a less strict interpretation. Its adherents tended to impose upon the church a broader "humanitarian" mission than the "Scriptural" mission advocated by the upholders of the first theory. They stood for a definition of moral evil or sin in the Scriptures by implication. Broadly speaking, it was the clash of these two opposing points of view which led to the great division of the church in 1844. The particular issue had to do with the question of the relation of the church to the institution of slavery.

During the earliest period the attitude of the Methodists on this question had been clearly defined. John Wesley, himself, had stigmatized slavery as a great evil, and the early Methodist preachers all seem to have been agreed on the subject. In 1784, when the Methodist Episcopal Church in America was formed, the organizing Conference adopted the General Rules which had been prepared by Wesley for the English societies.[1] Among these rules was one prohibiting "the buying or selling the bodies and

---

[1] *Cf. Minutes of the General Conference of 1784*, pp. 14-15; *cf.* also Sweet, William Warren, *The Methodist Episcopal Church and the Civil War* (Cincinnati, 1912), pp. 16-17.

souls of men, women, or children, with an intention to enslave them."[1] Moreover there was included in the conclusions of this Conference a sweeping indictment of the whole slavery system, and it was asserted that there must be found at once "some effectual method to extirpate this abomination from among us."[2] Since slavery had already crept into the Church, the Conference adopted rules requiring members who owned slaves in States where there was no legal obstacle to emancipation to provide for their gradual emancipation or to withdraw from the Church. If they refused to do so, they were to be expelled.[3] For some years these rules remained in force and were in a large measure complied with. For a few years, it appears, Methodist ministers boldly denounced slaveholding, and a number of slaves were freed by members of the societies.[4]

Nevertheless these rules met at once with opposition in the South, and the Church soon began to retreat from its well defined position of 1784.[5] With the change effected in the economic life of the South as a result of the invention of the cotton gin in 1793, the Church ceased to maintain an absolute condemnation of slavery on moral grounds.[6] Indeed, while the buying and selling of slaves was forbidden in its *Discipline* of 1786, nothing had been said of slaveholding.[7] In 1792 the Church receded still further. The law of 1786 was omitted from the *Discipline* and the only prohibition against slavery retained was that in the General Rules.[8] While from time to time the Church undertook to strengthen its position with regard to slavery, it was always with little success. By 1809 it had reached a point where it said nothing about slaveholding upon the part of individual members and only prohibited the election of slaveholders to official positions in States where emancipation was legally possible.[9] A few minor changes were made in the rules during the next few years,

---

[1] *Cf. Minutes of the General Conference of 1784*, pp. 14-15.
[2] *Idem.*
[3] *Idem.*
[4] Sweet, *op. cit.*, pp. 16-17.
[5] *Ibid.*, p. 17.
[6] *Cf.* Luccock, Halford E., and Hutchinson, Paul, *The Story of Methodism* (New York, 1926), pp. 340 ff.
[7] *Cf. Discipline of 1786*, p. 14.
[8] *Cf. Discipline*, 1792, p. 47; Sweet *op. cit.*, p. 17.
[9] *Journal of General Conference*, 1808, p. 211.

but from 1824 to 1860 nothing was said in its *Discipline* with regard to slaveholding by individual members, nor was slave-holding a bar to official position in States where emancipation was prohibited by law.[1] Since the Church no longer expressly prohibited slaveholding, its members might consistently claim that slavery, while it might become a great social evil, was not necessarily a moral evil or sin.

But the rise of the Abolition Movement during the Thirties soon made itself felt in the Church and resulted in a demand for a further definition of the attitude of the Church toward slavery. The agitation of the subject in the Church in the North, and especially in New England, increased rapidly and soon a number of Methodist Anti-slavery societies were formed.[2] It was during this period that the opposing theories with regard to the scope and functions of the church were first brought prominently before the communion and elaborated.

Anxious to preserve peace in the Connection, the authorities of the Church made it uncomfortable for those who kept the question alive. In the General Conference held at Cincinnati in 1836, numerous petitions were received from persons in the North asking for a restoration of the stricter rules on the subject of slavery that had formerly been in the *Discipline.* The General Conference replied by adopting a report condemning "modern abolitionism." It declared that it would be "inexpedient to make any change in our book of Discipline respecting slavery," and that "we deem it improper to further agitate the subject in the General Conference at present."[3] Moreover, when it was learned that two of the New England delegates to the Conference had taken part in the proceedings of an anti-slavery convention then being held in the city, resolutions were adopted censuring their conduct. These resolutions declared that the General Conference was "decidedly opposed to modern abolitionism, and wholly disclaim any right, wish or intention to interfere in the civil and political relation between master and slave."[4] The position of

---

[1]Matlack, L. C., *The Antislavery Struggle and Triumph in the Methodist Episcopal Church* (New York, 1881), pp. 71ff.

[2]*Ibid.,* pp. 87-89; Sweet, *op. cit.,* p. 20; Buckley, *op. cit.,* pp. 20-21. This early agitation appears to have been confined largely to New England.

[3]*Journal of General Conference,* 1836, p. 475.

[4]*Ibid.,* p. 447.

Methodism was further defined in a pastoral address issued by the bishops at that time. This paper exhorted the members of the Church to abstain from all abolition movements and urged them not to patronize any abolition publications.[1]

But "modern abolitionism" was not crushed out in the New England conferences, and trouble was soon experienced in other Northern conferences.[2] Within the next four years ministers were brought to trial in the Pittsburgh, the Erie, and in New York Conferences of the Church.[3] Young candidates were refused admission into the ministry because they advocated abolition. For ten years the Philadelphia Conference asked every candidate for admission, "Are you an abolitionist?" Unless the question were answered negatively admission was refused.[4] Despite such repressive measures Methodists in the North who favored abolition came with increasing frequency to assert that slavery was a great moral evil which the Church must use its influence to extirpate. These persons naturally espoused the latitudinarian theory of the scope and functions of the Church. In the South the opposing theory was soon asserted in various places. As early as 1837 the Georgia Annual Conference resolved that "*Whereas,* There is a clause in the Discipline of our Church which states that we are as much as ever convinced of the great evil of slavery; and *whereas,* the said clause has been perverted by some, and used in such manner as to produce the impression that the Methodist Episcopal Church believed slavery to be a moral evil; therefore, *Resolved,* That it is the sense of the Georgia Annual Conference that slavery as it exists in the United States is not a moral evil; *Resolved,* 2, That we view slavery as a civil and domestic institution, and one with which, as ministers of Christ, we can have nothing to do, further than to ameliorate the condition of the slave, by endeavoring to impart to him and his master the benign influence of Christ, and aiding both on their way to heaven."[5] The next year after the adoption of the above resolution the South Carolina Conference unanimously

[1]Sweet, *op. cit.,* pp. 20-21; McTyeire, *op. cit.,* p. 603.
[2]Matlack, *op. cit.,* pp. 112-120; Sweet, *op. cit.,* p. 21.
[3]McTyeire, *op. cit.,* p. 611; Sweet, *op. cit.,* p. 21.
[4]Sweet, *op. cit.,* p. 21.
[5]*Cf.* Matlack, *op. cit.,* pp. 103-104; Sweet, *op. cit.,* pp. 20-21.

adopted a resolution declaring that "We hold that the subject of slavery in these United States is not one proper for the action of the Church, but is exclusively appropriate to the civil authorities; therefore, *Resolved,* That this Conference will not intermeddle with it further than to express our regret that it has ever been introduced in any form, into any one of the judicatories of the Church."[1] Dr. William Capers, who had founded the first mission to the slaves, and who moved the adoption of this resolution, explained his position with regard to it. He said that "if slavery were a moral evil, that is, sinful, the Church would be bound to take cognizance of it; but our affirmation is that it is not a matter for her jurisdiction, and, of course, not sinful."[2]

When the General Conference of 1840 offered no relief to the abolitionists, the most uncompromising among them prepared to secede from the Church, and in 1842 they organized a new church, the Wesleyan Methodist Church, with non-slaveholding a condition of membership.[3] Despite the departure of the more unyielding abolitionists, the anti-slavery sentiment greatly increased in the Church in the North from 1840 to 1844. This was due in large measure to the fact that political agitation of the slavery question was forcing the issue upon the Church again. One move of this sort especially contributed to that end. In January 1842 a pro-slavery convention in Maryland recommended to the legislature that it adopt legislation which would result either in driving free Negroes from the State or in reducing them to slavery.[4] As many of the free Negroes in Maryland were members of the Methodist Episcopal Church, this action aroused the anger of many Methodists in the North and increased the anti-slavery feeling.[5] By 1844 sentiment in both New England and the South had so crystallized with regard to slavery that the leaders of the Church in each section felt compelled to disavow the attitude maintained toward the question in the other section. In the General Conference of 1844 a marked divergence was

---

[1]*Cf.* Matlack, *op. cit.,* p. 104; Sweet, *op. cit.,* pp. 20-21.
[2]Matlack, *op. cit.,* p. 104.
[3]Buckley, *op. cit.,* pp. 403-404; Sweet, *op. cit.,* p. 22.
[4]*Cf.* Norwood, John Nelson, *The Schism in the Methodist Episcopal Church, 1844* (Alfred, N. Y., 1923), pp. 55-56; Buckley, *op. cit.,* pp. 404-405; Sweet, *op. cit.,* p. 23.
[5]Norwood, *op. cit.,* p. 55.

apparent between the theories as to the scope and functions of the Church as held in the North and in the South, and especially as regards the attitude which the Church should maintain toward the institution of slavery.

During the preceding quadrennium James O. Andrew, of Georgia, one of the bishops of the Church, had, through inheritance, bequest, and marriage, become technically a slaveholder.[1] Although a resident of a State whose laws did not admit of emancipation, and therefore being guiltless of a breach of the law of the Church, Bishop Andrew was suspended in the performance of his episcopal functions, by the vote of a Northern majority in the Conference.[2] This action involved not only the question of the Church's attitude towards slavery and the question of its scope and authority, but also questions as to the nature and authority of the episcopal office and of the supremacy of the fundamental law of the Church. The deeper question at issue— that of the attitude which the Church should maintain toward slavery—was lost sight of during the discussions, while the legal, constitutional, and practical aspects of the immediate issue occupied the foreground. But the long days of debate served to increase the divergence between the North and the South with regard to the theories of the nature and functions of the church.

Northern speakers argued for an interpretation of the Scriptures and the *Discipline* which would make slavery a moral evil and demand the Church's interference. This conception was well expressed by the Reverend James B. Finley of Ohio, when he said: "It has been reiterated again and again that the Discipline of the Methodist Episcopal Church is conservative toward slavery. This assumption I most positively deny. Now, sir, how a grave body of ministers of the Methodist Episcopal Church can hold that this great moral evil can be justified and sanctioned by the Methodist Discipline, is a paradox to me. Any man who can say it is right for him to hold his fellow-being in bondage, and buy and sell him at pleasure, and *drive, whip, and half starve him,* and that

---

[1]Buckley, *op. cit.,* p. 412; McTyeire, *op. cit.,* p. 623. A thorough statement of his case is found in the letter addressed to the Committee on Episcopacy by Bishop Andrew and which is given in the proceedings of the Conference. Cf. *Journal of General Conference,* 1844, p. 73.
[2]*Journal of General Conference,* 1844, pp. 190-191.

this is connived at by the Methodist Church, I think must have
a queer view of the Methodist Church and her Discipline. I now
say in my place, before God, that whenever the Methodist
Episcopal Church shall sanction this doctrine, as much as I love
her, I will leave it and seek another community."[1]

The eloquent Dr. Lovick Pierce of Georgia, on the other hand,
declared that nothing had done so much harm in the South as
the intermeddling of the Methodist Episcopal Church with
slavery.[2] Dr. William A. Smith of Virginia, later the president
of Randolph-Macon College, complained that Methodists in the
North were placing Southern Methodists "in direct connection
with an abolition Church—a fanaticism, at once a grief to the
pious, and the scorn of the wicked, among whom we live."[3] The
theory of the scope and functions of the church most acceptable
among the Methodist leaders in the South was best expressed by
the Reverend Augustus Baldwin Longstreet of Georgia, already
nationally known as the author of his *Georgia Scenes,* and by Dr.
Smith of Virginia. Referring to a tendency manifest in the Conference to deal with matters beyond its cognizance, Longstreet
said to that body: "I have ever feared that you would begin to
presume upon your authority and power to operate reforms, not
by the simple, blessed principles of the Gospel, but by your ideas
of what will best conduce to the general interests of Methodism.
What is Methodism? If it be anything else than the pure gospel
religion, let Methodism go upon the winds far from my sight. . . .
Your rules about slavery have constituted you a high court of
judicature of the country, and made you judges of all the statute
laws of the States. . . . When Methodism first made its appearance among us, she found slavery overspreading the length and
breadth of the land. She entered her protest against it, and in
doing so she did more than our Saviour or any apostle ever did.
Our ideas of it now are not drawn up from any express precept,
but from a train of logical reasoning on general principles. The
Methodist Church went beyond anything that is found within the
lids of the Bible."[4] Dr. Smith warned the Conference that it was

---

[1]*Journal of General Conference,* 1844, p. 151.
[2]*Journal of General Conference,* 1844, p. 92; Buckley, *op. cit.,* p. 417.
[3]*Journal of General Conference,* 1844, pp. 143-144; Buckley, *op. cit.,* p. 422
[4]*Journal of General Conference,* 1844, p. 113.

fast losing its "conservative character and influence." He declared that "By years of departing from your plain duties which
appertain to you as a council of Christian ministers, to discuss and
settle the great and perplexing question of American slavery—*a
question which belongs exclusively to our national councils, and
one which statesmen of greatest distinction touch with a trembling
hand*—you are rendering yourselves odious to the political union.
Andrew's case and Harding's case are but incidents in this view
of the matter. No, sir, any interference whatever, on your part,
with this question, is insufferable! . . . the cause of Christ—the
cause of human salvation—demand that we concentrate our influence upon the one great object of spreading Scriptural holiness
over these lands—*the only legitimate object of ecclesiastical
legislation.*"[1] Bishop Joshua Soule, who, though a native of the
State of Maine, was soon to cast his lot with Southern Methodism,
elaborated further the position taken by these men. He declared
that "we are fully persuaded that, as a body of Christian ministers,
we shall accomplish the greatest good by directing our individual
and united efforts, in the spirit of the first teachers of Christianity
to bring both master and servant under the influence of that
Gospel which teaches the duty of every relation. . . . Do we aim
at the amelioration of the condition of the slave? How can we so
effectually accomplish this, in our calling as ministers of the
Gospel of Christ, as by employing our whole influence to bring
both him and his master to a saving knowledge of the grace of
God, and to a practical observance of those relative duties so
clearly prescribed in the writings of the inspired apostles."[2]

Upon the adoption of the resolution suspending Bishop
Andrew in the performance of his episcopal functions, the
Southern delegates drew up a "Declaration" protesting against
the proceeding as extrajudicial. They declared that this action,
together with the continued agitation of the slavery question in
the Church in the North and the frequent action on the subject
in the General Conference, would render a continuance of the
jurisdiction of the General Conference over the Southern conferences "inconsistent with the success of the ministry in the

---

[1] *Ibid.*, p. 144.
[2] *Ibid.*, p. 167.

slaveholding States."[1]   It was learned afterwards that, even before
the adoption of the resolution suspending Bishop Andrew, the
New England delegates had drawn up a paper declaring that it
would be necessary for their conferences to secede should Andrew
be left in the exercise of his functions.[2]   It was obvious that the
laity and public sentiment in both sections had forced the clergy
into an uncompromising position.

The dilemma was met by the parties agreeing upon a plan for
a "mutual and friendly division of the Church," to be acted on
if, and when, in the judgment of the Southern conferences, such
a division should prove necessary.   This Plan of Separation provided also for an equitable division of the property of the
Church.[3]   The following year the conferences in the slaveholding
States, through a convention of their representatives at Louisville,
took the steps necessary for the division of the Church.[4]   The
convention formed of the conferences represented in it a distinct
ecclesiastical organization, the Methodist Episcopal Church,
South.[5]   The Plan of Separation provided that all property which
had belonged to the undivided Methodist Episcopal Church and
which now lay within the limits of the Southern organization
should be forever free "from any claim set up on the part of the
Methodist Episcopal Church."[6]   Also, while the Plan made special
provision for allowing the conferences, circuits, and stations along
the border between the two connections to decide to which of
them they would adhere, it further specified that neither Church
should in the future undertake to extend its operations to the
territory embraced within the jurisdiction of the other.[7]   Thus in
1844 a distinctly Northern and a distinctly Southern Methodism
were created, the one inclining to a broad conception of the scope
and functions of the Church, the other adhering to a strictly
Scriptural definition.

---

[1] *Cf. ibid.*, pp. 200-212.
[2] McTyeire, *op. cit.*, p. 636. See also the account of this action given by the
Rev. James Porter, one of the New England delegates, in the *Methodist Quarterly Review*, vol. liii (April 1871), pp. 235-250.
[3] *Cf. Journal of General Conference*, 1844, pp. 217-219.
[4] McTyeire, *op. cit.*, pp. 641-643; Norwood, *op. cit.*, 82-101. The decision
in favor of separation was made by a vote of 95 to 2.
[5] McTyeire, *op. cit.*, pp. 642-643.
[6] *Cf. Journal of General Conference*, 1844, pp. 217-219.
[7] *Idem.*

From the time of the division in 1844 to the outbreak of the Civil War, a number of things served to increase the divergence between Northern and Southern Methodists as to the nature of the church, and to widen the breach between them. Although the *Discipline* of the Northern Church did not make non-slave-holding a positive test of membership until 1864, that body had little repose from anti-slavery agitation after its separation from the slaveholding conferences. The provision of the Plan of Separation which allowed conferences, circuits, and stations along the border to decide to which of the organizations they would adhere had resulted in the inclusion in the Northern body of a good number of persons living on slave territory.[1] It will be seen that other such persons were soon brought into its fold. It was soon apparent that the attitude of the border elements in the Northern Church toward the slavery question differed little from that of the Southern Church.[2] Realization of this fact led to a demand on the part of many members that the Church either withdraw entirely from slave territory or else adopt a rule entirely prohibiting slaveholding. This latter suggestion was vigorously opposed by the border members, and there was considerable talk prior to the General Conference of 1856 of a further division of the Church over the slavery issue.[3] Nevertheless an attempt to have the rule of the *Discipline* changed so as to make non-slaveholding a term of membership, was, after much debate, defeated in that Conference.[4] A similar attempt in the General Conference of 1860 resulted only in securing the insertion of a new rule in the *Discipline* that was merely advisory and admonitory.[5]

While the necessity of retaining its border conferences kept the

---

[1]*Cf.* Sweet, *op. cit.,* pp. 34-46; Matlack, *op. cit.,* pp. 190 ff.

[2]Sweet, *op. cit.,* pp. 34-38. In 1855 the *Northwestern Christian Advocate* warned the border elements of the Church that they were "on the road to the Church South by a philosophical necessity." *Cf.* Sweet, *op. cit.,* p. 35.

[3]*Ibid.,* p. 34.

[4]*Cf. Journal of General Conference,* 1856, pp. 112-129.

[5]This "New Rule" declared that "We believe that the buying, selling, or holding of human beings to be used as chattels, is contrary to the laws of God and nature, and inconsistent with the Golden Rule, and with that Rule of our Discipline which requires all who desire to continue among us 'to do no harm' and 'to avoid evil of every kind.' We therefore affectionately admonish all our preachers and people to keep themselves pure from this great evil, and to seek its extirpation by all lawful and Christian means." *Journal of General Conference,* 1860, p. 260.

Northern Church from making non-slaveholding a test of membership before the Civil War, abolitionist sentiment increased rapidly in its membership. The pulpit and press of the Northern Church sought energetically to influence the political contests that were being waged over the extension of slavery during the Fifties. Moreover its Annual Conferences often adopted reports on the slavery question with the purpose of influencing political action. During the debates over Clay's Compromise bill of 1850 the journals of the Methodist Episcopal Church took a strong stand against the measure.[1] The introduction into Congress of the Kansas-Nebraska Bill, which threatened the repeal of the compromise measure of 1820, evoked the strongest condemnation of the Methodist ministers and press in the North. While the debates were being carried on over that measure, the leading journal of the Northern Church declared that "To admit or tolerate slavery in the Territories, . . . justifies the reproaches of the civilized world upon the people of the United States."[2] *The Western Christian Advocate* of Cincinnati was rejoiced to point out that the religious press of the North was condemning the bill on "the general principles of morality and good faith." It declared that "We trust that every citizen who loves his country will use his influence against this bill."[3]

In the South the leaders of the Methodist Episcopal Church, South, desired to prevent all agitation of the slavery question. Holding to a strictly Scriptural mission for the church, they believed that it would be politically contaminated by an agitation of the subject. Hence the pulpit and press of the Southern Church decried all intermeddling on the part of the Church with the political contests over slavery. The sentiment in the Church with regard to these things was reflected in the changes that were made in its *Discipline*. Although the Southern body, in its *Discipline* in 1846 and 1850, retained the section on slavery as it was given in the *Discipline* of the undivided Church, no ruling on slavery appeared in the *Discipline* of 1854. Moreover, the General Conference of that year declared that the General Rule on slavery

---

[1] Sweet, *op. cit.*, pp. 42-43.
[2] *Christian Advocate and Journal*, March 2, 1854, as quoted in Sweet, *op. cit.*, p. 44.
[3] *The Western Christian Advocate*, as quoted in Sweet, *op. cit.*, p. 44.

had reference to the slave trade only.[1] In 1858 the General
Conference, by a vote of 140 to 8, decided to strike out entirely
the General Rule on slavery. It explained this action on the
ground that the rule was "ambiguous in phraseology, and liable
to be construed as antagonistic to the institution of slavery in
regard to which the Church has no right to meddle, except in
enjoining the duties of masters and servants as set forth in the
Holy Scriptures."[2] "Southern Methodist preachers, as such" were
warned by the press of the Church to "stick to their work of
great moral reform and allow the people who are competent to
attend to the affairs of the Nation and the State."[3]

Moreover the political agitation of the slavery question by the
Northern Methodists, with whom their relations were now
embittered, increased the dislike and dread of a "political church"
among Southern Methodists. "We most sincerely wish," declared
the editor of their chief journal when referring to recent discussions of the Kansas-Nebraska bill by the editor of the New York
Christian Advocate and Journal, "that he and all the religious
editors in this land would attend to their appropriate work, and
leave great National questions and State policies to the people as
citizens. . . . Better preach repentance and faith and holiness than
to meddle with the organization of States and Territories."[4]
Thus the position taken by the Northern Church had the effect
of confirming the Methodists of the South in their adherence to
a narrowly Scriptural definition of the scope of the Church and
in particular it inclined them to a narrow view of the functions
of the church where their exercise involved an interference with
political issues.

Meanwhile another series of differences had helped further to
widen the breach between the two sectional branches. Hardly
had the consent of the Northern majority been given to the
division of the Church in 1844 before the Plan of Separation was
denounced by a number of the journals and leaders of Methodism

---

[1]Elliot, Charles, *Southwestern Methodism* (Cincinnati, 1868), p. 109.
[2]*Ibid.,* p. 110.
[3]*Nashville and Louisville Christian Advocate,* as quoted in *Christian Advocate and Journal* and cited in Sweet, *op. cit.,* p. 45.
[4]*Nashville and Louisville Christian Advocate,* as quoted in *Christian Advocate and Journal* and cited in Sweet, *op. cit.,* p. 45.

in the North. They argued that the Plan had never been legally adopted and the Southern Methodists were branded as schismatics and secessionists.[1] As a result, the Northern Church not only refused to make the division of property as agreed upon, but in 1848 its General Conference repudiated the whole Plan, declaring it to be null and void. The Northern Church almost at once indicated a determination of returning to the South, by enlarging its conferences on slave territory wherever it found it practicable to do so. Because of its agitation of the slavery question, its attempts in this direction had met with small success prior to the Civil War.[2] In the General Conference of 1848 the Northern Church refused to establish fraternal relations with its sister Church of the South. It declined to receive officially Dr. Lovick Pierce of Georgia, who had been delegated by the first General Conference of the Southern Church to convey fraternal messages to the Northern body. The Conference declared that, as there were "serious questions and difficulties between the two bodies," it did not "consider it proper, at present, to enter into fraternal relations with the Methodist Episcopal Church, South."[3] The action of the Northern Conference was followed by an appeal to the courts on the part of the Southern Church for a vindication of its claims. Suits were entered in the United States Circuit Court for New York and for Ohio in 1849, for a division of the property of the Methodist Book Concern. While a decision was

---

[1]*Cf.* McTyeire, *op. cit.*, p. 648.

[2]McTyeire, *op. cit.*, pp. 660-663; Sweet, *op. cit.*, pp. 29-46; *Cf.* Pastoral Address in *Journal of General Conference*, 1856, pp. 199-200.

[3]The Conference of 1848 repudiated the Plan of Separation on the grounds that it was unconstitutional, its predecessor having lacked the authority to make such a division of the Church; that its adoption had been made dependent upon constitutional changes that were contingent upon the action of all of the Annual conferences and not merely upon the action of the conferences in the South; because of alleged violations of some of the provisions of the Plan with regard to the border. *Cf.* Report on the State of the Church in *Journal of General Conference*, 1848, pp. 154-164. In his *The Methodist Episcopal Church and the Civil War*, W. W. Sweet, in discussing the breach which developed between the two Churches and the reasons for the action of the Northern body, mentions merely the alleged violation of the compact as the cause of the repudiation. He says: "The Methodist Episcopal Church in the North claimed that the Church South had violated their agreement made in the General Conference of 1844, in that they proceeded immediately to organize a separate Church without waiting for the Annual Conferences in the South to vote upon the division, which action they claimed invalidated the whole plan of separation." *Cf.* Sweet, *op. cit.*, pp. 28-29.

given in favor of the Southern Church in the New York suit, the case in Ohio went adversely to it and was appealed to the Supreme Court of the United States. That body reversed the decision of the Ohio court and the Plan of Separation was upheld in all of its provisions.[1]

Disturbed as were its relations with its sister Church, the Methodist Episcopal Church, South, almost immediately after its organization in 1844 had entered upon a period of growth, internal peace, and financial prosperity that lasted to the outbreak of the Civil War. Preferring "the old gospel," the Southern Church was more evangelical than the Methodists in the North.[2] Revivals occurred almost every year in all parts of the Connection and the membership of the Church grew at a rapid rate. In 1846 the Methodist Episcopal Church, South, had 455,217 members; by 1860 the number had risen to 749,068.[3] Of this number practically one third—207,766 to be exact—consisted of Negroes.[4] Not only did the Southern Church convert to Christianity a larger number of slaves than any other Church in the section,[5] but it also brought a large proportion of the wealthy planter class into its fold.

Indeed, the Methodist Episcopal Church, South, had a special

---

[1]McTyeire, *op. cit.*, pp. 647-648.

[2]Luccock, Halford E., and Hutchinson, Paul, *op. cit.*, p. 341.

[3]*Cf.* McTyeire, *op. cit.*, p. 651.

[4]*Ibid.*, p. 670.

[5]Lewis G. Vander Velde in his *The Presbyterian Churches and the Federal Union,* p. 104, gives an estimate of the number of slaves in connection with Christian churches in 1861 as given in the *Education Journal* of Forsythe, Georgia, and quoted in the *Presbyterian Banner,* February 18, 1861. It is as follows:

Methodist Church, South	200,000
Methodist Church, North (Va. and Md.)	15,700
Missionary and Hard Shell Baptist	157,000
Old School Presbyterian Church	12,000
New School Presbyterian Church (supposed)	6,000
Cumberland Presbyterian Church	20,000
Protestant Episcopal Church	7,000
Campbellites, or Christian Churches	10,000
All other sects	20,000
Total	447,000

The *Educational Journal* estimated the number of colored church members at 465,000. Vander Velde points out that the difference of 18,000 from the total given above was presumably accounted for by free colored membership in the South.

claim upon the sympathy of the dominant social classes in the South, both because of the work it accomplished among the slaves and because of the attitude it had maintained toward the slavery question. The sympathy of the dominant planter elements for the Methodists of the South was clearly manifested at the time of the division of the Church in 1844. While plans were being matured for the division, political conventions representing the planting interests were held in various parts of the South in which warm expressions of sympathy for the Southern Methodists were adopted.[1] Such a convention, held on June 8, 1844, in Russell County, Alabama, a county containing a large number of wealthy planters, commended the Southern Methodists for the stand they had taken, and promised them the loyal support of every sect and denomination in the South.[2] Shortly after that time, the Governor of South Carolina, in his annual message to the legislature, animadverted upon the demotion of Bishop Andrew by the General Conference. He then commended the "becoming spirit" with which "patriotic Methodists of the South dissolved all connexion with" the Methodists of the North, and he declared that for their action the Methodists of the South were "entitled to lasting honor and gratitude" from the people of that section.[3]

Under such favorable auspices, and especially in the far South, the energy and zeal of the Methodist preachers had brought into the Southern Church a large number of wealthy planters. In the Black Belt plantation regions the Church was especially successful in reaching the cultivated and wealthy elements. Accounts survive of rich Methodist planters in South Alabama who drove to their churches in fine carriages, preceded by outriders.[4] Among these communicants were men of "princely liberality." Wealthy planters not infrequently built "chapels" or houses of worship for the Connection at their individual expense.[5] Charles Tait who

---

[1] Norwood, *op. cit.*, pp. 89-90; *Nile's Register*, vol. 66, pp. 312-313, 256, 288.
[2] *Nile's Register*, vol. 66, pp. 312-313.
[3] Norwood, *op. cit.*, p. 90.
[4] Communication of F. M. Grace in *Nashville Christian Advocate*, April 20, 1899; *Cf.* West, Anson, *A History of Methodism in Alabama* (Nashville, 1893), *passim*; Milburn, William Henry, *Ten Years of Preacher-Life* (New York, 1859), *passim*.
[5] Mrs. Robert L. Crawford, whose daughter, Mrs. Frank Crawford Vanderbilt later bestowed a great benefit on the Southern Church, built a chapel for the Connection near Mobile a short time before the Civil War. *Cf.* letter of

had large holdings in Monroe and Wilcox counties, in Alabama, was an outstanding communicant of this section. In addition to conducting his well-managed plantations Tait had a distinguished career as a statesman and jurist and his scientific and scholarly acquirements made him one of the most interesting men of his times. His piety and his devotion to Methodism are attested by his will in which he bequeathed to his heirs "forever in trust" the Chapel he had built "for the use and benefit of the Methodist Episcopal Church." Specifying the religious welfare of the slaves as a chief consideration, he expressed it as "my earnest request" that regular services be continued in this Chapel in order that "my black people, and those of the neighborhood" might "have the opportunity of religious instructions."[1] In Mississippi one of the planters most prominently identified with the Church was Edward McGehee, who owned a thousand slaves and numerous plantations. His fine estate, "Bowling Green," near Woodville in that State, was long a rendezvous for well known Methodist leaders.[2] Many of the planters who had been Episcopalians in Virginia and other older slave States were brought into the Methodist fold

---

January 18, 1938 to the author from Mrs. Janie McTyeire Baskervill of Bristol, Virginia.

[1]Charles Tait, a native of Virginia and a first cousin of Henry Clay, became while still a youth a tutor in Cokesbury College, Abingdon, Maryland. After reading law he removed to Georgia where he was made Rector of Richmond Academy at Augusta. Here he formed a close friendship with his associate, William H. Crawford, which lasted to the end of their lives. From 1803 to 1809 he was a judge of the Western Circuit of Georgia. During the next decade he represented Georgia in the United States Senate. Removing to Alabama in 1819, he was that year appointed by President Monroe the first Judge of the Federal Court in that State. In 1826 he retired to devote himself to his planting interests and to scientific study. Two years later he was offered, but declined, the mission to Great Britain. Shortly after settling in Alabama he made known to the scientific world the "Claiborne beds", one of the notable Eocene deposits of America. His scientific acquirements won membership for him in the American Philosophical Society in 1827 and election as a corresponding member of the Academy of Natural Sciences of Philadelphia in 1832. *Cf.* transcript of will of Charles Tait supplied the author by Mrs. Charlotte Vass Tait Beck of Camden, Alabama; *Dictionary of American Biography*, vol. XVIII, pp. 274-275.

[2]Hawkins, H. G., and Cain, G. B., "Historic Sites of Mississippi Methodism" (pamphlet, Vicksburg, 1934), p. 10; Letter to the author from the Reverend H. G. Hawkins, of Vicksburg, Feb. 12, 1935. McGehee, who was an elderly man during the Civil War, had settled near Woodville about 1808. He was outstanding in both the religious and industrial development in his world. He built the first railroad and the first cotton factory in the Southwest, and he loaned the money for the building of the Carondelet Street Methodist Church in New Orleans.

after their removal to the far South where they had gone in quest
of its rich cotton lands.[1]

Referring to the character of the membership in the Church
prior to the War, an unfriendly critic said in 1865: "In the more
Southern, and especially in the Gulf States, the Methodist Church
was the most popular and powerful in the country, and as such
comprised more of the culture, wealth and social influence of the
people than any other. This very class of the population was the
first to foment secession and rebellion, and has done more than
any other to keep it up until now. They were the slaveholders
and abolitionist haters of the first water. . . ."[2] The large element
of cultivation and wealth among the Southern Methodists during
the *ante-bellum* period was evidenced by a growing agitation that
took place within the denomination during the years preceding
the Civil War for "more culture in the pulpit to meet the demands of the pew."[3] One who had been familiar with·the
Methodist congregation at Tuscaloosa, Alabama, during the
Fifties, in after years said with regard to it: "Nor were the
Methodist families of those days less wealthy and elegant than
the members of other Churches. Our congregation in Tuskaloosa

---

[1] This statement is based on the author's personal knowledge of such families
in the South, upon conversations and correspondence with such men as Dr.
Peter A. Brannon, of the Alabama State Archives Department, Dr. Dunbar
Rowland, of the Mississippi Archives, and the Rev. H. G. Hawkins, of Vicksburg, Mississippi, a careful student of Methodist history in the Southwest, and
upon references in the records and literature of the Methodist Episcopal Church,
South. It is certain that in many of the Black Belt counties in the Gulf States
where there was a large number of wealthy planters, and where many Virginia
planters settled, the Protestant Episcopal Church gained almost no foothold.
In Dallas, Sumter, Marengo, and Montgomery, all Black Belt counties in
Alabama, that Church had, in 1860, altogether, only six houses of worship.
Cf. Statistics . . . of the Eighth Census, Misc. vol., p. 352. In Sumter, one of
the wealthiest counties in the State, it had not a single church edifice. It had in
the entire State at that time only thirty-three houses of worship. *Idem.*

[2] Letter of the Rev. George Lansing Taylor in New York *Christian Advocate,*
June 8, 1865. Bishop Clark in 1865 pointed out the fact that the Southern
Methodists in Tennessee had been largely drawn from this class, and he made
that the basis of objections to overtures being made to the Southern Church.
Cf. Letter of Bishop Clark in *Central Christian Advocate,* quoted in New York
Christian Advocate, Feb. 9, 1865. The Methodist journals in the North fre-
quently emphasized the fact that there was a large "aristocratic" element in
the Southern Church.

[3] Smith, George G., Jr., *The History of Methodism in Georgia and Florida,
1785 to 1865* (Macon, 1877), pp. 490-491. A good account of this agitation is
given in this work.

contained at that time such honored citizens as Gov. Collier, Judge Ormond, Dr. Guild, Mr. Harris, Mr. Vaughn, Alfred Battle, Dr. Garland, Prof. Benagh, the Owens and many others who were cultivated and refined people. They were both wealthy and liberal."[1] When in 1861 Civil War broke out the Methodist Episcopal Church, South, was not only the largest and financially the strongest Church in the South,[2] but it also had, as has been shown, a strong hold upon public sympathy in the section.

---

[1] It is interesting to note that there were included in this group the Governor of the State and Landon Cabell Garland, then president of the University of Alabama, and connected by blood with most of the distinguished and socially prominent families of Virginia.

[2] *Cf.* table of statistics, Appendix B, p. i.

CHAPTER II

O N the return of peace in 1865 the Methodist Episcopal
Church, South, faced a struggle for its very existence.
It found other organizations now sharing with it the
Methodist membership of the Southern States. With the changed
conditions brought about by the fortunes of the War the Northern
Church had seized the opportunity to effect an entrance into the
South and the methods by which it sought to accomplish its
purpose had injected a new element of bitterness into the re-
lations of the two Churches. The Northern Methodists were
conspicuously loyal to the Federal authorities during the War.
It was a boast of the Church that there was almost no element of
Copperheadism in its membership.[1] To its members the issue
had not remained merely one of the integrity of the Union, but
had taken on the aspect of a moral crusade against slavery.[2]

The ministry and members threw themselves with fervor into
the struggle.[3] In reply to an address of loyalty and sympathy
which had been made to him by the General Conference of the
Methodist Episcopal Church in 1864, President Lincoln, himself,
called attention to the fact that the Methodist Church had "sent
more soldiers to the field, more nurses to the hospital, and more
prayers to heaven than any."[4] Over five hundred of its ministers
served as chaplains in the United States armies, and four hundred
and fifty-eight were engaged in the service of the United States
Christian Commission, in which were combined a number of
agencies to promote the welfare of the soldier.[5] Methodist
ministers were active in promoting enlistments, and sometimes
the church itself was used for recruiting, thus imparting to the
undertaking a religious significance.[6] The six bishops of the

---

[1]Cf. *Journal of General Conference.* 1868, p. 565.
[2]Cf. Sweet, *op. cit.,* pp. 47-85.
[3]*Idem.*
[4]Cf. Luccock and Hutchinson, *op. cit.,* p. 356.
[5]Sweet, *op. cit.,* p. 139.
[6]*Ibid.,* p. 77.

Church who moved continually about the country, were untiring in their efforts to strengthen the morale of the North.[1] The Church press exerted an influence of far-reaching importance.[2] On the other hand, while no General Conference of the Southern Church occurred during the War, and, therefore, no official commitment was made by the Church to the Confederacy, the ministry and members of that body were in general no less ardent in their support of the Confederate Government.

Enjoying favor with the Federal authorities, the leaders of the Northern Church enlisted the aid of the Government in executing its purpose. In November 1863, one of its bishops, Edward R. Ames, induced the Secretary of War, Edwin M. Stanton, to issue an order directing the Generals commanding the Federal armies in the Departments of Missouri, the Tennessee, and the Gulf, to place "at the disposal of the Rev. Bishop Ames all houses of worship belonging to the Methodist Episcopal Church, South, in which a loyal minister, who has been appointed by a loyal Bishop of said Church does not officiate." The commanding officers were directed to give Bishop Ames "all the aid, countenance, and support practicable in the execution of his important mission."[3] Shortly afterwards similar orders directed that the churches of the Southern body in the Departments of North Carolina and Vir-

---

[1] *Ibid.*, pp. 142-157.
[2] *Ibid.*, pp. 111-132.
[3] *Cf.* McPherson, Edward, *The Political History of the United States . . . During the Great Rebellion* (Washington, 1865), p. 521, gives order:

WAR DEPARTMENT, ADJUTANT-GENERAL'S OFFICE
WASHINGTON, *November 30, 1862.*

To the Generals commanding the Departments of Missouri, the Tennessee, and the Gulf, and all Generals and Officers in the service of the United States in the above mentioned Departments:

You are hereby directed to place at the disposal of Rev. Bishop Ames all houses of worship belonging to the Methodist Episcopal Church, South, in which a loyal minister, who has been appointed by a loyal Bishop of said Church does not officiate.

It is a matter of great importance to the Government in its efforts to restore tranquility to the community and peace to the Nation, that Christian Ministers, should by example and precept, support and foster the loyal sentiment of the people.

Bishop Ames enjoys the entire confidence of this Department, and no doubt is entertained that all ministers who may be appointed by him will be entirely loyal. You are expected to give him all the aid, countenance, and support practicable in the execution of his important mission. You are also authorized and directed to furnish Bishop Ames and his clerk with transportation and

ginia be delivered to Bishop O. P. Parker of the Northern body, those of the Department of the South to Bishop E. S. Janes, and those in Kentucky and Tennessee to Bishop Matthew Simpson.[1] With the way thus opened for entering the South by the War Department, and with funds appropriated by its Board of Missions, the Church improved its opportunities.[2] Forcible possession was taken of many Southern Methodist pulpits. Churches were occupied in New Orleans, Charleston, Nashville, Memphis, Baton Rouge, Newbern, N. C., and other large towns.[3]

The Northern Methodists justified their course in occupying these pulpits on the ground that it was but a temporary expedient for aiding the Government in the task of putting down rebellion. One of the outstanding Northern missionaries who went to the South was Dr. John P. Newman, who afterwards became a bishop of his Church and an intimate friend and counsellor of President Grant. Early in 1864 the Reverend Newman was sent to New Orleans to take possession of the Methodist churches there.[4] Meeting with bitter hostility from the white Methodists of the city, and taunted with "church stealing," he attempted to defend his position. In an address to the public he declared: "We are denounced as Church robbers, are charged with having robbed the people of the South of their properties. My answer is: The right of Church property has never been disturbed as far as we are concerned. The General Government has seen fit to seize these Churches, but it has not conveyed their title to us. There has been no passing of deeds. We do not own an inch of this or any other Church in the South. . . . If there has been any robbing the accusation lies against the General Government. But the Govern-

---

subsistence when it can be done without prejudice to the service and will afford them courtesy, assistance, and protection.

BY ORDER OF THE SECRETARY OF WAR.

Cf. also, *Official Records of the Union and Confederate Armies* (Washington, 1891), vol. xxxiv, p. 311.

[1]*Official Records,* vol. xxxiv, p. 521; Sweet, *op. cit.,* p. 99.

[2]Some missionaries had been sent into the South as early as 1862. Cf. Simkins and Woody, *op. cit.,* p. 376. Early in 1864 the Board of Missions of the Church made an appropriation of $35,000 for work in the South. Its appropriations for Southern work were to be increasingly large for a number of years.

[3]Sweet, *op. cit.,* p. 96.

[4]*Ibid.,* p. 108; McPherson, *op. cit.,* pp. 523-524.

ment has committed no robbery. It was aware that these Churches
were occupied (so far as they were occupied at all) by congregations united by disloyal sympathies and by teachers disposed to
inculcate treason."[1] Despite disavowals of this kind, the representatives of the Northern body sought energetically to utilize
such points of vantage to gain a permanent foothold for their
Church in the South. When the General Conference met in the
Spring of 1864, steps were taken, at the instance of the bishops,
to follow up the advantages thus gained and looking to a further
penetration of the Southern States. The bishops urged upon the
Church the duty of entering the entire South.[2] To meet the
situation the Conference amended the constitution of the Missionary Society so as to provide for missions in the Southern
States, and it authorized the bishops to organize Annual Conferences in the South whenever, in their judgment, the interests of
their work should require it. The entire section was mapped out
for occupation.[3] Thus the Northern Church had already developed a following in a number of places in the South when
peace came. And it had made it apparent that it intended to
occupy the region independently of the Southern Church.

The action of the Methodist Episcopal Church in seizing the
Southern pulpits was the more surprising since it was not followed
to any comparable extent by the other Churches of the North. Although by 1861 there had occurred in every important Protestant
denomination represented in the South a division into Northern
and Southern branches, in no other denomination had there resulted so violent a break or such intense or long continued bitterness as in the Methodist. As the first of the great denominations
to split along sectional lines over the issue of slavery, the connectional character of Methodism had, as has been seen, led to complications of unusual bitterness. The break in the ranks of the
Presbyterians and Episcopalians, it must also be remembered, did
not occur until the eve of the Civil War.[4] The Protestant Episcopalians had taken no important part in the sectional dispute

---

[1]*Idem.*

[2]Luccock and Hutchinson, *Story of Methodism*, p. 343. Accounts of these
attempts are found in the Methodist journals of that time.

[3]*Journal of General Conference*, 1864, pp. 226, 253, 387-388.

[4]Vander Velde, *op. cit.*, pp. 3-17; Sweet, *op. cit.*, pp. 26-28.

before the Civil War. Moreover, while the division in the Baptist Church occurred the year following that of the Methodist, the independent or congregational form of government among the Baptists and Presbyterians enabled those denominations to escape much of the friction and bitterness that developed among the Methodists.[1] While somewhat after the orders were issued regarding the Methodist houses of worship similar orders were given respecting those of other important denominations, none of the other Churches of the North apppears to have taken advantage of the opportunity to occupy the buildings of a sister Church in anything like the same measure as the Methodists. Bishop Ames, according to the *Episcopal Methodist* of Baltimore, tried in vain to induce other denominations to pursue a similar course.[2] Bishop Whittingham of the Protestant Episcopal Church, that journal reported, rejected the Bishop's overture with contempt.[3] A leading Dutch Reformed minister, being in New Orleans at the time Bishop Ames was operating there, was urged, it was said, to seize the Presbyterian Church of the celebrated Dr. B. M. Palmer, but indignantly refused to do so.[4] In that city, where the Methodist seizures were most numerous, no other denomination appears to have availed itself of the opportunity of taking over a Southern church. In 1879 the editor of the New Orleans *Advocate* wrote with regard to the seizures that had been made there: "It is true, we believe, that similar orders were given respecting other Churches. Nevertheless the seizures were instigated by Bishop Ames and others of the Methodist Episcopal Church. To them belong the credit and glory of the measure, and they should be permitted to remain in possession of their laurels. No other Northern Church, so far as we have heard, ever stooped so low as to avail itself of ecclesiastical spoilation in New Orleans."[5]

Apart from the rivalry of the Methodist Episcopal Church and

---

[1]Sweet, *op. cit.*, pp. 26-27.
[2]*Idem*. Sweet gives in this place an account of the orders issued to the other denominations.
[3]*Episcopal Methodist* as quoted in Nashville *Christian Advocate*, Feb. 20, 1869.
[4]*Idem*.
[5]*New Orleans Christian Advocate*, August 14, 1879.

that of the Methodist Protestant Church, already at home in the region, the Southern Church found that the African Methodist Episcopal Church and the African Methodist Episcopal Zion Church had entered the South and were profiting by defections from its membership. Having been excluded from the section during slavery, both of these bodies came to the South during the War. As early as 1861 the African Methodist Episcopal Zion Church sent the Reverend James W. Hood, afterwards a bishop, to do missionary work in the South.[1] As soon as emancipation became an actuality, the other African body began preparations to send missionaries. The first African Methodist Episcopal congregation in the South was organized by the Reverend James Lynch at Savannah in 1865, and about the same time Daniel A. Payne, a minister who had been exiled thirty yeais before, returned to Charleston as a bishop, commissioned to establish the Church there.[2] The colored membership of the Southern Church was going over in droves to the African Churches and to the Methodist Episcopal Church. To many persons the continued existence of the Methodist Episcopal Church, South, seemed an impossibility.[3]

The internal condition of the Southern organization in 1865 was a cause for serious misgivings. Its administration was thoroughly disorganized. The *Christian Advocate* of New York in its issue of March 16, 1865, referring to the Southern Church, said: "So far as we can ascertain, most of its Conferences are virtually broken up, its circuit system is generally abandoned, its appointments without preachers to a great extent, and its local societies in utter confusion. Its Book Concern is overthrown; its Missionary Society, Sunday-School Union, and most of its other Church enterprises without power, if not without form. All has been submerged in the general wreck of the South." The bishops

---

[1] *Cf.* Sweet, William Warren, "Methodist Church Influence in Southern Politics", *The Mississippi Valley Historical Review*, Vol. I (March 1915), p. 549.

[2] Gaines, Wesley J., *African Methodism in the South; or Twenty-Five Years of Freedom* (Atlanta, 1890), p. 5; Simkins and Woody, *op. cit.*, p. 285.

[3] Smith, *op. cit.*, p. 410. In its issue of March 11, 1865, *The Methodist* of New York declared: "Southern Methodism may, in fact, be pronounced generally disorganized. The way is thus opened for the replanting of our standard throughout the South."

had been cut off from one another and could hold no consultation.[1] In 1865 the aged Bishop Joshua Soule in Tennessee had had no word from his colleagues for four years.[2] Owing to the fortunes of the War, there had been no effective episcopal supervision west of the Mississippi since the early days of the struggle.[3] The Texas Conference had seen no bishop for over four years.[4] There had been no session of the General Conference since 1858. New Orleans, which had been chosen as the seat of the Conference for 1862, was captured by the Federal army before the event took place, and the Conference was not held.[5] The Annual Conferences had met irregularly and had been but poorly attended.[6] In many regions where lines of communication had been broken up, the whole system of the itineracy was disrupted. The preachers had not known what to do.[7] Where it was possible to do so, most of them remained on their circuits and at their stations. A large number became chaplains in the Confederate army.[8] Others served as missionaries in the army, and a good number entered the army as commissioned officers or as privates. Some were forced to move as refugees before the advancing Federal forces.[9]

The institutions of the Church were equally disorganized. All of the weekly *Advocates* had suspended publication. Not one of the Church presses was at work. The central Publishing House of the denomination had been seized by the Federal military authorities at the time of the capture of Nashville in 1862. For the remainder of the War it was used as a United States printing office and for other purposes. Its material was confiscated and

---

[1] Smith, *op. cit.*, p. 490.
[2] *Cf.* letter of "Reynard" in New York *Christian Advocate*, July 20, 1865.
[3] *Journal of General Conference*, 1866, p. 3.
[4] Smith, *op. cit.*, p. 490.
[5] McTyeire, *op. cit.*, p. 664.
[6] *Idem.*
[7] Smith, *op. cit.*, p. 490.
[8] *Idem.*
[9] Although the records of the conferences of the Southern Church are incomplete for these years, W. W. Sweet has been able to show that there were at least 209 ministers who served as chaplains, and thirty-one who went as missionaries to the Confederate army. He has also listed 141 who served as regular soldiers and officers. *Cf.* Sweet, *op. cit.*. pp. 219-225.

the property badly damaged.[1] The Church had no official journalistic organ until this property was returned. The *Advocates*
which had served as the representatives of the Annual conferences
had fared little better. The *Southern Christian Advocate* of
Charleston, the official organ of the South Carolina Conference,
had been forced to flee before the Federal army, first to Augusta,
Georgia, and finally to Macon, where it suspended publication.[2]
The *Richmond Christian Advocate,* another very influential
journal, lost all of its visible assets in the fire which occurred in
Richmond at the time of its evacuation in 1865.[3]

Most of the educational institutions of the Church were also
in dire straits. With but few exceptions the colleges had been
forced to close their doors during the War. Their buildings had
stood abandoned and had deteriorated in value. Their endowments had been partially or totally swept away.[4] To nearly as
great an extent, the Missionary Society of the Church was crippled
in its operations. With the exception of the work done among
the soldiers, there had been a virtual suspension of operations
during the War. The Society was burdened with a large debt,
for which the Church at large felt responsible but which it would
be hard to meet.[5]

The actual loss of the denomination in church property was
large. Hundreds of church buildings had been destroyed. Many
had been burned; others had been dismantled to be used as
hospitals, warehouses, and stables. In a number of places within
the zone of actual war operations, handsome churches were
abandoned by their congregations and allowed to deteriorate. In
Knoxville, Tennessee, every one of the Methodist churches was
either destroyed or damaged by the use of the military.[6] Some
of the most important churches of the Connection were still in
the hands of the ministers of the Northern Church who had

---

[1]An idea of the damage done to this property is given by the fact that
thirty-three years later the Federal Government allowed $280,000 for damages
and rent on it, this being about fifty per cent of the amount claimed by the
Church. *Cf.* Du Bose, *op. cit.,* p. 190.

[2]Du Bose, *op. cit.,* p. 557.

[3]*Cf. Richmond Christian Advocate,* November 15, 1894.

[4]McTyeire, *op. cit.,* p. 664.

[5]Du Bose, *op. cit.,* pp. 14-15.

[6]*The Methodist,* January 14, 1865.

occupied them during the War, acting under the authority of the order secured by Bishop Ames from the Secretary of War.[1]

The loss of the Church in numbers had been great. By the end of the War there had been a decrease of thirty per cent of the membership of 1860.[2] The decline of white members during the war years amounted to slightly over one hundred and thirteen thousand.[3] The white membership of 1860, including 3,828 local preachers, was 542,489; in 1866 the number (including the same number of local preachers) was reduced to 429,233.[4] A colored membership of over two hundred thousand in 1860, was reported in 1866 as being only 78,742.[5]

More serious for the future of the Church than the losses in membership and property was the poverty which now hung like a pall over the Communion. Many of the most liberal patrons and supporters of the Church and its institutions were now reduced to abject need.[6] In common with other Southerners, the Methodists were entering upon a period of reconstruction and economic readjustment which made it appear that a grinding poverty would for years be their portion. In 1866 an editor of the Church declared that "in our Church, there was probably, before the war, more wealth than was ever held by the same number of professing Christians. . . . let us pray God to lead us into temptation no more. And it does seem sure enough, that in that direction we shall be gratified; that the field which we now cultivate will be noted henceforth for its poverty, as it was once remarkable for its wealth."[7]

Returning from the army, men of the South found their homes destroyed, their fields uncultivated and laid waste, their stock starving. Fields were without fences and streams without bridges. The implements of industry had been ruined or entirely destroyed. The basis of the only economic life with which the Southerner was familiar had been swept away. An indispensable considera-

---

[1] McTyeire, *op. cit.*, p. 673.
[2] Luccock and Hutchinson, *op. cit.*, p. 342.
[3] McTyeire, *op. cit.*, p. 670.
[4] *Idem.*
[5] The actual Negro membership in 1860 was 207,766. *Cf.* McTyeire, *op. cit.*, page 670.
[6] *Ibid.*, p. 664.
[7] *New Orleans Christian Advocate*, September 22, 1866.

tion was the role to be assigned to the ex-slave in the new order. And any solution of the question of the part which the freedman was to play was made difficult because every move of the Southerner was jealously watched from the outside by those who feared that the Negro would again be remanded to slavery and because the Negro himself was intent upon experiencing the full extent of his freedom. To add to the confusion, the question of the legal status of the Negro was soon made a political issue.

The loss of wealth invested in slaves resulting from their emancipation was by no means the only cause of economic distress in the South. During the years of greatest poverty the carpet-bag governments levied taxes which rose until they became confiscatory. For two or three years after the armies disbanded there were crop failures in many parts of the South, notably in Alabama and Georgia. Large districts were on the verge of starvation time and again, and were dependent upon food sent from more fortunate sections of the South and from the North. Scourges of yellow fever at times added to the distress.[1] In 1850, in the thirteen Southern States which were later to secede from the Union, the value of the taxable property, slaves not included, amounted to $2,498,790,267.[2] In 1880 the value of the taxable property in this same territory was only $2,370,923,269, showing a clear loss of approximately $117,000,000 in real and personal estate during a period of thirty years.[3] The Methodist Episcopal Church, South, shared in full measure the distress and privation of the times.[4]

It seemed that not only must the colleges and other institutions of the Church perish, but also the system of itineracy; this despite the fact that in many regions the people were unable to contribute to the support of a pastor. Even in more prosperous sections Methodist ministers sometimes appeared at their appointments on

[1]Frequent appeals were made in the Church papers for these sufferers.
[2]De Bow, J. D. B., *Statistical View . . . embracing a Compendium of the Seventh Census* (Washington, 1854), p. 190.
[3]*Report on . . . the Tenth Census* (Washington, 1884), Vol. 7, p. 25.
[4]An indication of the general poverty of its membership is reflected in an announcement of the *Raleigh Advocate* of its willingness to accept for subscriptions "corn, lard, fowls, butter, etc. . . . which would be equal to money if sent to us." Cf. *Raleigh Christian Advocate,* quoted in *Christian Advocate,* August 3, 1865.

large circuits on foot, and were commonly dressed in rough jeans. In 1866 the Reverend Enoch M. Marvin, of Missouri, attended the sessions of the General Conference of the Church at New Orleans in "brown jeans" until a number of his friends combined their resources to provide an "elegant broadcloth" for his ordination as a bishop.[1] Frequent admonitions were made to both pastors and the people regarding the necessity for sacrifice. In August 1865 the bishops of the Connection issued at Columbus, Georgia, a Pastoral Letter to the Church. "We beseech you, brethren," they said, "let no labor or sacrifice hinder you from preaching and hearing the Gospel. To accomplish this result your self-denials must be mutual and cheerful. . . . When and wherever, necessary, we commend to the preachers the example of the Apostle to the Gentiles in ministering to the Corinthians, 'working with your own hands.' "[2] The Tennessee Conference in a Pastoral Address in the same year declared that "the prospect is . . . we may suffer hunger and nakedness." "Where you cannot furnish your ministers with money, give them shelter, send them food; give them a portion of the products of your fields, your shops, your trade. By timely and united efforts the work of ministerial support may be made comparatively easy."[3]

Other conferences showed a like destitution.[4] In the Georgia and South Carolina Conferences many churches were unable to support their pastors, who were forced into secular pursuits.[5] They were "forced to field and bench and counter to get bread."[6] In South Carolina, during the four years following 1869, the average yearly income of the Methodist minister was still only about six hundred dollars.[7] The itinerant character of the work of the Methodist preacher required most of them to keep a horse and prevented their supplementing their salaries by farming or cultivating gardens.[8] They frequently found it necessary to sell

---

[1]McLean, Jno. H., *Reminiscences of Rev. Jno. H. McLean*, (Nashville), p. 142.

[2]*Journal of General Conference*, 1866, pp. 25-26.

[3]From an account in the scrap-book of the Reverend S. M. Cherry.

[4]Smith, *op. cit.*, pp. 490-492.

[5]*Ibid.*, p. 490; Simkins and Woody; *op. cit.*, p. 397.

[6]Smith, *op. cit.*, p. 490.

[7]Simkins and Woody, *op. cit.*, pp. 397-398.

[8]*Ibid.*, p. 397.

their horses in order to provide for their families.[1] Ministers were reported as unable to collect their salaries, and as "stripped of every earthly comfort."[2]

In 1860 there were in the Church 2,458 effective travelling preachers, and 266 candidates admitted on trial. By 1866 the number had dwindled to 2,116, with 114 admitted on trial. A further index to the general poverty in the Connection is given in the fact that while in 1860 the collection for superannuated preachers, and orphans and widows in all the conferences was $67,030, there could be collected in 1866 for these groups, now more needy than ever, only $35,444.[3]

A serious threat to the integrity of the Church existed in a belief held by many, even among its own members, that the Church was so thoroughly disorganized it would be impossible to reorganize it. Acting upon this assumption other religious groups were making overtures to its ministers and members for incorporation into their own bodies. Many were not disposed to offer resistance to such proposals. Some, losing hope for the future of the Church, looked with favor upon a proposed plan for a union of the Southern Methodists with the Protestant Episcopalians. In the confusion of the period, before the administration of the Church was again put in order, some of the Episcopalian leaders, especially among those of the North, sought to secure the Southern Methodists.[4] Some of the Methodists favored going over in a body to the Episcopalians, and were "coquetting" with a bishop of that denomination with regard to a union.[5] Others proposed to abandon the struggle and return to the Methodist Episcopal Church. A number of persons were reported as having gone to the Northern Church "under the impression that Southern Methodism was dead."[6] One of the Southern bishops felt constrained to enjoin upon his Connection the necessity for "saving the Church from the schismatic plans of the Northern Methodists and the subtle proselytism of the

---

[1] *Ibid.*, pp. 397-398.
[2] *Idem.*
[3] McTyeire, *op. cit.*, p. 665.
[4] *Cf.* Fleming, Walter L., *Civil War and Reconstruction in Alabama* (Cleveland, 1911), p. 637.
[5] Smith, *op. cit.*, pp. 490-492.
[6] *Nashville Christian Advocate*, April 4, 1867.

Episcopalians."[1]   The colored Methodists were leaving almost *en masse* for the Northern Church or for the African bodies.

The presence of the Federal troops for a number of years after the War proved unfavorable to the recovery of the Southern Church.   Federal military officials manifested a disposition to meddle in the affairs of the Church.   Its services were interfered with and its ministers told that they must pray for the President of the United States.[2]   On one occasion a Federal general issued an order interfering with the administration and discipline of the Church and threatening an officer of the Church with imprisonment should the order be disobeyed.[3]

The Methodist Episcopal Church, now seeking to gain a foothold everywhere in the South, maintained towards Southern Methodism an attitude which made its future appear extremely doubtful.   In conspicuous contrast to the distraction and poverty of the Methodist Episcopal Church, South, was the flourishing condition of that Church.   Always larger than its sister Church, the Northern Church at the beginning of the War had had 990,447 members.[4]   Although there had been a decrease of over sixty-eight thousand in its membership from 1860 to 1864, its losses had occurred chiefly in the conferences along the border.[5]   At the close of the War it had a membership of 929,259.[6]   Its contributions for missions actually increased sixty per cent during the years from 1860 to 1864.   In 1866, while the Southern Church was fighting for its very existence, the Northern Methodists celebrated the centenary of the establishing of Methodism in America with contributions of over eight millions of dollars. By 1884 its Church Extension Society, which had been established in 1864, had expended approximately two millions of dollars.[7]

This prosperity reflected the flush times that prevailed in the

---

[1]Smith, *op. cit.*, p. 492.

[2]Richardson, Simon Peter, *The Lights and Shadows of Itinerant Life: An Autobiography* (Nashville, 1901), p. 184; Fleming, *op. cit.*, p. 652; Jewell, Horace, *History of Methodism in Arkansas* (Little Rock, 1892), p. 211.

[3]New York *Christian Advocate*, September 28, 1865. This action was taken when the Rev. J. H. Caldwell of Georgia appealed to General Thomas against the authority of his presiding elder.

[4]Luccock and Hutchinson, *op. cit.*, p. 353.

[5]McTyeire, *op. cit.*, p. 664.

[6]Luccock and Hutchinson, *op. cit.*, p. 353.

[7]*Ibid.*, pp. 358-359.

North during the war years and the period of reconstruction. The rapid exploitation of the natural resources of that section, which took place with the progress of the industrial and agricultural revolutions, led to a vast increase of wealth. In 1850 the taxable property in the Northern States, including Maryland and Delaware in which the Southern Church was not represented, amounted to $3,473,000,000.[1] By 1880 its value had risen to $14,403,000,000.[2]

Of especial advantage to the Northern Church were the cordial relations which existed with the National Government. Because of the services it had performed and the influence it had exerted, favor was shown the Church in many ways by the Government. In the Summer of 1865 a bishop of the Northern Connection was reported as saying: "Of the *increase* of public wealth, which has been very large since the war began by reason of the stimulus given to manufactures and commerce, the increased prices of agricultural products, and the opening of new sources of wealth, such as oil wells, our Church has had her full share—perhaps more than her full share; for no Church has been more loyal than she, if any *as* patriotic, active and earnest in suppressing rebellion." "And when army contracts have been awarded, and grants to purchase cotton in rebellious States have been made, our people," he said, had not been forgotten or ignored. "Without unduly or dishonestly seeking to profit by the war, the attitude which our Church has borne to the Government has *naturally and necessarily* increased her wealth."[3] The favor shown the Church was of great advantage to it in pushing its forces into the South. Financial aid was sometimes furnished. During the years following the War the Government frequently contributed two hundred dollars, and in some instances five hundred, toward the erection of Methodist Episcopal houses of worship in the South. These gifts were made on the condition that such buildings might be used for Freedmen's Bureau schools when needed for that purpose.[4]

---

[1]De Bow, *op. cit.*, p. 190.
[2]*Report on . . . the Tenth Census*, vol. vii, p. 25.
[3]Speech of Bishop Edward Thompson before an educational convention at Delaware, Ohio, cited in *New Orleans Christian Advocate*, February 3, 1866.
[4]Matlack, L. C., "The Methodist Episcopal Church in the Southern States," *The Methodist Review*, Vol. LV (Jan., 1872), p. 105.

The return of peace and the removal of the exceptional conditions upon which the seizure of the Southern churches had been
justified made it necessary for the Methodist Episcopal Church to
define further its position with regard to the Southern organization. Its ministers in a number of places now refused, even at
the urgent request of the congregations, to yield the pulpits they
held. The Reverend John P. Newman, whose address was noted
above, thus refused to surrender the important Carondelet Street
Church in New Orleans. On an appeal to the Government at
Washington, orders were issued directing the return of such
churches to their legal owners.[1] In a number of instances they
were relinquished only after repeated orders from the Government and sometimes only when compelled by court orders to do
so. The Reverend Newman was ousted from the New Orleans
Church barely in time for its use in the sessions of the General
Conference in 1866.[2]

The attitude of many of the Northern missionaries in regard to
these churches was well expressed by the Reverend M. French,
who served as a chaplain in the Federal army and was stationed at
Charleston, South Carolina. In a letter to the New York *Christian
Advocate* in June 1865, in which he described conditions in
Charleston, he wrote: "The return of the paroled soldiers of the
rebel army has emboldened greatly the leading citizens. . . . In
Charleston, where they had cordially, or rather *labially,* received
a Northern missionary, they now, much encouraged by the return
of their former fellow-citizens and brethren, propose terms as to
the sittings of the people in the same sanctuary, dictate doctrines
to be taught, and assert the absolute necessity of the return and
settlement of former ministers, such, at least, as may have escaped
with their lives in fighting against the Union. 'Jeshurun is wax-
ing fat,' and gives fair warning that unless gratified, he intends
"to kick.' "[3] Numerous letters expressing such sentiments were
written by the missionaries to the Church papers in the North.
In refering to another of these communications from Charleston,
the editor of the New York *Advocate* declared: "Brother Lewis

---

[1] *Cf. Nashville Christian Advocate,* February 20, 1869.
[2] McTyeire, *op. cit.,* p. 673.
[3] Letter of M. French in New York *Christian Advocate,* June 1, 1865.

is having a *hard time* with 'the beasts of Ephesus,' such as Paul fought with. . . . We have very little to expect from the South Carolina Conference. . . . I fear the war is ending *too soon* and *too abruptly* for the good of the South or the peace of the Country."[1]

Indeed, to many Methodists of the North it had seemed that the restoration of unity in government must of necessity result in the reestablishment throughout the nation of a unified Methodism of unquestioned loyalty to the Federal Government. They held that territory recovered for the Union was also territory won for "loyal" Churches. To them it seemed that the reorganization of the Southern Connection would be an impossibility, and that even though that were not the case, the Government should not permit the continued existence of an institution which had, as they believed, played so large a part in the attempt to disrupt the Union.[2] Were the claims of such a Church to be respected in the reorganization and reconstruction which must be effected?

Not only did the Northern missionaries hold on to the pulpits they had occupied, but they began, in many instances, to assert a claim to them as of right.[3] Now, despite the decision of the

---

[1]Dr. Daniel Curry in New York *Christian Advocate,* May 18, 1865.

[2]The New York *Christian Advocate* in its issue of March 16, 1865, asserted the necessity for the Methodist Episcopal Church entering the South. The individual member of the Southern Church was to be kindly received and sheltered, but all of this was conditioned by a "first qualification." It declared that "one thing should be clearly understood, that if he does not avail himself of the amnesty act, we do not want him. . . . The flag of the republic and the flag of Methodism mus [sic] go forward over the revolted territory side by side." For similar statements see *ibid.,* Feb. 9, 1865. In its issue of Feb. 10, 1866, *The Methodist* of New York said: "Our Church has come out of the war with the consciousness of having taken a sublime part in crushing rebellion and destroying slavery, and she feels it to be an essential part of her calling to maintain hearty and loving loyalty to the United States Government . . ." Rev. E. N. Cobleigh, in the *Methodist Review,* Vol. LIV (Oct. 1871), when discussing the church property question in the Holston Conference of the Northern body, said: "There was a general feeling and belief among the laity . . . that as slavery was abolished—the original cause of the separation—hereafter there would be but one Methodist organization in the South, and that must be of necessity under the organization that had been loyal to the Government during the War."

[3]In a letter to the New York *Advocate* in 1867 the Reverend Thomas H. Pearne declared the intention of the Northern Methodist congregation in Knoxville, Tennessee, to hold on to the Church there. When a Methodist Episcopal Church had been organized in that city three years before, the house of worship of the Southern body, erected prior to 1844, had been turned over by the military authorities to the trustees of the Northern Church. The writer said

Supreme Court upholding the Plan of Separation and confirming
the title of such property to the Southern Church, the legal title
was declared to inhere in the Methodist Episcopal Church.[1] In
one or two regions, as in East Tennessee, where sentiment had
been divided during the War and there had been a large amount
of disaffection to the Confederacy, the Methodist Episcopal
Church had established itself with considerable ease in 1865.
As early as 1864, a portion of the Holston Conference, lying
chiefly in the mountainous sections of Tennessee and Virginia,
had withdrawn from the Southern Connection and set up a
"loyal" conference, because angered at an attempt which had been
made to coerce it politically. In 1866 this Conference adhered
to the Northern Church.[2] Two years before, at the convention in
which the new conference was organized, a resolution had been
adopted declaring that "the loyal members and ministers of the
Holston Conference are entitled in law to all the property belonging to said ecclesiastical organization and with the Divine
blessing we intend to claim and hold the same, and to rebuild

---

that "they have held it ever since, and they propose to hold it until proper
authority decides that we are not entitled to use it." New York *Christian
Advocate*, January 24, 1867.

[1]Little unfavorable comment appears to have been made in the Northern
Connection with regard to this policy. In April 1867 Dr. Daniel Curry, editor
of the New York *Advocate*, wrote that if "a local congregation in any part of
the South desires our ministers to occupy their house of worship and form a
society among them, they would certainly be justified in doing so; but in all
other cases it would be wisest to avoid all appearances of coveting what others
claim as their own." "We incline to think," he added, "that it will generally
be better for us to suffer the inconvenience of a lack of Church accommodations,
than to appear greedy of such acquisitions." New York *Christian Advocate*,
April 25, 1867.

In a communication to the New York *Advocate* in 1867 the Reverend W.
H. Pearne declared that if the property were to have been returned at all, it
should have been to the "loyal" portion of the membership of the Churches.
He regretted that the Northern bishops "by acquiescing in the order of the
Government," had allowed the return of some of the churches. This, he said,
had been a very unwise policy on their part, for it had led to a charge of
church stealing against the members of his church. New York *Christian
Advocate*, June 6, 1867. Several years later the editor of the *Central Christian
Advocate* declared that the Southern Church "is tenant by suffrance only. Our
right to this whole church property is indisputable; and though a quarter of a
century has passed without possession, that right is still intact and indefeasible,
and no competent, honest judge ever did or could render any other decision."
Central Christian Advocate, July 1, 1871.

[2]Price, R. N., *Holston Methodism* (Nashville, 1912), Vol. IV, p. 356.

the waste places of Zion."[1] Another resolution declared the purpose of the "loyal" members to transfer this property "at the earliest day practicable" to the Northern Church.[2] Thus in whole areas the houses of worship of the Southern organization were appropriated for the use of the Northern body and a claim of ownership asserted to them.

Of the position taken by many of the Northern missionaries one of their number later said: "No other denomination did just as we did in that matter. Temporary occupancy of pulpits in some instances occurred with others; but our ministers stood in the attitude of conquerors. They differed little in appearance from invaders. It did not so appear to them. It did so appear to the Church, South. It is so esteemed by them now. They may stigmatize it with unwonted severity we may think; but their ox is gored by our bull, and we do not feel the pain. We should remember that. . . . If our occupancy of the pulpits of the Church, South, had been only for the purpose of suffering the preaching of the word to deserted congregations, and, if on the return of their pastors and the restoration of peace, had been yielded up gracefully, it would have been better for the peace of the Methodist family. But such was not the case. Claims were set up to the property on questionable grounds. Possession was retained until compelled to relinquish by civil authority. . . . If this statement be correct, then our ecclesiastical relations with the Southern Methodists are, in this aspect, most unfortunate."[3]

The missionaries were particularly averse to surrendering those houses of worship which prior to the War had been used by blacks. The Northern Church was now winning over, in many instances, entire congregations of colored Methodists who sought to carry with them the property they had used. As the Negroes often had a large claim in equity on such buildings, much ill feeling resulted when they were withheld.[4]

Although a united Methodism was "the first thought in the

---

[1]*Cf.* Cobleigh, E. N., "Church Property Question in the South," *Methodist Review,* Vol. LIII (Oct. ,1871), pp. 614-641.

[2]*Idem.*

[3]Letter of L. C. Matlack in *Central Christian Advocate,* quoted in Nashville *Christian Advocate,* April 2, 1870.

[4]Although in many instances the slaves themselves had contributed largely to the construction of their churches, legal requirements had necessitated their

minds of Northern Christians," the thought was not that of an unconditional acceptance of Southern Methodists in the Methodist Episcopal Church, nor was it based on the idea of an organic reunion of the two great Methodist bodies of the country.[1] In 1864 the Northern bishops in their Episcopal Address had declared it to be their solemn judgment that none should be admitted to the Church "who are either slaveholders or tainted with treason."[2] The General Conference of that year provided that ministers of the Southern Church, in order to be admitted to the conferences of the Northern Connection, must not only comply with the requirements imposed upon ministers transferring from other Methodist bodies, but that they must give in addition "satisfactory assurances of their loyalty to the National Government, and hearty approval of the anti-slavery doctrine of our Church."[3] These additional requirements were retained for several years after the close of the Civil War.[4]

Despite all that had transpired, there is evidence to show that, if, during the first days after the War, the Northern Church had manifested a conciliatory and charitable spirit towards the Southern Methodists, a reconciliation might have been effected and a union consummated between the two bodies. The editor of the *Methodist Review* of the Northern Church declared in 1873 that "Immediately after the war and the reestablishment of the weeklies of the Church, South, we discovered in their columns a spirit of repentance, of conciliation and reunion, that inspired a just hope that, immediately appreciated and accepted, it might lead to early unification in Church as well as in State."[5] But the leading

---

being held for the congregations by white trustees. While the Negroes thus had, in equity, a just claim upon such property, the buildings, like all other denominational holdings, were the property of the Connection, and therefore subject to the disposition of the General Conference of the Church. In New Orleans, when an order was issued directing the return of the houses of worship to the Southern organization, an exception was made of the colored church buildings, and the Southern Church was forced to appeal a second time to the President to intervene. Cf. *New Orleans Christian Advocate*, February 3, 1866.

[1]Crooks, George R., *The Life of Bishop Matthew Simpson of the Methodist Episcopal Church* (New York, 1891), p. 433.

[2]*Journal of General Conference*, 1864, p. 279.

[3]*Ibid.*, p. 417.

[4]Cf. *Disciplines*, 1864-1869.

[5]Cf. *The Methodist Review*, Vol. IV (Jan., 1873), pp. 321-334. For similar statements see *Episcopal Methodist* as quoted in *Nashville Christian Advocate*,

officials and the press of the Northern body rapidly assumed an attitude of hostility towards the Southern organization and its members that gave the final blow to any prospect for a reunion of the two Churches at that time.[1] They did not for a moment leave in doubt their enmity to the Southern Church or their determination to impose stringent conditions upon the return of Southern Methodists to the Methodist Episcopal fold.

As early as January 1865 Bishop Clark of the Northern Connection had discussed in one of the Church papers the question of Methodist reorganization in the South. Referring to the members of McKendree Chapel of Nashville, in many respects the outstanding congregation of the Southern Church, he said: "It is well known that McKendree Chapel, by military order has been supplied by a loyal pastor from the old Methodist Church. It is due to truth and candor to say that comparatively few of the Methodists of the Church, South, in Nashville give any countenance to its occupancy, or even enter it as a place of worship. The great body of them are traitors, in fact, and have gone through the lines South. . . . The great proportion of those who have remained are traitors *at heart,* no matter how many times they may have taken the oath to secure amnesty privileges. These men look to the reorganization of the Southern Methodist Church. They will attempt reorganization at the earliest practicable period. *Then the issue will be joined.* A loyal Methodist Church will be set over against a disloyal. No pretense can disguise or conceal the plain issue. . . . And I mistake the tone of public sentiment, if the joining of the issue is not a prelude to a speedy and decisive triumph of that Christianity which is true to both God and Country." "What then," he added, "is our hope in Tennessee. It is not in winning back the old rotten and ruined aristocracy. . . . They are now too deeply steeped in treason for any medicine

---

February 20, 1869; *The Methodist,* March 8, 1865, and Pearne, *Sixty-One Years,* p. 313.

[1] W. W. Sweet in his *Methodist Episcopal Church and the Civil War,* p. 103, says that "the death blow at any attempt at a union of the Churches, North and South, at this time was struck by the bishops of the Methodist Church, South in a pastoral letter which they sent out over the South at the close of the war." The pastoral letter referred to was not issued until August 7, 1865, and months after the leaders and press of the Northern Church had demonstrated their unyielding hostility towards the Southern Methodists and their Church organization.

to work their cure. . . . To win such persons back to the bosom
of the Church is to plant in her very vitals the elements of moral
and spiritual weakness and ruin."[1]

Similar sentiments were soon expressed by leaders of the denomination in all parts of the North. The question of the reconstruction of Methodism in the South filled many communications to church papers during the first months. *The Methodist*
of New York, always more conciliatory than other Northern
Methodist journals, lost no time after the close of the War in
proposing that some terms of reunion be offered to the Southern
Church.[2] But its proposal drew forth expressions of disapproval
from prominent ministers in all directions. In a letter to the New
York *Christian Advocate*, Dr. Daniel Wise, an outstanding official
member, expressed sentiments that struck a responsive chord in
other quarters. "It is worse than folly," he declared, "to talk
of accepting their professions of loyalty and anti-slavery as conditions of their reception: Who believes in Southern professions?
. . . Those Southern Methodists have blood on their skirts, and
treason stains their reputation. They must purge themselves by
repentance, by sincere repudiation of their old sins, and by a
hearty desire to lead a new and better life."[3]

Even the liberal Dr. Abel Stevens, of New York, who was
foremost in advocating a lenient treatment of the Southern
Methodists, defended his course on the grounds of policy.[4] After
suggesting a plan of reunion based on a liberal financial aid to
the Southern conferences, he explained his position. "I am far
from being sanguine of its success," he said, "but its liberal offer
would do us credit in the sight of all the Christian world. And
do not its opponents perceive the moral vantage ground it would
secure us for the only other alternative policy we can follow in
the South? . . . If we can approach these multitudes after having
made a magnanimous and brotherly overture of reunion to the
leaders of the Church, South, the rejection of it by the latter will

---

[1]*Cf. Central Advocate*, quoted in New York *Christian Advocate*, February
9, 1865.
[2]Crooks, *Life of Simpson*, p. 146; *The Methodist*, March 25, 1865.
[3]New York *Christian Advocate*, June 8, 1865.
[4]In a letter to the New York *Advocate*, published in its issue of May 25,
1865, Dr. Stevens advocated immediate overtures of conciliation and reunion.
He urged that there be imposed no "fastidious, much less, invidious," tests.

give us a moral vindication and power of inestimable importance among these hosts."[1] To such men a general effort at reunion was an alternative policy to "a return to the South by efforts in detail" and each was to be "conducted in such a way as not to destroy the possibility of the other."[2] But there is little evidence that Stevens' appeal met with any considerable response among influential leaders of the Church. Typical of the antipathetic sentiments evoked by his proposal were those expressed by the Reverend R. M. Hatfield of Philadelphia. "I had hoped," he declared, "that we were done with war in the Church, but if these brethren propose to deal 'magnanimously' with these Methodist rebels, and allow them to slip back into the Church unchallenged, why we must buckle on the armor again."[3]

The press of the Northern Connection was not less outspoken against a magnanimous treatment of Southern Methodists. Not one of the official or independent Methodist weekly journals followed the lead of *The Methodist* in advocating reunion. All were quick to express disapproval.[4] Leadership in the opposition was assumed by the New York *Christian Advocate,* the most widely quoted and influential journal of the Church. Its editor, Dr. Daniel Curry, had, before the separation of 1844, been for several years a youthful member of the Georgia Conference, and he claimed to speak with authority on Southern questions.[5] Dr.

[1]Letter of Dr. Stevens in New York *Christian Advocate,* June 8, 1865.

[2]*The Methodist,* March 25, 1865.

[3]Letter of the Reverend Hatfield in New York *Christian Advocate,* June 8, 1865.

[4]The most widely read among the official journals were the *Christian Advocate* of New York; *The Western Christian Advocate* of Cincinnati; the *Northwestern Christian Advocate* of Chicago; and the *Central Christian Advocate* of St. Louis. Among the independent Methodist journals, *Zion's Herald and Wesleyan Journal* of Boston, and *The Methodist* of New York were most influential. The latter paper was founded just prior to the Civil War to oppose the radical anti-slavery stand taken by the *Christian Advocate* of New York, but when hostilities began it gave its support wholeheartedly to the National Government. With the return of peace it assumed at once a more conciliatory attitude towards Southern Methodists than any of the other journals. *Cf.* Thompson, *Life of Edward Thompson,* pp. 145-151, and Sweet, *op. cit.,* pp. 111-132. All of these papers continued to exert a wide influence to the end of the century save *The Methodist,* which ceased to exist early in the Eighties. All of these papers reported frequently on the developments in Southern Methodism and in Southern life.

[5]*Cf.* Buckley, *op. cit.,* p. 561.

Curry had, indeed, advocated a severe treatment of Southern Methodists prior to the proposal of *The Methodist*.

Early in February 1865 an editorial on "Church Reconstruction in Rebeldom," appeared in the New York *Advocate*. While admitting that in the future slavery would be a dead issue, the editor declared that while he was "decidedly inclined to agree with those who believe that our Church owes it to herself and to the people of the South to enter into and occupy all of that country, and that, too, independently of the pretensions of the local Methodism, which has become hopelessly debauched with pro-slaveryism and tainted with treason."[1] He expressed the opinion that there would be many whites, "who will reject the religious services of a set of men by whom they have been so fearfully misled" and that the freedmen would "not accept the services of those who so long desecrated the Gospel to the cause of their enslavement." "It is quite evident, therefore," he concluded, "that our Church must spread its institution all over the Southern States, and in doing so it will be compelled to sharply define its antagonism to the spurious local Methodism of the Country."

For months following the close of the War the tone of the paper became increasingly bitter towards the Southern Church. The leading editorials in almost every issue were devoted to a discussion of the situation. On various occasions the editor employed such expressions as "the treason-tainted Methodism of the South," "this degenerate, bastard Methodism" of the Southern Church, and "the Southern and apostate Church."[2] In an editorial in the issue of May 25, 1865, Dr. Curry said: "Southern Methodists are as a body precisely in that condition so aptly described in the Episcopal address of a year ago, as a disqualification to a reception among us: 'Slaveholders in heart and tainted with treason.' " He was convinced that "the less we have to do with the Methodist Episcopal Church *South*, or its ministry, as such, the better." If individuals would come out of that Church and purge themselves, they should be received by the Methodist

---

[1] New York *Christian Advocate*, February 9, 1865.
[2] *Cf.* New York *Christian Advocate*, May 25, 1865; *Ibid.*, May 11, 1865; *Ibid.*, April 25, 1867.

Episcopal Church. "Otherwise," he said, "we can have no fellowship with them." He warned the Church that a policy of "earnest and *antagonistic* aggression" must be adopted in the South or the field be abandoned. Referring to two Southern churchmen who had remained silent with regard to the issues of the War, and who were believed to be not unfriendly to the Union, he said: "As to the loyalty of Bishops Soule and Kavanaugh, we have not the least confidence in it or respect for it. We earnestly hope that our Church authorities will make no overtures to them or any of their class." In August 1865 the New York journal warned the Northern Church against postponing its work in the South while projects looking to reunion were being discussed. Such a delay, it argued, would enable the Southern Church to regain its position. It pointed out that nothing could be done toward such a consolidation for nearly three years. "Meanwhile," it said, "they may shrewdly hold out the olive branch to us and keep us in division and suspense, while they proceed to reorganize their dissolved conferences, reoccupy their abandoned stations, revive their publishing establishments— in a word regain their lost dominion. After a lapse of thirty months they will have got the start of us. . . ."[1]

The irreconcilable attitude of the New York *Advocate* became more pronounced with the passage of time, and it presently developed an outspoken policy of "disintegration and absorption" with regard to Southern Methodism. In October 1865 the *Advocate* declared that even though "the establishment of loyal anti-slavery Methodist Churches shall tend to 'disintegrate' churches of another kind, we may not therefore neglect to do our own duties."[2] On another occasion Dr. Curry urged his Church to carry to the South the Methodism of the early fathers. With that, he said, "we may not only maintain our place in the South, but certainly disintegrate the rival body, and absorb whatever of it shall be found worth preserving."[3] Looking back to

---

[1] *Ibid.*, August 31, 1865.
[2] *Ibid.*, October 5, 1865.
[3] *Ibid.*, April 25, 1867. In its issue of February 22, 1866, the New York *Advocate* said that "as with the State, so with the Church, the removal of slavery necessitates a disintegration and reconstruction. This general remark applies even more fully to Southern Methodism than to any other Southern

that time several years later, Dr. Curry asserted that the work of his Church in the South had become "of necessity, one of disintegration and absorption."[1]

Little disapproval was expressed by other official journals of the "disintegration and absorption" policy proclaimed by the "great official" of New York. They were, indeed, in most instances, hardly less antagonistic toward the South. Thus, the *Central Christian Advocate* of St. Louis, was firmly opposed to all conciliatory overtures. It urged pushing forward the enterprises of the Northern Church in the South and the absorption of Southern Methodism. Early in the Summer of 1865 it declared: "The only true theory of Methodist reconstruction is to *push on our work*. We must show the Southern people that we intend with our wealth and numbers, and culture and power, *to occupy the territory*, whether there be a Church South or not, and we shall soon find that we have restored the unity of Methodism in a manner honorable to ourselves, and eminently beneficial to all loyal men, black or white, in the Southern States. To this great work of evangelization let the Church address herself with all her powers. Other matters may remain in abeyance for a time, but this grand mission must be accomplished without delay. And we trust that the bishops will use every man within their reach, and every dollar appropriated for that purpose, to secure us in all the South the position and ascendancy to which we are entitled. Let them appeal to the Church and men and means will be cheerfully furnished to rear the pillars of an empire for Christ."[2]

About the same time *The Western Christian Advocate* at Cincinnati took a similar position. The *Western* deprecated all projects looking to a reunion of the Churches, and favored the plan for absorbing the Southern membership. It urged the cordial reception of all individuals who could subscribe to the requirements of the *Discipline* of the Church with regard to loyalty and slavery.[3]

---

ecclesiastical system, on account of its denominational unity and common pastorate."

[1]*Ibid.*, July 8, 1869.

[2]*Central Christian Advocate*, quoted in *The Methodist*, June 10, 1865.

[3]The position of *The Western Christian Advocate* is summarized in *The Methodist*, in its issue of June 10, 1865.

The influential *Northwestern Christian Advocate* of Chicago which was commended by *The Methodist* for its "fair-minded dealing" toward the Southern Methodists saw insurmountable obstacles to reunion.[1] Despite the fact that the "decided secessionist" bishops, Pierce and Paine, had at the close of the War issued manifestoes enjoining upon the Southern people loyalty to the National Government and "avoiding bitterness," the Chicago paper declared that such men would be an insuperable barrier to a reunion. "We would do everything honorable and righteous for a united Methodism," it said, "but we would hesitate long before consenting to do business under such men."[2]

Besides the unofficial *Methodist* among the weekly journals, only the *Methodist Review,* the official quarterly of the Connection, expressed any disapproval of the antagonistic policy that was advocated in the Northern journals. Dr. Whedon, editor of the *Review,* early in 1866 spoke a good word for the leaders of the Southern Church, pointing out that both they and the press of the Southern body had made professions of loyalty to the National Government. He urged that a charitable view be taken of their actions.[3] But his overture aroused a storm of hostile criticism.[4]

That the influence of the Church leaders and the press in

---

[1]*The Methodist,* June 10, 1865.

[2]*Northwestern Christian Advocate,* cited in *The Methodist,* June 17, 1865.

[3]It was the opinion of the editor that Bishop Andrew had "made deep and solemn confession," and that other Southern bishops were for reunion just after the surrender of Lee. *Cf. Methodist Review,* Vol. XLVIII (Jan., 1866), pp. 124-130.

[4]In referring to the hostile criticism occasioned by his overtures to the Southern Methodists, Dr. Whedon wrote in August 1866: "My own experience is, that with the efforts I, almost alone, have made with the Church, South, I have found that reasoning appeals, made as a reasonable Christian man, to Southern Methodism, do meet with a cheering response. Such a course, kindly and generally pursued for a few brief years, would, I believe, win them from the whole catalogue of sins Brother Wise arrays against them." Dr. Whedon then proceeded to warn his Church against a transgression of its mission in the South through "bad temper mistakenly supposed by us to be high moral sternness." "Thereby," he added, "we are destroying souls and ruining our country's peace." Letter of Dr. Whedon in reply to Dr. Wise in *Northwestern Christian Advocate,* as quoted in Nashville *Christian Advocate,* August 9, 1866. Dr. Whedon's article in the *Review* led to a prolonged discussion of the subject in the journals of the Northern Connection. On another occasion Dr. Whedon declared that he had "fought against the policy of disintegration and absorption" "at the risk of forfeiting our standing with our friends and the Church." *Cf. New Orleans Christian Advocate,* December 18, 1869.

advocating an antagonistic and aggressive policy towards Southern Methodism was not without effect in the Connection at large is evident from the action that was taken in some of the Annual conferences. Resolutions were passed calling on the Church to take vigorous measures to advance its work in the South, and defining the relation of the Church to the Methodism already there. In April 1865 the New England Conference adopted a long report on "the Reconstruction of the Church." It declared that the Church was called upon by "the Providence of God" to re-enter the South and plant there true principles in government, in morals, and in religion. The leaders of the Southern Church were "unworthy of renewing the land in righteousness which they have so long made less tolerable than Sodom and Gomorrah." Such men, the report declared, could not be trusted with the work of reunion, and would not accept overtures from the Northern Church even if it were so false to its principles as to make them. "We must," the report concluded, "first shun the temptation of making the former Church the center around which we shall reorganize our own."[1]

In October of the same year the West Wisconsin Conference put itself on record against reunion. It declared with regard to the Southern Church that "inasmuch as the ministers and members thereof, after instigating treason and rebellion, have not shown evidence of penitence and reformation . . . to receive them back with the *animus* and spirit which led to treason and rebellion, would be countenancing sin, and tend to the impurity of the Church."[2]

Shocked by the announced policy of "disintegration and absorption," Southern Methodists did not long remain in a mood favorable to the infrequent suggestions for reunion that were made at first. The South Carolina Conference in 1865 declared that such a suggestion after twenty years of "ecclesiastical warfare," even though urged by assurances of advantage to the Southern Church, "falls on cautious ears." "*Timeo Danaos, et dona ferentes*—

---

[1] This report was officially published in the New York *Christian Advocate* of April 27, 1865.

[2] *Cf.* New York *Christian Advocate*, October 12, 1865. Dr. Curry commended this resolution as the "sensible and Christian view."

'We fear the Greeks, even when they offer presents.' "[1] Such utterances were taken as a cause of offense in the North and made the occasion for bitter accusations.

To many persons in the Northern Connection, however, the sectional scope which their Church still retained seemed a matter of reproach. Feeling that the restored national unity should be supported by a "loyal" Methodism extending to all parts of the nation, they ardently desired to nationalize the Church by bringing into its fold a large Southern membership. That desire, nevertheless, did not prevent such persons from viewing the Southern Church and the position of the Southern people from a sectional standpoint. They felt that anything which prevented the acceptance. of the terms offered in the North was wicked.[2]

They were disposed to see in the unwillingness to entertain proposals for reunion evidence of a rebellious spirit, and in the determination to rebuild the Southern Church, an indication of disaffection to the national government.[3] In an editorial on "How to Treat the South," in September 1865, the editor of the New York *Advocate* declared that the ecclesiastical bodies of the South "sullenly refuse to hear of conciliation." "Can there be any other conceivable reason," he asked, "than that these rebellious priests still hope for 'something to turn up,' something that may re-

---

[1]*Cf.* Pastoral Address of South Carolina Conference, given in Shipp, *History of Methodism in South Carolina*, p. 5.

[2]"That they should not affiliate and ultimately become harmonious," declared a writer of the period in referring to the two Churches, "can only be the result of some great wickedness." *Cf.* Anon., "The Two Methodisms, North and South", *Quarterly Review*, Vol. XLVIII (April 1866), p. 278.

[3]The Southern Methodist press repelled with indignation the charges of disloyalty that were made against the Church. The *Episcopal Methodist* of Baltimore, declared that there is "a studied and persistent attempt made by the Northern religious journals to impress the public mind with the conviction that the Methodist Episcopal Church, South, in the maintenance of its independent ecclesiastical organization is disloyal to the Government." "The Southern Methodist Church today is more thoroughly loyal to the Government, more to be trusted, than the Northern Methodist Church. We are tired of strife and excitement. We intend to seek peace and pursue it. Our oaths have been taken in good faith, and we intend to keep them; and 'as much as in us lies,' we intend to live in peace with all men. We 'pray for all those in authority, that we may live quiet and peaceable lives in all godliness and honesty.' These avowals and pledges have been given to the Government, and we shall sacredly observe them; and in due time, we shall prove our fidelity and trustworthiness." *Cf. Episcopal Methodist*, October 11, 1865, cited in *Methodist Quarterly Review*, Vol. XLVIII (Jan. 1866), p. 126. The editor of the Nashville *Christian Advocate*, referring to such charges, said: "When it is intimated that

inaugurate the defeated cause of the South?"[1]   A few months later one of the missionaries in the South wrote to the New York *Christian Advocate:* "I am at a loss to account for the inveterate rancor cherished and manifested by adherents of the M. E. Church, *South,* towards us, except on the theory that they have not yet been divested of the hope and purpose to reestablish slavery, and to make treason not only respectable but successful."[2]

Even *The Methodist,* the fairest-minded of all the Northern journals on the subject,[3] adopted such an attitude on occasion. When the Southern bishops in their Pastoral Address issued at Columbus, Georgia, in August 1865, asserted the necessity for the continued existence of the Southern organization, *The Methodist* saw in their action only a design to foster treason against the Government. Individual members of the group had earlier issued separate manifestoes enjoining loyalty and submission to the Government,[4] and in the Pastoral Address the bishops again counselled peaceful acceptance of the situation "as citizens of a

---

the Church, South, refuses to recognize the North,—refuses to fraternize with the North, rejecting all overtures for Christian intercourse, and Church fellowship, and that this is a sign of disaffection to the Government of the United States, indicative of a rebellious spirit, the reader will be able to appreciate such insinuations. It is all for effect—all to make the impression on the minds of good people that we of the South are influenced by a bitter spirit of opposition, and that the sin of schism lies at our door."

[1] New York *Christian Advocate,* September 7, 1865.

[2] Letter of Thomas H. Pearne in *Christian Advocate,* April 26, 1866.

[3] The editor of the Nashville *Advocate,* in its issue of May 25, 1875, said that *The Methodist* "has drawn upon itself an almost incessant attack from the *Advocate* family of the Northern Church on account of its supposed friendliness to us."

[4] In a letter published in the Atlanta *Intelligencer* of July 25, 1865, Bishop Pierce said: "Accepting the issues of the war as the will of God in reference to the unity of the nation, and the government, let us all lead a quiet and peaceable life in all godliness and honesty. Do not leave your loyalty in doubt by unmanly repinings—by querulous complaint, or by refusing the terms of offered amnesty. Qualify yourselves for the duties of citizenship—for the speedy restoration of civil government. Let us seek to repair the desolations of the land by a prompt and vigorous industry, and prevent the further demoralization of society by multiplied works of faith and love." *Intelligencer,* quoted in *The Methodist,* August 12, 1865. Bishop Paine urged the ministers under his control to "use their influence, both publicly and privately, for the promotion of peace and quietness among all classes, and especially among the ministers and members of the Methodist Episcopal Church, South." *Cf. Methodist Quarterly Review,* Vol. XLVIII (Jan. 1866), p. 125.

common country," and called upon their flocks "to pray for all that are in authority."[1]

Despite these deliverances The *Methodist* now charged the Southern bishops with disloyalty. "Hating freedom and Union as much as they dare," it said, "they will not consort with us. This, stripped of its disguises, is the meaning of their manifesto. . . . It is clear that these Southern leaders have learned no wisdom from the past; that they cherish with fondness the souvenirs of the rebellion; that they are determined to foster in the minds of their flocks the opinions and the spirit which led to rebellion. Loyal men will indignantly ask for what end this is done? Is it their design to make the Southern Methodist Episcopal Church the nursery of future treasons and future outbreaks against the authority of the Union?" The bishops, this journal declared, had in their Address, "written the death warrant of Southern Methodism." They had had an offer of oblivion of the past made to them, but henceforth they would be "known and read of us all."[2]

The position assumed by the Methodist Episcopal Church in the South was the more remarkable in that no other Northern Church on the return of peace sought to occupy the section in the same way that it did. None of them entered the South in all of its departments and agencies as did the Methodist Church. The unique character of the Methodist occupation was emphasized by one of the leading ministers of the Northern Church in 1884. In a communication to the New York *Christian Advocate* Dr. Abel Stevens pointed out that the Church was exerting an influence in the section not only through the school, as was largely true of the other Northern bodies, but also through the pulpit and the press; that it had gone there "in its completeness of aims and agencies." He said: "It was almost peculiar in this respect, for nearly all other Northern Churches have arrived at but partial work in the South. The Congregationalists for example, have next to ourselves done most for the great field, but it has been chiefly educational work. They have built about two hundred churches there. The Presbyterians and Baptists have erected even fewer churches, though active in education; but the Methodist

---

[1] *Cf.* Pastoral Address in *Appendix* of *Journal of General Conference*, 1866.
[2] *The Methodist*, September 9, 1865.

Episcopal Church has built no less than 3,385 since 1864, 'each of which represents about a hundred communicants added to the Church since that date.' "[1] Dr. Stevens also pointed out that it had recently been estimated by one of the outstanding missionaries in the field that all the other Northern Churches together had not built more than a hundred churches among the Southern whites, whereas the Methodist had erected 1,540 houses of worship for white congregations.[2]

Although the Congregationalists, Baptists, Presbyterians, and other religious groups of the North put forth considerable effort in the field for the uplift of the Negro, the work of these bodies was in no small measure supplementary to that of local Churches. In no other denomination was there any considerable agitation for the disintegration and absorption of a sister Church in the South.[3] Although the Protestant Episcopal Church alone among the Churches which had been divided by the sectional dispute effected a reunion before the end of the century, whatever subversive influences were exerted by other Churches were directed at the Negro membership of the Southern bodies. In no other denomination than the Methodist did the activity of Northern missionaries result in the detachment of a large membership from a Southern body with its subsequent transfer to a Church of the same faith in the North.[4]

Although perplexed by the situation confronting them and uncertain at first as to whether their organization could survive, the leaders of the Southern Church quickly resolved that it must live, and they soon showed no less determination, than did their co-religionists of the North, to make their Church a vital influence in the life of the Southern people. The first indication of this determination appeared as early as June 1865 in the form of the "Palmyra Manifesto." This document was the outgrowth of a "movement for the deliverance" of the Church, led by the Reverend Andrew Monroe, a patriarch of the denomination in

---

[1] New York *Christian Advocate*, April 3, 1884.
[2] This estimate was made by the Reverend J. C. Hartzell at New Orleans.
[3] Vander Velde, *op. cit.*, pp. 49ff; Simkins and Woody, *op. cit.*, pp. 375. 381; Fleming, *op. cit.*, pp. 639-646; Mohler, Mark, "The Episcopal Church and National Reconciliation", *Political Science Quarterly*, Vol. XLI (Dec. 1926), pp. 567-596.
[4] Vander Velde, *op. cit.*, p. 104; Fleming, *op. cit.*, p. 645.

Missouri.[1] He issued a call for a meeting of the preachers and official members of the Southern Church within the bounds of the Missouri Conference at Palmyra on the twenty-second day of June, 1865. The call was made as general as the times would allow, and chiefly through private correspondence.[2] Twenty-four preachers and about a dozen laymen responded. This body of men adopted a paper setting forth the necessity for the continued existence of the Southern Church. In form, it was a report of a Committee on the State of the Church, but in effect it was a sort of manifesto against those who wished to absorb Southern Methodism.

The report, a very long one, announced the judgment of the leaders that they considered the maintenance of a separate and independent ecclesiastical organization "of paramount importance and our imperative duty."[3] The reasons for this were "many and numerous." After reciting the differences between the two bodies since the time of their separation, the report declared that to affirm that all these differences had been swept away with the institution of slavery must be the result of ignorance or of a desire to mislead the public. Besides, for the Southern Methodists to go into the Methodist Episcopal or any other Church would be "to admit the charge that with the institution of slavery we stand or fall."[4] Further reasons were then enumerated for the unwillingness to be absorbed by Northern Methodism. Referring to the Northern overtures for reunion, the report declared: "The only consolidation or reconstruction they would accept would be that we turn over to them our Church property and interests and influence; yield the whole field; confess that we have been wrong; indorse the politics of their Church as a condition of membership; and become political hucksters instead of Gospel ministers; then even our motives would be suspected, and we looked upon with contempt for our cowardly truckling to party and power."[5] The leaders asserted that their flocks had been consulted as far as

---

[1]Lewis, W. H., *The History of Methodism in Missouri for a Decade of Years from 1860 to 1870* (Nashville, 1890), p. 173.
[2]*Idem.*
[3]*Ibid.*, p. 175.
[4]*Ibid.*, p. 176.
[5]*Ibid.*, p. 177.

practicable, and that they demanded with "great unanimity" the maintenance of the Church organization.[1]

The Manifesto closed in the following words: "It is, therefore, due to the great mass of the people who oppose the prostitution of the pulpit to political purposes, it is due to our large membership who have been converted and gathered into the fold of Christ under our ministry, and who love our Church doctrines and discipline too fondly to seek any other fold now—it is due every principle of self-respect and ecclesiastical propriety that we maintain with firm reliance upon the help of the Great Head of the Church, our organization without embarrassment or compromise."[2]

The Palmyra Manifesto came as a breath of life to the Southern Church.[3] Its message was carried quickly throughout the South and its effect on the tone and spirit of the Church everywhere was instantaneous. The *Episcopal Methodist* of Richmond, Virginia, declared that in that State and the Carolinas it was "like life from the dead."[4] It gave courage and confidence to Methodists in all parts of the South, and the evidence indicates that it had a large influence in shaping the policy of the bishops and other leaders of the Church with regard to the future.[5]

There were soon reverberations to the call from Palmyra. A month after the Manifesto was issued, Bishop Pierce in Georgia published a letter in which he declared that, after much reflection, "my deliberate judgment is, that our true policy is to maintain our present organization."[6] Within another month the policy proclaimed at Palmyra received further recognition when it was definitely adopted by the bishops of the Church in the Pastoral Address which they issued at Columbus, Georgia.

In this address the bishops discussed the whole situation with which the Southern Church was confronted. After enjoining

---

[1]*Ibid.*, p. 178.
[2]*Idem.*
[3]There is no mention of the influence exerted by the Palmyra Manifesto in the standard histories of Methodism.
[4]*Episcopal Methodist,* quoted in Lewis, *Methodism in Missouri,* p. 178.
[5]According to Lewis, *Methodism in Missouri,* pp. 178-179, both Bishop Kavanaugh and Bishop Marvin reported that the Manifesto exerted a large influence on the spirit and policy of the Church.
[6]Letter of Bishop George F. Pierce in Atlanta *Intelligencer,* July 26, 1865, as quoted in *The Methodist,* August 12, 1865.

loyalty to the Government and a charitable treatment of the Negro membership in the Communion, they turned to the subject of the relations between the two Methodisms. The question of reconstruction or reunion had, they declared, within the past few months, been brought prominently before the public by the denominational journals and the published addresses and resolutions of the ministers and members of the Northern Connection. This fact made it incumbent upon them to explain their own position. To this end they reviewed the history of their relations with the Northern Church from the time of the separation in 1844, and explained that the abolition of slavery had in no way affected the questions concerning slavery which had been in dispute at the time of the division. Nor, they added, were the differences over slavery the only ones, or the only principal source of disagreement. Then dwelling upon the difference in spirit which animated the two groups, they declared: "While testifying with pleasure to the nobler conduct and sentiments of many brethren among them, we must express, with regret, our apprehension that a large proportion, if not a majority of Northern Methodists have become incurably radical. They teach for doctrine the commandments of men. They preach another Gospel. They have incorporated social dogmas and political tests into their Church creeds. They have gone on to impose conditions upon discipleship that Christ did not impose. Their pulpits are perverted to agitations and questions not healthful to personal piety, but promotive of political and ecclesiastical discord, rather than those ends for which the Church of the Lord Jesus Christ was instituted."[1] This statement clearly indicated the acceptance by the Southern Methodists of a "Scriptural" mission of the Church as contrasted with the broader conception of that mission which had come to be accepted in the Northern Church.

The bishops declared that without such a change in the tone and temper of Northern Methodism as they saw no immediate prospect of, they could "anticipate no good result from even entertaining the subject of reunion with them."[2] "Let us abide in our own lot," they said, "and be true to our calling, doing

---

[1]*Cf.* Appendix to *Journal of General Conference,* 1866, pp. 25-28.
[2]*Ibid.,* p. 28.

what we can to spread scriptural holiness through these lands, and to oppose the tide of fanaticism which threatens their overthrow."[1] In conclusion, they alluded to the conduct of the representatives of the Northern Church in appropriating and claiming the property of the Southern Church, and they warned the Church of a systematic attempt, already inaugurated by the Northern body, "to disturb, and, if possible, disintegrate and then absorb our membership individually."[2]

After it was apparent that the Southern leaders were reassembling their flocks and reviving their institutions, and despite the obstacles to any friendly intercourse between the two Churches, certain leaders of Northern Methodism were disposed to ignore such obstacles and began to press upon the Southern Church proposals for reunion which were, under the circumstances, both ill-timed and ill-advised. Notwithstanding the fact that the Northern Church was unwilling to recognize the validity of the Plan of Separation and sent no fraternal greetings to the Southern body during the General Conference at New Orleans in 1866, two of the Northern Annual Conferences made overtures looking to reunion to that Conference.[3] In responding to these overtures the Southern Church made it clear that it was unwilling to treat for union under such conditions.[4] Other independent and local

---

[1] *Idem.*

[2] The bishops deplored, "not less as loyal citizens than as Christian men," the effect which such "an unprovoked conflict" must have in stirring up the popular feelings. They disclaimed all responsibility for "the passions that will be aroused and the influences that will be generated, more or less, not only in the membership of both communions, but in those who sympathize with them."

[3] *Journal of General Conference,* 1866, pp. 26-27; Neely, *op. cit.,* pp. 149-152; New York *Christian Advocate,* April 12, 1866; *ibid.,* May 10, 1866. The New York East Conference sent a telegram to the Conference bearing its salutations and inviting the Conference to join in a concert of prayer on April 8, 1866, for the restoration of national peace and concord and the restoration "of Christian love and sympathy" between the Churches. Shortly afterwards the New York Conference invited the General Conference to appoint a commission to treat on the subject of reunion with a similar body to be appointed by the Northern bishops.

[4] Although the General Conference returned the salutations of the two Northern bodies and cordially agreed to unite in prayer for "the very desirable object expressed in the fraternal message" of the New York East Conference, it declared that it could not consent "to appoint commissioners on the plan proposed."

ventures looking to the establishment of fraternal relations and reunion were no more successful.[1]

Undaunted by the outcome of such negotiations, the bishops of the Northern Church in 1869 made an overture for reunion to the Southern bishops.[2] Two of their number were deputed to confer with the Southern leaders during their annual meeting at St. Louis with regard to "the propriety, practicability, and methods of reunion."[3] In a communication to the Southern churchmen the Northern bishops expressed the opinion that as the division of Churches of "like faith and order" had been productive of evil, their union would be productive of good and that since slavery had been the chief cause of separation, the main obstacle to the restoration of unity had been removed. They declared that it would be a reproach to the leaders of the separated bodies should they wait until prompted by their flocks to seek the union which "both the love of the country and religion invoke and which the providence of God seems to render inevitable at no distant date."[4]

The Southern bishops seized the opportunity thus offered them to make clear the attitude of their Church toward the Methodist Episcopal Church. As one of their number later declared, they "replied at sufficient length to be understood."[5] They reminded

---

[1]*Journal of Baltimore Conference*, 1870; Nashville *Christian Advocate*, March 19, 1870; New York *Christian Advocate*, November 9, 1871. Such attempts to cultivate fraternal relations between local organizations of the two Connections were, as a rule, made in regions where both Churches had a hold upon the dominant white population, as in Maryland and Tennessee. The Holston Conference of the Southern body, which four years previously had resolved not to recognize or introduce members of the Holston Conference of the other Church, in 1871 tabled, by a vote of 37 to 51, a resolution which declared that "it is proper that such of their ministers as may be present at our sessions should, in their individual capacity, receive the usual courtesies." *Cf.* New York *Christian Advocate*, November 9, 1871. In 1870 the Baltimore Conference of the Southern Connection declined to receive in their official capacity two fraternal messengers sent by the Baltimore Conference of the other Church, declaring that their respective General Conferences alone were competent to initiate such intercourse. *Journal of Baltimore Conference*, 1870, pp. 32-33.

[2]Letter of Northern bishops in New York *Christian Advocate*, May 20, 1869.

[3]*Idem.* Bishops Janes and Morris, and later Bishop Simpson.

[4]*Idem.* The Northern churchmen acknowledged that there were difficulties "growing out of the controversies of the past and the tempers of the present," but expressed the hope that the high regard in which Janes and Morris had been held in the South might aid in removing them.

[5]*Cf.* McTyeire, *op. cit.*, p. 680.

the Northern bishops that in the nature of the case, any discussion of reunion must necessarily be preceded by the consideration of another question—that of the establishment of fraternal feelings and relations between the two bodies. "Heart divisions must be cured," they told the Northern leaders, "before corporate divisions can be healed." They made it equally clear that their Church would entertain no overtures of any kind looking to a closer relation between the two connections in which were not involved a recognition of the validity of the Plan of Separation. They would be ready to remedy, on terms honorable to all, the evil effects which had resulted from the unhappy relations existing since 1848. "But you could not expect us to say less than this," they said, "that the words of our rejected delegate have been ever since, and still are our words."[1] It would be well, they said, for the parties to "keep distinctly in mind our mutual positions." Pointing out that the commissioners had referred to the cause "which led to the separation from us of both the Wesleyan Methodists of this country and of the Methodist Episcopal Church, South," they said: "We cannot think you mean to offend us when you speak of our having separated from you, and put us in the same category with a small body of schismatics who were always an acknowledged secession. Allow us in all kindness, brethren, to remind you, and to keep the important fact of history prominent, that we separated from you in no sense in which you did not separate from us. The separation was by compact and mutual, and nearer approaches to each other can be conducted with hope of a successful issue only on this basis."[2]

Declaring that an understanding of their position with regard to the part that slavery had played in causing the separation would aid in any future negotiations, they explained their views in the following words: "Slavery was not in any proper sense the cause, but the occasion only of that separation, the necessity of which we regretted as much as you. But certain principles were developed in relation to the political aspects of that question, involving the right of ecclesiastical bodies to handle and deter-

---

[1] Reply of Southern bishops as given in the *St. Louis Christian Advocate,* and quoted in New York *Christian Advocate,* May 20, 1869.
[2] *Idem.*

mine matters lying outside of their proper jurisdiction, which we could not accept; and in a case arising, certain constructions of the constitutional powers and perogatives of the General Conference were assumed and acted on, which we considered oppressive and destructive of the rights of the numerical minority represented in that highest judicatory of the Church."

Another serious hindrance to fraternity between the two connections, the Northern churchmen were reminded, existed in the conduct of the missionaries and other agents of the Methodist Episcopal Church in the South. The bishops declared that the avowed purpose of the missionaries "to disintegrate and absorb our societies that otherwise dwell quietly," had been "very prejudicial to that charity which we desire our people to cultivate toward all Christians, and especially those who are called by the endeared name of Methodists." Their course "in taking possession of some of our houses of worship," the bishops said, "has inflicted both grief and loss on us, and bears the appearance to disinterested men of the world, of being not only a breach of charity, but an invasion of the plainest rights of property." Having indicated the only grounds upon which fraternal intercourse would be possible, the Southern leaders disclaimed for themselves all authority to act with regard to the "propriety, practicability, and methods of reunion."[1]

---

[1]The response of the Southern bishops was given wide publicity by the Church press both in the North and in the South. The discussions provoked by it served to show that Southern Methodists were a unit with regard to the position taken by their bishops and that the events of the past few years had developed among them a strong opposition to any organic union with the Northern Church. The Southern journals expressed full approval of the stand taken by the bishops. The Richmond *Advocate*, in its issue of June 10, 1869, said: "The reunion of Methodists is, as we have seen, a question for a better day. They have not yet made peace. They have not yet restored amity. . . . And when the question shall become a practical one it will be found to require grave consideration." All the Southern journals agreed that the question was not one for practical consideration. A number of them expressed the opinion that whatever grounds of hope for conciliation and reunion had existed at the close of the War had been destroyed. The Richmond *Advocate,* in its issue of June 24, 1869, said: "We will be candid enough to say that with the lights now before us, we consider reunion neither possible nor desirable." The editor of the Nashville *Advocate,* on October 23, 1869, said: "The editor of this paper has no authority to pledge the Church to any policy, but he thinks that the ministry and membership, almost to a man, will agree with him when he says he wants no organic union of the two Churches. If the Northern Church were to repudiate the Hamline Doctrine, which gives the delegated General Conference conventional powers—a doctrine emphatically endorsed in the October

Although the Southern bishops had specified the recognition of their Church as a legitimate branch of American Methodism as a condition indispensable to any closer approach between the two groups, a similar proposal for reunion was made the following year. Bishop Janes and Dr. W. L. Harris presented to the General Conference at Memphis in 1870 a communicaton conveying fraternal messages from the Northern Church and asking that the Conference appoint a committee to treat with a committee of the Northern body on the subject of reunion. It was discovered, however, that these gentlemen acted under authority of a commission created by the Northern Conference of 1868 which was empowered to treat with commissions from other Methodist bodies "that may desire a union with us."[1]

Although receiving the commissioners in their personal capacity and extending personal courtesies to them, the Memphis Conference adopted a resolution declaring that their commission "could not be construed without great violence" to its language, as constituting "a committee to bear us fraternal greetings."[2] Furthermore, the Conference stated that had the commission been "fully clothed with authority to treat with us for union, it is the judgment of this Conference that the true interests of the Church of Christ require and demand the maintenance of our separate and distinct organization." It also took occasion to say that the response made by the bishops to the overture of the Northern bishops the preceding year had its full endorsement, and that it "accurately defines our position with reference to any overtures which may proceed from that Church, having in them an official and proper recognition of this body."[3]

Thus it had quickly become apparent after the War that there

---

number of the *Methodist Quarterly,* the most important periodical published by that Church—and were to cancel the legislation and extra-judicial action, based thereon, which caused the division of the Church—still we should not want an organic union." The discussion of the response thus served to show that there had been little change of sentiment in either Church with regard to the disputed issues between them. *The Methodist* of New York expressed surprise that the Southern leaders should hearken back to "a past that is utterly dead," and the *Northwestern Christian Advocate* declared the spirit of the two Churches to be "as varient as the styles of the two Episcopal Communications." *Cf.* Nashville *Christian Advocate,* June 5, 1869.

[1]*Cf. Journal of General Conference,* 1870, pp. 230-231.
[2]*Idem.*
[3]*Idem.*

would in the future be two separate and distinct Methodisms in the South and in the nation. There would be in the South not only the old Southern Methodism, which had its centers of power in that section, and which inclined to hold to a conservative or "Scriptural" view of the legitimate sphere of the functions and associations of the Church, but there would be also a Methodism whose vital centers were in the North, and which was disposed to accept a more inclusive view of the proper activities and associations of the Church. Both of these forces were sectional in that each tended to view the problems which confronted the Southern people in the light of the prevailing sentiment of that section in which it had long held its chief seats of power. As we shall see, these characteristic traits were important factors in determining the nature of the influence which Methodism was to exert in Southern society from 1865 to 1900.

CHAPTER III

Conditions Determining Southern Methodist Influence, 1865-1900

FIGHTING for its very life, the Southern Church in 1865 entered upon a new era. Almost at once it showed strong powers of recovery and the willingness to make a new departure. A group of young progressives which had developed in the Church during the years preceding the outbreak of the War now served the Connection in good stead.[1] Inspired by the Palmyra Manifesto and heartened by the action taken by the College of Bishops at Columbus, the leaders of the organization set about repairing and bringing order out of the chaos into which the machinery of the Church had fallen.

Soon preachers were at their charges, quarterly and Annual Conferences were being held and well attended, and the institutions of the Church resumed their activities.[2] The central Publishing House of the Connection sprang into life again as soon as it was relinquished by the military authorities, and *The Christian Advocate,* the official journal of the entire Church, issued regularly from Nashville. Of even greater importance, perhaps, was the revival of the *Advocates* which served as official organs of the several Annual Conferences. One by one, they made their reappearance, and the spirit of courage and determination shown in their columns was of inestimable value in the rebuilding of the Church.[3] The editor of the *New Orleans*

---

[1] Smith, *op. cit.,* p. 492.

[2] *Journal of General Conference,* 1866, pp. 16-17; *New Orleans Christian Advocate,* January 27, 1866.

[3] The papers which had been established before the War, and which now revived to play an important rôle in Southern Methodism, were the *Raleigh Christian Advocate* (founded 1855); the *New Orleans Christian Advocate* (established 1851); the *St. Louis Advocate* (dating from 1849); the *Texas Christian Advocate* (established 1847); the *Southern Christian Advocate* (founded 1836); and the *Richmond Christian Advocate* (dating from 1832). It was customary for each conference of the Connection to adopt some one journal as the representative of its interests, and each of these papers enjoyed throughout the period the support of a varying group of conferences. From time to time as new journals were established, the individual conferences transferred their support from one to another. Among the journals which were in existence for a part of this period, and which exerted a strong influence, the

Advocate said of the other *Advocates* early in 1866 that "it does one good like a medicine to read the tone and spirit of these messengers."[1] The New Orleans *Advocate,* itself, stood foremost in imparting to the Connection a note of optimism and hope, and in stressing its prospects. In an editorial on "the Situation," early in 1866, it asked the question, "Can we, do we survive?" In answer, its editor declared that in all the elements of strength the Connection was as well off as before the War. Moreover, he envisioned new opportunities. The work of the Southern Church in the past had been in vast fields occupied by the Negro and from which the white laborer had been excluded more and more each year. "The future vineyard of the Church" would lie "amid thousands of small farms and a constantly increasing white population." "Those missionary labors which hitherto have been expended on plantations to be reaped only in Heaven will hereafter be spent on farms and reaped both on earth and in Heaven." Especially favorable to future success, he pointed out, was the spirit of "unity, unanimity and energy," which characterized "every department of Southern Methodism."[2]

With the machinery of the Church already set in motion, the bishops called a meeting of the General Conference in New Orleans at its regular time in April 1866. This gathering proved to be one of the most important in the history of Church councils in America. It was soon apparent that the party of young progressives would dominate the Conference, and the necessities of the times inclined the usually conservative minds to accept measures which otherwise would have been distasteful to them.[3]

---

most important, with the dates of their establishment, were: the *Wesleyan Christian Advocate* (1878), published at Macon, Georgia; the *Alabama Christian Advocate* (1881); the *Holston Advocate* (1872); the *Central Methodist* (1866), of Catlettsburg, Ky.; and the *Arkansas Methodist* (1881). Mississippi was the only Southern State in which no Methodist journal was published throughout the period, 1865-1900. The Mississippi conferences generally found it convenient to recognize as their special representative the *New Orleans Christian Advocate.* A sketch of the weekly press of the Southern Church is given in Du Bose, *History of Methodism,* pp. 551-557.

[1] *New Orleans Christian Advocate,* January 27, 1866.
[2] *Ibid.*
[3] Price in his *Holston Methodism,* Vol. III, p. 152, says that the ministry was inclined to "any reasonable measures which would give it a stronger hold on the laity and on the men of the world." *Cf.* also, McTyeire, *op. cit.,* p. 667, and Smith, *op. cit.,* p. 493.

Of the five bishops who had been conspicuous in the old regime, three were now relieved of active participation in the direction of Church affairs. The aged Bishops, Andrew and Early, were retired from active work, and the venerable Soule, who had been too feeble to attend the sessions, died within a year.[1] The New Orleans Conference introduced a new and vigorous leadership which guaranteed to the Church an important influence in Southern life.

Never before had there been such a need for strengthening the episcopal office or so great a concern felt with regard to the men who would be chosen to fill it.[2] The Conference named four new bishops, and these men, with the others who were elected to the episcopal office before the end of the century, constituted what was probably the ablest body of ecclesiastical leaders in the South during that period.[3] It is significant that among the men chosen at New Orleans was Holland N. McTyeire, who had already distinguished himself as the outstanding leader in all forward movements.[4]

The New Orleans Conference also effected in rapid succession a series of changes in the economy of the Church that were of great importance for the future.[5] Indicative of the determination to strike out along new lines was the adoption of a motion to change the name of the Church. Though the proposal was later defeated in the Annual Conferences, in so far as the Conference could do so, provision was made for renaming it "The Episcopal Methodist Church."[6] To provide for a more rounded ministry,

---

[1]*Journal of General Conference*, 1866, p. 60; Smith, *op. cit.*, p. 494. Bishop Early was prematurely retired and informally censured because of his rulings with regard to political matters during the War. *Cf.* Price, *op. cit.*, Vol. IV, p. 305.

[2]*Cf.* Smith, *op. cit.*, p. 494; Du Bose, *op. cit.*, p. 12.

[3]The men elevated to the Episcopal office at this time were Holland N. McTyeire, William M. Wightman, Enoch M. Marvin, and David S. Doggett.

[4]Smith, *op. cit.*, pp. 492-494.

[5]So general was the demand and expectation with regard to alterations in the polity of the Church that a special committee, called the "Committee on Economy," was appointed at the beginning of the Conference to consider and make recommendations on the memorials and other papers having to do with proposed changes. *Cf.* Du Bose, *op. cit.*, p. 12.

[6]*Journal of General Conference*, 1866, p. 88. This provision later failed of ratification when presented to the Annual Conferences for confirmation. *Cf.* Du Bose, *op. cit.*, p. 13. Designing to discard the notion of a purely sectional

HOLLAND N. MCTYEIRE
BISHOP OF THE METHODIST EPISCOPAL CHURCH, SOUTH

the pastoral term was lengthened from two to four years.[1] The rigid requirement of a six months' probationary period for admission to membership in the Church, and that of compulsory attendance upon class meetings were abolished.[2] Church conferences were legalized, district conferences suggested, and a committee for revision of the *Discipline* of the Church, which was to report to the next General Conference, was appointed.[3]

Of not less importance to the influence of Methodism in Southern society was the provision for lay representation in the conferences and courts of the Church.[4] Lay representation was the commanding question before the Conference, and the interest manifested in it foretold the importance of this innovation in the future. By this act, the clergy made a voluntary relinquishment of power unprecedented in any important ecclesiastical body.[5] The new provision brought into the counsels of the Church a new energy and new talents. Henceforth many of the most distinguished and capable laymen were drawn into the service of the Church, and their talents utilized in furthering its interests. The names of eminent educators, lawyers, jurists, statesmen, and business men now became familiar in the records of the Church, and they brought the advantage of their specialized training and

Church, and to prepare the way for operations which it might be called upon to undertake in the North, the Conference adopted the following resolution: "*Resolved,* That the geographical line defining the territorial limits of the Methodist Episcopal Church and the Methodist Episcopal Church, South, established by the General Conference of 1844, has been officially and practically repudiated by the Methodist Episcopal Church, therefore we are bound neither legally or morally by it; and that we feel ourselves at liberty to extend our ministrations and jurisdiction to all beyond that line who may desire us to do so." *Journal of General Conference,* 1866, p. 88.

[1]The Conference actually voted to remove the time limit on appointments altogether and to submit this decision to the Annual Conference for ratification. This, however, was not done. Bishop Pierce, the outstanding conservative among the younger leaders of the Church, fearing that the economy of the Church was imperiled, threatened to resign his office at once should the abolition of the time limit be made operative. An able and eloquent leader, he was, in some respects, conservative to the point of being reactionary. Because of his opposition, the vote was reconsidered, and the term extended to four years. *Cf.* Smith, *op. cit.,* p. 494.

[2]McTyeire, *op. cit.,* p. 667.

[3]Du Bose, *op. cit.,* p. 12.

[4]*Journal of General Conference,* 1866, p. 62. The Conference adopted this measure by a vote of 95 to 50.

[5]The Reverend B. M. Palmer, of the Southern Presbyterian Church, declared that "the history of the Church presented no parallel" to the action. *Cf. New Orleans Christian Advocate,* June 2, 1866.

experience to the management of its affairs.[1] Moreover, their presence in its councils served to impress upon the public mind the large amount of culture and wealth in the denomination. The intimate association with Southern Methodism of such outstanding Southerners as Chancellor Landon Cabell Garland, Justice Lucius Q. C. Lamar, and President James H. Carlisle served greatly to enhance its influence.[2]

As to the critical condition of the colored membership of the Church, the New Orleans Conference took timely action. It set into operation a plan for organizing the Negro members into separate circuits, missions, districts, Annual Conferences, and ultimately into a separate General Conference. This plan resulted four year later in setting them off as an independent ecclesiastical organization, the Colored Methodist Episcopal Church of America.[3]

Having mapped out their course and overhauled their economy preparatory to ventures in untried waters, Southern Methodists turned hopefully toward the future, and, until the end of the century, little desire was expressed in the Connection for further changes in its economy. Nor was the Church disturbed during those years by any serious differences over doctrine. It entered upon a period of unusual internal peace and of remarkable recovery. As early as 1871, the *New Orleans Christian Advocate* could observe that "such internal tranquility is scarcely to be found in any other Church."[4] Such statements were frequently heard to the close of the century. In the Episcopal Address delivered in the General Conference of 1876 the Southern bishops declared that "a more homogeneous ecclesiastical community does not exist on the American Continent," and that almost universal harmony prevailed among both ministry and laity.[5] Again in

[1]*Cf.* Du Bose, *op. cit.*, p. 39; *Cf. Journals of General Conference*, 1866-1900, *passim*. President Carlisle of Wofford was in the first Conference in which the laymen were represented, and appeared regularly thereafter. Duncan, *Carlisle Memorial Volume*, p. 26.

[2]A secular paper of the day in assessing the influence of the Church in Southern society declared that there were in its membership "every range of culture, from the honest country-bumpkin to the robe of ermine and the seat of civic dignity." *The South* (New York) quoted in Nashville *Christian Advocate*, January 20, 1872.

[3]McTyeire, *op. cit.*, p. 671.

[4]*New Orleans Christian Advocate*, June 8, 1871.

[5]*Journal of General Conference*, 1876. See Pastoral Address.

their Pastoral Address of 1894 the bishops reported that the Church was "remarkably free from strife and factions."[1] There was in the Connection, they felt, "as near an approach to unity in doctrine, and also in general approval of our general polity as could be expected."[2] This internal quietude made possible for the Church a period of rapid growth and increasing financial prosperity.

The increasing prosperity of the Church was reflected in the growth of communicants. The membership, numbering 507,975 in 1866, was reported in 1870, despite the loss of almost its entire colored contingent, as 535,040.[3] From 1870 to 1874, there was an increase of 126,299, the largest gain which had ever been made during a similar period.[4]

In a period of rapid urban growth throughout the country, Methodism made great strides in the cities of the South. To be sure, early in the post-war period some concern was felt regarding the effectiveness of the itinerant system as a means of urban evangelization. Lack of aggressiveness in the cities was said to constitute a weak spot in Methodism.[8] In 1876 one of the journals of the Southern Church said that, of the eleven largest cities of the South, the smallest of them had the largest ratio of white Methodists to the population.[2] It also pointed out that the

---

[1]*Journal of General Conference,* 1894, p. 21.

[2]*Idem.* For some years during this period the membership of the Methodist Episcopal Church, South, increased at a more rapid rate than that of any other large Christian group.

[3]These figures are based on those given in the *Methodist Almanac,* 1870, p. 41, and in McTyeire, *op. cit.,* pp. 664, 670.

[4]Baltimore *Episcopal Methodist,* quoted in *New Orleans Christian Advocate,* January 20, 1876. According to the *Episcopal Methodist,* which based its calculations on the *Census* of 1870, the ratio of white Methodists to the population in these cities was as follows:

CITIES	WHITE POP.	METH. MEM.	RATIO TO POPULATION
St. Louis	228,000	1,317	1 in 218
Baltimore	228,000	1,332	1 in 216
New Orleans	141,000	1,048	1 in 134
Richmond	28,000	1,774	1 in 15
Louisville	85,000	2,170	1 in 39
Memphis	24,000	1,022	1 in 23
Charleston	22,000	783	1 in 25
Nashville	19,000	1,531	1 in 12
Mobile	18,000	822	1 in 21
Savannah	15,000	694	1 in 21
Atlanta	12,000	1,685	1 in 7

largest increases in Methodist membership in these cities from 1870 to 1874, were generally in those having the smaller populations, Atlanta, the smallest, having the largest increase. "Why is this?," it asked. "Has Methodism no mission to the great cities of our country? Have we been unmindful of the potential influence of metropolitan centers of trade and population? Or is there some secret in the mission system of the smaller towns? Let us pause and reflect."[1]

But these doubts concerning the ability of Methodism to cope with city conditions were soon found to be unjustified. During the years from 1880 to 1888, the rate of increase of membership in the larger urban centers surpassed that in the Church at large. Thus, the rate for Atlanta, Nashville, Richmond, Louisville, St. Louis, Baltimore, New Orleans, Augusta, and Macon was fifty-five per cent as against thirty-seven for the entire Church.[2] In a number of cities the Methodist membership advanced at a faster rate than the population itself. By 1886 the Nashville *Advocate* could declare that "the notion that the system is unsuited to the city population has been exploded." "Look at Baltimore, Richmond, Atlanta, Nashville, Louisville," it said. "Methodism has grown with their growth, the ratio of its increase exceeding that of the population in general."[3]

---

[1] *Ibid.* The *Episcopal Methodist* compiled the following chart, showing the increase in Methodist membership in the cities from 1870 to 1874:

CITIES	METH. MEM. 1870	METH. MEM. 1874	INCREASE
St. Louis	1,317	1,237	dec. 80
Baltimore	1,382	1,447	65
New Orleans	1,048	1,127	79
Louisville	2,170	2,284	114
Richmond	1,774	2,297	523
Memphis	1,022	1,119	97
Charleston	783	931	151
Nashville	1,531	2,318	787
Mobile	822	883	61
Savannah	694	768	74
Atlanta	1,685	2,273	588

[2] *The Methodist Review,* Vol. VI (April 1899), pp. 208-209.
[3] Nashville *Christian Advocate,* March 13, 1895. The *Advocate* explained that, in certain places where Methodism had not relatively maintained its ground, it had been due to exceptionally unfavorable conditions or to a mistaken policy by which some congregations had cut themselves off from the currents of Methodistic life around them and which had developed "a narrow un-Methodistic spirit in them."

The white membership of the Southern Church, which in 1866 was smaller than in 1854, doubled in the next fifteen years.[1] By 1885 the membership numbered 860,687, almost exclusively white.[2] This remarkable growth is to be accounted for in large measure by the capacity of the Church for keeping awake the revival spirit among the people.[3] It is notable that its greatest gains in membership were made in those years when the revival spirit rose highest. To a people recently disappointed in their fondest hopes, impoverished, humiliated, and despondent of the future, a religion that could offer an emotional experience which would turn men's thoughts from the ills of this world would make a strong appeal. Methodism offered "an experience in grace" which made men strive to secure the happiness of another world and made them forget the cares and vanities of this life. Such a release it offered freely to every individual and to a degree hardly to be expected even in the other evangelical Churches with their more rigid theologies.[4] It held out to all who would renounce the world not only such an experience, with the prospect of happiness in the future, but also the possibility of a "second blessing" of "Christian perfection" in this world. Its adherents could claim for themselves the "witness of the Spirit."

Throughout the period from the Civil War to the close of the century revival fires burned brightly in the denomination.[5]

---

[1]McTyeire, *op. cit.*, p. 670.

[2]*Journal of General Conference*, 1886, p. 16.

[3]Simkins and Woody, *op. cit.*, p. 402, assert this to be the chief source of the power of the Church in South Carolina during the period of Reconstruction.

[4]In its issue of April 23, 1896, the editor of the Nashville *Advocate* said: "What good does it do to tell all men that they can be saved if they will, when in the next breath you declare that only the elect can be saved? . . . It is well enough for Methodists to keep these things in mind. They must not forget that they are put in trust with the most catholic and comprehensive version of the Gospel that the world had ever heard. Beyond any other people, it is their privilege to make a *bona fide* offer of pardon, cleansing and deliverance to every soul outside of hell." The conditional character of the offers of salvation made by other denominations, the writer admitted, were, in this period, more often "suppressed or at least allowed to remain unspoken."

[5]The ground was prepared for these outbursts by the persistence of the spirit of a great religious awakening which had occurred shortly before the outbreak of the Civil War, and which was called the "Great Awakening of 1858." There were frequent revivals in the South during the War and they exerted a strong influence in the Confederate army. *Cf.* Candler, *Bishop Charles Betts Galloway*, p. 14. The emphasis which the Southern Church placed on its "Scriptural" mission tended to keep alive the revival spirit during the post-war period.

"Gracious revivals" were reported year after year in all parts of the South. As early as 1866, a "perfect blaze of revivals" was recorded in various places. The files of the Methodist journals of that time abound with accounts of these emotional outbursts. In 1866 during a great awakening in the Church in South Carolina, a minister, "whose face shone like that of Moses," spoke "a language of melting tenderness."[1]

While, due perhaps to the general decline in the roughness of American life, the Methodist revivals of this period were more restrained than those of *ante-bellum* times, their influence was none the less powerful and at times the old manifestations were present.[2] Although it was often lamented that "a tacit, genteel ritualism" had replaced the fervor of former times, the old time intensity frequently expressed itself, especially in the camp meetings which had long been utilized by the denomination as a means of evangelization. These meetings were held in groves in which rough pulpits and benches had been erected and in which there were "tents" for overnight protection.[3] Of such a meeting in Louisiana, a lady at Opelousas wrote in 1883: "The Holy Spirit came at the very beginning, and was manifest at every service. The preaching was powerful, earnest and plain, and God honored it to the saving of souls. There was not a single dull service. There were conversions and sanctifications at every altar service. The work went right along together. Souls would get converted at one service, and then go right back to seek the second blessing, and praise God. They got it, too. Some would come into the experience during the sermons, and would praise God aloud, and, amid tears and groans and shouts, the altar was filled with seekers after pardon and holiness. Conviction was deep and awful, and the cries for mercy and shouts of victory, mingled with the prayers and praises of the saints made a scene never to be forgotten. Sometimes the tide of salvation rolled so high we could scarcely sing for the joy that welled up in our souls. The glad

---

[1] *Cf. Southern Christian Advocate,* quoted in Simkins and Woody, *op. cit.,* p. 400.

[2] Simkins and Woody, *op. cit.,* p. 402, give this explanation.

[3] Simkins and Woody, *op. cit.,* pp. 400-402, give an interesting account of such meeting places in South Carolina. It was estimated that there were in that State in 1875 approximately twenty-four such assemblies.

hallelujahs and amens would ring out between the lines."[1] Of another such revival in South Carolina it was reported that "It would be hard to conceive of a more beautiful and touching spectacle than that of hundreds of people leaving their work for a few days to devote themselves to praise and prayer. . . . Every service was well attended, every sermon seemed endowed with special power from on high and many were born to newness of life. . . . The communion service at night was a scene almost painful in its awful solemnity; the sacred vessels were on the rude table; there were deep Rembrandt shadows from which would merge a face radiant with a light which was not of this earth. . . . The presence of God was acknowledged by the cheering of the cast-down, the comforting of the weary, the supporting of the weak, and triumphantly attested by the exultant songs of the new-born soul."[2]

In connection with the revivalism of the times there developed a "movement" within the Church which threatened to rob it of much of its strength, but which, through the reaction it caused, ultimately added to its power. The disorders resulting from the War and the distractions of the Reconstruction period led many persons to believe that the moral integrity of the Church was threatened. The young men of the time, despondent of the future, were thought to be on a certain road to ruin.[3] "Here as most everywhere," declared a Methodist minister in South Carolina in 1866, "the Church has suffered terribly. Morals have become lax, backsliding frequent and in some localities the Church is in a condition to dishearten its ministers."[4] A cure for these things was seen in the doctrine of entire sanctification, which tended to turn men's minds from the consideration of social phases of life

---

[1]Letter of Mrs. Emma Foster, in *New Orleans Christian Advocate*, October 5, 1883.

[2]Account in *Southern Christian Advocate*, quoted in Simkins and Woody, *op. cit.*, pp. 401-402. With regard to a meeting at Sandy Springs in that State, it was said: "The old people and the preachers say that they had never seen the like. Some of the scenes beggar description. One afternoon the services continued from the 3 o'clock sermon until midnight, giving the regular preacher no time to preach." Cf. *Southern Christian Advocate*, cited in Simkins and Woody, *op. cit.*, p. 401.

[3]*Cf.* Simkins and Woody, *op. cit.*, p. 398.

[4]Letter of the Reverend H. G. Wells, in *Southern Christian Advocate*, quoted in Simkins and Woody, *op. cit.*, p. 398.

to that of individual religious experience, and which had always been prominent in Methodist theology. John Wesley, himself, had taught that inherited depravity or "inborn sin" remains in the human soul after conversion, but that it could be removed by the "second blessing" of "entire sanctification," through which one might attain unto a state of "Christian perfection" or "holiness."[1] And Wesley had declared the mission of the Church to be that of spreading "Scriptural holiness over these lands." The alarm occasioned by the evidences of moral laxness in the Church caused the doctrine of entire sanctification to be brought prominently before the Communion. In the Episcopal Address of 1870 the bishops admonished the Church of the necessity for a quickening of the conscience with regard to it. "We fear," they said, "that the doctrine of perfect love which casts out fear and purifies the heart, and is the 'measure of the stature of the fulness of Christ,' as a distinct and practicable attainment is too much overlooked and neglected."[2] Soon an extraordinary interest was manifested, almost simultaneously in many parts of the South, in this doctrine. There were reports from many places "of lamenting on account of the decadence of holiness, inquiries as to its nature, arguments urging the necessity for it, and exhortations to seek it."[3]

By 1878 the Nashville *Advocate* could announce that an interest in holiness was pervading the entire Church. In September of that year, it said: "Venerable and holy men are calling attention to it. Multitudes of awakened believers are seeking it. . . . The movement is the natural recoil of the religious mind from the rampant worldliness of the time. There is left no alternative for the Church; it must be engulfed by the world or oppose to it a stronger resistance; it must sink to the same level or rise to a higher life."[4]

But already the intense interest in holiness had given rise to "angry disputings" over its nature. A group of specialists had

---

[1]This "residue theory," which draws a distinction between a "justifying faith" and a "consecrating faith," was set forth by Wesley in his sermons on "Sin in Believers" and "Repentance in Believers."

[2]*Journal of General Conference,* 1870, p. 164.

[3]*Cf.* Nashville *Christian Advocate,* September 21, 1878.

[4]*Idem.*

arisen who proclaimed themselves the only true exponents of "Christian perfection."[1] These special advocates of holiness, who themselves professed "entire sanctification," attempted "to stand at the gate of Heaven" and exclude "all who will not or cannot produce their shibboleth."[2] The movement inevitably attracted to it elements of fanaticism which threatened the integrity of the Church.[3] It had the effect of imparting a spirit of "universal censoriousness" to many of its exponents.[4] To add to the confusion, a new type of evangelist appeared in the Church at that time. While every Methodist minister was held to be properly an evangelist, there now appeared the evangelist as a specialist. Devoting themselves to a special work, these new evangelists were not subjected to the restraining influences with which the regular travelling ministry was hedged about.[5] They came and went as they chose. The potentialities for extravagance in such an order were reflected in the doctrinal preaching of many of these men. While often powerful agencies in preserving the moral integrity of the Church, such men not infrequently identified themselves prominently with the holiness movement and imparted to it a new extravagance and radicalism.[6]

---

[1]*Cf.* Episcopal Address in *Journal of General Conference,* 1878, p. 33. Since the days of Wesley Methodists had been involved in controversies on the subject of holiness. Hitherto, however, the controversies had generally taken the form of disputes with other denominations over the possibility of attaining to entire sanctification in this world. Now, Methodists quarrelled with Methodists over the nature of holiness, and their controversies generally had to do with the question of whether holiness was achieved through a gradual transformation or whether it was an instantaneous work. The uncertainty as to the character of the transformation led to the assertion of exclusive claims by those who claimed to have arrived at a state of "Christian perfection."

[2]*Cf. Southern Christian Advocate,* June 16, 1887.

[3]A minister of that day, in a communication to the *Pentecostal Herald,* a journal devoted to the promotion of holiness, said with regard to these elements: "But many holiness people—so-called—are fallen, and are impregnated with divers forms of fanaticism, crankism, 'damnable heresies,' come-out-ism, and strong hydra-headed doctrines of devils. They are split up into little sects, factions and fads, each claiming to be the only true body of Christ; and while they excommunicate all others from the kingdom of God, they themselves manifest the most intolerant bigotry." Letter of the Reverend W. W. Hopper in *Pentecostal Herald,* quoted in *New Orleans Christian Advocate,* July 26, 1900.

[4]*Cf.* Nashville *Christian Advocate,* August 3, 1878.

[5]These men were "local" preachers and were not subject to scrutiny and examination by a Quarterly Conference as were the regular itinerants.

[6]In its issue of November 2, 1893, the *New Orleans Christian Advocate* described the new order of evangelists as the "wild, irresponsible, self-made system of evangelism now operating within the Church."

When the doctrinal specialists, possessed of ideas "hard to be understood by the common mind," could not carry the great body of the Communion with them, they tended to draw apart and organize themselves, independently of the Church, into associations for the promotion of holiness, or to leave the Church entirely. In their Pastoral Address of 1878 the bishops warned the Church that "fanatical distortions" of the doctrine were being taught by "factious leaders."[1] The tendency of the movement to "other worldliness" and its anticipation of the pre-millennium days were found to be unfavorable to experiences in practical religion.[2]

The agitation reached a high pitch during the Eighties. Whole congregations were disrupted by disputes over entire sanctification.[3] At that time the journals of the Connection fairly bristled with controversial articles on the subject. Editors repeatedly voiced their embarrassment at the large number of communications received and as to what disposition should be made of them.[4] Holiness associations multiplied and calls were issued for holiness conventions.[5]

Shocked at the radical doctrines that were being spread and alarmed at the effects of the holiness movement on its authority, the Church sought energetically to combat these influences by an authoritative and sane exposition of the doctrine of entire sanctification. The journals of the Connection insisted that the ministry must not allow its function of expounding the doctrine of holiness to be usurped by extremists and that every pulpit must speak forth boldly on the subject. The editor of the *Southern Christian Advocate* said in 1887: "No self-constituted and irresponsible 'association,' with its many objectionable features, must be allowed to stand forth before the world as the only, or even as the chief,

---

[1]*Cf.* Pastoral Address in *Journal of General Conference,* 1878, p. 33.

[2]My attention was directed to this phase of its significance by Dr. D. B. Raulins, a recent editor of the *New Orleans Christian Advocate.*

[3]The Reverend S. P. Richardson reported that when he assumed the pastorate of the St. James Church in Augusta, Georgia, in 1890, he found the congregation about equally divided in a dispute over this doctrine, with bitter feelings on both sides. Some of the members had already gone to St. Johns in that city, and others were preparing to go. *Cf.* Richardson, *Lights and Shadows,* p. 240.

[4]Such a complaint was made by the editor of the Nashville *Christian Advocate* in its issue of December 12, 1889.

[5]*Cf.* Nashville *Christian Advocate,* January 10, 1885; *ibid.,* December 12, 1889.

exponent of holiness. The honor and the very existence of the Church is involved in this. . . . The Church must assert her prerogatives and be true to her character. She cannot allow a handful of men, however good and sincere they may be, to assume a work and responsibility which God himself has laid upon her. . . . The Church has her work to do and her rights to preserve. She must not neglect the one or surrender the other. . . . The remedy then is in the Church herself. She must vindicate the claim that her highest aim is to spread Scriptural holiness over the land. In order to do this every Methodist pulpit must continue to ring out clear and strong on the doctrine of the higher Christian life, and every preacher must exemplify the doctrine he preaches. The Church must also discountenance all those who seek to usurp her functions or rob her of her honor. She must allow no 'church within the Church,' by showing its utter uselessness, as well as its harmfulness. She must allow no divisions in her own ranks."[1] In the General Conference of 1894 the bishops admonished the Church with regard to the duty of expounding the doctrine and warned it that there existed within its bounds "a party with holiness as a watchword; they have holiness associations, holiness meetings, holiness preachers, holiness evangelists, and holiness property. . . . The effect is to disparage the new birth, and all stages of spiritual growth from the blade to the full corn in the ear, if there be not professed perfect holiness."[2] The admonition was not without effect. The Conference took action to bring the new evangelists under the more direct control of the Church. It provided for the incorporation of a new section in the *Discipline*, declaring that "No local preacher shall enter the recognized territory of any of our pastoral charges for the purpose of conducting protracted or revival meetings except upon the invitation of the preacher in charge."[3]

The special emphasis which the Church came in this way to place upon the doctrine of holiness served to augment the spirit of revivalism in the Communion. The late Eighties—after the holiness movement was in full stride—were a time of extraordi-

---

[1]Dr. W. D. Kirkland in *Southern Christian Advocate*, June 16, 1887.
[2]*Cf.* Pastoral Address in *Journal of General Conference*, 1894, p. 25.
[3]*Ibid.*, p. 111.

nary revivals. The increased revival activity was reflected by the growth of Methodist membership. In 1885 the net gain was reported as the largest in the history of the Church.[1] The following year the Connection boasted of a net increase of over 75,000.[2] During the years from 1886 to 1900, an increase of 186,156 was recorded. By the latter date the total had mounted to over a million.[3] The rapid growth of the Southern Church continued through the remainder of the century. "The success of the Methodists in the South is worthy of special note," wrote an eminent Baptist minister and editor in 1895. "In former years it was not a rare thing for rich Methodist families to go over to the Episcopalians; and not infrequently, too, their talented and inspiring young preachers were restless until they finally found more congenial surroundings in the old mother Church, in whose fellowship John Wesley lived and died. But it is different now. The Methodists excel us all in wealth and in numbers in nine-tenths of the larger cities and towns of the South, and no preachers are more loyal to their Church than they."[4] At the last General Conference of the century the bishops reported a membership of 1,487,431. And the 2,116 travelling preachers of 1866 had increased to 5,989 in 1898.[5]

The growth in membership was accompanied by a proportionate increase in wealth and church accommodations. In the post-war days of poverty the people supported the Church and its institutions in a spirit of devotion and sacrifice. Better economic condi-

---

[1]*Cf.* Nashville *Christian Advocate*, April 9, 1887.

[2]*Cf.* Nashville *Christian Advocate*, April 9, 1887. "Thank God," wrote the editor of the Nashville *Advocate*, when referring to this gain, "the great body of the Methodist preachers is composed almost solidly of evangelists in the best sense of the word." He declared that he was rejoiced "at the revival news which is reaching us daily from our cities." The Methodists noted with satisfaction that they were provoking others to "love and good works." In the Episcopal Address delivered in the General Conference in 1886, the bishops said: "We gratefully note an increased spiritual activity in all of the Protestant Churches. That they have entered upon methods of revival, and have employed Evangelists after the manner of our Church and seem ready to adopt the system which has been approved among us by habits of an hundred years. Whatever Methodism is worth revivals are worth." *Cf.* Pastoral Address in Nashville *Christian Advocate*, May 15, 1886.

[3]*Journal of General Conference*, 1890, p. 31.

[4]Letter of Dr. Alfred E. Dickinson, editor of the Richmond *Religious Herald* in the *Independent*, as quoted in the Nashville *Christian Advocate*, April 4, 1895.

[5]*Journal of General Conference*, 1898, p. 20.

tions among the membership were quickly reflected in the improved financial condition of the Church. In 1850 the value of the church buildings and parsonages approximated $3,771,502; in 1883 their value was reported to be $13,323,592.[1] This increase of approximately 253 per cent, it must be remembered, was made notwithstanding the fact that during that time a decrease of approximately $117,000,000 had occurred in the value of the property of the Southern States.[2] An indication of the rapidly improving financial condition of the Church appeared in the fact that in 1884 its members contributed a Centennial offering of $1,375,000.[3] By 1890 the United States *Census* showed that the value of the church property owned by the Connection in the sixteen Southern States and the District of Columbia had risen to $17,775,819.[4] The wealth of the Church increased steadily to the end of the century. At the General Conference of 1898, the aggregate value of all the property of the Connection was reported as $35,000,000. That sum indicated an increase of approximately two millions of dollars during the preceding quadrennium.[5]

To understand more fully the capacity and power of the Methodist Episcopal Church, South, for influencing Southern society, it must be compared with the other Methodist bodies in the section, and the strength of the whole body of the Methodist communicants must further be compared with that of the other religious groups there. Though the growth of the Southern Church in numbers and wealth was paralleled by corresponding gains in the Southern conferences of the other large Methodist bodies, it must be remembered that the numerical gains of such other Methodist groups were predominantly in Negro membership. And in the cases of the two African Churches and the Colored Methodist Church the increase was entirely one of colored members.

---

[1] McTyeire, *op. cit.*, p. 670.

[2] *Idem.* McTyeire points out that while, during the same period, there was an increase of 342 per cent in the value of the church buildings and parsonages of the Northern Church, there was during the same time an increase of 314 per cent in the value of the real and personal property in the Northern States.

[3] *Journal of General Conference*, 1886, p. 18. The objects for which the individual contributions were to be used could be designated by the donors, and practically all of that amount was expended on local projects, only a small amount having been designated for foreign missions.

[4] *Statistics . . . of the Eleventh Census*, Vol. XVI, pp. 38-43.

[5] *Journal of General Conference*, 1898, p. 20.

The Southern membership of the Methodist Episcopal Church, which in 1865 had amounted to about a hundred thousand, was reported in 1896 as 547,403.[1] Despite the fact that the work of the Northern Church in the South was heavily subsidized by Missionary and Church Extension funds contributed by Methodists in the North, and despite the avowed desire of the leaders in the North to displace the "white Methodism" of the Southern States, only a minor proportion of this increase represented gains in white communities. The Northern body found it difficult to gain a foothold among the Southern whites save along the border and in certain regions where Union sentiment had been strong. Although by 1869 the Northern Church had organized nine new conferences in the States lying below the border and large sums were annually being spent to advance the interests of the Church, it failed to gain a hearing among most of the whites in the territory included in those conferences.[2]

Aside from the character of its requirements for membership, this failure to impress itself on the dominant race was due to the unconciliatory attitude of the Northern body towards its sister Church of the South, and to the strongly sectional viewpoint of the agents it sent into the Southern States. The uncompromising attitude of these workers toward the former ruling classes of the South effectively closed to them all doors where the influence of those classes was still felt. The missionaries apprehended a revival of the "Bourbonism" of the old South, and they saw manifestations of it under various forms, such as Southern historical societies, anniversary celebrations, and Confederate monuments.[3] The journals of the Northern Church abounded with communications from them denouncing these manifestations. Their attempts to exert an influence in Southern politics, it will be seen, also served to prevent their exerting an influence over the great mass of whites.

In 1868 a minister of the Northern Church in Virginia, while

---

[1] *Journal of General Conference*, 1896, p. 411.
[2] These conferences were organized as follows: Holston Conference, 1865; Mississippi Mission Conference, 1865; South Carolina Conference, 1866; Tennessee Conference, 1866; Texas Conference, 1867; Virginia Conference, 1867; Georgia Conference, 1867; Alabama Conference, 1867. *Cf. General Minutes*, 1867, *passim*.
[3] *Cf.* Fleming, *op. cit.*, p. 649.

predicting "a glorious triumph of our form of Methodism," admitted that the ministry of all the other denominations in that State opposed his Church, and that "our occupancy of this territory as ministers of the M. E. Church, and its organization into circuits and stations, is denounced by them as anti-Christian and seditious." He said that the other denominations would regard the "expulsion and final exile" of the Northern Church as "a merited punishment for our presumption in entering it."[1] The Reverend Lucius C. Matlack, a presiding elder of the Northern Connection in Louisiana, reported in 1870 that not only were the Southern Methodists a unit in their opposition to the presence of his Church in that State, but that the mass of whites not Methodists "make our loyal and Northern affinities all sufficient reasons for standing off from us."[2] Of the more than eight thousand members reported by his Church in Louisiana, not over two hundred were white. And those whites, he said, were all in three of the New Orleans churches—Ames Chapel, the Felicity Street Church, and the Second German Mission. In the six other churches of the city and in all the others in the entire State, not one white member was to be found. "Such," he lamented, "is the record after five years of labor have been expended here."[3] The situation in South Carolina was even more extreme. As early as 1866 the Northern Church there had been declared to be "a living and efficient agent through which sinners are converted to God," yet it had not at that time a single member among the white population of the State, nor did it gain any before the end of the century.[4]

Exclusive of its border conferences, the Northern Church had in the entire South in 1895 a white membership of only 72,680.[5]

---

[1]Letter of W. T. D. Clemm in New York *Christian Advocate*, January 16, 1868. The writer declared that his Church was "mispresented and abused beyond all precedent, and its ministry and people subjected to manifold and unusual annoyances." "And foremost and most unscrupulous in this unhallowed persecution," he said, "are those who were formerly our ministerial brethren."

[2]Letter of the Reverend L. C. Matlack in New York *Christian Advocate*, quoted in *New Orleans Christian Advocate*, October 27, 1870.

[3]Letter of the Reverend L. C. Matlack in New York *Christian Advocate*, quoted in *New Orleans Christian Advocate*, November 19, 1870.

[4]Simkins and Woody, *op. cit.*, pp. 376-377.

[5]*Cf.* J. T. Davies, Jr., "The Two Episcopal Methodisms in the South," *The Methodist Review*, Vol. IV (January 1897).

Of this number over forty-one thousand were in three of its conferences, the Holston, the Blue Ridge, and the Central Tennessee, in all of which Union sentiment had been strong during the War.[1] After thirty years of labor the Church had gathered in the States of South Carolina, Georgia, Florida, Alabama, Louisiana, Arkansas, Texas, and Virginia only 31,000 white members.[2] But its black membership grew by leaps and bounds. Although it had not a single communicant in the middle and far South in 1861, by 1896 it reported 254,211 there.[3]

According to the statistics of the Census of 1890, the Methodist Episcopal Church had in that year in the Southern States a property in church buildings worth $12,351,585.[4] The total value of the property of the Northern Church in the South was reported in 1896 as being $17,822,133.[5] The great bulk of this property was made possible by funds contributed by Methodists in the North.

The large contributions made by the Missionary, Church Extension and other societies of the Northern Church for the whites in the South were chiefly for the benefit of a class residing in the mountain and back country regions, generally very poor and illiterate. The Alabama Conference of the Northern Church was described by one of its bishops in 1883 as being typical of the white element in the Church in the lower South. He said of it: "I held the Conference in a little log church in the woods. Windows it had none save holes cut through to let in the light. The nearest house was three quarters of a mile distant, where the principal man of our Church and of that section lived. The pigs made their bed under the floor of the house, and the chickens roosted all around. And this leading man eked out an existence

---

[1] *Idem.*

[2] *Idem.* In that region, during the four years preceding 1895 there had been an increase of only about six and two-thirds per cent in its white membership. *Cf. General Minutes,* 1891, 1895, *passim.* In 1865, the Holston Conference of the Southern Church, which lay chiefly in the mountainous regions of Tennessee and Virginia, reported a white membership of 46,408, only slightly over a thousand members having been lost since 1860. By 1866 its white membership had dropped to 23,021.

[3] *Journal of General Conference,* 1896, p. 411.

[4] This estimate is based on the returns of the *Statistics . . . of the Eleventh Census* (Washington, 1894), Vol. XVI, pp. 38-43.

[5] *Journal of General Conference,* 1896, p. 411.

from a miserable farm of forty-five acres. He could neither read nor write, and he was glad that his little boy could do both for him."[1] With a white membership primarily of this kind, it is obvious that whatever influence the Northern Church might exert on the dominant classes in the South must of necessity be an indirect one.

As compared with other faiths in the Southern States, the collective strength of Methodism, all branches included, served to make it perhaps the most potent religious force in Southern life.[2] According to the Eighth Census, in which denominational strength was measured in terms of church accommodations and the value of

---

[1]Speech of Bishop Wiley before the General Missionary Committee of the Methodist Episcopal Church, as reported in *The Western Christian Advocate,* and cited in the Nashville *Christian Advocate,* December 8, 1883. Excerpts from the speeches of the other bishops were also given. At this meeting the bishops debated the advisability of their Church continuing its work among the whites. Bishop Randolph S. Foster expressed the opinion that, to a large extent, the work was unsatisfactory. He said: "With the best of intentions we have used a good deal of money there, and tried to do a good deal, which, to me has seemed unnecessary to perform, because others were there who ought to do it, and who would have been likely to do it, if we had not attempted it." He was of the opinion that in a number of conferences the people had learned to depend upon the financial aid given them from the North and were not exerting themselves for their own improvement. In response to this statement of opinion, Bishop Wiley said: "But suppose that we must have to concede that a large portion of white people in our Southern country are very poor and ignorant, or even debased, and that they have been very badly trained in all educational and benevolent matters; and suppose that there are multitudes that might be included in that class, what is our duty in the premises?" In a speech before the same body in 1891 Bishop Foster declared that he had never favored the work of his Church among the whites, save on the border. He said that the Church had undertaken to project itself upon the Southern population under circumstances that made it doubtful whether more harm than good had been done in Alabama, Mississippi, Georgia, Louisiana, North Carolina and South Carolina. He advocated a curtailment of appropriations "until those who come to us simply to get the fat will leave us." *Cf.* Nashville *Christian Advocate,* December 5, 1891.

[2]The Negro Methodist organizations experienced a remarkable development in the Southern States during this period. The African Methodist Episcopal Church, which in 1864 had a membership of only 20,000, twenty years later reported the number of its communicants as 391,044. The African Methodist Episcopal Zion Church, whose members in 1864 had been only 6,203, boasted of 300,000 in 1884. The membership in both of these Churches, and that of the Colored Methodist Episcopal Church, which was organized in 1870, increased steadily to the end of the century. These estimates are based on the figures given in *The Methodist Almanac,* 1864, p. 28 and in McTyeire, *op. cit.,* p. 687.

church property, the Methodists ranked first among the religious groups in the Southern States, as they did in the nation at large.[1] Although by 1890 the Census showed a somewhat larger Baptist membership in the South and a larger number of church accommodations in that denomination,[2] Methodism remained in other respects the strongest denomination in the section.[3] This was true as regards the value of church property. In 1890 the value of the Methodist property exceeded that of the Baptists by over eight millions of dollars.[4] Moreover, in comparing the capacity of these denominations for influencing society, it should be noted that, while in the same year the number of Baptist communicants exceeded that of the Methodists by over two hundred thousand, the Negro membership of the Baptist Churches exceeded that of the Methodist by approximately the same amount. The table

---

[1]*Statistics . . . of the Eighth Census*, Misc. Vol., pp. 252-501. This estimate is confirmed by the figures given in Goss, C. C., *Statistical History of the First Century of American Methodism* (New York, 1866), pp. 110-112. This work gives the number of Southern Methodists in 1865 as 708,949. The number of Southern Baptists, as estimated from reports of 1862, is given as 640,806. Since the Southern Methodists lost approximately 113,000 members during the War, it is evident that the difference in numbers between the two denominations was larger in 1862, or as large, as in 1865. *Cf.* table of statistics, Appendix B, p. i.

[2]*Cf.* table of statistics, Appendix A, p. i.

[3]It is probable that the superiority in the number of communicants and in church accommodations assigned to the Baptists in the Census of 1890 was exaggerated. Because that denomination lacked central control in the government of its churches and a thorough system of returns and reports, the statistics prepared by officials of the Church were not always trustworthy. The absence of well kept records in the denomination made it impossible for the Government officials who prepared the Census reports to use the Church records for verifying their own calculations. The *Statistics . . . of the Ninth Census,* Vol. I, p. 502, reported that the Baptists were notably inaccurate in their records. The want of frequent church reports, it said, admitted of dead churches being listed as active, and tended to exaggeration with regard to numbers. The same authority declared that the Methodists, because of their peculiar organization and their special efforts to maintain a careful system of records, were able to furnish statistics that were unusually reliable. The Episcopal form of government and the plan of changing its ministers periodically enabled the Church to know at all times the true condition of the organization in all its parts. The Methodists were said to be foremost among religious groups in this respect. Because of the difference in the manner of preparation of statistics in the two communions, it is probable that the difference in numerical strength between the Methodists and Baptists was much less than the Census reports would indicate.

[4]*Cf.* table of statistics on the value of church property, Appendix A, p. i.

below gives with approximate accurateness the Negro membership of the two denominations in the South in that year:

METHODIST AND BAPTIST NEGRO COMMUNICANTS IN THE SOUTH IN 1890[1]

	African Methodists (eight bodies)	Baptists	Conferences of Meth. Epis. Church	
Alabama	129,167	142,437	Central Ala...	8,924
Arkansas	37,445	63,786	Central Mo...	7,219
Delaware	3,823	————	East Tenn....	37,124
Florida	38,715	20,828	Florida	3,683
Georgia	108,793	200,516	Lexington ...	9,283
Kentucky	28,097	50,245	Little Rock ..	3,697
Louisiana	24,453	68,008	Louisiana ...	13,642
Maryland	15,284	7,750	Mississippi ..	27,771
Mississippi	54,145	136,647	No. Carolina.	7,212
Missouri	12,579	18,613	Savannah ...	15,113
North Carolina	131,026	134,445	So. Carolina .	36,172
South Carolina	137,250	125,572	Tennessee ..	8,123
Tennessee	55,120	52,183	Washington .	29,143
Texas	45,318	111,138	West Texas..	8,828
Virginia	27,855	199,871	Delaware ...	15,061
West Virginia	216	4,233	Texas	11,931
District of Columbia..	4,913	12,717		
	————	————		————
Total	854,200	1,348,989		242,926

Total Negro Methodists.........1,096,496.
Total Negro Baptists............1,348,989.

The connectional character of the Methodist polity contributed much toward making the Southern Church a potent influence in society. Its whole system is consolidated and given compactness through the supervision of a college of bishops. The Methodist episcopacy, unlike that of other Churches, is of the character of a general superintendency, rather than a diocesan episcopacy. The

[1]*Statistics . . . of the Eleventh Census,* Vol. XVI, pp. 38-43. It is very difficult to determine the exact number of Negro Methodist communicants in the South during this period because of the policy which the Methodist Episcopal Church followed in its records of making no distinction whatever with regard to color. By 1890 the colored membership of the Northern Church almost everywhere had been organized into conferences composed entirely of Negro members. By adding the number of communicants in such conferences to the membership of the African Churches, one can arrive at a fairly accurate estimate of the number of Negro Methodists in the South. But such an estimate lacks complete accuracy because the colored conferences did not conform to State lines and in some instances extended to States outside the South.

authority of the bishop, through the medium of subordinate officials, is exercised throughout the bounds of the entire Church.[1]
The bishops act as presiding officers in the quadrennial General
Conference, the highest judicatory and the legislative body of the
Connection, and in the Annual conferences, which are regional
administrative and deliberative assemblies in which the travelling
ministry meets with representatives of the laity to transact the
business of the Church. The bishops report upon their administration, and upon the execution of the law of the Church in the
Annual conferences to the General Conference. In the Annual
Conference they assign to the travelling ministry work for the
coming year.[2] What the individual assignment shall be is determined by the bishop who is presiding, in conference with the
presiding elders of the conference.[3] Because of its centralized
government, the whole body of the Church can be easily moved by
its leaders, and the impulse of any movement within the denomination makes itself felt throughout the entire Connection in a
measure difficult of realization in a body with a congregational or
independent form of government or in one under a diocesan
episcopacy.

"There is illimitable power in a system which sends men to
every community whether they are wanted there or not, and holds
them there by force of law until they create a church and crystallize
a public sentiment in its favor," wrote a Southern Methodist editor
of the period when discussing the itineracy as a factor in the
success of Methodism. "This is the glory of our Church. It goes
ahead of calls and stays in spite of rebuffs and frowns. The success of Methodism in any place may be greater or less; but it never

---

[1] The presiding elder, to whose authority the itinerant preacher is subject,
acts as the local representative of the bishop.

[2] The General Conference is composed of delegates chosen to represent the
travelling ministry and others chosen to represent the laity. In it are not only
reviewed the administrative acts of the Annual conference but appeals are
heard regarding administrative decisions made there. The General Conference
is the patron of all of the pupits of the Connection. The trustees of all church
property hold it for the General Conference.

[3] This conference is informally designated as the "bishop's cabinet." In the
Annual conference is reviewed the results of the year's activities within its
jurisdiction, the minister's character is examined and passed upon, and he is
expected to report on the spiritual and financial condition of the churches under
his care. Young ministers are examined on courses of study which have been
prescribed for them.

retires from any field which it once enters. It has no vacant pulpits, whether in the largest cities or in the far off mountain coves. Nor has it any unemployed preachers. There is work for every effective man in its ranks, and he is protected by the whole power of the Church while doing it. . . . In other communions preachers sometimes stand all day long 'in the market place' because no man hath 'hired' them."[1] Thus the connectional system derived no small measure of its strength from its itinerant feature. Adherents of other denominations charged that the Church was oppressive in government and administration.[2] Its episcopal system was said to have no parallel save that of the Jesuit order.[3] The driving power which Methodism derived from the character of its polity gave it an advantage over other denominations in influencing social policy.[4]

The Methodist press and the function of the Church as an educator were, it will be seen, among the most potent means through which the power of the denomination was conserved and its influence extended in the South during the period from 1865 to 1900. As has been pointed out, the Church showed the utmost energy in reorganizing its press. By 1870 its communicants were supporting twelve weekly journals.[5] Twelve years later twenty weekly papers were being published in the interest of the Church,

---

[1] Dr. E. E. Hoss in Nashville *Christian Advocate,* June 3, 1891. Dr. John P. Newman, of the Northern Church, asserted that the central government of Episcopal Methodism gave it "a supreme authority over the humblest laymen within her communion." *Cf.* letter of Dr. J. P. Newman in *The Methodist,* February 4, 1865.

[2] Although the era of bitter disputation between the denominations in the South was past, reverberations of such controversies as that occasioned by Graves' *The Great Iron Wheel* prior to the Civil War were sometimes heard.

[3] A Protestant Methodist minister of the period wrote: "The Jesuits, or Society of Jesus, had ulterior aims never dreamed of in the philosophy of the Methodist Episcopacy, but as a militant system designed for absolute supremacy over men's minds, and a subordination of all outlying interests to a great central force the likeness is most striking." The idea of the system, he averred, was in the vision of Ezekiel of a "wheel within wheels and a fire infolding itself." It was for the purpose of making men "content under the yoke of a higher estate" that they were "invested with authority over the lower." *Cf.* Drinkhouse, *History of Methodist Reform,* p. 543.

[4] Bishop R. H. Wilmer, of the Protestant Episcopal Church expressed the opinion that the Baptists, while also possessing a large membership and wealth, did not "exercise the same power with the Methodists" because they lacked unity in organization and compactness. *Cf.* Wilmer, *The Recent Past,* pp. 99-100.

[5] *Cf. New Orleans Christian Advocate,* July 30, 1870.

exclusive of its Sunday school journals.[1] Moreover, a number of
the papers of the Northern Church enjoyed a considerable circulation in the South and they kept in close touch with developments
in the Southern body and reported and commented upon them.
Two of the journals of the Methodist Episcopal Church were
published in Southern States throughout most of this period.[2] An
idea of the extent of the influence exerted by the press of the
Church was given in the results of a survey made in 1870, in
which it was found that nine per cent of the Methodist communicants of the South were subscribers to church papers. The Presbyterian was the only denomination which could boast of a larger
percentage. Twenty-seven per cent of its communicants were reported as subscribers.[3] But while the proportion was higher
among the Presbyterians, it should be remembered that the Methodists outnumbered the adherents of that faith by more than three
to one in the Southern States.[4] Moreover, the Presbyterian journals
were private enterprises and could not speak for the denomination
with the same degree of authority that the Methodist journals, as
official organs of their Church or of some of its conferences, could

[1]Statement in Nashville *Christian Advocate,* cited in *New Orleans Christian
Advocate,* January 5, 1882. In its issue of January 28, 1875 the New Orleans
Advocate declared that these journals exerted an indirect influence of highest
importance on Southern society and that "their mission is to conserve and
benefit society."

[2]The two papers published in the South were *The Methodist Advocate* of
Atlanta (later published in Chattanooga) and the *Southwestern Christian Advocate* of New Orleans. The establishment of the former was authorized by the
first General Conference of the Church which convened after the Civil War.
The *Southwestern* which was founded in 1873 as an independent enterprise, by
the Reverend J. C. Hartzell, then serving as pastor of the St. Charles Street
Church of his connection, was made an official organ in 1876. It was in reality
a revival of the *New Orleans Advocate,* a journal which was founded by Dr.
J. P. Newman in 1866, and edited by him until it ceased publication in 1869.
The *Southwestern* became a sort of official mouthpiece for the Negro element
in the Northern Church, and after the early Eighties its editors were colored
men. For a number of years the two journals published in the South were
extremely sectional in tone and they did much to prolong sectional ill feeling
in the South. They took a decided position on all the controversial issues
which then troubled Southern society and they frequently provoked the Southern
journals to sectional outbursts. A good history of the *Southwestern* is given in
its issue of June 28, 1923.

[3]*Cf. New Orleans Christian Advocate,* July 30, 1870. This survey was made
by George R. Rowell and Company, of New York. It was found that only
four per cent of the Baptists and one and a half per cent of the Catholics in
the South were subscribers to church periodicals.

[4]*Cf.* tables of comparative denominational strength in Appendix A, p. i.

claim.[1] The connectional character of Methodism gave to its organs a very wide influence within the denomination. It cannot be doubted but that they exerted a profound influence on a large portion of the Southern people, for in many regions little other than religious periodical reading matter was used. It was asserted in 1885 that the Methodist papers "seem at places to entirely supercede secular literature." The same unfriendly observer declared that the Southern Church had in its journals "facilities for the speedy control of public opinion almost incredible in the North."[2]

There were Methodist institutions of learning in every part of all the Southern States. In a period when the educational system was in chaos and the States themselves could not perform the function, Methodist schools did a work which otherwise must have been, in a large measure, left undone. By the year 1878 the Methodist Episcopal Church, South, was maintaining ninety-five educational institutions. Of these fifty-five were listed as colleges, two as universities, and the remainder as academies or secondary schools.[3] As will be seen, this Church, through force of circumstance, was able to direct the most potent movement in liberal higher education in the South during the period, 1865-1900. The zeal of a renaissance was manifested in the Methodist educational activity of the time. The opportunity for influencing the public mind through its function as an educator was thus one of the chief sources of the influence of the Southern Church.

The power of the Church was greatly enlarged during this period through its growing recognition of the religious needs of youth and its provision of special agencies designed to supply them. Realizing that during the post-war years many children would receive no other formal education than what could be acquired in the Sunday schools, the Church undertook to make these schools effective agencies for religious instruction. The General Conference of 1866 gave much thought to the matter. It abolished the old Sunday School association which had been dis-

---

[1]*Cf.* Vander Velde, *The Presbyterian Churches*, p. 132.

[2]Letter of "A Southerner" in the New York *Nation*, quoted in Nashville *Christian Advocate*, August 28, 1885.

[3]These statistics are taken from an official tabulation given in the Nashville *Christian Advocate*, June 15, 1878.

rupted by the War, and made the Sunday school a part of the Church itself. It made provision for a graded series of literature, to consist of "a regular progressive series of catechisms,"[1] and for the resurrection of the Sunday school journal of the Church, which had not been published for several years.[2] The Book Editor was authorized to add suitable books to the Sunday-school library from time to time, and it was ordered that sacred music be made a feature of the schools.[3] Further effectiveness was given to the system in 1870, when the General Conference created the office of Sunday School Secretary and named for the position Dr. Atticus G. Haygood, one of the most able ministers of the Connection.[4] Under his direction an effective uniform system of lessons was adopted.[5] In 1878 a Sunday School Board, of six members, with the Sunday School Editor as chairman, was created and given charge of all of the connectional Sunday school interests.[6] By 1882 there were 462,321 pupils and 62,444 teachers enrolled in the 9,310 Sunday schools of the Church.[7] In 1886 the bishops of the Connection were moved to declare that "The Church is at last coming to a just appreciation of the claims of the 'child in the midst,' and is making something like adequate provisions for his religious wants."[8] The activity along such lines, and especially among the poor, received a new impulse from the "mission" work done by the Woman's Missionary Society and the Church Extension Society, which were organized in 1878 and 1882 respectively.[9] The interest in Sunday schools continued unabated to the end of the century, at which time the Church

---

[1]*Journal of General Conference*, 1866, p. 82.
[2]*Cf.* Du Bose, *op. cit.*, pp. 157-158.
[3]*Cf. Journal of General Conference*, 1866, pp. 82ff.
[4]Du Bose, *op. cit.*, p. 158.
[5]*Idem.*
[6]*Idem.*
[7]*Cf.* statistics given in Pastoral Address in *Journal of General Conference*, 1882, p. 2.
[8]*Journal of General Conference*, 1886, p. 50. In its issue of July 6, 1877, the New Orleans *Advocate* said: "We should not lose sight of the great end of Sunday schools as the means of instructing children who have no religious advantages at home, and children whose parents do not go to church, and are indifferent, if not inimical to religion. . . . It may be expedient to organize mission schools in the cities, but every school, to a considerable extent, should be a mission school—aggressive, and intent on helping and saving those for whom nobody cares."
[9]*Cf.* McTyeire, *op. cit.*, pp. 676-678.

could boast of 849,101 pupils and 102,703 teachers, enrolled in 13,940 schools.[1] The Church was then publishing nine Sunday-school periodicals, with a combined circulation of 1,131,800.[2]

A further recognition of and provision for the religious needs of youth were made in the young people's societies which were formed and made a part of the organic system of the Church.[3] Although a part of the Young People's Movement, a development which manifested itself to some measure in all of the great Protestant bodies of the day, the "leagues" which were formed in the Methodist Churches for furthering the interests of religion tended to emphasize denominational life and loyalty, whereas in other bodies it inclined to be more diffusive and non-denominational.[4] Such leagues began to appear in the Methodist Episcopal Church, South, as early as 1882, and they were soon found at widely scattered places in the Connection.[5] In 1890 the General Conference gave its sanction to the formation of such "Young People's Leagues."[6] It declared their purpose to be the "promotion of piety and loyalty to our Church among the young people, their education in the Bible and Christian literature and in the missionary work of the Church, and their encouragement in works of grace and charity."[7] Put at first under the control of the Sunday School Board, the leagues were in 1894 formed into a separate connectional department, the "Epworth League."[8] The General Conference of that year also authorized the publication of a journal for the promotion of the interests of the League.[9] Local chapters were soon established in all parts of the South and the membership increased rapidly.[10] The League brought a new and vigorous

---

[1]Boswell, *A Short History of Methodism*, pp. 143-144.
[2]*Idem.*
[3]*Journal of General Conference*, 1890, p. 84. Du Bose, *op. cit.*, pp. 73-76, gives a good account of the origins of the Epworth League.
[4]Du Bose, *op. cit.*, p. 73.
[5]Du Bose, *op. cit.*, p. 74, points out that such a society was organized in the Shearn Methodist Church in Houston, Texas, as early as 1883. The genesis of the Epworth League in the Southern Church was independent of that formed in the Northern Connection, although the latter was formed a year earlier. *Cf.* letter of the Reverend H. M. Du Bose in Nashville *Christian Advocate*, October 14, 1897.
[6]*Journal of General Conference*, 1890, p. 184.
[7]*Cf.* Du Bose, *op. cit.*, p. 74.
[8]*Ibid.*, pp. 74-75; *Journal of General Conference*, 1898, p. 21.
[9]Du Bose, *op. cit.*, p. 110.
[10]*Ibid.*, p. 75.

force to the support of the Church in all of its undertakings. That it acted as a leavening force is shown by a statement made by the editor of the Nashville *Advocate* in 1895. Referring to the claims made for the League by its Secretary, Dr. Samuel Steele, and to the participation of its members in the devotional exercises and business affairs of the Church, the editor declared that, in taking the lead in such affairs, "they are impressed with the necessity of circumspection, and consistency in their daily life—much more so than they could ever be as silent lookers-on in the great congregation. We do not know but Dr. Steele is fully justified in saying that the League can be largely relied on to save our young men and women from the follies of fashionable society and from the grosser sins of the world."[1]

Apart from considerations of numerical and financial strength and the advantages derived from the general character and special features of its economy, a number of things tended to make the Southern Church a potent influence in society. An important element of its power came from the advantages it enjoyed for reaching non-Methodist elements in the population. Because of the unique relations which existed between the Southern Methodists and their co-religionists of the North and because of their relation to the disputed issues which had led to war in the Sixties, Southern Methodism occupied a position of peculiar prominence in the public mind that gave to it a broad popular sympathy. Representatives of the Northern Church attacked the Southern body for its connection with the former ruling classes and the Methodist Episcopal journals frequently paraded the public men of the South most obnoxious to Northern sentiment as being connected with Southern Methodism. Although somewhat misinformed as to the true character of the relations between the two Churches, the comments of a secular paper of that day illustrate well the feeling of sympathy for the Southern Church entertained by the non-Methodist population because of these things. In 1877 the Atlanta *Constitution* said: "Considering the fact that the Northern Methodists hounded on the war, and, since the cessation of hostilities, have contributed numerous anathemas and a large amount of money to keep up the strife, it is a little singular that

---

[1] Dr. E. E. Hoss in Nashville *Christian Advocate*, June 6, 1895.

the Southern Methodists should be continually suing for fraternity. Any fraternity between the Southern and Northern Methodists would be a humbug and a delusion. It is well enough for citizens to fraternize, but what has the Southern Church to do with the imposters who brought the country to grief, and who were most appropriately named the 'hell-hounds of Zion'."[1]

In many places during the post-war period, and especially in the far South, the Methodists possessed wealth and culture enough to enable them to dominate socially.[2] Such leadership was facilitated by a tendency, apparent before the War and now more pronounced, to abandon the peculiar customs which had distinguished the denomination and to place less emphasis on the stricter Methodist notions in regard to dress, ornaments and amusements. "Southern Methodists," it was observed shortly after the War, were "resolved to be like other people."[3] An old-timer declared in 1871 that it had come to pass that "Young Methodist sisters, seated among the scornful, cannot be distinguished from them."[4] "Organs, choirs, and promiscuous sittings,"

---

[1]Atlanta *Constitution,* quoted in the *Methodist Advocate,* June 13, 1877.

[2]Simkins and Woody, *op. cit.,* p. 403, show this to have been true even in the older States like South Carolina, in some sections. They state that the Methodists could dominate in towns like Spartanburg and Cokesbury in the same manner that the Episcopalians did in Charleston and Columbia. They point out that they were able to do this "through routine educational and moral efforts without the emotionalism" necessary during an earlier period. In such places, they state, the Sunday services, weekly prayer meetings, and the Sunday school were directed by well educated ministers, and were of prime importance in the maintenance of the denomination. In Georgia a very large proportion of the public leaders and statesmen were prominently identified with Methodism. Among them were Henry W. Hilliard, Henry W. Grady, L. Q. C. Lamar, B. F. Hill, General John B. Gordon, Walter B. Hill, Alfred H. Colquitt, Mrs. Rebecca Felton, and her husband, Dr. William H. Felton. Of this group, Colquitt, Hilliard, and Dr. Felton were local Methodist preachers.

[3]Smith, *Life of Pierce,* p. 580. In a letter to the Church, published in the *Wesleyan Christian Advocate* in 1884, Bishop Pierce said: "We hear of progress, and civilization, and refinement; and the popular inference is that these things have brought along changes of manners and customs which demand of the Church a relaxation of her rules for the convenience, and accommodation, and social prestige of her members. But this very idea is vicious, and full of corruption—a plea for back-sliding and degeneracy. Neither wealth, nor culture, nor society can purchase exemption from the great law of *self-denial,* nor authenticate any enlargement of our moral liberties. The terms of discipleship, as laid down by Christ, are inflexible." Cf. *Wesleyan Christian Advocate,* quoted in Nashville *Christian Advocate,* February 16, 1884.

[4]Letter of "Old Fogy" in *New Orleans Christian Advocate,* June 8, 1871, In 1877 the venerable Dr. Lovick Pierce, one of the outstanding figures in Southern Methodism since the time of his rejection as a fraternal messenger by

lamented a bishop of the Church about the same time, "have pretty nearly petrified Methodism in our larger towns. Oh that Methodists were content to be a peculiar people."[1] "Nothing," declared this same bishop on another occasion, "is left in many places but a petrified respectability."[2] The outstanding educational work of the Church inevitably won for it the respect of the more cultivated elements.[3] Despite the fact that the Church had continued to be conservative with regard to ministerial training, and had not made a formal theological schooling an indispensable qualification for entering its ministry, it had done much to encourage theological study in its own colleges, and there were in the Connection many learned and eloquent preachers.[4] Of the able body of men who composed the College of Bishops from 1865 to 1900, several stood forth among the most commanding public figures of the day. They were distinguished as being

---

the Northern Church in 1848, sent a communication to the Nashville *Advocate* on this subject. Referring to an inquiry which had recently been made with regard to the wearing of jewels by Methodists, he said: "I am greatly troubled at the inquiry—and the more so, as I see the inquirer is an itinerant Methodist preacher, having to read the General Rules to his people—and still more so, because within a few years past, I have had the mortification to see Methodist preachers' wives and daughters—all in Church—ear-ringed and jeweled to the extent of their money and pride. Of course they all look upon Mr. Wesley as a Scriptural *ignoramus,* and upon Paul and Peter as if joking upon the credit of inspiration. . . . The growing practical contempt of our General Rules, by allowance, in the Church has been to me the unmistakeable diagnosis of our moral death." *Cf.* Nashville *Christian Advocate,* March 10, 1877.

[1]Smith, *Life of Pierce,* p. 537.

[2]*Ibid.,* p. 578.

[3]Evidences of this were frequently seen in the secular press in connection with references to Vanderbilt University.

[4]A strong movement developed in the Church just after the Civil War in favor of establishing an institution to be devoted solely to the purpose of furnishing a formal theological training, and, although this movement was defeated, it will be seen that its supporters had their project incorporated in the plans for a great central university for Southern Methodism which resulted in the founding of Vanderbilt University. *Cf. Journal of General Conference,* 1866-1900, *passim.* Dr. Stuart Robinson, one of the best known ministers of the Presbyterian Church in America, was reported to have declared that the Reverend Holland N. McTyeire was the ablest preacher in the South. *Cf.* Price, *op. cit.,* Vol. IV, p. 439. Bishop George F. Pierce was commonly reputed to be one of the greatest orators that America had produced. The Atlanta *Constitution* asserted that as a pulpit orator he was incomparable and it reported that Lord Macaulay had declared one of his sermons to be "the finest specimen of English he had seen from any American." *Cf.* Atlanta *Constitution,* quoted in *Wesleyan Christian Advocate,* Sept. 17, 1884. A correspondent of *Zion's Herald* (Boston) in 1865 described a sermon preached by Bishop Pierce in the Georgia Conference which met soon after the close of the Civil War in the following words: "His hortatory appeals to the ministry, which were mingled

among the foremost leaders in progressive thought along various lines.[1]

A further important means of affecting the non-Methodist elements of society lay in the capacity of the Methodist Episcopal Church, South, for influencing the other large Protestant denominations of the section. The disapproval which those bodies felt of the invasion of its territory by the Northern Church naturally inclined them favorably towards it. Moreover, the Methodists held to almost no particularistic doctrines, and in all of the fundamentals of othodox belief they occupied common ground with them. "Whatever else may be believed by the Presbyterian, Baptist, Lutheran, Congregationalist, Episcopalian," wrote a Southern Methodist in 1890, "every one of them believes all that is in the Twenty-five Articles; or even if there should be anything here which he cannot heartily indorse, he can unite with his Methodist brethren upon the simple terms by which the Methodist himself became a member—'a desire to flee from the wrath to come and be saved from sin'."[2] With the Baptists and Presbyterians, who with the Methodists formed the great bulk of the Protestant communicants in the South, the Methodists were, save in regard to minor doctrinal points, in hearty agreement. While Methodists disagreed with Baptists and Presbyterians over special doctrines, and often furiously, their essential agreement on fundamentals, their common dislike and dread of Catholicism, and their puritanical and anti-ritualistic leanings frequently led to a good measure of coöperation between their Churches.[3] They often joined in union services, assembling together for preaching, in

---

throughout the sermon, sometimes rose to a pitch of pathetic eloquence truly sublime and overwhelming, and wrought with matchless power on the clerical portion of his audience." Cf. Zion's Herald, quoted in Nashville Christian Advocate, January 4, 1866.

[1] This is particularly true of Bishop McTyeire, who as president of the Board of Trust of Vanderbilt University, was in a position to exert a wide influence, and of Bishop Atticus G. Haygood, who gained a wide reputation and power as Agent for the Slater Fund and as a writer of liberal and progressive views.

[2] Dodd, T. J., "Methodism and Advanced Thought," The Quarterly Review, Vol. IX (October 1890), p. 54.

[3] A Protestant Episcopal Bishop of that time declared with regard to the Baptists that, while they were in fact illiberal, they had, "by their fraternizations with other Christian people in preaching, etc.," acquired a credit for liberality that was undeserved. Cf. Wilmer, The Recent Past, pp. 100-101.

prayer meetings, and in revival services. While the Protestant Episcopalians generally held apart, they, too, sometimes united in such services.[1] Methodism was frequently asserted to be a "feeder" of other denominations during the second half of the nineteenth century.[2] Its "revivals of religion," it was claimed, "helped to fill their pews, besides imparting vitality to their organizations."[2] This function was recognized by the Church as a legitimate part of its labors. "To meet the fact . . . and to recognize this catholic and unsectarian purpose as a part of our aim and work," said the editor of the New Orleans *Advocate* in 1866, "is certainly a noble and magnanimous position."[3]

Because of its fundamental accord with the other large Protestant bodies in the section, any movement inaugurated in the Methodist Episcopal Church, South, naturally made itself felt in those bodies. The extent of the influence exerted in this way is indicated by the fact that in many parts of the South the Methodists and Baptists together had a virtual monopoly of the church

---

[1] *Cf.* Simkins and Woody, *op. cit.*, p. 408. Although so nearly akin in doctrine and origin to the Methodists, the Protestant Episcopalians, because of certain exclusive pretensions and their dislike of emotional religion, puritanism, and levelling tendencies, held apart from the Methodists more than the other Protestant denominations did. This is the more surprising since a considerable part of the membership of the Protestant Episcopal Church was drawn from the Southern Church, and, as has been pointed out, a large number of the Episcopalians families of the older slave States had turned Methodist on moving to the far South. Moreover, as the New Orleans *Advocate* pointed out in 1870, it "is notorious that no small per cent of Episcopalian ministers were Methodist ministers and the children of Methodist parents." *Cf. New Orleans Christian Advocate,* July 9, 1870. "They do not claim," said a bishop of the Methodist Episcopal Church, South, when deriding certain assumptions of the Protestant Episcopalians, "to be more holy, but more genteel and respectable." *Cf.* letter of Bishop George F. Pierce in *Southern Christian Advocate,* quoted in Simkins and Woody, *op. cit.*, p. 408. Bishop Wilmer of the Protestant Episcopal Church attributed the lack of a hold on "the masses" by his Church to their "indwelling spirit of social jealousy." *Cf.* Wilmer, *The Recent Past,* p. 63. "Verily, what means it," asked Bishop Pierce, "that Episcopalians of high and low degree can call us sects, without clergy or sacraments, and set themselves up as the Church, the only Church, no man objecting to this fustian and nonsense, this brag and bluster; and forsooth if you or I or any other decent man beg leave to dissent, or try by Scriptural arguement, by history and fact, to show that Methodism is somewhat too, then we are ignorant, vulgar, ill-bred." *Cf.* Smith, *op. cit.,* p. 506.

[2] *Cf. New Orleans Christian Advocate,* May 26, 1866.

[3] An unfriendly critic declared in 1885 that the Church had the means of influencing for good or evil nearly every household in the South. He felt that it exercised a direful influence on the Southern character through its "emotional 'revivals of religion,' whereby the process of instantaneous conversion is sub-

membership. According to an estimate made by the New York *Nation* in 1885, the two denominations together constituted 90 per cent of the total church membership in the eight States from Virginia to Louisiana. This estimate revealed that in Alabama and Mississippi the combined membership of the Methodists and Baptists reached the high average of 95 per cent of the total; in Georgia 94 per cent; in South Carolina 91 per cent. At the same time, the *Nation* pointed out, the combined membership of the two denominations in the nation at large comprised but 47 per cent of the total.[1] According to the Eleventh Census, the combined membership of the two denominations in the eight States mentioned above and in the four other Southern States of Arkansas, Texas, Tennessee, and West Virginia amounted to nearly 80 per cent of the entire church membership in 1890.[2]

The improvement of its relations with the Northern Church served to make possible for the Methodist Episcopal Church, South, a new power in society. When it had been made apparent that the Southern Methodists were unprepared for reunion and would entertain no overtures looking to a closer approach not based on terms honorable to themselves, the way was cleared for the establishment of formal fraternity. Undeterred by any expectation of reunion for the present, leaders in the Northern body were more inclined to strive for an amicable adjustment of differences. The sentiment in favor of establishing a friendly intercourse now gained ground rapidly, and in 1872 the Northern General Conference declared with reference to the Southern Church that, "recognizing that Church and its people as a portion of the great Christian Church and Methodist family, we wish them abundant success in their efforts to promote the cause of Christ

---

stituted for the calm, sober years of reflection that should logically precede all religious conviction." Letter of "A Southerner" in *Nation,* quoted in Nashville *Advocate,* August 29, 1885. To the editor of the *Christian Observer,* who had written him with regard to the Methodist revivalist, Sam Jones, that he preferred taking his theology "out of deep, old wells, and with a Greek bucket and a Hebrew windlass," an Alabama Presbyterian wrote: "Of course I know that, and how scholarly your defense of a learned clergy always is—but when you hear that almost every friend you have in Huntsville has come to Christ through this man, I know you will want to hear something of his way—a way that is absolutely Apostolic in its simplicity," Letter of Flake White in *Christian Observer,* quoted in Nashville *Advocate,* April 4, 1885.

[1]*Nation,* quoted in Nashville *Advocate,* October 3, 1885.

[2]Estimate based on figures given in Appendix A, p. i.

and his Gospel." At the same time the Conference authorized a delegation of three to visit the General Conference of the Southern body in 1874 for the purpose of placing "ourselves in the truly fraternal relations toward our Southern brethren which the sentiments of our people demand, and to prepare the way for the opening of formal fraternity with them." While the Conference asserted the necessity of the Northern Church occupying the Southern territory in perpetuity, it expressed the wish to avoid all unfriendly rivalries with "our brethren of the Church South."[1]

The overture of the Northern Church was cordially received. The General Conference at Louisville in 1874 took pains, however, to guard against the impression that it would favor reunion, and it urged the necessity of an adjustment of all the troubles between the two bodies as a basis for real fraternity.[2] Following its suggestion the two Churches created commissions to adjust all matters outstanding between them.[3] The report of the joint delegations, known as the Cape May Commission, was accepted as a finality by the two Churches. The settlement agreed upon in 1876 did much to advance practical fraternity. The action of the Commission was directed toward making it possible for the two Methodisms to dwell amicably together on Southern soil. In adopting the report the Methodist Episcopal Church officially recognized the Methodist Episcopal Church, South, as "a legitimate branch of Episcopal Methodism in the United States, having a common origin" with itself. The Commission adjudicated claims to the property in dispute between the Churches. This it did both in particular cases and on general principles. It also sought to ensure peace between the two connections by adopting rules regulating the occupation of places by them in the future.[4]

---

[1] *Journal of General Conference*, 1872, pp. 402-403. Stating that it did not propose to discuss at that time the relations between the two bodies since 1844, the Conference declared that it was "content to let past events go into history or be forgotten, as the case may be."

[2] *Journal of General Conference*, 1874, pp. 542-548. The Conference adopted a report on the subject which said: "We deem it proper, for the attainment of the object sought, to guard against all misapprehension. Organic union is not involved in fraternity. In our view the reasons for the separate existence of these two branches of Methodism are such as to make corporate union undesirable and impracticable. The events of the past thirty years have confirmed us in the conviction that such a consummation is demanded neither by reason nor charity."

[3] McTyeire, *op. cit.*, p. 684.

[4] *Idem.*

Atticus G. Haygood

Although the rivalries between the two Methodisms in the South continued to be productive of ill feeling after 1876, and frequently took the form of the setting up of "altar against altar,"[1] the future of the Methodist Episcopal Church, South, was now secure, and the adoption of the Cape May Report marks the beginning of a transition from a period in which the policy of the Church had of necessity been largely one of defense and self-preservation to one in which it could employ its energies in constructive purposes. It foretold a reaction from the conservatism, in policy and administration which had characterized the Connection since the time of its organization. The Church was animated by the confidence always begotten by a wholesome sense of power.[2]

The new trend was clearly indicated in an article of the Reverend David C. Kelley which appeared in the *Quarterly Review* of the Southern Connection early in 1882. Declaring that he spoke for a large class in the South, the writer asserted that "so far from continuing to hold the doctrine that the Church must abstain from all teaching on civil questions, the true doctrine is that wherever a moral question has been adversely acted upon by the State, the necessity for fearless, outspoken truth becomes the more urgent upon the part of the Church." The effort which had been made to relegate slavery to the State as a purely civil institution, he pointed out, could now be regarded only "as a temporary parallax in the vision of good men under great trial." He urged that the Church would not adhere to the old view because of considerations of consistency. He protested against the idea that "because some of our fathers—wise and good men—should have, in great pressure, in the midst of the smoke and confusion of

---

[1]As late as 1898 the editor of the Nashville *Advocate* could declare: "No matter who is to blame, it is a fact that in hundreds and thousands of villages and hamlets the unedifying spectacle is presented of two little Methodist meeting houses standing over against each other, and maintaining an eager and often unholy rivalry for preëminence. . . . In this connection we wish to call public attention to the fact that during the past two or three years as many as twenty-five feeble congregations, not one of which has the remotest chance of becoming self-supporting, have been organized by the officials of the Methodist Episcopal Church in the State of Texas. These congregations, in every instance, are made up of malcontents and seceders from our Communion. The pastors sent to them by Episcopal authority are a burden upon a depleted missionary treasury. Is this right: In the name of fraternity, we insist that it is not." *Cf.* Nashville *Christian Advocate*, April 14, 1898.

[2]*Cf.*, Du Bose, *op. cit., passim.*

battle, declared that slavery was a civil institution, and drawn therefrom the false conclusion that the Church must maintain towards
it a perpetual silence, that we at this late date shall be bound to
regard their declaration as the lamp of truth." Considerations of
consistency would shut the Church out from exercising any influence on "the liquor question, the Sunday-law question, gambling
in its protean forms, and other ever recurring matters of vital
interest to the Church and to the world, all of which have both a
civil and a moral side." History, he declared, had "written slavery
as the cause of the separation" of the Churches, "never to be
rewritten." The writer proceeded to give evidence to show that
the Church was reacting from its old conservatism. "In visiting
Conferences for the past two years," he said, "it has been a matter
of deep interest to watch the efforts to put this new wine in the
old bottles. In every case we have witnessed, but one, the attempt
to restrain temperance resolutions by applying the old rule, that
this belongs to the State, and must not be meddled with by the
Church; the wine has burst the bottles, and the old leaders have
found that their appeal to history falls on deaf ears. This is
peculiarly so in the most active Conferences where progress in
every Church activity is most marked." He pointed out that resolutions with regard to prohibition and Sunday-laws, of the same
general character as the anti-slavery resolutions which forty years
before had flooded the conferences of the Methodist Episcopal
Church, were now being passed by large majorities in the conferences of the Southern Church.

Although the Methodist Episcopal Church, South, continued to
emphasize its "Scriptural" mission to the end of the century, it
will be seen that its interest in "practical religion" grew steadily.
A number of things other than the adjustment of its difficulties
with the Methodist Episcopal Church and the sense of power
resulting therefrom operated to give the Southern Church a
broader conception of its mission, and to impress upon it, more
and more, the importance of bringing its influence to bear on
practical affairs. There can be little doubt that the example set by
the Methodist Episcopal Church with regard to matters of practical
religion awakened it in many instances to a realization of the
necessity for the performance of good works. The close juxta-

position of the two bodies in the South inevitably invited a comparison of activities that would provoke an emulation in good works. The shortcomings of Southern Methodists in such matters were constantly advertised by the Methodist journals of the North. This was done with regard to both particular instances and general policies. The journals of the Southern Connection were frequently charged with "censurable silence" with regard to matters of social and moral reform. Southern Methodists were said to be morally incapacitated for undertaking the regeneration of society.[1] When it was implied in 1887 that the Northern Church was not needed in the South, because the doctrines preached by the two Churches were the same, a correspondent of the New York *Christian Advocate* declared that such a statement "must be taken with some degree of allowance." "If the doctrines be the same," the writer said, "the principles outgrowing are vastly different, and the practices more widely so."[2] That the taunts of Northern Methodists were not without effect on the Southern Church was indicated by the remarks of the editor of the New Orleans *Advocate* in 1881. Referring to the charges brought by the Northern journals against the press of his Church, he said: "The Northern politicians and religious meddlers have been so long and strenuously insisting upon the social and industrial and other shortcomings and sins of the South, that some of our own press are beginning to echo their senseless and conceited jargon. We are glad to see that the Nashville *Advocate* has a true conception of the situation."[3] In 1883 the Reverend W. L. C. Hunnicutt of

---

[1] Such charges were made in the New York *Christian Advocate* in its issues of September 7, 1865, January 25, 1866, and October 12, 1871. The spirit in which many of the taunts against the Church were made was indicated in the remarks made by the Reverend J. M. Buckley, when he assumed the editorship of the New York *Advocate* in 1881. Referring to the Southern Church, he said: "To taunt those who are doing what they can for their people and for the cause of Christ by referring to past events, or to narrow and bitter men among them, belongs not to the 'Church constructant,' nor to the Church nobly militant, but to the 'Church termagent'." *Cf.* New York *Christian Advocate*, April 17, 1881.

[2] Letter of "A Voice from the Border South" in New York *Christian Advocate*, January 20, 1887.

[3] *New Orleans Christian Advocate*, February 3, 1881. The Nashville journal had maintained the position that the religious journals of the North, and especially those of the Methodist Episcopal Church, were denouncing and magnifying the evils of Southern society for party effect, and that it would give no countenance to such a course. The New Orleans *Advocate*, in its issue of

Mississippi complained with reference to the policies which Dr. Atticus G. Haygood had urged as editor of the *Wesleyan Christian Advocate* that it seemed to him that Dr. Haygood had advocated a "Northern, as contradistinguished from our Southern, view on almost every question on which they would be expected to differ."[1]

Forces of a subtler character were inclining the Church to a broader conception of its legitimate functions and activities. New forms of skepticism and unbelief were threatening its authority. By the late Seventies American scientists everywhere were committed to the support of Darwin's theory of biological evolution.[2] At the same time textual or "higher" criticism, imported from the German universities, was calling into question the authority which heretofore had been accorded the Scriptures.[3] Subjecting the Bible to historical analysis, the new science declared it to be not a work all of one piece and inspired in all its parts, but one combining history, prophecy, folklore, and poetry, which had been assembled during a period of a thousand years. While the Southern people were generally orthodox in their religious views, and there was less of skepticism in the public mind of the South than in the North,[4] the Church could not ignore such threats to its

---

August 3, 1876, again expressed such an attitude. It said: "At any rate we are not to be forced into a premature denunciation of the white people of the South by the clamor and innuendoes of Northern religious partisans."

[1]Letter of "W. L. C. H." in *New Orleans Christian Advocate*, October 25, 1883.

[2]*Cf.* Schlesinger, A. M., "A Critical Period in American Religion," (Pamphlet), p. 3.

[3]*Ibid.*, pp. 5-6; *Cf.* White, *Warfare of Science with Theology*, II, pp. 288-396.

[4]The conservatism of the religious mind of the South, as contrasted with that of the North, was frequently commented upon by the Methodist journals of the South. In its issue of July 6, 1882, the *New Orleans Christian Advocate* said: "The South can congratulate herself on what some may sneeringly term 'conservatism' or 'old fogyism,' but what is really an orthodox and evangelical religion. The isms and heresies of the North cannot live and thrive in the South. Universalism, Unitarianism, Agnosticism *et id omne genus* have scarcely a name in our borders. In that respect we are behind the times, and there may we ever remain, plodding along 'the old paths'." In its issue of June 6, 1883, the Nashville *Christian Advocate* said: "Southern Methodists are a solid, conservative sort of people, who do their own thinking, and act on their own convictions. They are not given to sudden excitements, nor do they follow any leader, or commit themselves to any new movement until they have closely examined the credentials of the one and the tendency of the other. They have never been swept off their feet by any sudden tide of popular opinion; and when any man they have loved and trusted goes wrong, they refuse to follow him." On another occasion the Nashville *Advocate* declared: "Southern Metho-

authority as it saw implied in the teachings of the new science and scholarship. Moreover it was alarmed at the crumbling of orthodoxy in the North which resulted from such developments as Christian Science, Ethical Culture, the Theosophical Movement, and from the influence exerted by the "notorious infidel," Robert G. Ingersoll.[1] In the increasing secularization of the Sabbath which took place in urban districts and especially in the North, during the post-war period, the Southern Church saw an especially ominous portent of the influence exerted by such movements.[2] The alarm which it felt with regard to these developments inclined the Church to adopt new methods of combatting such influences and to redouble its efforts in that direction. That the threats to orthodoxy were causing it to take a new conception of its legitimate functions was made clear by the bishops in the Pastoral Address delivered in the General Conference of 1878. Referring to the condition of the Church during the quadrennium then drawing to a close, they said: "The startling diffusion of new and imposing forms of unbelief, within the period of which we speak, has placed the entire Christian Church in the presence of a formid-

---

dism is true to its conservative traditions, and is manifestly more disposed to develop along lines already marked out than to hazard doubtful experiments or revolutionary measures. It is so busy cultivating the fields it occupies that it has no desire to waste its energies in fitting out North Pole expeditions of ecclesiastical or doctrinal discovery." *Cf.* Nashville *Christian Advocate,* May 23, 1885.

[1]*Cf.* Schlesinger, *op. cit.,* pp. 9-18. An account of the rise and the novel teachings of these new movements is given in this article. Socialism was very much feared as a vehicle for the dissemination of such views. In 1886 the *Episcopal Methodist* of Baltimore warned the Church that "The socialist, under the garb and guise of a working-man, is influencing the men of toil, who want rest and recreation after the labors of the week; and into greedy ears he is pouring the glowing promises of much better times for the laborer when the capitalist shall have been robbed and the Churches shall have been destroyed. We must pay more attention to home missions, especially in our large cities, and the old grapple with lowly life must begin anew; and we must prove that we believe every man a brother, possessed of an immortal soul, for whose salvation we are deeply concerned. . . . Either the Church must do the pioneer work thoroughly or 'the enemy will sow tares while we sleep,' and by our own indolence and indifference we will contribute to the loss of souls and the upturning of the very foundations of society." *Episcopal Methodist,* quoted in Nashville *Christian Advocate,* May 1, 1886. The Methodist journals pointed out often the "essentially infidel" element in all such movements. They were especially opposed to Spiritualism on such grounds. *Cf.* Nashville *Christian Advocate,* September 27, 1883.

[2]In 1880 the *Episcopal Methodist,* in referring to the increasing desecration of the Sabbath in the cities, said: "There is a foreign population among us who have imported into this country their infidel and socialistic ideas, and are

able and self-confident antagonism, which is forcing upon her the vital questions of her true foundation, her legitimate affinities, and her best modes of successful defense. All alike are obliged to accept this gage of War. We too must adjust ourselves to these exigencies."[1] Again in 1890 the bishops reminded the Church that it must carry forward its work in "an age when the functions of the pulpit and pastorate are largely usurped by the secular press and platform, and doctrines are widely disseminated (sometimes from the pulpit itself) subversive of the word of God and of the foundations of spiritual life."[2]

Although the old fear and dislike of a "political" Church survived in the denomination and the continued emphasis on revivalism tended to keep men's minds diverted from the affairs of this world, yet these things did not serve to counterbalance the new tendencies. Indeed, the ability to keep awake the revival spirit added greatly to the power of the Church in all of its undertakings. Referring to a revival which had recently taken place there, a physician at Gadsden, Alabama, wrote in 1886: "From this time forth there will be in Gadsden less profanity, less whiskey-drinking, less Sabbath breaking, less theater-going. As to the german, its back is broken, and there are not enough patrons left to give it a decent burial."[3]

Editors and ministers of the Methodist Episcopal Church, South, came to speak out boldly on public questions where moral issues were involved.[4] In 1882 the editor of the official journal of the Connection expressed his approval of the influence that was being

---

seeking to engraft them upon our institutions and social customs. Our only safety is in resisting every encroachment of the kind. Otherwise our liberties will be endangered, and every sacred formula and venerable tradition transmitted to us with our birthright of freedom set at naught. There is nothing we should guard with more jealous care than the observance of the Sabbath. Let that be ignored, and the very foundations of public morality and private virtue will be undermined." Cf. Episcopal Methodist, quoted in New Orleans Christian Advocate, April 29, 1880.

[1]Cf. Pastoral Address in Journal of General Conference, 1878, pp. 30-31.

[2]Journal of General Conference, 1890, p. 27.

[3]Letter of John P. Rawls, M. D., in Nashville Christian Advocate, April 10, 1886.

[4]As early as 1876 the Tennessee Conference called upon the Nashville Advocate to give in place of so much writing on "the dogmatic" and "ecclesiastical questions," more articles "which deal with questions that arise in the every day experience of Christian lives." Cf. Tennessee Conference Journal, 1876, pp. 240-241.

exerted by the ministers in the movements for reform that were then being waged. He said: "The minister of the Gospel who stands silent, with his finger in his mouth, while the battle for moral reforms that involve the life of the Country, incurs the secret contempt of even the vicious elements, of whom he is the ally. When the victory is won without his help, he will be sorry that he mistook pussillanimity for prudence."[1] That same year the editor of the *Wesleyan Christian Advocate* commended the Nashville *Advocate* for having recently instituted a column for observations on the affairs of the country at large. He deplored the fact that the editor had put his observations in small print, as though half apologetic about them; but he ventured the opinion that they would be put in large print by and by. "The representative paper of a Church of more than a million members has a right to animadvert on the way things are going in America, to warn the country of the dangers ahead, and to urge the people to lives of noble daring along all lines of righteousness, truth, and charity," he said. "Outside and apart from all partisan politics—such as the tariff, woman's suffrage, and the like—there are many and far-reaching subjects on which Christian people need information and advice."[2] In 1889 Dr. O. P. Fitzgerald, the editor of the Nashville *Advocate,* lamented the fact that an experience in grace seemed to suffice for so many persons. The insistence of early Methodist preaching on experimental religion, he said, partly accounted for the fact that so many in the Church were "slow to fall in the line of progress and work for the great moral movements of the day." But he added: "Better sentiments are prevailing, and the attitude of the Church is changing. We would not intimate that the Church is losing sight of the vital principles of the Gospel, or ceasing to insist on experience in grace, but that the ministry and membership are learning more and more, and giving more and more emphasis to the importance of practical religion—of 'bringing forth fruits meet for repentance.' Hence the activity in all religious and benevolent enterprises."[3]

The extent to which the denomination occupied itself with

---

[1]Nashville *Christian Advocate,* February 19, 1887.
[2]*Wesleyan Christian Advocate,* quoted in Nashville *Christian Advocate,* March 5, 1887.
[3]Nashville *Christian Advocate,* February 16, 1889.

practical affairs is indicated by the alarm which was expressed by another editor of the Nashville *Advocate* in the mid-Nineties. In 1894 Dr. E. E. Hoss wrote: "In many places the old theme of personal religion has been virtually banished. Into its place are put mere discussions of current issues, the most of which have, it is true, pronounced moral phases. We feel sure that the final outcome of this policy will be disastrous beyond measure. No amount of interest in matters that are occuring in this world can be an effective substitute for an intelligent concern in matters that lie within the sphere of the world to come."[1]

That Southern Methodists had ceased to be apologetic with regard to their attempts to influence social policy was evinced by the out-spoken manner in which this same editor discussed current issues. Only a few years after Dr. Hoss had deplored the decline of personal religion he wrote an "Open Letter" to the General Assembly of the State of Tennessee, in which he pointed out that open and notorious lobbying in that body by the liquor interests had been unrebuked by its members. In his letter to the legislators Dr. Hoss said: "If such a thing should ever happen again, we promise to make it too warm for the comfort of the gentlemen in question and of the Senators who debase themselves by allowing so brazen a performance."[2]

As with the pulpit and press, so the deliberative bodies of the Church came more and more to deal with problems of practical and social interest. These bodies debated at great length matters of public policy. Special committees were appointed and standing committees created to consider and report on such matters. Resolutions were passed and petitions adopted and sent to legislatures and public officials calling upon them to take action with regard to public issues. The coöperation of other denominations was invited, and the work of special organizations designed to secure such ends was commended and encouraged. It will be seen that the representative bodies of the Methodist Episcopal Church, South, came with increasing frequency to adopt reports, resolutions, and petitions with the purpose of influencing social policy.

From what has been said in this chapter, it is obvious that the

---

[1]*Ibid.*, November 1, 1894.
[2]*Ibid.*, November 17, 1898.

strength of Southern Methodism in wealth and numbers, the advantages it derived from the general character and special features of its economy and from its peculiar relation to Southern society, the compactness it acquired through its contest with Northern Methodism, its fundamental accord with the other large Protestant bodies of the section, its ability to keep awake the revival spirit among a large portion of the population, and its changing conception of the scope and mission of the church, all combined to make it a potent influence on social reform in the South during the years from 1865 to 1900. The extent to which the Methodist Episcopal Church, South could exert such an influence becomes apparent when one reflects that during those years religion played a dominant rôle in the life of the Southern people. In 1880 a thoughtful observer of the times expressed it as his opinion that since the Civil War "The controlling sentiment of the Southern people in city and hamlet, in camp and field, among white and black has been religious."[1] And in 1885 a distinguished Methodist minister and editor declared that "There is no part of the world in which ministers of the Gospel are more respected than in the Southern States."[2] Nor were its opportunities for influencing society unrecognized by the Church. "Never at any former period," exultingly announced a committee of Southern Methodists when referring to their Church in 1870, "Never at any former period, had the Methodist Church so strong a hold upon public sympathy, never were its opportunities for usefulness so great as at the present time."[3]

---

[1] Haygood, Atticus G., *The New South* (pamphlet, 1880), pp. 9-10.
[2] Dr. O. P. Fitzgerald in Nashville *Christian Advocate*, October 17, 1885.
[3] *Cf. Journal of General Conference*, 1870, p. 235.

CHAPTER IV

METHODIST FACTORS IN POST-WAR SECTIONALISM

THE struggle to maintain its position of ascendency in the Southern States which was forced upon the Methodist Episcopal Church, South, during the period following the Civil War was essentially a sectional one, and, as such, exerted a marked influence on the outlook of Southern society. As has been seen, the dominant and articulate classes in the greater part of the South looked upon the Northern Church as an alien body when it sought to occupy the section and sympathized with the Southern Church in objecting to its presence there. To the end of the century the Methodist Episcopal Church was regarded by the great majority of Southerners as a "Northern Church" on Southern soil. The Northern and Southern churchmen continued to wage bitter controversies over all the issues on which the two sections differed at the time, and in so doing kept those issues prominently before the public mind. The degree to which the Methodist Episcopal Church, South, may be charged with responsibility for prolonging sectional ill feeling among the Southern people can be best understood therefore in the light of the position maintained there by the Northern Church.[1]

Hardly had hostilities ceased in 1865 before the journals and the deliberative bodies and officials of the Methodist Episcopal Church began to announce that their Church had an important mission to fulfill in the regeneration of Southern society which they said must now take place. "Never before was such a mission given to any people," declared the editor of the New York *Christian Advocate* early in 1865. "It must be our great business

---

[1] Referring to a great benefaction which had recently been conferred by a Northern business magnate upon the Southern Methodists and the people of the South, a secular Southern journal expressed the hope in 1873 that the gift would result in the "obliteration of that sectional bitterness for which the Methodist Church is in a great measure responsible." Asking how it was that when such men of the world could forget and forgive "the saints" could not do likewise, this journal volunteered the opinion that "The Methodist Episcopal Church, North, and the Methodist Episcopal Church, South, have both sinned enough to forgive each other." Cf. *Memphis Avalanche,* quoted in New York *Christian Advocate,* April 3, 1873.

through the years of the immediate future to reconstruct Southern society on the basis of free labor and universal education, in the absence of class legislation, and with all men, as of a common brotherhood, equal before the law."[1] "Our Church," wrote a missionary of the Northern body, "has a great, glorious, and important mission to fulfill in the South; greater, more imperative than in the North."[2] Another of the missionaries in the South when urging young ministers to come there declared that "To reform society here by the Gospel of Christ is a work so vast, so certain to be accomplished by faith and work, as to assure the laborer a place in history beside the immortal founders of our missionary Church."[3] The editor of a journal established by the Northern body in New Orleans, when discussing the reason for the existence of the paper explained that "The field is large. Society is to be recast in a higher mold."[4] It was frequently said that the Church had been providentially called to the performance of this task. "We are called upon by the providence of God," declared the New England Conference, "to enter that territory and plant there the true principles in government, morals, and religion."[5]

All of the plans of the Northern Church for the regeneration of Southern society, it must be noted, were based on sectional concepts. They were the expression of "Northern" or "New England" ideas, and they were urged upon the Southern people in a manner that proved irritating to those for whose benefit they were designed. They were invariably founded upon the assumption of a superior morality and civic virtue in the North. "This country," said the editor of *The Methodist Advocate* when referring to the South in 1869, "is to be rejuvenated with new and in the main peculiarly 'Northern' ideas. . . . The Methodist Episcopal Church is to be one of the most potent agencies in the renovation of the South. This Church is to become one of the leading if not the

---

[1] Dr. Daniel Curry, in New York *Christian Advocate*, April 6, 1865.

[2] *Cf.* letter of the Reverend E. N. Cobleigh in New York *Christian Advocate*, November 1, 1871.

[3] *Cf.* letter of the Reverend Isaac J. Lansing in New York *Christian Advocate*, November 19, 1874.

[4] *Cf.* Reverend J. C. Hartzell in *Southwestern Christian Advocate*, July 3, 1873.

[5] *Cf.* Proceedings of New England Conference as given in New York *Christian Advocate*, April 27, 1865. For similar statements see *ibid.*, April 6, 1865.

strongest Church South as well as North."[1] A decade later the New York *Christian Advocate* declared that "the actual people of the South will learn that their future peace and prosperity are to be found, not under the leadership of the old traitors and conspirators, but under the direction of Northern ideas and Northern liberty."[2] "There is a struggle now going on as to the character of the Methodism of the future in this section," said the Atlanta journal of the Northern Church in 1881. "Shall it be under American or Southern ideas? This is the bone of contention between us and the Southern Church."[3] "It is evident to every deserving mind," said a Northern editor at New Orleans when discussing the regeneration of Southern society, "that New England has developed a stronger arm, a more active brain, a greater love of freedom, and a higher form of civilization."[4]

The arrogant standpoint from which the plans for the regeneration of the Southern people were frequently conceived is well expressed by an editorial which appeared in the *Central Christian Advocate* in 1867. Referring to a criticism which had recently been made by the *St. Louis Advocate,* a journal of the Southern Church, of the spirit it had manifested toward the South, the *Central* said that "the real business of the Protestant Churches of the North is to bear down upon the South with all their forces. We inform the *St. Louis Advocate* that we are going to map out, and then spread over the South, bearing with us free schools, equal rights, free speech and a thoroughly Christian civilization. We expect to put down by the free ballot and the true Gospel every form of barbarism including all the untold villainies of slavery. We intend to keep right on, and when there are enough school teachers, radical voters and Yankee notions all over the South, we

---

[1]*Cf.* Dr. E. Q. Fuller in *Methodist Advocate,* December 29, 1869.
[2]*Cf.* Editor J. H. Fowler in New York *Christian Advocate,* November 13, 1879.
[3]*Cf. Methodist Advocate,* March 30, 1881. Referring to the conditions of Southern society as described by Albion W. Tourgee, a carpet-bag official, in his book, *Bricks without Straw,* the New York *Advocate* said in its issue of September 18, 1879: "We see in this state of society in the South a divine call to us to go down there with knowledge and grace for the poor whites, and all such as are willing to hear, and out of these raise up a new sentiment and new ideas to control that land. It is the way out. . . . We are called of God to create a new race of rulers for the South."
[4]The Reverend L. P. Cushman in *Southwestern Christian Advocate,* March 8, 1883.

expect Wendell Phillips, William Lloyd Garrison, and other fanatics, to swing round that circle through Arkansas, Texas, Mississippi and South Carolina and talk *just as they please* without the slightest molestation. You must really grin and bear it. We will not stop for 'line upon line,' leaving out the 'n' if you like. We will leave 'whining' to your ancient friends, the bloodhounds, now out of office with the slaveholders, and whimpering to the chagrined rebels, who have been suppressed but not taught."[1] That such a sectional outlook persisted as late as 1890 is indicated by the remarks of a writer in the *Methodist Review*, who declared: "The calm, resolute spirit of the North encounters the wild, reckless expressions of the South with cool, convincing logic and the philosophy of fairness and right."[2]

The plans of the Northern Methodists, it is true, revealed little desire for vengeance for vengeance's sake. None were to suffer save those who blocked the way of reform. Such plans were always given with much advice as to how the happiness of the Southern States could be promoted.[3] Nevertheless stern lectures were read and many harsh words were uttered. Sweeping indictments were brought against the civilization of the section.[4] The

---

[1]Editorial of *Central Christian Advocate* as given in "an exchange" and quoted in *Southern Christian Advocate*, May 24, 1867.

[2]*Cf.* Pearne, Thomas H., "The Race Problem—The Situation," *The Methodist Review*, Vol. LXXII (September, 1890), p. 694.

[3]A typical expression of the concern felt for the future of the section was made by the Reverend E. Q. Fuller in 1878. He said: "A century of freedom, peace, and enterprise, directed by intelligence will make the South the pride of America, the admired of all lands, the garden of the world. The ministers and teachers of the Methodist Episcopal Church are not toiling in vain in these States. . . . Shall not the strongest Church in America continue to do something for the darkest corner of our land for its future safety and welfare?" *Cf.* Fuller, E. Q., "Our Southern Field," *Methodist Quarterly Review*, Vol. IV (April, 1878), p. 225. The editor of the New York *Christian Advocate*, in its issue of December 7, 1871, said: "The work of reconstruction in that terribly-afflicted portion of our nation is to be social and religious, as well as political." He added that his Church was laboring to convert the Southern people from "their wide estrangements from the right." "Its work in that direction is recognized by those who are laboring for the pacification of the country, and because of its influence for good it is disliked by those who, not despairing of the revival of the 'lost cause', would resist all tendencies at social reorganization." In a report issued in 1868, the Freedman's Aid Society declared: "Our schools have rendered essential aid in the work of restoring social order. . . . Our teachers have been pioneers in the work of reconstruction and are laying a foundation upon which the most enduring superstructure can be reared." *Cf. Report of Freedman's Aid Society*, 1868, p. 12.

[4]*Cf.* Simkins and Woody, *op. cit., passim.*

civil and religious leaders of Southern society were frequently declared to be morally disqualified for the work of political and social reform. They were said to be incapable of just action where the freedmen were concerned. The Methodist journals constantly upbraided the former master class for errors of the past. They were tactless in ignoring the feelings and the past experiences of the people whom they sought to help. Bishop Clark asserted that "the very conscience of the professedly religious portion of the South was debauched; that the ministry had been guilty beyond the power of language to describe in that they were debauchers, and I fear that both preachers and people were back-slidden into a depth out of which even the mercy of God might fail to lift them."[1]

The Methodist Advocate in 1872 warned Northern Methodists that they must not leave "the poor down-trodden white people of the South" under the influence of "the pro-slavery, man-stealing, Negro-whipping, whiskey-drinking, Ku Klux Churches to which so many of them belong."[2] The New York *Advocate* referred to the South as "that sinful and unrepentant region," and it deplored the tendency to subserviency to Southern ideas which persisted in the North despite "the revelations of Southern meanness and atrocity."[3] It was frequently said that the moral deficiencies of the Southerners were innate and much doubt was expressed as to the possibility of their reformation. In 1885 a Northern Methodist minister who had recently visited the South said that "In many respects the moral convictions of the Southern people have been wrong, and wrong on such fundamental principles as are necessary for the surest and best advancement of society. The original influence of those early settlers, the Spanish and the French, has not yet become a vanished quantity, and more, the signs of its vanishing are not so hopeful as we could desire. . . . That Spanish love of gold which led the gold hungry explorer to

---

[1]*Cf*. Bishop Clark as cited in *National Baptist* and quoted in Simkins and Woody, *op. cit.*, p. 375.

[2]*Methodist Advocate*, January 24, 1872.

[3]*Cf*. New York *Christian Advocate*, May 25, 1865. The editorial in which the South was referred to as a "sinful and unrepentant" region was written by the Reverend Gilbert Haven of Boston, one of the contributing editors of the journal, who was later made a bishop and assigned to work in the South. During his official residence at Atlanta Bishop Haven did much to antagonize Southern sentiment.

get gold even without giving any kind of equivalent made a good supporting back-ground to American slavery, one of the greatest wrongs of which was to take labor without giving any adequate remuneration for the service rendered."[1]

The great majority of the Southern people had emerged from the War with their dislike of Yankees increased and their devotion to Southern principles intensified. They were unwilling to recognize any but the unmistakable accomplishments of the War, the emancipation of the slaves and the restoration of the Union.[2] After it had become apparent that the North would not demand the penalties which some had feared, every suggestion of reform from that quarter was resented and combatted. The Southerners saw in the plans for their regeneration sponsored by the Northern Methodists only the malice of a hypocritical foe. The lack of tact and the harsh words from the North added greatly to the sectional bitterness. The assumptions of moral superiority were repelled with scorn. The charges made by the Northern Methodists often appeared to be malicious indictments of a whole people. In 1879 a Tennessee Unionist who had fought for the North to the end of the War said of the New York *Christian Advocate:* "No kind word for the South ever graces its columns—no sentiment in all the articles bearing upon the relations of the two sections of our country that indicates that the editor or his correspondents had ever taken a lesson in the school of fraternity. . . . But on the other hand it has unkind thrusts, bitter charges, and denunciations and petty spleen."[3] A secular journal asserted in 1880 that Bishop Gilbert Haven was noted for his "unrelenting hostility" toward the Southern whites and that he had "by his speeches and writings proved himself to be among the most mendacious revilers of the South."[4] The Roman Catholic *Southern Cross* of Savannah, Georgia, charged that the Atlanta *Methodist Advocate* was inspired with "a venomous hatred of the Southern people."[5] Nothing has been considered more unfraternal on our part than calling

---

[1]Letter of the Reverend E. M. Wood in New York *Christian Advocate,* August 6, 1885.

[2]*Cf.* Simkins and Woody, *op. cit., passim.*

[3]Letter of "X" in Nashville *Christian Advocate,* May 17, 1879.

[4]*Cf. The Commonwealth,* quoted in New York *Christian Advocate,* February 5, 1880.

[5]*Cf. Southern Cross,* quoted in *Methodist Advocate,* January 10, 1877.

attention to facts," said a Northern Methodist editor when discussing the defective foundations of Southern society. "When we tell of the destitution of Churches and schools in any locality as a reason for pushing forward our work we are said to be 'abusing the South'."[1]

But it was in connection with their attempts to control the political destinies of the Southern people that the Northern Methodists aroused the bitterest sectionlism. Proudly conscious of the part which their Church had played in preserving the Union, they regarded it as "an essential part of her calling to maintain hearty and loving loyalty to the United States Government, and to aid in elevating those who have been delivered from bondage."[2] For the achievement of these ends they believed that it would be necessary for the Republican party to be continued in power. They were, almost without exception, adherents of that party.

Northern Methodists continued to think in terms of "party lines based on loyalty and disloyalty to the United States Government."[3] Despite the fact that the Democratic party had renounced the issues which had been discredited by the War and had announced a "new departure" in policy, the Methodists persisted in regarding it only as a safe refuge for those who were "tainted with treason." They thought it folly to suppose that those who had been Copperheads and traitors had abandoned their purposes. "Earnest and active men," said Dr. Daniel Curry, editor of the New York *Advocate,* "seldom reverse the objects for which they labor; aggregate bodies of men never. They who a few years ago sought to betray the country into the hands of the enemy, the Vallandighams, the Woods, and the Seymours of the years of the war, are now what they were then. Their affiliations with certain political associations prove nothing as to themselves, but very much as to the character and designs of such associations. . . . It is only common sense to conclude that the political organization which can attract to itself such materials is unsafe and unpatriotic, and a dangerous one."[4] In 1880 the Reverend L. P. Cushman, who was soon to assume the editorial chair of the *Southwestern Christian Advocate*

---

[1] *Cf. Methodist Quarterly Review,* Vol. LXX (March, 1888), p. 256.
[2] *Cf. The Methodist,* February 10, 1866.
[3] *Cf. Southwestern Christian Advocate,* July 1, 1875.
[4] *Cf.* New York *Christian Advocate,* September 6, 1866.

at New Orleans, expressed the opinion that the Democrats constituted the lowest and most depraved elements of Northern society.
"It is well known," he said, "that the Congregationalists, Presbyterians, Baptists and the Methodist Episcopal Church, all large,
intelligent and influential denominations, have for some cause
failed to reach the great mass of the Democrats in the North."
He marvelled that Horatio Seymour had once "addressed a blood-
thirsty mob of these ragged, blear-eyed, ulcerous, filthy wretches
that were hanging upon society like a large festering carbuncle,
as his friends."[1]

The Methodists of the North feared the Democratic party
especially as a vehicle by which the hated "Bourbons" of the
South might be restored to political control in the nation. In an
editorial on the presidential campaign of 1880 in the *Southwestern
Christian Advocate,* the Reverend J. C. Hartzell admitted that the
chief candidates of both parties were of good character. But he
said: "As the contest proceeds all questions of minor importance
will drop out of sight, and the only question will be—whether it
is best to leave the Nation under the control of the North, which
overthrew the Confederacy, abolished slavery and saved the Republic from destruction, or to let its control pass over to the
representatives of the late Confederacy, which believed in slavery
and fought a short time since with desperation for four years to
destroy the Nation."[2]

Persuaded that the achievements of the War could be preserved
only through Republican control, the Methodists anxiously hoped
for some means of guaranteeing the success of the party. In
common with other Republicans, they ardently desired to nationalize it by bringing within its fold a large Southern contingent. It
was obvious that the former master class could not be brought into
the Republican organization in sufficient numbers to secure the
adoption of legislation embodying its program. The adoption of
"black codes" in the Southern States had quickly made it apparent
that the whites of the South were unwilling to accept Northern
views with regard to measures for their regeneration.

The Methodists promptly urged that the ballot be conferred

---

[1]Letter of L. P. Cushman in *Southwestern Christian Advocate,* April 1, 1880.
[2]*Cf. Southwestern Christian Advocate,* July 1, 1880.

upon the Negro as a means of nationalizing the party and as a matter of right. The New York *Advocate*, early in 1865, advocated Negro suffrage as a "measure which is urged upon the Country equally as right and as expedient."[1] In an editorial on "The Suffrage Question" in February 1866, the same journal declared: "To consummate the act of emancipation by Mr. Lincoln, there must be local legislation and the administration of the law in the spirit of that proclamation. Such legislation and administration cannot be expected from the pardoned rebels of the South, and without the votes of the freedmen no others than such can be chosen to office. The government in behalf of law and order in the South needs the vote of the freedmen quite as much as they themselves need it. This probably is the strongest argument that can be urged in favor of Negro suffrage."[2]

The other journals of the Church quickly followed the lead of the New York *Advocate*. In July 1865 *The Methodist* declared

---

[1] New York *Christian Advocate*, May 11, 1865.

[2] *Ibid.*, February 1, 1866. During the preceding May the *Western Christian Advocate* had said: "It must be understood that disloyalty disfranchises. Those who have conspired to overthrow the Government, who have voluntarily borne arms against the republic, or who have given material aid and comfort to the rebellion must be deprived of the ballot, if not in perpetuity, at least for a considerable number of years. Such men have proved themselves unworthy of the immunity of citizens in a free State, and cannot with safety again be endowed with the franchise. . . . There must be no restriction of suffrage on account of color or previous condition. All loyal men must have the privilege of the ballot, whether white or black, whether formerly slave or free." *Cf. Western Christian Advocate*, as quoted in New York *Christian Advocate*, May 18, 1866. In a letter to the New York *Advocate* in June 1865, Dr. J. P. Newman said: "Unopposed by the black man's vote, these traitors will reinstate themselves in office and power, perpetuating the disloyal sentiment, and keeping rife the bitter sectional animosities of the South, while the loyal men, whether white or black, will have no voice that can be heard in the politics of their own State." *Cf.* letter of Dr. J. P. Newman in New York *Christian Advocate*, June 29, 1865. "The truth is," wrote the Reverend W. T. Gilbert from New Orleans, "that the rebels, though beaten in the field are still masters of the situation; and now, as before, the Negro is our only hope. The superior of intelligent Southerners in regard to a hearty adhesion to free government and an honest patriotism, and the superior of the poor whites both in intelligence and patriotism, he should be recognized, as he is in fact, preëminently the American citizen of the Southern country." *Cf.* letter of W. T. Gilbert in New York *Christian Advocate*, June 15, 1865. Another correspondent of the New York *Advocate* said in July 1865 that the plan for conferring the suffrage upon the freedmen "may be ridden over by madcaps, and another civil war may be the result. But if so it would be principally between the blacks and their oppressors, the latter of whom must and will be then exterminated, as were the Canaanites, which they as richly deserve." *Cf.* letter of Alfred Brunson in New York *Christian Advocate*, July 6, 1865.

that God had willed that the Negro should vote. "It is God's decree," it said. "Why cannot the Southern people, to whom this problem is committed, anticipate events, and enfranchise the black man by a magnanimous stroke, rather than be conquered again by Northern ideas?"[1] By October 1866, the Chicago *Northwestern Christian Advocate* could announce that the press of the Connection was unanimous in urging Negro suffrage.[2]

Presently the Methodists became outspoken in their championship of the candidates and policies of the Republican party, as such. Pulpit and press were distinguished for their partisanship. Ministers took great pains to inform their congregations of "the true condition of public affairs." Clergymen of the highest rank publicly supported Republican presidential candidates in their addresses and writings. Subscribers to the Church journals were told that any one who opposed the continuation of the Republican administration was "practically an enemy to the peace of the country."[3] "Our scarred and war-worn veterans, who because of their labors and sufferings for the country more highly appreciate its privileges," said the editor of the New York *Advocate* in 1866, "will scarcely consent that they who during the war sympathized with their enemies and declared their own heroic actions failures, shall now be intrusted with the administration of the nation's affairs. We have confidence in the great heart of the nation, in the public conscience, in the power of our holy religion, in the public intelligence that will not be hoodwinked. . . . God save the Republic!"[4]

During the presidential campaign of 1868 the New York *Advocate* warned the country that the success of the Democratic party would be the signal for a renewal of rebellion.[5] *The Methodist* declared that it firmly believed that the safest remedy for the troubled conditions of the times would be the election of General Grant.[6] In 1872 Dr. Curry argued that the Negroes still needed the protection of the party which had given them their freedom

---

[1] *Cf. The Methodist,* July 1, 1865.

[2] *Northwestern Christian Advocate,* quoted in *New Orleans Christian Advocate,* October 13, 1866.

[3] *Cf.* New York *Christian Advocate,* August 6, 1868.

[4] Dr. Daniel Curry in New York *Christian Advocate,* September 6, 1866.

[5] New York *Christian Advocate,* August 8, 1868.

[6] *The Methodist,* October 31, 1868.

and that the consolidation of the new order "requires that its completion shall be intrusted to the same hands that have so successfully brought it thus far on its way."[1]   The Republican party, declared a Northern Methodist editor at New Orleans in 1873, "has the proudest record of any political organization on earth!"[2] "We have one word of advice to our colored leaders," he said on another occasion. "Stand firm to the party that has done for you all that has been done."[3]

The representative bodies of the Church were no less zealous in committing themselves politically. They developed a practice admirably suited for the purpose. During the Reconstruction period the adoption of reports "on the state of the Country"—a custom which had originated during the War—came to be a regular feature of the procedure of the Annual Conferences of the Northern Church. In these reports every phase of the political situation was carefully dealt with. They were, in the main, thoroughly partisan deliverances, designed to influence action on political issues before the country. As the controversy over reconstruction measures waxed hotter, the reports became increasingly bitter. In 1867 a Presbyterian journal, the *Free Christian Commonwealth* of Louisville, Kentucky, remarked that such reports had become an institution of Northern Methodism. "One would suppose," it said, "that in sheer disgust, Northern Presbyterian church courts would give up their miserable demagoguery, after seeing how far their Methodist allies can outstrip them in the business of 'firing the Northern heart'."[4] Such pronouncements

---

[1]*Cf.* New York *Christian Advocate,* August 11, 1872.

[2]*Cf.* The Reverend J. C. Hartzell in *Southwestern Christian Advocate,* November 20, 1873.

[3]*Cf. Southwestern Christian Advocate,* July 17, 1873. The *Northern Christian Advocate,* referring to a letter which Bishop Haven wrote to the *Independent* in 1872, and which strongly supported the candidacy of Grant, admitted that it was "a political partisan letter" and designed to serve party purposes. "In the letter before us," it said, "he has certainly spoken like a man, but whether like a bishop is the question." *Cf. Northern Christian Advocate,* quoted in Nashville *Christian Advocate,* August 17, 1872.

[4]*Cf. Free Christian Commonwealth,* quoted in *Richmond Christian Advocate,* November 4, 1867. Referring to a report which had recently been adopted by the Cincinnati Conference, Dr. Stuart Robinson, the editor of this journal, said: "We were not prepared—bad as we know Northern Methodism to be—to consider that in any other light than an ebullition of ignorance imposed upon by some leader of the Rev. Col. Moody pattern, who had managed to get the more decent and honorable men into a position to whip them into the service of

were likewise not infrequently made in the lesser conferences and preachers' meetings of the Connection.

It soon became obvious, moreover, that the press, the pulpit, and the representative bodies of the Northern Church were practically unanimous in supporting the radical Congressional program for the reconstruction of the Southern States and in opposing the less rigid requirements of the plan advocated by President Johnson. They were untiring in their efforts to influence the political contests that were waged with regard to reconstruction policies both in the nation at large and in particular States. As the debate over reconstruction measures became more furious, their deliverances became increasingly bitter. By October 1866, the *Northwestern Christian Advocate* could declare that "The whole Methodist press is now, we believe, without an exception, on one side of the present national controversy. It is thoroughly radical for the restoration of the Southern States on the most uncompromised principles of universal rights and loyalty; the rebuke and legal punishment of treason, the protection of Southern loyalists; the enfranchisement and elevation of our emancipated population; and the stern repression of every remnant of the rebellion."[1]

The responsibility of the Church with regard to Southern reconstruction was constantly stressed by the *Advocates* and leading officials of the Connection. It was said that the presence of the Church in the section must be "a guarantee for loyalty and correct notions of national authority as extensive as her spread is wide and as intense as her influence is great."[2] "We claim the South," declared the editor of the New York *Christian Advocate* in 1879, "because the Republic which we have recently saved by Methodist conscience and Methodist bayonets, now demands at our hands another salvation by Methodist ideas and faith. Nothing is gained

---

political demagogues, in view of the approaching election. But it turns out that this was but the opening ball of the ecclesiastical campaign of Methodism for the year of grace 1867. Every other Conference seems to follow suit."

[1] *Northwestern Christian Advocate,* quoted in *New Orleans Christian Advocate,* October 13, 1866. The *Northwestern* asserted that the Methodist press "is a power in the land; we doubt whether there is another journalistic power equal to it. . . . it wields a force that may in the highest sense be called the 'balance of power'."

[2] *Cf. Pittsburgh Advocate,* quoted in Nashville *Christian Advocate,* August 31, 1878.

by shutting our eyes to the fact, that the preservation of the Union and the reign of moral law all over the South depends more upon what is done by our Church, with its nation-wide extent and its millions of adherents, than upon any other force in the field. Born with the Republic, the Methodist Episcopal Church has become the guardian of American liberties."[1] During the same year one of the Northern bishops emphasized the duty of the Church. Referring to the advantages to be had through a removal to Texas, he said: "Here then, ye men of the colder North, set up your penates. . . . occupy the land. . . . Surround our still unrepentant States with this cordon of love. Thus you will free America from the fear of the reoccupancy of the seats of national authority with its unreconstructed enemies." "Texas is to be the ransomer of America. It is to be the future fighting ground of union and disunion, of Northern and Southern ideas. It is to be the field where the rebellious and slavery-loving and feudal-holding systems are to meet freedom and equality in stirring, if not in bloody conflict. It is to be the coming Kansas in our coming war."[2]

The *Advocates* constantly warned the Government against a lenient treatment of the former Confederates and insisted that the Southern whites were still in a latent state of rebellion. As early as April 1865 Dr. Curry of the New York *Advocate* declared that "We apprehend that there is more danger of excessive clemency than of too much severity."[3] The following September this same

---

[1] *Cf.* Dr. J. H. Fowler in New York *Christian Advocate*, March 20, 1879. In 1878 the Reverend E. Q. Fuller wrote: "It may prove that the defenders of the Union, after having preserved the nation from disruption and ruin, untimely surrendered to opposing principles, and that other struggles are inevitable. But eternity and almightiness are attributes of right, and through the mercy of God the end will be glorious. In any case, a great and effectual door is open before the Methodist Episcopal Church in the South, and fearful responsibility attaches to its course in reference to this section." *Cf.* Fuller, E. Q., "Our Southern Field," *Methodist Quarterly Review*, Vol. LV (April, 1878), p. 238.

[2] Letter of Bishop Haven in *Southwestern Christian Advocate*, July 17, 1879.

[3] *Cf.* New York *Christian Advocate*, April 13, 1865. Dr. Curry also said at that time: "That the chief conspirators, if taken, should suffer death as a public example, lest their great crimes should appear but venial, may be necessary and only right. That all who have engaged actively in the rebellion should suffer for it the forfeiture of the rights of citizenship would be only just and reasonable, and that more than this should be visited upon the leaders of the foul revolt may be demanded by the public safety." Shortly after the assassination of Lincoln, Dr. Curry, declaring that act to be an indication of "the dark and dampening turpitude of the spirit of rebellion," said: "We hope hereafter to hear much less of public clemency toward public enemies than we have heard for some weeks past." *Cf.* New York *Christian Advocate*, April 20,

minister, in an editorial on "How to Treat the South," warned Congress that the people would hold it sternly to its duty. He urged that more stringent methods be employed. "What is to be done with this infatuated people?" he inquired. "Evidently the process of reconstruction must assume some new phases. . . . Meanwhile the president is wisely slow in the exercise of his pardoning prerogative; could we reach his ear we would say 'the slower the better; wait and see what this people deserve . . .' " Dr. Curry declared that the attitude of the Southerners had made it necessary that the provisional governors who had been appointed there "should be replaced by military control wherever this truculent spirit is much longer exhibited. The Confiscation Act should become a renewed consideration with the Government."[1] *The Methodist* warned the nation that what had already been done was an indication of what the whites of the South would again do should civil government be too quickly restored.[2] On another occasion it declared that "The policy of conciliation is but an experiment. It is already carried to an extent without parallel in all history. If it is abused—if our generous treatment of the conquered is to be repaid with insult . . . there may be a reaction which will be neither pleasant nor comfortable. . . . The South

---

1865. During the summer of 1866, the *New Orleans Advocate,* a journal which had recently been established in that city by Dr. J. P. Newman, said: "Five millions of Union people in the South protest against continuing a policy under which they have experienced an increasing insecurity of property and life, and under which rebellion is rapidly repairing its strength. Our blazing Churches, scattered schools, and slaughtered citizens cry out against such mistaken clemency. Never before was it known that after a great war the victors were placed at the mercy of the vanquished and made to bear their maddened spite. Never before was the engine of government so disastrously reversed. Never before was an illustrious nation so quickly placed on the downward grade to ruin. It is time to put down the brakes. We stand absolutely alone in the history of the world in our fearful experiment of clemency. Our policy must be changed or our country will be imperiled." *Cf. New Orleans Advocate,* quoted in *New Orleans Christian Advocate,* September 8, 1866.

[1] *Cf.* New York *Christian Advocate,* September 7, 1865.

[2] *Cf. The Methodist,* November 4, 1865. Just at the close of the War, *The Methodist,* in referring to the former governing class of the South, said: "The thought that such miscreants may ever be permitted to pollute the Capital with their presence is enough to make a loyal American's blood boil within him. The only portion possible for these men is that which they have chosen— infamy now and forever." *Cf. The Methodist,* April 22, 1865. In its issue of May 13, 1865, when speaking of Lee, it said: "He belongs to a class that needs to be humbled. The *chivalry* of the South, so called, have given this war to the country; it is solely and emphatically their work; and our best wish for them is that they may find the *level* which is their greatest dread."

has not yet recovered its civil rights, and may so act as to protract its period of probation."[1]

By March 1866 the New York *Advocate* announced that things were going "fearfully and ominously wrong in the insurgent States" and that the spirit of rebellion "only awaits a sufficiently favorable opportunity" to reassert itself. It declared that the North might expect "any new folly" until "by reflection and by the infusion of a better population" the section could attain a better judgment. It concluded that "The whole civilized world will say that after the moderation of the Government any severities necessary for the complete and prompt restoration of order and safety in the South are justifiable, and we hope the country will not trifle with fastidious questions of policy, but go to work energetically to do up and dispatch out of the way this whole question of Southern law and order. Our financial safety and the liability of the national debt to repudiation demand it, the business and industry of the nation require it, the welfare of suffering Unionists and of the faithful and gallent freedmen claims it, and the majesty of the law commands it."[2]

Early in 1867 Dr. Curry urged that "the time for partial remedies is past; the case calls for something radical and complete." Referring to the obstacles with which President Johnson might block such action, he suggested that recourse might be had to impeachment. "Whether or not the time has come for action must be determined by the facts with which we are not conversant," he said. "If, however, facts shall be brought out showing cause for impeaching and removing the President, we presume it can and will be done, and the country will sustain the action." The country, he observed, was growing impatient to know what Congress would do.[3] Shortly afterwards the New York *Advocate* stated that it believed that the Congressional plan of reconstruction, while stringent and decisive, was as clement as it should be. "A nation must morally stultify itself," it said, "if it would for the sake of a hasty pacification cover up by strained or ambiguous phrases such turpitude." Referring to the persistent attempts of

---

[1]*Ibid.*, September 16, 1865.
[2]*Cf.* New York *Christian Advocate*, March 29, 1866.
[3]*Ibid.*, January 31, 1867.

the South "to dignify its unholy struggle and to glorify the rebel leaders," he expressed satisfaction at the thought that the "new military regime will summarily put an end to them, and to many other intolerable after symptoms of the rebellion. General Sheridan is beginning the needed work in New Orleans."[1]

When proposals were made for ending military government in the various Southern States, they were vigorously opposed. On one occasion the New York *Advocate* suggested that the interests both of the South and of the nation at large would be advanced if the late Confederate States were deprived of political representation indefinitely. "We conclude, therefore," it said, "that no great interest of the South or of the whole country would suffer, if for the next ten years no rebel State should be completely 'reconstructed'."[2]

When, after the restoration of civil government, local and sporadic disturbances occurred and the Republican administrations in the Southern States were threatened, the Methodist journals frequently hinted that it would be wise and necessary to restore military government. Referring to the impenitence of the Southern people as reflected in sentiments recently expressed by Jefferson Davis, Dr. Curry said in 1873: "The people of this country remember very well who it was that so effectively tamed the wild spirits of rebellion in New Orleans. They may not for themselves desire that the peace of the country should be put under the same protection; yet probably nothing could so effectively reconcile

[1] *Ibid.*, April 4, 1867. In the issue of May 23, 1867, Dr. Curry said with regard to the trial of Jefferson Davis: "Meanwhile hundreds of thousands of the best sons of Northern families sleep on unavenged in their patriotic graves throughout rebel territory. Some assassins, some prison-keepers, have been brought to justice in vindication of the laws; not one of the leaders of the great crime, not one really responsible man, has been brought to condign punishment. The politicians, the administrators of the country have these matters in hand; the people look on and ponder them; eyes dim with weeping for their dead read the facts, and continue to weep. The great heart and head of the people remember and reason and are beginning to demand what is the significance and what the moral consequence of this unheard-of policy."

[2] *Ibid.*, October 4, 1866. "Why should anybody at the South oppose it?" said the *Advocate* with regard to Congressional reconstruction. "Its moderation as to the extent of the demands made by the 'radicals' is wonderful. It is a peace offering, and should be accepted as such. It may be added that it is probably the best offer for the South that will ever be made to it, and if this is not accepted the result will be that the recusant States may go further and fare worse."

them to that extreme as this Southern madness."[1] In an editorial on "These United States," the *Methodist Advocate* of Atlanta declared in 1875 that the return to territorial government in the South might yet become necessary. And it volunteered the opinion that "Righteous military rule, wisely administered under the Constitution and with the support and supervision of Congress, would be the best possible government for portions of the South at the present."[2]

The following year the same journal, in an editorial with the caption "Shall the Southern States Be Reduced to Territories?" asserted that it was not "impossible that this question may become one of grave importance." "That something decisive must be done is evident," it said, "unless a radical change in the conduct of the Confederate whites takes place, of which there is no probability."[3] "A peril scarcely less fearful than that encountered when armed rebellion was clutching at the nation's throat is now upon us," exclaimed the New York *Advocate* when reporting a political outrage which had occurred in Grant parish, Louisiana, in 1873. It insisted that the "same spirit of rebellion is still rampant through all the South, and waits only the opportunity of probable success to again inaugurate a reign of terror." It felt that it would "be criminal in the National Government to ignore these facts." "The Southern States," it argued "have since their formal reconstruction abundantly demonstrated their incapacity for self-government; the duty of the National Government in the emergency is obvious and imperative. We shall see by its action in this Louisiana emergency what we have to hope."[4] With reference to such disturbances Dr. Arthur Edwards of the *Northwestern Christian Advocate,* in an editorial on "Facing the Crisis", said in 1879: "If rebels persist,—the people will not fail to speak on the subject. We have a notion that the world has never seen such wrath as will be shown by a patient North in case it resumes

---

[1]New York *Christian Advocate,* quoted in *New Orleans Christian Advocate,* September 18, 1873.

[2]*Methodist Advocate,* April 28, 1875. In 1875 the Boston preachers' meeting telegraphed a vote of thanks to President Grant and General Sherman for their action in suppressing the legislature of Louisiana. *Cf. The Bulletin,* quoted in *New Orleans Christian Advocate,* January 28, 1875.

[3]*Methodist Advocate,* August 16, 1876.

[4]New York *Christian Advocate,* April 24, 1873.

original jurisdiction. Appomattox were a love feast in comparison."[1]

The "Reports on the State of the Country" which were adopted in the several Conferences of the Northern Connection cautioned the people against an apathy which might result in the Government falling into the hands of its "enemies." They called for the most stringent measures in dealing with the South. Congress was warned that it must "proceed carefully, wisely and firmly in the work of reconstruction, removing if necessary, by constitutional means, every obstruction of whatever character or position."[2] In 1866 the New York Conference adopted a report in which it was declared that "it is our calm, and settled conviction, uninfluenced by passion, strife, or sectional prejudice, that expediency, constitutional law, justice, and the Bible all unite in demanding that at least some of the leaders of the rebellion be punished with death."[3] During the same year the New England Conference, by adopting a similar report, resolved "That we consider the recent action of our present chief magistrate, in frustrating the benign legislation of the representatives of the people, as most alarming and disastrous in its character, it causes defeated treason to show again a defiant front; it seriously imperils the beneficent results of our glorious victories gained by such lavish outlay of blood and treasure, it causes deep sorrow and discouragement to every true friend of his country and of mankind; it frequently results in the torture and murder of some of our most devoted citizens, and threatens ultimately to foment an exterminating war of races."[4]

---

[1]Cf. *Northwestern Christian Advocate,* quoted in *Wesleyan Christian Advocate,* March 1, 1879.

[2]Cf. Proceedings of Rock River Conference, as cited in the *Free Christian Commonwealth* and quoted in *Richmond Christian Advocate,* November 14, 1867.

[3]Cf. Proceedings of New York Conference, as given in New York *Christian Advocate* and quoted in *New Orleans Christian Advocate,* May 12, 1866.

[4]Cf. *Minutes of New England Conference,* 1866, p. 38. The Troy Conference, in 1866, after thanking Congress for having passed the Civil Rights Bill over the presidential veto, asserted that "while we agree with *Vice-president* Johnson, that treason should be made odious and punished, we regret that under the administration of *President* Johnson nothing of the kind has been done." Cf. Proceedings of Troy Conference, as reported in New York *Christian Advocate,* May 13, 1866. The New York East Conference, about the same time, said: "We must now look to Congress and the people. We thank the Senate for passing the Civil Rights Bill over the veto. This act sends a thrill of delight through the loyal heart of the nation, and gives hope that the great

In 1867 the Central Ohio Conference declared that "We believe it the duty of every friend of his country to keep in remembrance the issues of the late terrible war, and that as armed rebellion was put down by the bayonet, so disarmed rebellion must be by the ballot, if the American people would secure the union of these States and perpetuate liberty to all. . . . We believe that the belligerent States should be reconstructed by the plan proposed by Congress, and we look forward with hope to the time when this reconstruction shall be consummated and every loyal citizen enjoy equality before the law and the right of suffrage. . . . It is a source of humiliation that there should be a difference between the legislative and executive departments of our Government, and that this difference should manifest itself so frequently upon the part of the latter by arbitrarily removing good men from office whose only offense is that of carrying out the enactments of Congress and the wishes of the great loyal heart of the country. But it is to be hoped that at no distant date this difficulty will be removed, when passion will no longer oppose reason, or obstinacy, common-sense, and the two departments be one in feeling, one in design, and one in effort."[1] The General Conference of the Northern Church announced in 1868 that it was "an occasion of no small rejoicing" in the Church that, "so far as is known to us she numbers not in her whole communion *one single rebel* against our noble government. Then let our youthful nation and Church march on together, following this joint battle-cry, For God and our country."[2]

As has been mentioned, the churchmen performed valiant service during the periods of political excitement preceding presidential elections and in other such emergencies, boldly avowing

---

moral results which philanthropists and far-seeing statesmen had ardently wished should follow the sanguinary contest, are not to be sacrificed to the animosities or ambitions of aspiring men." *Cf. Report* of New York East Conference as given in New York *Christian Advocate,* April 9, 1866.

[1]*Minutes of Central Ohio Conference,* 1867, pp. 29-30.

[2]*Journal of General Conference,* 1868, p. 565. The Conference also declared that "we must enter our solemn protest against any system of reconstruction which does not secure hearty loyalty to the Federal Government, and place all men equal before the law in all the rights and eligibility of citizens without distinction of class or color."

their partisanship.[1] Alarmed by the narrowness with which their party had escaped defeat in 1876, Methodist journals and leaders redoubled their efforts during the campaign of 1880. "We believe it to be our Christian duty to give our readers information touching the more important interests in the presidential campaign," said the Atlanta *Methodist Advocate* in July 1880. "It is of great moment, because if carried by the Republicans, as it will be, the redistribution of the members of Congress will leave the Confederates in a hopeless minority, and the solid South, if it should remain solid, would be rendered powerless for harm, while the election of Hancock would almost inevitably lead to serious complications, if not to national disaster." The *Advocate* declared that the "Bourbon" papers teemed with such falsehoods that "we ought to do what we can to correct misapprehensions."[2] "All must now admit," remarked the editor of this same journal on another occasion, "that the party of law and order, of Protestantism, of the intelligent masses, is the Republican, and for that

---

[1]That the political action of the Northern Church was sometimes an embarrassment to it is evidenced by the action taken in some of its Southern Conferences with regard to office-holding among its ministry. In 1875 the Louisiana Conference adopted a resolution declaring that "whatever may have been the necessities in the past requiring or justifying the holding of any political office by the members of this Annual Conference, we are satisfied that the time is now passed, and from this time forth we affectionately urge our brethren to abstain from political combinations, and that in case any brother persists in refusing to do this it is in our judgment sufficient ground for his location by the Conference." Cf. *Journal of Louisiana Conference,* 1875, p. 258. In 1869 the Tennessee Conference adopted a preamble and resolution in which it stated that *"Whereas,* Brother W. H. Pearne has seen proper to accept the office of Chief of Police of Memphis, Tenn.: and *whereas,* we as a conference deem the holding of said office incompatible with the functions of the ministerial office and hurtful to the reputation of the Church; therefore

Resolved That, so soon as can be, without material injury to himself, Brother Pearne be requested to resign said office." Cf. *Proceedings* of Tennessee Conference as given in *Western Christian Advocate* and quoted in Nashville *Christian Advocate,* October 23, 1869. In 1885 the Georgia Conference, stating that "Inasmuch as some misapprehension has existed and still exists in reference to our position as a church in the South," resolved that "the Methodist Episcopal Church, while mainly supporting the great Government of the United States, is in no sense allied to any political party, nor will allow its policy to be dictated by the views and interests of political parties or leaders; that our work in the South is simply to preach the law of God and the Gospel of Christ . . . , leaving our members and friends to determine upon the political relations and course of action which they ought to choose and hold." Cf. Resolution as reprinted in *Journal of Georgia Conference,* 1885, p. 23.

[2]Dr. E. Q. Fuller in *Methodist Advocate,* July 20, 1880.

reason this Church is largely on that side."[1]   The Reverend J. C. Hartzell of the New Orleans *Southwestern Christian Advocate* expressed surprise at this time that Southern Methodist editors should raise an outcry when Dr. Fowler of the New York *Advocate* "sees in the ascendency and proposed measures of the Democracy in Congress danger to the Republic, and says so."[2]

Although with the passing of Reconstruction such partisanship became less pronounced, commitments and activities of this kind were not uncommon to the end of the century.[3]   "It is to be hoped," said the *Southwestern* in 1888, "that the verdict at the polls will be the restoration of the protectors of the American Constitution and industrial system to power; and the casting out of an administration limp and halting at every turn where wise statesmanship was called for. . . .   The election of Grover Cleveland would mean a postponement of the day of political retribution, and give warning of a serious menace to the peace and institutions of the country."[4]   "And now with a Republican president and administration," exulted the South Carolina Conference of the Northern Church in 1897, "it is not too much for us to hope for a revival of industry and business and for 'better times'."[5]

During such periods of excitement all of the old war-time issues were revived and paraded before the public for political effect. The specter of slavery was constantly invoked to perform a political service.   For more than two decades it was periodically charged that the entire body of upper-class whites in the South were bent on restoring slavery, and that, failing that, they would seek to force the nation to pay for the slaves which had been liberated. "In our opinion," declared the New York *Methodist* in 1868,

---

[1]*Ibid.*, September 22, 1880.
[2]Dr. J. C. Hartzell in *Southwestern Christian Advocate*, April 17, 1879 In the issue of November 6, 1879 of the New York *Advocate*, Dr. Fowler exultingly announced that his Church could continue its work in the South for another quadrennium because "God still protects us by the National presence. If this protection continues another term of years we must so push our work that it will be forever impossible to drive us out."
[3]With the election of Dr. J. M. Buckley as editor of the New York *Christian Advocate* in 1880, that journal ceased to concern itself with political developments, and it at once adopted a conciliatory and friendly tone towards the Southern people.
[4]*Cf. Southwestern Christian Advocate*, November 8, 1888.
[5]*Cf.* "Report on State of the Country" in *Journal of South Carolina Conference*, 1897, p. 29.

"just as surely as exclusive power comes back into the hands of the recent leaders of the rebellion, so surely will they in some form restore slavery."[1] In an editorial on "The Prolonged Conflict," Dr. Fuller of the *Methodist Advocate* warned the country in 1871 that "The majority of those who were slaveholders hope by some means, fair or foul (no matter which) to recover pay for their slaves."[2] In a second discussion of the question that year Dr. Fuller said editorially: "We have heretofore given repeated warnings of the appearance of one interest that rises above all others in the South. Religious, social, educational and political questions, in the minds of many of the former slaveholders, revolve around this point, namely, *pay for slaves liberated during the war.* . . . The determination to restore slavery in some form or to secure payment from the Government for slaves, is the controlling principle with many party leaders, and multitudes sympathize with them, and the mass even are indifferent or leaning that way. . . . Some of the white 'Union men' of the South would have no serious objection to taxing the North thousands of millions to reimburse the South for losses in the war, while secessionists would rejoice in any calamity that would befall the nation."[3]

In an editorial headed "1861—1879", Dr. Fowler of the New York *Advocate* warned the country in the latter year that an attempt was making to force the Government to compensate former slaveholders. He said: "This week the Legislative department of the United States falls into the hands of the men who ruled in 1861. They have the same spirit which actuated them when they went out. The field was the weak place in '61; therefore they struck with the sword. The treasury is the weak place now; therefore, we may expect the blow there."[4] Shortly after the November elections of that year the New York *Advocate* said: "The fourth of November has come and gone. It remains for us to interpret the meaning of the day. . . . The elections of November 4 mean that . . . the North do not intend to pay the 'germinal bill of damages' now offered at the doors of Congress for collection, and already grown to $2,200,000, and that, with the addition

---

[1]*The Methodist,* September 19, 1868.
[2]*The Methodist Advocate,* September 6, 1871.
[3]*Ibid.,* August 9, 1871.
[4]*Cf.* New York *Christian Advocate,* March 20, 1879.

of fabulous lists of slaves and State debts, and other claims such as
the Rebel debt which will become the Nation's debt whenever the
Rebel South becomes the Nation, will easily grow to $10,000,000,-
000. The North do not intend to pay this bill. . . . The North
can conduct a determinative war for half the money."[1]

Much was made of the so-called rebel atrocities which occurred
when political excitement was intense. The Methodist journals
teemed with accounts of outrages against defenceless Negroes and
Southern "loyalists." Such outrages were declared to be not
occasional and sporadic outbursts but the result of the unappeased
wrath and vindictiveness of the former ruling class. The missionaries formed a corps of volunteer reporters to their Church journals and the secular papers in the North, and from week to week
filled their communications with accounts of deeds and plans of
violence. To their own experiences these correspondents added
any reports they could gather from others. Many accounts of
outrages based only on hear-say evidence were retailed by the
Church papers, and sometimes humiliating retractions had to be
made.[2] The letters of the missionaries often represented the
Southern whites as animated by an inhuman hatred of the Negro,
and as ready to slaughter the entire black population on the least
provocation. Harrowing accounts were given of ex-slaveholders
who amused themselves by mutilating their former slaves and by
burying them alive.[3] "Many friends of the colored people who
have lived here much longer than myself," wrote a correspondent
of the New York *Advocate* from Newbern, North Carolina, in
1866, "agree with me in thinking there is a deep plot, tacitly

---

[1] *Ibid.*, November 13, 1879.

[2] That these journals encouraged such reports is evident from a statement
made by the *Southwestern Christian Advocate* in its issue of October 18, 1888.
It said: "Our correspondents in lawless portions of the country need have no
fear in furnishing us their names when detailing outrages committed in their
sections. Names are wanted for identification not for publication." In its
issue of October 4, 1888, the *Southwestern* declared that outrages were being
perpetrated on "inoffensive, intelligent colored citizens" merely "because they
are brave and honest Republicans." In 1890 Dr. A. E. P. Albert, the colored
editor of the *Southwestern*, acknowledged that one of the supposed victims, the
harrowing account of whose death he had given in detail the week before, was
still alive, and that he had published the report "as we gathered it from a
letter from a resident of Donaldsville, to a friend in this city." Cf. *Southwestern Christian Advocate*, May 29, 1890; *ibid.*, June 12, 1890.

[3] Cf. New York *Christian Advocate*, June 15, 1865; *ibid.*, March 8, 1866;
ibid., April 6, 1876.

formed, to bring on an insurrection of the blacks, in order to furnish a pretext for massacring them, and obnoxious Northern men with them. It is not uncommon for Northern men to be followed in their intercourse with colored people by spies and informers, in search, as I imagine, of some plausible pretext to be used against them in case of an outbreak. Our Northern business men do not seem to be the objects of suspicion, for their interests are too obviously in favor of preserving quiet to have any possible ground for fear respecting them. . . . If the people here had the power to oppress the colored people, as many of them are disposed to do, I am inclined to think that the worst fears would be speedily realized."[1] It was asserted that thousands of colored people were being killed.[2] Writing from Georgia with regard to the situation there, a teacher of the Freedmen's Aid Society of the Northern Church said in 1875: "My impression is that the South will be devastated by another war. Leading men here assert that the United States Government must pay for the slaves it emancipated. The bad passions which made the former war are as prevalent, as unreasonable, as furious, as they were fifteen years ago. I would not wonder if we were fleeing from Georgia for our lives in less than a year; and as I review history, past and present, of ours and other lands, I fear that God will make this whole land a wilderness. . . . Centuries of wrong and oppression and suffering cry unto God for vengeance. May God have mercy upon us when he draws his sword and bends his bow."[3]

The editors who filled their columns with accounts of outrages often accompanied them with comments and suggestions of retaliation which, under the circumstances, were incendiary. They talked much of "just retribution." They declared that further endurance upon the part of the blacks would be impossible. The Negro was spoken of as "a lamb in the midst of wolves." He was told that it "cannot be that God's day of vengeance is far away."[4] In an article which was given a place of prominence on

---

[1]Letter of "J. E. R." in New York *Christian Advocate*, October 28, 1866.
[2]*Cf.* letter of R. M. Hatfield in New York *Christian Advocate*, cited in Nashville *Christian Advocate*, October 28, 1876.
[3]*Cf. Report of Freedmen's Aid Society*, 1875, p. 87.
[4]*Cf. Northern Christian Advocate*, quoted in Nashville *Christian Advocate*, November 4, 1876.

the editorial page of the New York *Advocate* in 1876, the Reverend R. M. Hatfield declared that "God who gave the deer his antlers and the eagle his talons has not left the black man 'naked to his enemies.' He will not always submit to be a lamb in the midst of wolves." The writer said that the Southern people were sowing the wind in such a fashion that the result could be nothing but a whirlwind. "Present appearances," he thought, "indicate that the crop of tribulation and anguish will be large."[1] The efforts which, in attempts to restore white dominion, were made through fraud and intimidation to prevent the exercise of the suffrage by the blacks, excited the journals to unwonted exertions along such lines. "The rights of the freedmen are allowed them by the laws of the Country," said the *Methodist Advocate* in 1871, "and yet, as if forgetful of the past, and reckless of the future, multitudes of Southern people continue to deny them rights and trample them in the dust. Even the right of suffrage, which to the mass is most dear, important and powerful for good, is denied them by intrigue and violence. . . . And now a shout of gladness is heard through all the land in the hope that the political rights of the oppressed are about to be wrested from them by those who, had they been hung as rebels to their country, the history of six thousand years would have justified the act—or those who, had the oppressed destroyed them when they had the power to do so, the civilized world, although standing aghast at the deed, could only have said, 'This is but retribution.' Barely escaping fearful destruction, they seem still to covet it, and determined not to rest until they have brought it upon themselves."[2]

The migration of large numbers of Negroes to the North during the late Seventies and the Eighties served as an occasion for much inflammatory speech. This "exodus" was the outgrowth of the general dissatisfaction felt in a period of financial depression and of the agitation of political demagogues, as well as the result of political terrorism. It was commented upon in nearly every instance, however, from a sectional and partisan standpoint. Parallels were frequently drawn between the situation of the Negroes in the South and that of other peoples whose oppressors had been

[1] Communication of R. M. Hatfield in New York *Christian Advocate*, October 5, 1876.
[2] *The Methodist Advocate*, January, 1871.

destroyed.[1] In a long editorial entitled "Let My People Go", the editor of the New York *Advocate* in 1879 reflected upon the similarity of the visitations sent upon the South and those of the day of Pharaoh. After describing the wasting of the land by the sword, he said: "Next came the yellow fever, till the whole South moaned like a sick baby, and whimpered for help. The North rushed to the rescue with millions of money and with many martyrs. Relief and returning security revive the old spirit. . . . Who shall say what the next impulse may be? Shut in, robbed, deserted, butchered, with no hope but death, yet with the memory of having worn the blue and having met in honorable battle these same oppressors, what if the dark angel should go forth as of old? This is not impossible. We beseech these people to heed the voice of God in history! The Egyptians refused to let God's poor slaves go out to freedom; but before the end came, they were glad to have them go forth with their treasures, that they might bury their own dead in peace. . . . The fear that the colored people will go may soon give place to a greater fear that they will not go. May the repentance and just dealings of the whites enable God to avert this calamity! . . . In this hour the Church must not stand back any more than did Moses. We must deliver the command, 'Let my people go'."[2]

Declaring that he had for some time been watching for the colored man to strike, Dr. Fowler said shortly afterwards: "It now comes to light that so great has been the pressure upon these ignorant, helpless people that longer endurance is impossible. . . . Terrorized, mobbed, bulldozed, cheated, kept poor and dependent, they have not enjoyed the gift of freedom. . . . There are two ways up from bondage to manhood: one is by migration, as Israel went from Egypt; the other is by the sword, as Israel went into Canaan. Both were necessary under the old dispensation. Let us

---

[1] "How He will reveal His wrath we cannot say," said the *Northern*, "but Hayti may be the prototype of a possible solution and penalty. It will be remembered that in that unhappy Island prior cruelty and massacre gave a hint to the blacks concerning the effectiveness of torch and sword. The analogous hint given by bloody white murderers in the South must necessarily have sunk deep in the hearts of many black men who have been wronged far, far beyond description. May God avert such a calamity from the South." *Cf. Northern Christian Advocate*, quoted in Nashville *Christian Advocate*, November 4, 1876.

[2] Dr. J. H. Fowler in New York *Christian Advocate*, May 1, 1879.

hope that one will suffice under the new dispensation."[1] On another occasion the same editor when referring to this exodus likened the Southern Negro to a giraffe which, after having been bullied for years by an elephant in a zoo, turned with sudden ferocity one day and mangled the snout of its tormentor.[2] The New York journal urged the National Government to send steamers to transport the "thousands lining the shores of the Mississippi seeking deliverance from murder and assassination," and it declared that this policy might "save much blood-letting at a later date."[3] *The Methodist Advocate* expressed the opinion that no doubt one purpose of the Divine mind in suffering the repeated wrongs against the Negro was to awaken in him "responsibility of manhood and self-defense and protection of home." "It is not the law of retaliation, even under the code of 'an eye for an eye and a tooth for a tooth,' that we would inculcate," the *Advocate* explained, "but the higher and older one of self-defense. . . . That these lessons are needed at this time must be apparent to reflecting minds."[4]

Atrocity stories of former days were often revived and pressed into service. "Some people think that it is in poor taste and poor charity to wave the 'bloody shirt'," said the editor of the New

---

[1] Dr. J. H. Fowler in New York *Christian Advocate,* April 10, 1879.
[2] *Ibid.,* May 22, 1879.
[3] *Idem.*
[4] *The Methodist Advocate,* February 8, 1871. In an address before the Freedmen's Aid Society at the Metropolitan Church in Washington, D. C. in 1875, the Reverend Townsend of Boston declared that the crimes against the Negro, if long continued, would admit of no expiation but bloodshed. Dr. Townsend read to the audience a poem describing a vision which, although he had constantly sought to banish it, remained with him. It was as follows:

> "Is seen a black and calloused hand,
> It seizes quick and flings abroad a fire-brand,
> Lurid skies appear; at morn, at eve the same;
> Roofs of city and villages are aflame;
> Gleaming brands and gleaming eyes—terrific glare;
> Ashes in the sunny South are everywhere.
> Is seen a hand of blacker shade,
> It seizes quick and wields in might a crimson blade,
> Women mad with dread, and with disheveled hair,
> Screech murder! the bloody hand does not forbear;
> Deeply craped and crimsoned now is all that's fair;
> Hush! the mangled corpse is lying everywhere.
> O'er the sunny land descends a lengthened night;
> Tempest, cloud, and darkness thickly shroud the light.

* * *

York *Advocate* in 1879, "but that depends upon whose shirt it is, and who crimsoned it with gore. If it is red with the blood of our preachers and members it stands us in hand to look after it." He declared that the Methodist Episcopal Church must claim the South because it was "trampled by sin," and because "its coarse and bloody despotisms are too public to need illustration." He reminded his readers that while "Dr. Blackburn, who fought women and children with small-pox virus, occupies a Governor's chair, and the hero of Fort Pillow, who buried prisoners alive, has a seat in Congress, the crimes of this bloody land cannot be hid."[1] "The spirit of '61, revived in '79, must be judged by its history," wrote the same editor on another occasion. "The poisoning of Harrison and Taylor, and the attempted poisoning of Buchanan and the shooting of Lincoln, the killing of every President who was assisted by a Vice-President who could serve the South better, makes the election of a temporary President of the Senate suggestive. The spirit that murders thousands of citizens for the control of the South can hardly be expected to hesitate at killing two more men for the control of the nation. Billions of money with which to pay for the slaves make sufficient motive for anything. Hayes and Wheeler will do well to insure their lives soon."[2]

Jefferson Davis was frequently paraded as a menace to the public safety. He was spoken of as "the bloody dregs and *debris* of the 'lost cause'," and as "the chief conspirator in the worst rebellion against the best government for the most fiendish pur-

---

Nights must have an end. The sun at length does rise,
Other scenes and visions gaily greet mine eyes;
Gleeful children, homes and lands enchanting fair;
Freedmen are enlightened, honored freemen there;
'Tis now another race; forgotten are the dead;
Blessed is the sunny South; but fifty years are fled."
Cf. Report of Freedmen's Aid Society, 1875, p. 89.

[1] New York *Christian Advocate*, November 6, 1879. An article by "M" which was given a conspicuous place on the editorial page of the New York *Advocate* in its issue of January 28, 1875 warned the country that "The men who starved to death our soldiers at Andersonville, attempted to burn New York, and planned to send clothing infected with yellow fever from Bermuda into the cities of the North, have all been forgiven."

[2] New York *Christian Advocate*, September 6, 1871.

poses ever known in history."[1] Referring to a political outrage which had recently taken place in Mississippi, the New York *Christian Advocate* said in its issue of September 4, 1879: "There remains but one more step in the infamy of Mississippi, and that is the election of the perjured and bloody traitor, Jefferson Davis, to the United States Senate. He is the bloodiest man on earth. One word from him would have stopped the starving of our brave men in Richmond. But it suited his nature better to feast on the delicacies sent by Northern mothers to their sick sons in the famine pens."

The Northern Methodists aroused the bitterest hostility to themselves and contributed much to sectional ill feeling in the South through the countenance and the actual support which they gave to the carpet-bag administrations in the Southern States. Believing the carpet-bagger a necessary instrument for effecting the regeneration of the South, the Church condoned the abuses of the governments controlled by him, and sought to utilize him for the furtherance of its own interests in the section. Declaring that the urban population of the South was noticeably less antagonistic to the carpet-bagger than the people of the open country, the editor of the New York *Advocate* said in 1871: "The social reconstruction of the South must proceed from the cities to the country, and whatever social elements shall prevail at those centers will largely influence the whole body. Here, then, is our opportunity to utilize those 'Northern colonies,' and by serving them in the Gospel secure to ourselves their co-operation and influence. And this can be done only by planting a mission, with a respectable and fairly commodious house of worship, in each of the considerable cities of the South. To do this will require the expenditure of relatively large sums of money for a number of years; but we are satisfied that money for that purpose could be readily gotten, and in no other way could it be put to better account."[2] "One reason why

---

[1] *Ibid.*, July 18, 1878; *ibid.*, May 22, 1879. The New Orleans *Picayune* said of the Reverend J. C. Hartzell of the *Southwestern Christian Advocate* in 1880 that it was unaware that he possessed any other claim to distinction, but that "in the department of bloody-shirt and outrage literature he has secured a position of undisputed prominence." *Cf.* New Orleans *Picayune*, quoted in *Southwestern Christian Advocate*, March 11, 1880.

[2] Dr. Daniel Curry in New York *Christian Advocate*, December 14, 1871.

we deem it important for Northern Churches to go Southward,"
said *The Methodist* the following year, "is that it may be possible
for Northern men to settle in the late slave States without any
abridgment of their liberty of opinion or speech or conduct, as
secured by national law. If, for being what they are, they are to
be socially ostracized, then we wish them to be able to take society
with them for their social protection. . . . This is plain talking,
but the case demands the utmost plainness."[1] Aid was frequently
solicited in Northern cities on such grounds for building churches
in the Southern cities, and much was said in the Church journals
with regard to the difficulty of the upkeep of such churches after
changes had occurred in the political situation.

Bishops and other high dignitaries of the Church lent countenance to the carpet-bag regime by visiting and addressing legislatures which were dominated by Northern politcal adventurers and
their Negro and scalawag allies. Dr. Daniel Curry after a visit to
the legislature of South Carolina and an audience with the notorious Moses in 1874, declared that in no other part of the country
"would any considerable change of the national administration
operate so disastrously."[2] The churchmen frequently sought
energetically to vindicate the character of the carpet-bagger when
it was attacked. At an anniversary celebration of the Freedmen's
Aid Society in New York City in 1878 Bishop Gilbert Haven
sought to repel the invidious character which had attached to these
politicians. He said: "How maligned has been that grandest
word of the age—the carpet-bagger. How Northern pen and
tongue have joined with Southern tongue and pen in abusing these
martyrs of today, chosen of God and precious. So have the sons
of this world always mocked at the sons of God. . . . Carpet-bagger
is the true knight-errantry of the age. . . . Deserted by the Government he has elected, and the nation he has recreated, the carpet-bagger will yet save that nation, will again restore a true and
honest and patriotic government, that shall protect every citizen
in his every right."[3] When Horace Greeley had given a very
damaging description of the carpet-bagger in 1871, the New York

[1]*The Methodist,* quoted in *New Orleans Christian Advocate,* December 5,
1872.
[2]*Cf.* New York *Christian Advocate,* April 9, 1874.
[3]*Ibid.,* November 14, 1878.

Advocate asserted that "We have the best of reasons for doubting that such is the general character of the Northern people who have gone South since the war," and it expressed the opinion that the men who were in control of the State governments in the South were "not a jot below the full average of society either North or South."[1] Shortly after his visit to the South Carolina legislature in 1874 Dr. Curry declared that he "would venture the opinion that, compared with the various administrations—national, State and municipal—that of reconstructed South Carolina will not fall below the average, whether in honesty or wisdom." He said that the outcry of the native whites was made, not because they were oppressed or because they were denied equal rights, but merely because they, as a minority, were not permitted to rule. This, he thought, seemed "hardly a sufficient reason for pity."[2]

"Of these governments," wrote the Reverend J. C. Hartzell at New Orleans in 1879, "it is popular now to speak disparagingly, but the future historian will not so speak of them. . . . Those governments had some bad men, but the per cent of these was no larger than may be found in some of the governments that have taken their places."[3] In a communication to the *Independent* in 1874, Bishop Gilbert Haven lamented the fact that the North was "crying peace, hugging her defiant enemies to her breast and heaping up epithets against those who are her true and faithful friends."[4] The New York *Advocate* that same year deplored the fact that the secular journals of the North were beginning to create "pity for the sorrows of 'the prostrate States'." It declared that "the proverbial rapacity of new officials in the exercise of fiduciary authority" was a thing to be expected. Therefore, "the indebtedness of the Southern States since the War is only what might have been anticipated."[5]

When it became apparent that the carpet-bag administrations might be finally overthrown, eloquent pleas were made in their

---

[1]*Ibid.*, June 22, 1871.
[2]Dr. Daniel Curry in *ibid.*, April 9, 1874.
[3]*Cf.* Hartzell, J. C., "The Negro Exodus", *Methodist Quarterly Review*, Vol. LVXIII (October, 1879), pp. 736-737.
[4]Letter of Bishop Gilbert Haven in *Independent*, quoted in New York *Christian Advocate*, September 24, 1874.
[5]New York *Christian Advocate*, August 27, 1874.

behalf. Methodist leaders and journals entreated that the Federal troops, which had been stationed in the South for the enforcement of the Congressional plan of reconstruction and which were the last prop of the carpet-bag governments, should be left there. Bishop Haven insisted that there was no more despotism in South Carolina in 1877 than in Massachusetts, and he pleaded that the radical administration there be upheld. "Friends of the South, of humanity, and of Christ, patriots who mean to keep what your fathers and brothers died to obtain," he implored, "give not South Carolina over to her foes within and without. . . . If we keep South Carolina aright, we shall win all the rest."[1] When President Hayes began to withdraw the troops from the South in an attempt to conciliate Southern opinion, the New York *Advocate* warned the country that "a policy which abrogates authority and substitutes for it surrender and purchase will beget contempt and disturbance." "We see no reason why the troops should be taken out of Louisiana and South Carolina," it said. "Communities that do not need the presence of the troops will not object to their presence. We may as well look the facts in the face. We want the soldiers left in Louisiana and South Carolina, in the interest of peace. . . . Let us be wise above our generation."[2]

The missionaries at the South rendered a more active service in supporting the carpet-bag governments. They were generally extreme partisans, and many of them assumed a position of political leadership, employing all the methods of political drill-sergeants. The missionary and the carpet-bag politician were therefore frequently identical. In 1870 the Reverend Lucius C. Matlack declared that the representatives of his Church in the section had not only sustained a very equivocal relation to Southern society because of their Union sympathies, but that "the action of some as politicians, has been unfortunate, and has given the Church a false position." "The right of every man to act politically is under-

---

[1] Letter of Bishop Haven in New York *Christian Advocate*, March 29, 1877. In a letter to the same journal, published in its issue of October 22, 1879, Bishop Haven lamented the fact that "a gush of sentiment" had taken possession of the whole North in 1872, compelling the nation "to abandon its only friends and defenders." The nation had "consummated its bloody folly in the base surrender to her vilest enemies of Louisiana and South Carolina, the States that alone had stood between the Union and its foes, for the chief magistry, the commander-in-chief of her armies and navies."

[2] New York *Christian Advocate*, March 29, 1877.

stood," he said, "but for Methodist missionaries who are sustained by church-funds to become partisan politicians—advocating on the stump Republican nominations—and even taking nominations to office—which in some cases were accepted, and the ministry forsaken therefor, is not right. Our opponents, Churchmen and otherwise, know well that such action does not increase piety. They know, also, that the salary of office is double that of preacher. . . . The effect of this in affixing the stigma of self-seeking and office-hunting preachers to our ministry, is a constant and pressing evil. . . . and all our Southern Conferences should be as united in their sentiments against that as they are a unit in favor of lay delegation." He emphasized the fact that the partisan political action of the ministry had made it necessary that the Church examine carefully its attitude towards the South.[1] After a visit to the Pinchback Legislature in 1873, Bishop Haven reported that there were four, and perhaps more, ministers and at least one presiding elder of the Louisiana Conference of the Northern Church in that body. Although the Bishop admitted that such a participation in political affairs was perhaps a "doubtful expedient," he felt that in the cases of the present ministers it was pardonable, for "so often they are almost the only men who represent the views of the people that are able to speak well, or are experienced in public affairs."[2] In 1869 Bishop Matthew Simpson expressed the opinion that the violence which was directed against the members of the Texas Conference at that time was inspired, not by the fact that they belonged to the Northern Church, but rather by the belief that they were "identified with Radical movements."[3]

The number of Methodist ministers who sought and obtained office under the carpet-bag governments seems to have been quite large. The *New Orleans Christian Advocate* estimated in 1868 that there was at that time an average of almost a hundred men supported by the Northern Church in each Southern State who were engaged in promoting the work of reconstruction. An indi-

---

[1] Letter of Lucius C. Matlack in *Central Christian Advocate,* quoted in Nashville *Christian Advocate,* April 2, 1870.

[2] Communication of Bishop Haven on "The Newest South" in New York *Christian Advocate,* January 23, 1873.

[3] *Cf.* Letter of Bishop Simpson in New York *Christian Advocate,* February 18, 1869.

cation of the frequency with which Northern Methodist ministers
sought to influence politics is seen in the numerous attempts that
were made to intimidate the more aggressive individuals among
them. In 1879 the Atlanta *Methodist Advocate* published a list
of thirty-four outrages which had been committed upon the
persons of such ministers during the years since the War.[1] A
Congressional investigation, made in 1871, also revealed the fact
that the Methodist missionaries were prominently identified with
the carpet-bag administrations throughout the South. In that year
the radically controlled Congress appointed a "Joint Select Committee To Inquire Into the Condition of Affairs in the Late Insurrectionary States." The investigation was designed for the
purpose of furnishing campaign material for the radicals in the
approaching presidential election of 1872, and the report which
was drawn up by the committee abounded with accounts of political outrages. Throughout the twelve volumes of this famous
"Ku Klux Report" the ministers of the Methodist Episcopal
Church figure prominently in the disturbances that are recorded.
The Republican majority members of the committee pointed out
the fact that one of the "marked characteristics of the Ku Klux
operations" was "the persecution of that branch of the Methodist
Church known as the Methodist Episcopal, as distinguished from
the Methodist Episcopal Church South." The Democratic minority
members, when emphasizing the political coercion which had
been attempted by the agents of the Freedmen's Bureau, called
attention to the fact that "many of the agents of the Bureau were
preachers, and had been selected as being the most devout, zealous
and loyal of that religious sect known as the Northern Methodist
Church."[2] The Report revealed that the political activity of the
Methodist ministers had often resulted in their being visited by
members of the Ku Klux Klan and other bodies of masked men.
Some of the Methodist houses of worship which had been used as
Radical headquarters were burned and some of the more violently
partisan ministers were flogged or warned to moderate their ser-

---

[1] *The Methodist Advocate,* quoted in New York *Christian Advocate,* July
24, 1879.
[2] *Cf. Testimony Taken by the Joint Select Committee to Inquire Into the
Condition of Affairs in the Late Insurrectionary States* (Washington, 1872),
Vol. I, p. 70.

mons. In certain sections of the South the partisanship of the Northern Methodists caused them to be spoken of as "the Republican Methodists," as distinguished from the Southern or "Democratic" Methodists.[1]

Ministers of the Methodist Episcopal Church filled offices of every grade from that of membership in a local constabulary to those of congressman, State university president, and federal senator. The career of the Reverend James Lynch, a colored member of the Mississippi Conference, serves well to illustrate the political influence exerted by many of the preachers. Lynch, who had served as editor of an African Methodist journal prior to connecting himself with the Methodist Episcopal Church shortly after the War, became a member of the Mississippi Mission Conference in 1867. Bishop Simpson in that year appointed him presiding elder of the South Mississippi District. Throughout the period of his incumbency of this office Lynch was actively engaged in promoting the interests of the Republican party in that State. The *Journal* of the Mississippi Conference for the year 1873 tells that in 1867 he was employed "by the Congressional Reconstruction Committee, of which Thaddeus Stevens was chairman, to canvass the State in the interests of Reconstruction." "In this field of effort," the *Journal* states, "he took an active part in the calling of the Constitutional Convention." Although he was a successful candidate for the State senate in 1868, he never qualified since the proposed radical constitution was not ratified. The following year Lynch, with J. J. Spellman, began the publication of the *Colored Citizen's Monthly,* a journal "devoted both to the interests of religion and of the Republican party." During the Fall of that year he was advanced to the position of Secretary of State in the carpet-bag administration of Mississippi. After attending the General Conference of his Church in Brooklyn in 1872, Lynch proceeded to the Republican National Convention at Philadelphia in which President Grant was renominated. The Conference *Journal* informs us that he at once "entered most heartily into the campaign." But his career was suddenly cut short, we learn from the same source, when he died that year a victim to overwork.[2]

---

[1]Fleming, *op. cit.,* p. 639.
[2]*Cf. Journal of Mississippi Conference,* 1873, pp. 37-40.

The career of the Reverend Arad S. Lakin in Alabama is typical of the course pursued by a number of the missionaries in attempting to make their Church a dominant political influence. Lakin, who was pronounced by Bishop Haven to be "in no undeserving sense the head of our Church work in the South," was declared by his friends to be "the best stump speaker in the State."[1]

His stormy administration in North Alabama was characterized by continuous efforts to influence the course of politics. Bishop Mallalieu said of him that he had experienced "about as many perils, possibly more, as the Apostle Paul," and Bishop Haven reported that he had "been 'run out' of more than one county by the Ku Klux" and had been "plotted against as often as Paul was by the Jews, and as unsuccessfully."[2] Lakin, who had served as a chaplain in the Federal army, had been dispatched by Bishop Clark in 1865 to build up a following for the Church in Alabama. This he sought to do while serving as presiding elder of the Montgomery District by playing upon the political prejudices of the Union men of North Alabama and upon those of the Negro. He became a corresponding editor of the Atlanta *Methodist Advocate* when that journal was established in 1868, and in that capacity he sought energetically to advance the interests of the radicals. He maintained an extensive correspondence with other ministers and with laymen, taking great pains to gather up accounts of outrages, which he retailed through the columns of the *Advocate* for political effect.

When the carpet-bag administration in Alabama was threatened and disturbances occurred as the result of election excitements, the Reverend Lakin importuned the Federal military authorities to station troops in those districts where Radical control was endangered. Early in 1870 the Reverend T. W. White of the Village Spring Circuit, who had been made Superintendent of Education in Blount County, found his tenure of office precarious. At White's request, his presiding elder, the Reverend A. B. Watson, wrote Lakin that there were "a great many threats cir-

---

[1]*Cf.* communications of Bishop Gilbert Haven in *The Methodist,* November, 29, 1873.

[2]Letter of Bishop Mallalieu in *Western Christian Advocate,* quoted in *Southwestern Christian Advocate,* February 9, 1888.

culating through the county and we must have help if we can get it."[1] He asked that Lakin would assist in making a requisition for some troops "to preserve the peace." This, Lakin undertook to do at once. He addressed an appeal to General Samuel W. Crawford, the local military commandant, declaring that Blount County was in a "perfect reign of terror."[2] He stated that unless aid were forthcoming the "Union men" of the county would be forced to take the law into their own hands. When the Congressional investigation of conditions in the Southern States was made in 1871, Lakin rendered an important service to the Radicals. He was called before the committee in Washington, and, pouring out accounts of violence and atrocity, he represented the South as in a continuous state of terrorism.[3]   Although Lakin solemnly denied that he ever introduced politics into his sermons, there is an abundance of evidence to show that he did. He appears to have been equally ardent at political conversion as in his efforts at evangelization, and among the Southern people he acquired a reputation as a mischief-maker and an agitator. He himself sought office on several occasions, and in 1868 he was made president of the University of Alabama. This position he never filled, however, because of the intervention of the Ku Klux Klan.[4]

In South Carolina the missionaries were more successful in obtaining the rewards of office. The Reverend Henry J. Fox managed to hold, for several years, the presidency, of the University of South Carolina. In 1867 the Reverend B. F. Whittemore,

---

[1]*Testimony of Select Committee*, Vol. IX, pp. 1207-1209.

[2]*Idem.*

[3]The Democratic minority members asserted that Lakin had appeared before the committee "brimful of gall, bitterness and falsehood, which he poured out before us in such a way that it is hardly possible to determine which of the ingredients predominated." *Cf. ibid.*, Vol. I, p. 493.

[4]Lakin was commonly believed to be untruthful; he was said to have a "jaundiced eye", a "magnifying eye." Even Bishop Haven admitted that he was "as full of tropes as Beecher or Spurgeon or Longfellow, though, like the last he sometimes gets the figures mixed in the effluence of his fancy." *Cf.* letter of Bishop Haven in *The Methodist*, November 29, 1873. The *Independent Monitor*, published at Tuscaloosa, the seat of the University, in its issue of September 1, 1868, gave an account of the mob which frightened Lakin away from the institution. In the issue of March 4, 1869, of the same journal, a cartoon appeared in which Lakin and an associate were represented as hanging by ropes from a tree. Lakin was pictured with a carpet-bag in his hand on which was inscribed the word "Ohio." A mule, with the symbol "K. K. K." written on his side, was represented as walking out from under him. *Cf.* Fleming, *op. cit.*, p. 613.

of Malden, Massachusetts, was reported as a member of the South Carolina Mission Conference, and that same year he became Superintendent of Schools for the State. Under the carpet-bag administration of Scott, Whittemore was chosen as one of the representatives of the State in Congress. Although he was found guilty of having sold the appointment to a West Point cadetship and expelled from Congress in 1870, he was triumphantly re-elected by his Negro constituents.[1]

The highest office attained by any of the missionaries was that held by a Negro, the Reverend Hiram R. Revels. For a time Revels served as an official in the Freedmen's Bureau. Then, after locating at Natchez, Mississippi, he was soon made presiding elder of that district.. He was first elected to the state senate, and shortly afterwards was chosen to represent Mississippi in the United States Senate.[2]

The chief political service rendered by the missionaries who did not themselves seek office consisted of their efforts to guide the Negro politically. It was no secret in the Church that they assumed this function. When it was feared in 1867 that the Southern whites might conciliate the Negro and dominate him politically, the editor of the New York *Advocate* hastened to reassure his readers on that head. "That the Negro voter can be generally or seriously abused by Southern politicians we do not fear," he said. "The freedmen know quite well the value of their new rights and how they got them. . . . We are willing to trust him to whatever the conciliatory policy of his former master can acquire over him; especially as not only Northern politicians, but Northern missionaries, will see to it that he shall understand well his own rights and interests."[3] In 1877 a Negro, who disclaimed being a professor of religion, wrote the Reverend E. Q. Fuller of the Atlanta *Methodist Advocate* that he had found that journal "a guide both spiritually and politically for the colored race." "Every Tuesday for the last three months," the writer said, "some one of my friends wants to go to the post-office after my paper before I am ready to go after it, because they know they

[1]*Cf.* Sweet, W. W., "Methodist Church Influence in Southern Politics", *The Mississippi Valley Historical Review*, Vol. I (March, 1915), p. 556.

[2]*Ibid.*, p. 558.

[3]Dr. Daniel Curry in New York *Christian Advocate*, April 4, 1867.

can get a true statement of public affairs." And commenting upon this letter, Dr. Fuller asserted that thousands of "intelligent and thoughtful colored people are of the same opinion."[1]

Most missionaries did not seek to gain political control over the Negro merely through incidental advice given in sermons. Quite often journals like the *Southwestern Christian Advocate*, which teemed with political discussions, were read to congregations from the pulpit.[2] Many of the Northern ministers took an active part in the organization and management of the "Union Leagues," which were formed to provide political instruction for the Negro. In the League meetings, where everything was done to influence the colored man through impressive ceremonies and solemn ritual, the missionary played an important part. For the Negro, who was likely to confuse the political with the religious, the minister's presence aided in imparting a religious significance to the ceremonies. The effect was striking when the minister tendered solemn oaths, obligating the blacks to vote for the Republican party.[3] The Negro was told that since his freedom was a gift from God, he would be punished by slavery in this world and by damnation in the next if he should vote the Democratic ticket.[4] The Methodist houses of worship were frequently used as headquarters for the Leagues and the missionaries were on hand to open their meetings with prayer and to administer oaths.[5] Frequently the Northern missionary stood all day at the polls directing the voting of the Negroes and warning them against the influence of the white leaders of the South who sought to conciliate them and win their political support.[6] In order to maintain their control

[1]*Cf. Methodist Advocate*, January 10, 1877. In 1880 the Louisiana Conference of the Northern Church adopted a preamble and resolution which declared that "*Whereas*, The Church through her ministry is the God-appointed guardian of human liberty in all its relations, *Resolved*, That the Presiding Elders for 1880 be appointed a committee on the Civil and Religious Rights of our people, and that they be instructed to collect such facts and information upon their condition, and publish whatever in their judgment is wise, and also that they be a committee of correspondence with similar committees appointed by other Conferences." *Cf.* Proceedings of Louisiana Conference as given in *Southwestern Christian Advocate*, January 29, 1880.

[2]*Cf.* statement of Dr. J. P. Newman in New York *Christian Advocate*, March 12, 1868.

[3]Fleming, *op. cit., passim*.

[4]*Cf.* Deposition of Robert Aldrich in *Testimony of Select Committee*, Vol. III, p. 174.

[5]*Testimony of Select Committee*, Vol. XI, p. 105. Lakin was generally believed to be active in the formation of Leagues.

[6]*Cf.* Haygood, Atticus G., *Our Brother in Black* (New York, 1881), p. 97.

over the blacks such men frequently sought to inspire them with a distrust of all Southern whites. The colored people were often warned that they must regard the white men of the South as their natural enemies.[1] To act with them politically would certainly result in their reenslavement. Moreover, the Negroes were told that they were hated by the whites.[2] By 1875 the New York *Methodist* acknowledged that the editor of the Atlanta *Methodist Advocate* was chargeable with having incited riot in the South in that he "has sought to inflame race animosities and to keep alive race antipathies."[3]

By thus alienating the blacks from their former masters the missionaries aroused an intense bitterness towards the North. After quoting at length from the editorials of the *Methodist Advocate* in 1871, the Cartersville, Georgia, *Express,* a secular journal, declared that it was right that the Southern people should know something of "the animus of certain *luminaries*—'Northern lights'—who have come South to teach our people righteousness." "Go home, *Doctor* Fuller," it said, "and let the poor Negroes alone. They will improve slowly and behave themselves if your sort will cease to put mischief into their heads. Go home, and preach the Gospel to those who may be willing to hear you, and cease to vex your righteous (!) soul about the sins of the Southern people. . . . Go home, and may joy go with you, and peace be left behind you."[4] The Atlanta *Constitution* branded Fuller as a "hypocritical saint" who was acting as a radical emissary. It asserted that he was seeking to irritate and inflame the Southern people with the hope of maddening them to acts of violence.[5] Even the Nashville *Bulletin,* a Republican journal, denounced the

---

[1] *Cf. Testimony of Select Committee,* Vol. VIII, p. 208.

[2] When the *Independent,* a radical journal published at Selma, Alabama, predicted a race war, and expressed the hope that the blacks would "wipe out the whites," the editor of the *Southwestern Christian Advocate* condoned its action. Declaring that the *Independent* had not been the worst of the sinners, he merely deplored "the unguarded utterances so calculated to stir up the venmon [sic] of a people who are void of charity and toleration." *Cf.* Dr. A. E. P. Albert in *Southwestern Christian Advocate,* September 5, 1889.

[3] *Cf. The Methodist,* October 13, 1875. In 1879 the Alabama Conference of the Northern Church adopted a resolution which stated that, but for the aid rendered by the Atlanta and New York *Advocates,* the Northern Church would be almost powerless in the South. *Cf.* Proceedings of Alabama Conference as given in *Methodist Advocate,* December 3, 1879.

[4] *Cf. Express,* quoted in *Methodist Advocate,* September 20, 1871.

[5] Atlanta *Constitution,* cited in *The Methodist Advocate,* August 23, 1871.

Methodist Advocate for the bad blood it was stirring up between the races. "Doubtless if 'lovers of the Union' were made up of such envenomed characters as the editor *of the Advocate,*" it said, "the Southern States would exclude the whole pack, and we, as part of the Southern States, would help to sick the dogs on."[1] The attempts of many of the representatives of the Northern Church to inspire the Negro with a distrust of the Southern whites resulted in the expression of sentiments reflecting much bitterness towards the North.

The Methodist Episcopal Church, South, as has been said, bitterly resented the way in which the Northern Church undertook to occupy the Southern States. Regarding its action as schismatic, Southern Methodists strongly objected to its presence in the section. Forced to defend itself against the "disintegration and absorption" policy of the Northern Connection, the Southern Church constantly appealed to the popular feeling against any Northern interference in Southern affairs. Fully aware that the dominant and articulate classes in the greater part of the South sympathized with its attitude towards the Northern Church, it sought continually to emphasize the sectional character of that body and its anomalous position in the South. Thus the conduct of the Northern organization was constantly brought to the public notice and much resentment was awakened towards the North.

The aims and policies of the Methodist Episcopal Church were at all times opposed on the ground that they were the outgrowth of Northern ideas and prejudices. Representatives of the Southern Church addressed their pleas to sectional prejudice in various forms. Convinced of the correctness of the attitude of their Church toward the Methodism of the North and towards the issues of the War, the Methodists of the South adopted an unbending attitude toward all efforts to convert them to Northern views. The spirit of "humble penitence and conciliation," which Northern churchmen had seen in the Southern Methodist leaders just after the close of the War did not long prevail. The bishops, while they deplored the effect which a feud .between the two Methodisms must have upon the popular mind of the South, promptly disclaimed all responsibility for the controversies that

---

[1]Nashville *Bulletin,* quoted in *Methodist Advocate,* April 28, 1875.

were developing and for their unhappy results.[1] In 1882 the *New Orleans Christian Advocate* asserted that "We hold as strongly as ever to the position that the course pursued by the Southern Methodist Church was right from first to last, and there is not one measure from the action of the Southern delegates in 1844 to the finale of the Cape May Commission that we would recall or wish undone. Neither the principles nor the facts of our past history are to be abandoned or forgotten. . . . We believe the Southern Church stands today where she has stood from the first. There may be individual divergences, but the great body of our people are true to the principles of our past record."[2]

The press and leaders of the Southern Church did much to make the people of the South conscious of their sectional identity. Foremost among its journals in this respect, perhaps, was the New Orleans *Advocate*. "No," exclaimed that paper during the stormy days of Reconstruction in 1869 when discussing the question of the separate existence of the Church, "her work is to live with her own people, and if need be go down with them."[3] The journals of the Connection were quick to resent any disparagement of Southern views and principles. Referring to the comments made on the Cape May settlement by a Northern editor, the Nashville *Advocate* said in 1876: "Many of our readers will be sorry to see that reference to 'slavery as the sum of all villainies'—they do not so consider it—nor do they consider 'the cause of the Union the cause of God.' They are willing for Northern men so to think . . . but . . . so to speak . . . has a tendency to alienate the South more and more from the North. . . . We beg of our dear brethren of the North to cease these fanatical denunciations. Keep such sentiments *in petto,* their utterance does no good but much harm."[4] "Our Northern brethren . . . do not seem to be aware what Southern men think, and how they feel when their *secession* is called a 'rebellion'," said the same journal in 1877. "Drop that ugly word—if you *think* it, do not *print* it—that is if you want

---

[1]*Cf.* Pastoral Address in *Journal of General Conference*, 1866, p. 28.
[2]*Cf. New Orleans Christian Advocate,* February 9, 1882.
[3]*Cf. ibid.,* May 29, 1869. The *Advocate* declared that even "If the Church South could deliver herself from the common pressure by placing herself under the aegis of a body that prayed and fasted to induce the Lord to impeach the President, she would not, could not do it."
[4]Nashville *Christian Advocate,* November 18, 1876.

fraternity."[1] The New York *Christian Advocate* asserted in 1875 that the Methodist press of the South was "as sympathetically responsive as is the thermometer to the temperature of the atmosphere" to the "great reactionary sirocco in favor of the pro-Southernism of the *ante-bellum* period which is sweeping over the whole country."[2]

The *Advocates* constantly reminded the Southerners that they were a different people, and they held up to ridicule and repelled with scorn the assumptions of superior Northern or New England civilizations. Declaring that the "civilization of the two sections, and the customs and character of the people are in many things diverse," the New Orleans *Advocate* gave warning in 1880 that "the mission and objective point of the Northern mind and purpose" was that "the South must be reconstructed and recast in the moulds of Northern thought and opinion." The accomplishment of this purpose, it felt, would be a great calamity, for there was much that was distinctly Southern which ought to be preserved. "To obliterate State lines, unite the Churches, and surrender society to the unchallenged dominance of Northern fashions and opinions, would be a disaster to Christendom." Then, after admitting that there was both good and bad in the civilization of each section, it said: "One broad distinction is that the Southerner, as a matter of honor and principle, minds his own business, while the inborn nature of the North is to meddle. The South is tolerant, courteous and refined in its contact with people in the ordinary associations of life. The North has a prying, inquisitive disposition, and is bent on bringing every one to its way of thinking and doing." Thus, the *Advocate* explained, the North was seeking to force the South to accept Northern ways "in religion, in politics, in society." Such a consummation in the field of religion, it felt, would be especially disastrous. "There is a south side to Churches and religion, not so much in regard to their creeds, articles of religion and Church polity, as in the type of piety that prevails. Methodists and Presbyterians in the South profess the

---

[1]*Ibid.*, March 10, 1877.
[2]*Cf.* New York *Christian Advocate*, February 25, 1875. The *Advocate* explained that "The political spirit and *status*" of the Southern Church "are, despite all its disclaimers, intense and pronounced, and they are as obvious to the intelligent and unprejudiced observer as are the color of the Ethiopian or the spots of the leopard."

same faith as Methodists and Presbyterians in the North, and yet they are not the same people. The political meddling of the Northern Churches is, of course, one difference. . . . There is a secularity about them, and a style that brings them into near fellowship with worldly enterprises and organizations. They *run* things up there—Churches as well as factories and railroads. The style of their preaching is in contrast with ours, and is largely of the politico-sensational order. The North has been over-run with professional evangelists, whose methods and teachings have in many instances done harm. People raised in these Churches, and imbued with their spirit, if converted, are apt to be essentially defective in the higher traits of Christian character. With many excellent people and exemplary Christians among them, and with much that is good and worthy of imitation in their Church work, there is a spirit and practice, and a type of religion, that we should regret to see in our Southern Churches." "To Northernize our Churches," the journal concluded, "would be a calamity of unspeakable magnitude."[1]

The press and leaders of the Church constantly dwelt upon the vindictiveness of the North. The *Advocates* assured the public that "Whatever of hatred there is between the two sections, the most bitter, implacable and inveterate is on the side of the North."[2] It was told that "There are thousands in the North who would rejoice to have the Negro's heel on the white man's neck."[3] "We are free to say," asserted the New Orleans *Advocate* in 1866, "that complete and wonderful as the victory is which has been achieved over us by Northern skill and arms, we have yet to see the first exhibition towards us of grace, love of magnanimity, either in that Party or in those Churches, which mainly contributed to the result. The continued effort to make out that a revolution of eight millions of people, and a war of proportions beyond precedent, is a mere Pennsylvania Whiskey Rebellion, evidences the truth we affirm."[4] When the political situation seemed darkest in Louisiana in 1873, the New Orleans *Advocate* warned the Southern people that they must "be guarded and walk circum-

---

[1] *Cf. New Orleans Christian Advocate,* January 29, 1880.
[2] *Ibid.,* June 23, 1866.
[3] *Cf.* Nashville *Christian Advocate,* July 21, 1877.
[4] *New Orleans Christian Advocate,* June 23, 1866.

spectly" for they were completely at the mercy of the North. "We are entirely at the mercy of the conquerors, and must accept such treatment at their hands as they choose to bestow," it said. "It will be a good while yet before the North will be capable of doing us justice, or of truly understanding things as they are here. . . . If we are to be delivered from the present oppression and prospective disasters which now anticipate, the relief must come from those who have brought these calamities upon us."[1]

The Southern papers constantly reported, copied, and commented upon the bitter attacks that were made on the South in the religious journals of the North. In 1879 the *Wesleyan Christian Advocate* asserted that the religious papers of the North could no longer "deny themselves the luxury of a stab at the long-suffering South. It has become their second nature to treat our people bitterly and unjustly; they are in bondage to an unlovely and unchristian habit of mind that prevents them from seeing or expressing the truth as to the character and spirit of the Southern people. Alas! That it should be so. Many years have passed since the South—crushed, conquered, humbled—surrendered. But these editors—these religious editors—do not forget, and they do not forgive."[2] "But can it be possible," asked the Nashville *Advocate* in 1876 when referring to recent editorials in the Northern journals on the treatment of the Negro in the South, "that Christian editors—Methodist editors—would rejoice to see the torch and sword applied in South Carolina and in other Southern States? They say 'May God avert such a calamity from the South.' But this reminds us of the reply of the criminal when the Judge passed sentence of death upon him, ending with the customary formula, 'And may God have mercy on your soul.' He replied, 'I never knew one to prosper after your prayers'."[3]

It was a matter of constant amazement to the Southern *Advocates* that Northern Methodists should be so much more vindictive than others. They frequently dwelt on the particular bitterness of the Methodist journals. "The fire of revenge burns steadily in the hearts of our Northern brethren," said the New Orleans *Advocate* at the time of Jefferson Davis's discharge from prison in

---

[1] *Ibid.*, May 8, 1873.
[2] *Wesleyan Christian Advocate*, March 1, 1879.
[3] *Cf.* Nashville *Christian Advocate*, November 4, 1876.

1867. "The release of Mr. Davis gives no satisfaction to their Methodist journals. They think he ought to be hung. They are much afraid that his being out will elate the Southern people and give occasion to new outbursts of rebellious temper. They are resolved to believe that the entire South is still in a state of latent war. They harp on two strings—the rebellion and the freedman."[1] "Why is it that the Methodists of the North are so much more malignant and mendacious than others?" asked the same journal in 1873. "This has been a problem to us of long standing: Why they should be so much worse than people of other denominations, and, beyond comparison, worse in their invincible prejudices than the worldlings of their section. In comparison with Northern Episcopalians, Presbyterians or sinners, their tender mercies toward us would be most cruel and vindictive. It is impossible to enlighten them and they persist in reading but one side, and in viewing everything through the distorted and vicious medium of a fanatical bias." "They are utterly deaf and blind to truth, and willingly lend themselves to multiply and disseminate lies and misrepresentations." Declaring that the Southern people "have endured patiently, and are still enduring an amount of oppression and wrong to which no Northern State would submit," the *Advocate* concluded that "The most hopeless indication of the persistent injustice and outrage to which our people are to be subjected is the tone of the Northern Methodist press."[2]

On another occasion the New Orleans journal asserted that the letters of the missionaries which filled the columns of the *Advocates* of the Methodist Episcopal Church had done more than anything to convince the people of the North that "there is a mine of pent up malice in the" South. "We honestly believe," it said, "that but for them there would be between the South and the North tenfold the unanimity, mutual forbearance, and hearty reconciliation there now is."[3] Declaring that he was unwilling to believe that the better-minded Methodists of the North could endorse the bitter utterances of their ministers and journals, the

[1]*Cf. New Orleans Christian Advocate*, June 1, 1867.
[2]*Ibid*, May 15, 1873.
[3]*Ibid.*, May 2, 1873.

editor of the Richmond *Advocate* announced in 1875 that the hue and cry was being taken up all along the line from Boston to Chicago. In an editorial entitled "Firing the Northern Heart", he cited the statement of a Boston minister, made recently in a preachers' meeting, that strychnine and the shotgun should be employed in repressing the Southern "Bourbons."[1]

Many of the distinguished churchmen, in their communications to the *Advocates,* touched upon the bitterness of the Northern Methodists. Typical of their observations were the comments of the Reverend Atticus G. Haygood in a letter to the Nashville *Advocate* in 1874. Acknowledging that *"some* papers in the North while telling us of our faults have told the truth about us," he said: "But none have been so bitter, so relentless, so slanderous, as four or five of the Advocates of the Northern Methodist Church. At times they have not lacked honeyed words—but their sting is so sharp and bitter, their tender mercies are cruel. The present chief of our defamers is Bishop Haven. No detective with salary dependent upon the number of indictments procured, could be more diligent in searching out accusations against our people. His receptivity for slanders upon the South are enormous. He is never satisfied, and he never doubts—whale-like, he rushes with open mouth through the sea of 'evil reproach' and 'takes' in ('up') all that comes. Does he hear an outrage alleged to have been committed by a Southern white man? He receives it, affects to believe it, asserts it, publishes it. And he gives wide circulation to what he writes. He has access to the whole Northern Methodist press, and upon occasion goes beyond. Witness a recent letter in the *Independent* loaded down with accusations and slanders. . . . Nothing that the Southern white men do pleases him. In his eyes we are all bad. One cannot read a letter from Bishop Haven and not learn the bitterness of his hatred of our people."[2]

Throughout the period from the Civil War to the end of the nineteenth century representatives of the Southern Church invoked the Southern dislike of "Northern isms." The people were cautioned particularly against allowing "Northern fanaticism" to enter their religious undertakings. They were warned that they

---

[1]*Cf. Richmond Christian Advocate,* February 4, 1875.
[2]*Cf.* letter of A. G. Haygood in Nashville *Christian Advocate,* October 10, 1874.

must be continually on guard against "the mania of New England abolitionism." The New Orleans *Advocate* asserted that the workings of such fanaticism would demand "the most serious and patient consideration of our wisest and best citizens."[1] The dangers to be apprehended from Northern fanaticism with regard to political contamination and in connection with the problem of the Negro were most frequently stressed. When discussing the question of the education of the Negro in 1865, the Mississippi Annual Conference said: "If we allow the abolitionists to take this whole matter into their hands, they will send among us a class of teachers, men and women, who will be very detrimental to our and the Negro's interest. They will give them lessons on all the 'isms' of New England; will make them lawless and fanatical; will cause the Negroes to love Northerners and hate Southerners."[2] Two years later the aged Bishop Andrew discussed the religious status of the Negro in a letter to the Nashville *Advocate* and lamented the fact that "the spoilers" had come, bringing wih them "the New England gospel."[3]

In combatting the rivalry of the Northern Church, the Methodists of the South constantly appealed to the traditional Southern dislike of ecclesiastical interference in politics. Although there were occasional departures from the rule, the leaders and journals of the Southern Connection were generally careful to avoid anything that might be interpreted as political action upon the part of the Church. They were quick to make the political intermeddling of the Northern religious leaders a matter of reproach. With obvious reference to the position of Northern Methodism, the General Conference at New Orleans in 1866 took occasion to thank God that the Methodist Episcopal Church, South, "has in no wise become complicated with political affairs; but keeping in mind her own high mission, has been content to perform her legitimate duties."[4] Shortly after that time the New Orleans *Advocate* announced that "the Churches of the North are bidding against each other for place and power. Willing equally to affili-

---

[1] *New Orleans Christian Advocate,* September 19, 1868.
[2] *Cf. Journal of Mississippi Conference,* 1865, p. 11.
[3] Letter of Bishop James O. Andrew in Nashville *Christian Advocate,* January 31, 1867.
[4] *Cf. Journal of General Conference,* 1866, p. 17.

ate with politicians, it is a struggle who shall be able to wheel into action the largest and best drilled membership. So far the Methodists claim to have done, by large odds, more than all others." The *Advocate* declared that it was doubtless the desire to compete in this contest that had led to the coalescing of the Old and New School Assemblies of the North which had recently taken place. "We rejoice indeed," it said, "that there is a body of Presbyterians in the South separate and distinct from this coalesced Presbyterianism. We have no right to question these two Assemblies when they profess love for each other, but it is evident that they indulge in a good deal of outside hate; hatred for sin of course; for slavery, if there is any left; but O how they do hate disloyalty—in the South—anywhere; they look on it 'as the sin of witchcraft' especially when it refuses to pray for two-thirds of Congress. . . . And so these people in the North, Assemblies and Conferences, go on; under the plea of 'loyalty,' they rake over the ashes of war for the coals of vengeance. Afraid lest the Country and the Church should fall back again into a tranquil state of peace, they talk of rebellion and cry for justice, and band together in order to swell their power and clamor."[1]

More disposed than any of the other Southern journals to comment upon local political developments, the New Orleans paper sometimes spoke its mind in a fashion that, in a Northern journal, would have been denounced as meddling in politics. In August 1866 the *Advocate* charged that Northern ecclesiastical interference had been an important factor in precipitating the Convention troubles in Louisiana which had recently resulted in riot and bloodshed. In an editorial on "The Great Conspiracy," it said: "The churchmen of the Presbyterian and Methodist Churches in the North are largely identified with this attempt of violent revolution. In fact these godly gentlemen who are scattered throughout the South, taking ecclesiastical guardianship of hundreds of thousands of the freedmen of the South, have a very large interest in this new order of things which is to be precipitated. . . . They are on hand to open conventions with prayer which are avowedly to subvert the reigning government of

---

[1] *New Orleans Christian Advocate,* June 23, 1866.

the State; to take a 'guardianship' of the Negro, which ends in madness, riot and blood. These gentlemen constitute no mean part of the extensive machinery in motion to fan the worst passions of the Negro and to inflame anew the half-extinct coals of civil strife. The Lord judge between us and them!"[1]

When the New York *Methodist* asserted in 1866 that the mission of the Southern Church had ended with slavery, the New Orleans *Advocate* retorted: "If seeking importance in the filthy ways of political preferment constitutes a 'mission' then ours is certainly gone. If by formal deputation to the President the political power of the Church is claimed, and insisted upon as an essential element in the Country, as the true way to conserve and maintain the mission of the Church then ours is hopelessly gone. . . . But what shall we say of a Church which claims to be Christian, but which under the plea of 'loyalty,' drapes itself in its Country's ensign, wraps it around the pulpit until the preacher can barely be seen peering through this symbol of the earth, and which, with the lust of the ecclesiastical whore of the Apocalypse is only less scarlet in its clothing because there is no more of the color in the banner."[2]

The bishops of the Methodist Episcopal Church, South, openly rebuked the political meddling of the Northern Methodists. In a Pastoral Address in 1867 they declared that they were constrained to protest against the conduct of the Methodist Episcopal Church in the section. "Northern Methodist missionaries are sent," they said, "not to neglected places, but where our congregations abound, and where the doctrines of Methodism are fully preached according to the standards once held in common with us by the Church that sends them. . . . In some communities they have succeeded in misleading ignorant and unstable persons, by cries of 'the old Church,' and the hardly disguised threat that those who abide with us will draw on themselves confiscation and civil disabilities —all of which evils are to be escaped by alliance with them! By an open and shocking prostitution to political partisanship, they have found a doubtful foothold among some who are ready to

---

[1] *Ibid.,* August 11, 1866.
[2] *Ibid.,* April 7, 1866.

use a Church or any other instrument for the furtherance of their purposes."[1]

The assertion was frequently made that the Methodist Episcopal occupation of the South was essentially a political movement; that the Church was seeking to build up a "Northern" party in the section. Early in 1867 the *Southern Christian Advocate* warned the public that "The effort that is making at some points to disturb the harmony of the Church, by attempting to take advantage of differences of opinion among the people on political questions, to array brother against brother, requires some notice that the effort may be forestalled. The effort itself betrays the animus of those engaged in the so-called missionary operations in the South, and deserves rebuke as utterly unworthy of those bearing the Christian name. It adds to the innumerable proofs that the entire movement of the Northern Methodist Church is of a political character, intended to build up a Northern party in the South. Religion is the pretence; to add to the political power of a sectional party, to which that Church has allied itself, is the real purpose, and all the utterances of their missionaries and perverts, and of their new-fledged religious papers in the South prove it. Politics and not religion make up the staple of these sheets, and of the letters of those missionaries to the Northern papers."[2] "We say it more in grief than as conveying news to the Southern people," announced the Nashville *Advocate* in 1872, "that Northern Methodism is using, training and mustering the Negro for political uses. That Church in the South is mainly made up of Negroes, and is in fact a wing of the radical party. Plain words these, but true to the letter, and capable of proof from their papers, pulpits, and programmes."[3] The *Holston Methodist* stated in 1875 that in the South the Methodist Episcopal Church was "an arm of the radical administration, which will be withdrawn as soon as that administration retires to the shades of private life."[4]

The Methodist support of carpet-bag administrations and radical

---

[1] *Cf.* Pastoral Address as given in *New Orleans Christian Advocate*, May 25, 1867.

[2] *Cf. Southern Christian Advocate*, April 12, 1867.

[3] *Cf.* Nashville *Christian Advocate*, March 9, 1872.

[4] *Cf. Holston Methodist*, quoted in *Southwestern Christian Advocate*, March 11, 1875.

policies in the South was denounced in terms that aroused much bitterness. In a communication to the Nashville *Advocate* in 1867 Bishop Holland N. McTyeire pointed out that an important element of the membership of the Southern Church in Tennessee was composed of Union men whose "anti-secession and government record is unimpeached." "But what of that?" he said. "Just nothing with *loyal* conferences and Churches, and preachers. Loyalty means their party platform for reconstructing the Southern States. They favor the extremest measures. Having begun confiscation on their own account, of course they favor it in full."[1] By 1868 the New Orleans *Advocate* asserted that the Methodist missionaries had already "made the name of the Church they represent a stench in the nostrils of nine-tenths of the best citizens of the South, which will remain for half a century." In an editorial on "Missionaries in Sheep's Clothing," it stated that these workers "have urged policies and dictated constitutional clauses that looked more to petty revenge than to wholesome government; they have brought out candidates and attempted to control appointments from a commanding general's down to that of a city watchman's; they have industriously excited and arrayed the colored voter of the South against the white man, and have illustrated all the depths of a political whipper-in."[2] On another occasion the New Orleans paper charged that in order to support the carpet-bag administration in Louisiana the *Advocates* of the Northern Church had reported "the most barefaced falsehoods about the South" and about events in that State, even after such statements had been repeatedly corrected. Citing a false report which had recently been made concerning the constitutional convention of Louisiana, it said: "But this correction will never be made, nor will any truth be stated by those Radical Journals which may conflict with their prejudices."[3]

Referring to the sums which had been appropriated for work in the South by the General Missionary Committee of the Methodist Episcopal Church in 1871, the Nashville *Advocate* said: "In these appropriations one may get an idea of the Ku Klux howlings

---

[1] Letter of Holland N. McTyeire in Nashville *Christian Advocate*, July 25, 1867.

[2] *Cf. New Orleans Christian Advocate*, May 2, 1868.

[3] *Ibid.*, September 15, 1866.

that are to be kept up for another year: they are paid for misinformation, false and harrowing accounts from the South will be furnished abundantly by the Northern press. A band of men is kept on pay by a missionary society that will be felt in local politics and in the Presidential election just ahead."[1] "These are the men," wrote the Reverend J. W. Rush of Mobile with regard to the Methodist missionaries, "who have indorsed by their sermons, prayers, letters, conversations, that infamous system of carpet-baggism which has corrupted our Legislatures and courts, absorbed and squandered our wealth, prostrated all our material resources, and pushed up the poor negroes to the very verge of a gigantic social war."[2] The support given to the Negro in politics was often represented as a manifestation of the unrelenting vindictiveness of the white man of the North. The New Orleans *Advocate* asserted that it was an outgrowth of his "unappeased rage" and of his desire for "an illustration of his great power over the white man of the South."[3] Declaring that the handwriting had come out on the wall against "the political measures which have well-nigh ruined the fairest portions of the South," the Richmond *Advocate* said in 1875: "Does the great M. E. Church intend to come forward to uphold the men who have been the instruments of uncounted evils to this country? If so, we wish to know it."[4]

Apart from the fact that Southern Methodists regarded the Northern occupation of the section as schismatic, they deemed the actions and affiliations of the representatives of the Methodist Episcopal Church there sufficient grounds for excluding them from all fellowship with themselves. As a result the missionaries were socially ostracized by their co-religionists in a fashion that caused much sectional bitterness. Aggrieved at his presence and seeing in him only the politician and the incendiary, the Southerner sought to avoid contact with the missionary whenever possible. Since practically all doors among the upper class whites were closed to him, the church worker was often entirely dependent

---

[1]Nashville *Christian Advocate*, December 9, 1871.
[2]Letter of J. W. Rush in *New Orleans Christian Advocate*, September 24, 1874.
[3]*Cf. New Orleans Christian Advocate*, July 4, 1868.
[4]*Cf. Richmond Christian Advocate*, February 4, 1875.

upon the Negro for companionship and home life. A Kentucky minister in 1875 expressed well the attitude of hauteur maintained towards the societies of the Northern Church. Declaring that probably not over two hundred whites in the majority of the Southern cities knew even the location of such societies, the Reverend C. W. Miller said: "Now to complain of our people that they do not show 'proper courtesy' to an organization whose obscurity removes it from attention, and whose affiliations, *ipso facto,* bar social intercourse, an organization which, consequently, our people *courteously* let alone, is an exceedingly silly thing. But to make this 'courteous letting alone' the occasion for applying to us the epithets 'foolish,' 'bitter,' 'abusive,' 'whatever they may be, let us be Christians and gentlemen,' etc., . . . is an exhibition foreign to the friendly which they pretend to seek to establish between us."[1]

When, upon occasion, some ministers, more charitable than others, recognized the work that was being done by Northern clergymen, and visited them, they were made to feel the displeasure of their colleagues.[2] Although Southern Methodists were more often disposed to show courtesies to visiting Northern clergymen, even the highest dignitaries were ignored when they had made themselves offensive to Southern sentiment. When Bishop Gilbert Haven appeared on the floor of the General Conference at Atlanta in 1874, he was neither introduced nor given a seat within the bar, as was customary in such cases. Declaring that the Bishop had recently baptized the baby of the notorious Governor Moses of South Carolina, the Nashville *Advocate* said with regard to the Atlanta incident: "Some of our Northern friends express their wonder that we do not fraternize with such men as Haven, Fox, *etc.,* when they come down South. We wonder that they should wonder at it. Just think of South Carolina Methodists herding with the men who are cheek by jowl with the ursurpers and oppressors and plunderers of the State, and whose names are synonyms for all meanness and wickedness."[3]

---

[1] *Cf.* letter of the Reverend C. W. Miller in Nashville *Christian Advocate,* May 22, 1875.

[2] *Cf.* Mathews, John, *Peeps Into Life* (Roanoke), p. 205.

[3] Nashville *Christian 'Advocate,* June 27, 1874.

Although with the adoption of the Cape May Report and the passing of Reconstruction the opposition to the Methodist Episcopal Church in the South became less pronounced, many persons continued to the end of the century to feel aggrieved and resentful at its presence there. This resentment expressed itself in ways that did much to prolong ill feeling toward the North. The sentiments of many were voiced by the *Florida Christian Advocate* in 1888, when it said: "The Northern Methodist Church is doing a great work in the North. . . . It is more fully the embodiment of Northern thought and feeling and energy and peculiarities, in connection with religion, than any other body of men can be. It is at home and knows how to work. But this is not true respecting the South. Here it is an importation, a stranger, and not suited to the state of things. It comes into the South as a superior to an inferior; comes as an accuser with the conviction that the Southern people are disloyal citizens; comes doing the evil work of reviving sectional feeling and old buried recollections of the past; comes with impracticable plans and exciting views of Negro equality; comes as a special favorer of a particular political party; and, coming thus, it cannot have a mission of usefulness in the South, and must fail."[1] The New Orleans *Advocate*, when copying and commenting upon the above editorial, expressed a desire to commend it "to a certain class of our readers."[2] Belated attempts to influence the political situation and criticisms of the treatment of the Negro in the South continued to evoke bitter criminations.[3] In 1890 the Nashville *Advocate* announced that

---

[1]*Cf. Florida Christian Advocate*, quoted in *New Orleans Christian Advocate*, May 17, 1888.

[2]*New Orleans Christian Advocate*, May 17, 1888.

[3]When, in 1880, the editor of the New York *Advocate* referred to the women missionaries of his Church in the South as "Florence Nightingales", "spurned and neglected and insulted by Southern women, who are not worthy to loose their shoe latchets, and who are content to have their own children half-brothers and half-sisters to these poor colored people," the New Orleans *Advocate* said: "How such vulgar and scurrilous defamation as is uttered by the leading official journal of the Northern Methodist Church can be received without rebuke by the more decent people of the North is more than we can understand. This recent slander of our Southern women and men ought to arouse an indignation stronger than that aroused by Butler's infamous order. If such sentiments as those uttered by Dr. Fowler are inspired or tacitly indorsed by Northern Methodists here, the fact ought to be proclaimed. Our people should at least maintain an attitude of self-respect towards those who so maliciously misrepresent them." *Cf. New Orleans Christian Advocate*, February 26, 1880.

William M. Baskervill

nearly all of the "Methodist journals in the Northern States are insisting with clamorous voice upon the passage by the Federal Senate of the Lodge election bill, which was recently put through the lower House of Congress."[1] Referring to this matter in a communication to the *Advocate,* the Reverend John E. Edwards of Virginia said: "Bishop Joyce, of the Northern division of Methodism, but voices the prevailing sentiment of his Church when he advocates the passage of the Force bill by the United States Senate, and pledges hundreds of thousands of Federal bayonets to see it enforced at the polls. No legal measure is proposed the object of which is to degrade the South that does not find a million Northern Methodists ready to indorse it, and to promise material aid in seeing it executed."[2] A liberal-minded editor of the Nashville *Christian Advocate* in 1886 deplored the fact that it was still the case that when "a belated sectionalist in one part of the country utters a croak he starts the whole frog pond, North and South."[3] It is true that there were various influences at work among the Methodists, as in society at large, the tendency of which was to break down the old animosities and draw the sections together. But the position maintained by the Methodists often necessarily operated against this trend and served to keep alive sectional feeling.

Thus there can be little doubt that the struggle of the Southern Church against "disintegration and absorption" and the attitude it bore toward its sister Church of the North and towards the issues growing out of the clash between the sections had a marked effect on the popular mind and upon the course of social reform in the South. Men who were supposed to be influenced by Northern ideas were frequently denounced as being affected with "monomania," "negrophilism," and "Yankee fanaticism."[4] Reform movements having their origins in the North were suspect. The extent to which society in the South was affected in this way is suggested in the remark of a correspondent of the *New Orleans*

---

[1]Nashville *Christian Advocate,* August 16, 1890.
[2]Letter of the Reverend John E. Edwards in Nashville *Christian Advocate,* November 8, 1890.
[3]Dr. O. P. Fitzgerald in Nashville *Christian Advocate,* June 26, 1886.
[4]For such charges against Dr. Atticus, G. Haygood see accounts in *New Orleans Christian Advocate* of September 13, 1883 and October 3, 1883.

Christian Advocate who lamented in 1883 that "the day is not yet passed when a man must be able to pronounce a sectional shibboleth before he is entitled to speak from the pulpit or the platform on the moral and religious questions of the day."[1]

---

[1]Letter of "J. W. M." in *New Orleans Christian Advocate,* October 4, 1883.

CHAPTER V

WHAT to do with the free Negro had long been considered one of the gravest problems with which the Southern whites had to deal. Since the days of Jefferson and Patrick Henry the difficulty of arriving at an adequate solution had led men of liberal and humanitarian principles to accept the institution of slavery, and had prevented even those not actuated by economic self-interest from agitating for its abolition. The South was now suddenly confronted with the necessity of disposing of the problem in a practical way. The urgent need for a prompt adjustment of the six millions of former slaves, many of them but a few generations removed from the barbarism of Africa, left little time for debating the Negro's capacities and rights. Freed from all those restraints to which he had been accustomed, the black man showed an instability, which to the Southerner seemed to necessitate that he be subjected, for the present at least, to some sort of restraining influence. Of what nature should that control be? The several Southern legislatures soon undertook to dispose of the matter by adopting "black codes," designed to regulate the conduct of the Negro in various ways. It was but natural that the Methodists, who had manifested so great an interest in the salvation of the slaves and who had converted so many of them while in bondage, should now feel a deep responsibility for the welfare of the freedmen.

The leaders of Southern Methodism lost no time in proclaiming the obligation of their Church. With one accord the spokesmen of the denomination acknowledged the urgent duty of the Church to provide for the spiritual interests of the blacks. Pulpit and press discussed the question at length, and representative bodies at once took the matter under consideration. The laity were urged actively to coöperate. They were constantly reminded of the unpreparedness of the Negro for the situation in which he found himself. A fervent hope was expressed that the Africans would see fit to accept the spiritual guidance of the Church.

In the Columbus Pastoral Address of August 1865 the bishops reminded the people of the work which had been done for the blacks in the past. Admitting that the Church might have done more, they expressed gratitude that it had not done less. Reminding their flocks that the colored membership of the Connection had been greatly reduced by "recent changes and casualties," they pointed out that further defections to Churches "offering greater social inducements for their adhesion" would doubtless occur. "If they elect to leave us," the bishops said, "let them go with the assurance that as heretofore we have been, so we will continue to be their friends, and in every suitable way aid their moral development and spiritual welfare. We must still keep a place for those who remain with us and for others who after a brief experiment elsewhere, may wish to return. While no factious opposition, on the one hand, should be offered to the exercise of their fullest liberty in choosing their ecclesiastical associations; on the other hand no desire of being rid of a responsibility should incline you to treat their action, on so grave a matter, with indifference, or let them take their way in ignorance of all the issues involved. Give them exact information and patient explanation. Act faithfully and kindly in all things toward them, as becomes those who truly care for their souls."[1]

Almost simultaneously with the pronouncement of the bishops the Baltimore *Episcopal Methodist* discussed the duty of Southern Methodists with regard to the Negro. An editorial on "Our Relations to the Colored Population of the South", in its issue of August 2, 1865, is interesting as a full expression of sentiment on the subject. It is especially significant as revealing the attitude that obtained in the Connection before partisan and political agitation prejudiced the popular mind. Referring to the new obligations toward the ex-slaves which circumstances had imposed, the journal said: "The *first* is, to recognize their civil freedom as an undoubted fact; to collect them together and organize as independent congregations, in precisely the same manner that distinguishes the white population, so far as their training will allow; to make them realize that, henceforth, they must perform for

---

[1] *Cf. Journal of General Conference*, 1866, pp. 26-27.

themselves the functions of regularly constituted Churches, and measure up to the stature of their completeness.

"The second is the supply of their pulpits with judicious white ministers until such time when native preachers of approved qualifications shall arise among them. This is sound policy. Preachers, white or black, imported from the North, infected with extreme notions, and burning with fanatical ardor, would inflict incurable damage upon these nascent Churches. This they have already done by their political harangues, and their vindictive temper. . . .

"The third imperative duty is the organization of Sabbath schools, no longer upon the system of oral, but of literal instruction, in which the thousands of ignorant children shall be taught to read the word of God. This we believe to be a solemn debt which the South owes to the African race. It ought to have been paid long since. She ought to claim the privilege of paying it now, and, no doubt, will rejoice to cancel it at once. . . .

"As soon as practicable, a fourth duty would be to furnish them with day schools, in which as the intervals of labor would permit, they might acquire the ordinary branches of education, to prepare them for the pursuits upon which their secular advancement depends. And, finally, when, in the course of events, they shall be fitted for it, to furnish them with ministers of every grade, of their own color, to perfect the idea of their ecclesiastical, as well as their civil independence."[1]

Much concern was expressed as to the condition of the blacks in the Annual and lesser Conferences of all parts of the South during the days immediately following the War. The kindliest feeling was evinced for their spiritual and temporal welfare. The best methods for promoting their moral and religious interests were debated at length. The South Carolina Conference, unforgetful that the first mission to the slaves had been established within its bounds, asserted in November 1865 that it felt "a deep and abiding solicitude" for the religious and moral welfare of the freedmen, and that it would continue to put forth its "best efforts in their service and for their good."[2] The Conference

---

[1] Cf. The Episcopal Methodist, August 2, 1865.
[2] Minutes of the South Carolina Conference, 1865, p. 14.

issued a Pastoral Address, enjoining upon the people the duty of promoting the development of the race. The Address stated that "It can hardly be supposed that within the limits of a Conference whose Church-members have furnished in their annual contributions, more than thirty thousand dollars to extend the privileges of the gospel to the Negroes, any Christian man can be found willing to forego the laudable effort to elevate the race in the scale of intellectual, moral, and religious improvement." It expressed the opinion that the same methods as used in the past, slightly changed to fit the new conditions, could be employed in the work of evangelization. "Continue as heretofore," the laity were told, "your arrangements for their [the Negroes'] accommodations in all the churches, that, frequenting the schools of catechetical instruction, and occupying their accustomed places in the house of God, they may receive from the lips of a pure and spiritual ministry the messages of the Gospel, and rejoice with you in the participation of the benefits of a common salvation."[1] This Conference also advised the Quarterly conferences within its bounds to grant to suitable colored persons licenses to exhort and to preach when this might be done in conformity with the laws of the State.[2]

In December 1865 the Mobile Conference announced that its Church edifices were open to the blacks for worship as in the past, and that they were cordially invited to attend all services. It resolved to continue missions among the freedmen, and that, whenever possible, they should be organized into circuits, stations, and charges, officered by their own race and supplied with white or colored pastors. The Conference requested its presiding bishop to appoint "one of our best and most influential ministers" as a missionary to the colored inhabitants of Mobile, with a liberal sum for his support. It also recommended that pastors in charge promote the education of colored children, as far as it should seem advisable to do so. Referring to the recent defections from the Church, the Conference resolved: "That whenever they decide to leave our organization for one exclusively of their own race, unwise as we regard it, yet, as our spiritual children for whom we

---

[1] Cf. Pastoral Address as given in Shipp, Albert M., The History of Methodism in South Carolina (Nashville, 1884), p. 5.
[2] Minutes of the South Carolina Conference, 1865, p. 11.

have long sacrificed and toiled and prayed in the past, they shall go forth with no bitterness on our part, but rather with blessings."[1] The Georgia Conference of that year, after declaring that the freedmen "appeal to our patriotism, to our philanthropy, and Christian charity," asserted that this appeal would not be in vain. "They are now emphatically *the poor who are to have the gospel preached unto them*," the Conference said.[2]

The Montgomery Conference discussed the question of the Negro's needs in great detail. Acknowledging that the attitude of the freedmen towards the white population had greatly changed, it nevertheless declared that "We cannot see any necessity for a change in the relations of our colored members. They are still entitled to our pastoral care and to all their rights and privileges and the means of salvation, as heretofore." Pointing out that insuperable conditions had prevented the reorganization of its abandoned missions and a continuation of its old methods of working among the Negro population, the Conference asserted that the Church was, notwithstanding, "bound by every humane and Christian consideration, to labor as much as ever" for the colored man's salvation. But the old system of missions, the Conference explained, could not be restored at once. In the first place, the former masters, who had helped to support the missionaries financially, now no longer felt the sense of intimate dependence and responsibility which they had formerly felt for the Negroes, and hence this source of aid was cut off. Moreover, a disposition to drifting and instability persisted among the blacks, causing them to wander off from their old homes in large numbers. Employers who would otherwise have been disposed to contribute toward supplying religious instruction for the freedmen in their hire were unwilling to make pledges because of the uncertainty as to what labor they could procure for the coming year. The Missionary Society was not in a condition to warrant drafts being drawn upon it for the support of the workers, and it appeared inadvisable to send pastors forth dependent for "support upon contributions from the Negroes themselves."

While holding that the best religious interests of the blacks

---

[1]*Journal of Mobile Conference*, 1865, p. 14.
[2]*Minutes of the Georgia Conference*, 1865, p. 11.

would be served by their continuing with white Churches, the Conference stated that its principal black congregation had recently been allowed to go peaceably over to an exclusively colored organization, and it urged that, should similar defections follow, the Negroes be treated with kindness and forbearance, and be accorded all their rights. As to the colored population in general, it said: "Our people should take into consideration the social and constitutional infirmities and disabilities of the race, and their signal unpreparedness for the situation in which, without their own procuring, they find themselves. . . . Be kind and patient towards them, and by all humane and Christian reasons try to help them to a better future than a severe philosophy of all the facts seems to promise."[1] The following year the Montgomery District Conference similarly expressed a tender concern for the well-being of the Negroes: "So many views, honestly entertained in other days, must be changed: so much prejudice, the result of education and interest under the old order must be uprooted: so complete a victory over self, involving self-denial and sacrifice, must be obtained: that nothing less than Divine grace can enable us to see the subject in the new light of new relationships."[2]

The hope was frequently expressed that the Negroes who had been led to leave the Church might be induced to return. It was said that most of them would soon discover that they had left their "truest friends," and would want to come back. When proposals were made to transfer the ownership of houses of worship where entire congregations had gone over to exclusively colored organizations, it was advised that such action be deferred pending their probable home coming.[3]

During the confusion of the first days following the War, it is true, colored members were in some instances advised by their ministers to seek the African Churches or to set up organizations

---

[1]Cf. Proceedings of Montgomery Conference, as given in New Orleans Christian Advocate, January 27, 1866.

[2]Cf. Report of Proceedings of Montgomery District Conference, at Opelika, Alabama, in New Orleans Christian Advocate, September 22, 1866.

[3]Cf. Minutes of South Carolina Conference, 1867, pp. 44-45; cf. statements made in General Conference of 1866, as given in New York Christian Advocate, April 28, 1866; cf. Proceedings of Louisville Conference in Nashville Christian Advocate, December 4, 1869.

of their own.[1] But the Church as a whole sincerely regretted such departures. And it was for the purpose of retaining its old hold upon the rapidly dwindling Negro membership that the General Conference in 1866 adopted a plan for organizing colored circuits, missions, district and Annual Conferences, and ultimately a colored General Conference. In conformity with this idea, and to "promote union and harmony among the colored people," the New Orleans Conference authorized the bishops to negotiate with the bishops of the African Methodist Episcopal Church for a union with that body on the basis of the new plan.[2]

Much was expected as a result. "Why turn them over to the tender mercies of those who neither understand their nature or their wants?" asked the Mississippi Conference in 1866. "We feel assured," the Conference said, "that there is no disposition either to neglect their training, or shift the responsibility on others. But the question is how, in their new and changed relation, can they be best provided for. It must be evident to the most casual observer that the old plan of involuntary provision for them will not answer. They feel that it is not of their own choice, and hence, the first opportunity which presents itself, they set up for themselves, though in doing so they go away from their best friends. Now how is this difficulty to be met? By letting them alone and holding ourselves aloof from them? We think not, but advise the *wise* provision of the last General Conference." In that way, the Conference thought, the Church would appeal to "a lever power within themselves by which to elevate them."[3] About the same time the Montgomery District Conference expressed a profound concern for the success of the new plan. It reminded the Church that "A pure Christianity, of the highest gospel type, will be needed to give the system vital energy, and render it effective."[4]

In its issue of August 8, 1867, the *Richmond Christian Advocate* could announce with gratification that much had been accom-

---

[1]*Cf.* Sullins, D., *Recollections of An Old Man* (Bristol), p. 327; *cf.* statement of Bishop McTyeire as reported in New York *Christian Advocate,* November 26, 1868.

[2]*Journal of General Conference,* 1866, p. 73.

[3]*Journal of Mississippi Annual Conference,* 1866, pp. 13-14.

[4]*Cf.* Proceedings of Montgomery District Conference as reported in *New Orleans Christian Advocate,* September 22, 1866.

plished in binding the blacks to the Church. It stated that Bishop Paine had employed a well-qualified agent to aid in organizing the colored people into separate Conferences. While admitting that the problem was hedged about with difficulties and embarrassments, the *Advocate* nevertheless expressed the opinion that much had been lost through inactivity, and it urged upon the Church an aggressive policy. As a result of the new methods, a number of the Conferences were able for two or three years to report considerable gains in colored membership. The *Southern Christian Advocate* stated "the refreshing news" that many colored persons were even joining mixed Conferences during 1866 and 1867.[1] A number of colored converts were brought into the Church on the Weston and the Platte City Circuits in Missouri, and at one place they were given permission to build a gallery for their accommodation in a white Church.[2] Despite such gains the Negro membership continued to decline.

Whatever hopes Southern Methodism entertained for regaining its lost influence at that time were thwarted by forces that were operating in an opposite direction. To begin with, the Church, in common with the other large religious bodies in the South, was slow to perceive the full implications of emancipation as regards the religious life of the Negro. It was unprepared to revise radically its conception of the proper place of the blacks in the Connection. Though the Negro was cordially urged to remain in the Church, it was expected that he would continue in an inferior and subordinate relation. There was no disposition to concede him any real voice in the management of the affairs of the Church. He was admitted to neither an unrestricted pastoral nor legislative relation. The freedmen, on the other hand, felt that they should enjoy freedom and equality in their Church life. While the plan adopted by the General Conference secured them a large measure of control in their own Church affairs, the autonomy thus accorded was limited in the sense that the General Conference, which it was expected would ultimately be formed, would sustain a relation of dependence to the old Conference. It

---

[1] *Cf. Southern Christian Advocate,* quoted in Simkins and Woody, *op. cit.,* p. 384.
[2] Lewis, *op. cit.,* p. 281.

was further limited by the inclination of the white leaders to exercise "a judicious and exact superintendence" over the affairs of colored groups.

Moreover, to have new Church affiliations was considered at that time a symbol of one's freedom.[1] Another consideration existed in the social inducements held out to the blacks by other Methodist organizations. In them the individual colored member enjoyed a full voice in the management of the affairs of his denomination. One gained a new sense of social importance from an unrestrained mixing with the congregation, after having been confined to definite and inferior quarters. Pride of official position was an outstanding trait in the character of the newly enfranchised Negro. The Methodist organizations composed exclusively of ex-slaves naturally offered a fuller opportunity for the gratification of the ambition for advancement in the pastoral relation; in the Methodist Episcopal Church likewise the colored preacher was a man of greater consequence than in the Southern Church. In colored Churches, moreover, the blacks had an opportunity for unrestrained religious emotions, such as could not be expected in worship with the whites.

But perhaps the chief reason for the failure of the Southern Church to regain its former following of colored communicants was the influence exerted by the Methodist Episcopal Church. Against all efforts of the Southern Methodists to work among the Negroes, the agents and representatives of that body opposed an untiring resistance. The colored man was taught that the leaders of the Southern organization were his natural enemies, that the fixed purpose of these leaders was to restore slavery.[2] The Negroes were told, moreover, that Southern Methodists were morally unfitted to give "religious sympathy and guidance" and that they were incapable of ministering to the spiritual wants of "loyal" people.[3] They were urged to repel the overtures of the Southern Church as a means of guarding both their physical freedom and their spiritual safety.

Missionaries of the Northern Church increased their influence

---

[1] Fleming, op. cit., passim.
[2] Cf. New Orleans Christian Advocate, December 5, 1872.
[3] New York Christian Advocate, December 7, 1871.

among the blacks by advocating radical measures for their benefit. As has been seen, they and the Church journals urged Negro suffrage, and many of them favored at least a partial confiscation in behalf of the former slaves. Thus shortly after the War the Reverend J. P. Newman declared that "Both retributive and compensative justice demand that property in the South should change hands, and a just God will see to it that those who have been robbed of their earnings for generations shall not fail to obtain their share. Everything is now drifting that way, and in the golden age coming the planters of the South will be black men." Dr. Newman asked if the Church could afford to discard this "rising class of the community who are destined to possess the wealth of the State."[1] Such men aroused the Negro to a bristling sense of race consciousness. They continually appealed to the blacks on the basis of the "equality of relations" enjoyed in the Northern Church, denouncing the separation of the races in the Southern Church as a most wicked manifestation of caste spirit. Even the exclusively colored organizations were condemned as fostering the spirit of caste. Referring to the successful work of his Church among the Negro population, the Reverend Lucius C. Matlack said in 1872; "The equality of relations enjoyed by black and white was the rallying cry which gathered the people to us. That is now the triumphant and unanswerable argument which our preachers use with rival colored organizations."[2]

The political regimentation of the freedmen, accomplished in large measure through the influence of the missionaries, enabled the Northern Church to oppose an all but insuperable barrier to the work of the Southern organization among the blacks. Negroes were taught to consider as traitors to their race any blacks who acted with their former masters in politics. Congregations were led to ostracize socially any colored man known to have voted the Democratic ticket.[3] Those who acted with the whites in religious matters were accused of being politically subservient to them. The line of cleavage came to be religious as well as political.

---

[1] Letter of the Reverend J. P. Newman in New York *Christian Advocate,* June 29, 1865.

[2] *Cf.* letter of "L. C. M." in New York *Christian Advocate,* April 4, 1872.

[3] *Cf.* Fleming, *op. cit.,* p. 564. This writer also states that such action frequently resulted in expulsion from the colored Churches.

The Colored Methodist Episcopal Church, because of its friendliness to its parent Church, was declared to be a fit place for only such as desired to be in slavery. It was derided as "the Rebel Church," the "Democratic Church," the "old slavery Church," and "the kitchen Church."[1] The spirit manifested toward the Methodist Episcopal Church, South, and the Colored Methodist Episcopal Church is reflected in a comment made by the Atlanta *Methodist Advocate* in 1871. Referring to the organization of the colored Conferences of the Southern body into an independent General Conference, it said: "They are evidently out of the Church, South, and we congratulate them on getting out, though by the back door, through the kitchen."[2] Again in 1874 the Atlanta *Advocate* said: "The Colored Methodist Episcopal Church of America, South or of South America, or whatever it may be called, has the rickets, spinal complaint, and consumption. Instead of Gospel milk and meat, it has been fed upon Confederate politics, hatred to Yankees and official vanity till the poor thing is too dyspeptic to digest wholesome food and too blind to find it, while in the range of its research it is as destitute of nutriment for mind and spirit as a spring brook of oysters. . . . Poor thing! It is a fit place for nobody but such as prefer to be in slavery and ignorance rather than free and educated, and so has but a narrow and not widening field for operation."[3]

The New Orleans Preachers' Meeting of the Northern organization issued a circular letter to "our people," condemning the formation of the new Church. This paper expressed "our hearty condemnation" of the action of the Southern Church in establishing the new body, because "its unchristian 'color' is the badge of heathenish caste," and because "such a Church is at enmity with the fundamental principles of republican government, as that is most perfectly set forth in the fifteenth Amendment to the Constitution of the United States of America."[4] Against such influences exerted by the Methodist Episcopal Church, and, to a

---

[1] *Cf.* Phillips, C. H., *The History of the Colored Methodist Episcopal Church*, p. 71.

[2] *The Methodist Advocate*, January 4, 1871.

[3] *Cf. The Methodist Advocate*, quoted in *Southwestern Christian Advocate*, December 3, 1874.

[4] *Cf.* Circular as cited in *New Orleans Christian Advocate*, July 30, 1870.

lesser degree, by the African Churches, the Methodist Episcopal Church, South, found it exceedingly difficult to make any headway.

Moreover, it must be admitted, an apathy with regard to the religious instruction of the blacks had developed in the Church. In some measure this feeling had its origin in the profound despondency entertained by many persons with regard to the possibility of the advancement of the Negroes under the new order. The deep pessimism which prevailed among some persons was reflected in an editorial on "The Decadence of the Negro Race," which appeared in 1867 in the *Richmond Christian Advocate*. Referring to a report on the condition of the blacks under governmental care, which had recently been issued by General O. O. Howard, the editor expressed a gloomy outlook as to the future. He felt that, situated as the colored race was, one of three things must occur: the Negro must be subjected to the control of the superior race; amalgamation must take place; or the Negro's ultimate extinction must be expected. "And such," said the editorial, "must be the doom of the Negro." The whites had no desire for the re-enslavement of the blacks, but they would never amalgamate with them. The indolence, thriftlessness, and improvidence of the race, together with the circumstances by which the Negroes were surrounded, would result in their rapid extinction. The whites owed much to the African and should do all in their power to give him the few blessings and comforts he could enjoy "while his race lingers in the path of its destiny."[1] Such views were naturally not conducive to special exertions for the advancement of the blacks.

Apart from the apathy fostered by such ideas, the extravagances of the Negro's worship during the period immediately following the Civil War caused many whites to become indifferent to his religion, or even hostile to it.[2] The gravest apprehensions were felt that the blacks, removed from the direct influence of the whites in religious matters, were relapsing into heathenism.

The growing indifference towards the Negro's spiritual condition was reflected in occasional expressions of concern made in the Church with regard to his religious instruction. The Rich-

---

[1] *Richmond Christian Advocate,* October 31, 1867.
[2] *Cf.* Fleming, *op. cit.,* passim.

mond *Advocate,* while commending the work done in organizing the colored people into separate charges and conferences, said in 1867: "But it is, after all, to be feared that there has been and is too much apathy, among the preachers and people on this subject. We cannot but deem it of the highest importance, in every aspect of the subject, that this apathy should cease. The Presiding Elders of the districts and preachers in charge should rouse themselves to carry out the provisions of the Discipline which they have solemnly vowed to keep and not to mend."[1] In a "Report on the Religious Interests of the Colored People," the Mobile Conference asserted in 1869 its "fear that the Methodist Church generally has not evinced that concern to have them continue with us, that it should have done. In some instances, the use of our houses of worship has been allowed them with reluctance, and in some places they have been advised and encouraged to seek communion and church fellowship with other organizations. We are happy to know that there are many noble exceptions to this remark."[2]

By 1870, and with the establishment of the colored General Conference, the direct efforts of the Southern Church for the colored man's religious welfare and instruction virtually ceased. When petitioning the General Conference for a separate establishment that year, the colored conferences, while expressing their gratitude to the Church, said: "We believe that the time has now come when a General Conference can be organized for our race; under other circumstances it might be advisable to wait until our ministers were better educated. But in order that there should be no alienation on the part of our people we ask that you form at once and authorize the organization of a Colored General Conference. . . . It is known to your venerable body that many influences are being brought to bear against us because of our relation to the Church, South. We have been harrassed, persecuted, and abused."[3] Henceforth the efforts of the Methodist Episcopal Church, South, for the benefit of the race were made almost exclusively through the agency of the Colored Methodist

---

[1] *Richmond Christian Advocate,* August 8, 1867.
[2] *Cf. Journal of Mobile Conference,* 1869, p. 19.
[3] *Cf.* Memorial from the colored conferences, as given in *Daily Christian Advocate,* May 27, 1870.

Episcopal Church. But it is significant that the fundamental law of the new organization prohibited the introduction of any white person into the membership of the Church.[1]

The Southern Church now withdrew so completely from all direct labors for the Negro's spiritual interests that, for a number of years, any expression of concern for the welfare of his soul upon the part of its representatives was a matter of surprise to him. In 1886 a minister of the Methodist Episcopal Church, South, declared that "Southern christians—white men—have well-nigh, I might say altogether except incidentally, ceased to preach the Gospel, or to feel that they are any longer charged with the responsibility of looking after the moral and spiritual welfare of the Negro.[2]

With the passing of Reconstruction however, an active and growing sense of responsibility for the religious welfare of the blacks began to manifest itself in the Church. This was evidenced primarily through a concern for the education of the blacks, and found practical expression in a movement to provide trained Negro leaders for the race. The significance of this development appears in the light of the changed sentiment toward the education of the colored people which had grown up during the years from 1865 to 1870, both in the Methodist Episcopal Church, South, and among the Southern people generally.

As has been mentioned, the journals and representative bodies of the Church asserted the need for some provision for the education of the Negro immediately after the War. Indeed, there were among the leaders of the Church a number of men who had always favored at least an elementary book learning for the blacks. This they had deemed essential to the Negro's spiritual welfare. The usually conservative Bishop George F. Pierce had spoken forth boldly on the subject. Although repudiating the idea of erecting "the fancied rights of any people into a higher law than divine revelation," Bishop Pierce had, during the troubled days of

---

[1]*Cf.* Proceedings of Organizing Convention as reported in Nashville *Christian Advocate,* January 7, 1871.

[2]"There are doubtless individual exceptions to this," he said, "but they are so seldom as to elicit surprise from the Negro when spoken to by a white man about his soul; this I happen to know from personal experience." *Cf.* letter of the Reverend W. C. Dunlap in Wesleyan *Christian Advocate,* March 6, 1886.

the War, urged the Georgia Legislature to provide some education for the colored people. In an address before that body, in which he espoused new legislation on matters connected with religious interests, the Bishop said in March 1863: "There is another statute of Georgia adverse, as I believe, to the will of God and the true interests of humanity. I mean the law which forbids us to teach our Negroes to read. . . . If the institution of slavery cannot be maintained except at the expense of the black man's immortal interests, in the name of Heaven, I say—let it perish. . . . To make the Negro suffer for the sins of the Yankee is the grossest injustice, and yet this is the practical effect of our law. . . . A Bible in every cabin will be the best police for the country, and despite the ravings of a brainless fanaticism, subjugation and order will reign throughout the land."[1]

During the first days after the War Annual Conferences in all parts of the South expressed themselves warmly in favor of education for the blacks. The intellectual advancement of the Negro was asserted to be a duty of the first importance devolving upon the Southern people. Southerners were reminded of the devotion shown by the slaves to their masters during the late struggle. The dangers to be apprehended from the presence of a great body of illiterate blacks were dwelt upon. The Montgomery Conference promptly resolved that it would recommend "to our people to countenance and encourage day schools for the education of colored children, under proper regulations and trustworthy teachers."[2] The Mobile Conference, it will be recalled, urged that Methodist ministers be instructed "to promote, as far as they deem advisable, the education" of colored children.[3] The Mississippi Conference discussed the subject of the Negro's education at great length. The blacks are among us, the Conference said, "and will, in all human probability, remain so. They have not now masters to care and provide for them and to prevent their running into fanaticism and dissipation. They need more knowledge now than when in a state of slavery, because they must now exercise their own judgment in providing for themselves, whilst formerly others

---

[1] Cf. Smith, op. cit., pp. 474-475.
[2] Cf. Proceedings of Montgomery Conference as given in New Orleans Christian Advocate, January 27, 1866.
[3] Cf. ante, p. 258.

provided for them. Again, laws, civil and criminal, will be enacted by our Legislature for the government of the Negroes.
These laws they ought to be able to read. Surely none will deny
this. Formerly their owners informed them of the laws governing them, but now there is no one whose especial duty it is to do
this. . . . Again, formerly they had owners whose duty it was to
furnish them with religious instruction; but now it is not so. God
has given us and them, and all men, His Holy Word to read and
search. The reading of that word instructs the mind and the
heart, and better prepares man for usefulness, happiness, and
heaven. Who will have the hardihood to assert that the reading
of the Bible by the Negroes will do them harm, or will be of no
service to them? . . . Again if they are left without any mental
culture, they will sink deeper and deeper into ignorance and
superstition, and fanaticism, and be easily led by wicked and
designing men into the commission of crime." "But who," asked
the Conference, "are to superintend their education—abolitionists
or Southern people? The Committee answers emphatically,
Southern people."[1]

Having exhorted the Southern whites to undertake such instruction, the Mississippi Conference then adopted a resolution
stating its own duty in the matter. It declared that "it shall be
the duty of the Presiding Elders in charge of circuits and stations,
to organize schools, where they can do so to advantage, for the
education of the Negro, and where it can be done in accordance
with the Statutes of the State."[2]

That such action in the Annual Conferences had met with the
approval of the Church at large was shown by the measures which
were adopted by the General Conference when it met at New
Orleans during the Spring of 1866. Referring to the need for
educating the blacks, the Conference declared that the interests
of both the white and colored people "are materially dependent
upon the intelligence and virtue of this race," and that "our hearts
prompt us to this philanthropy." The Conference adopted a
resolution recommending "to our people the establishment of day-

---

[1]*Journal of Mississippi Annual Conference*, 1865, pp. 10-11.
[2]*Cf.* Proceedings of Mississippi Annual Conference, as given in *New Orleans
Christian Advocate*, January 20, 1866.

schools, under proper regulations and trustworthy teachers, for the education of colored children."[1]

Much was hoped for from the Sunday school as an agency for educating the Negroes. It was natural that Sabbath schools should be looked to as a means of furnishing the rudiments of learning in a section where the idea of elementary public schools had never taken deep root. The Annual Conferences, during the period immediately following the War, frequently suggested the use of Sunday schools for this purpose. Thus the Montgomery Conference resolved in 1865 "That we consider it a duty incumbent on our members and worthy of the best pastoral care and oversight, that Sabbath Schools be organized for the benefit of the colored children and youth, wherever practicable, in which they may be taught the principles of the Christian religion, and also to read the Word of God."[2]

For several years members of the Methodist Episcopal Church, South, were active in teaching Sabbath schools for black children. In its issue of August 8, 1867, the *Richmond Christian Advocate* reported that the education of Negro youths was being looked after in both day and Sunday schools. The editor stated "from personal observation during a recent visit to a part of Randolph-Macon District that considerable attention is given to Sunday schools for colored children. Some of the most intelligent and worthy white members of the Church are zealously and successfully working in these schools." "It is true," declared the Mississippi Conference late in 1866, "that a strong opposition to the moral and intellectual advancement of the Negro is very unjustly and unkindly felt, and very unreasonably manifested in

---

[1]*Journal of General Conference*, 1866, p. 39.

[2]Proceedings of Montgomery Conference as given in *New Orleans Christian Advocate*, January 27, 1866. The Georgia Conference declared in 1866: "The Negro, as an element in society, should be educated. Our people should be encouraged to gather the children, and the old where they can, into Sabbath Schools, and teach them the Word of God. . . . They must have the Gospel from intelligent teachers, and they will, and do turn to us for instruction." Cf. *Minutes of Georgia Conference*, 1866, p. 17. The Louisiana Conference urged "as the legitimate expansion of former efforts, that every available means heretofore used in white schools, be introduced into the Sabbath Schools for colored children." Cf. *Journal of Louisiana Conference*, 1865, The New Orleans General Conference in 1866 urged that "special attention be given to Sunday-schools among the colored people." Cf. *Journal of General Conference*, 1866, p. 59.

limited sections of the country. Yet we should the more readily undertake the work of establishing Sunday-chools among" them.[1]

The leaders of the Methodist Episcopal Church, South, rendered an important service to the cause of colored education during the first years after the War through the encouragement and aid which they gave to the schools which were established for the Negro by the Freedmen's Bureau and by agencies in the North. The Freedmen's Bureau, organized in 1865, although having other functions, was primarily serviceable as an agency in promoting the education of the freedmen.[2] During the five years of its existence the Bureau contributed $5,250,000 to schools for the Negro. Beginning in 1865, it took hold of schools already established, built others, hired teachers, and coöperated with Church and benevolent corporations in the educational work which they had undertaken. By 1869 it had created a great system of elementary Negro schools, both day and evening, with 2,500 teachers and 250,000 pupils.[3]

The favorable attitude of the Methodist Episcopal Church, South, was of much advantage to the Bureau in extending its work. Outstanding leaders of the denomination used their influence to arouse interest in the work. General Wager Swayne, who had charge of organizing the work in Alabama, wrote with special approval of the encouragement and assistance given by the Church through the Reverend Holland N. McTyeire, who was at all times in favor of colored schools.[4] In November 1866 the Reverend Charles K. Marshall of Vicksburg issued a "Letter to the People of Mississippi," urging the people of that State to approve and encourage such schools. Declaring that the "education of the freedmen's children in the common branches of learning taught in our schools is undoubtedly a duty we owe alike to ourselves and to them," Dr. Marshall entreated that the Southern people accept the benefits of the recent offer of Major-General

---

[1]Proceedings of Mississippi Annual Conference as reported in *New Orleans Christian Advocate*, December 22, 1866.

[2]Boone, Richard G., *Education in the United States* (New York, 1889), p. 351.

[3]*Ibid.*, p. 352. Although the other functions of the Bureau ceased in 1869, its educational work was continued for a year longer in some States.

[4]*Cf.* Fleming, *op. cit.*, p. 457.

T. J. Wood, which made available certain facilities and funds for educating colored children. Emphasizing the danger of leaving the Negro uneducated, he said: "He will come in contact with the worst class of white men, who will take every advantage of his ignorance, credulousness, and prejudice, to defraud and mislead him. Nothing but cultivation in the line of things where his greatest necessities will meet these opposing elements, can in any degree insure his enjoyment of the fruits of his labor. All good persons, all brave and magnanimous men will from habit, former long standing and friendly relations, and because it is proper, just, and right in itself, endeavor to promote the enlightment, and cultivate the friendship of the colored man, and will protect him, alike against the Southern cormorant and the ferocity of the Northern wolf."

The writer admitted that it was but natural that "some fastidious persons among us look with aversion upon African schools and their teachers, because of the relation they stand in to the 'Lost Cause,' as well as on account of the fact that the poor white man is taxed, without representation, to pay, in part for those schools, while the same poor white man's little ones have neither school, nor teacher, nor Bureau, to take care of them." But Providence would take care of these things. Moreover, if Southerners did not undertake the education of the blacks, there were those in the North who would gladly accept the work, and who, with some worthy exceptions, would bring with them to the South "the most embittered feelings of hate and aversion for everything of their own color."

Dr. Marshall urged Mississippians to accept positions in the schools which had been established. "Our Commonwealth," he said, "abounds with men and women who need employment; they understand the colored man's nature and capacities; they can render both races a lasting service; and they ought to be invited to take charge of the schools, or go at once, with true purpose of usefulness, and organize schools for themselves." In conclusion the writer declared that "For one—and I am not in a lean minority—I am willing to receive such aid, and promote the objects aimed at with a hearty good will."[1]

In 1867 Bishop Wightman issued a Pastoral Address to the colored communicants of the Mobile Conference, assuring them that the Southern whites entertained the sincerest concern for their well-being and advancement, and warning them that their freedom would benefit them only to the extent that they learned self-control. This they must acquire through disciplining their minds. "There are millions of free people in other countries— tens of thousands in our own country—who have to fight poverty, starvation, distress, in a hand-to-hand battle every day. Freedom in itself and by itself puts no bread in peoples' mouths; no clothes on their backs; no shoes on their feet. If they are sick freedom cannot cure them without a doctor." Then, after urging the blacks to see that their children received the advantages offered by the Sunday schools, he said: "As far as you can do so, I advise you to send your children to the day schools also, and encourage them to improve their minds. This improvement will qualify them to meet the responsibilities and perform the duties of the station in life in which it has pleased the providence of God to place them. It will teach them true self-respect. They will be modest, orderly, and well-behaved in proportion as they become intelligent, and are acquainted with the true value of industry, frugality, and order, provided they are brought up in the nurture and admonition of the Lord."[2]

Early that same year the bishops issued a Pastoral Address reminding the white communicants of their duty to foster and encourage the schools which had been established for the blacks. Calling attention to the resolution which had been adopted by the General Conference the preceding year, the bishops said: "This resolution in spirit, requires what we trust every one of you will be forward to do—the moral as well as the material support of such schools and teachers as it describes. We must not wait for public opinion to form itself right on this subject, but contribute to its formation. Anything like ostracism of those honestly en-

---

[1]*Cf.* letter of Dr. Charles K. Marshall in Nashville *Christian Advocate,* January 31, 1867.

[2]*Cf.* Pastoral Address as given in Nashville *Christian Advocate,* March 28, 1867.

gaged in this work is a violation of this pledge to each other, to the colored people, and to God. For moral incendiaries and political propagandists, who abuse school teaching to other purposes, this resolution challenges no sympathy, but so far as we may prevent it, let no man or woman be treated with less respect, or be thought less of, merely because he or she teaches a Negro school. Against such prejudice, from whatever source arising, let us make common cause with them."[1] It was under the inspiration of such leaders that, when the first colored conference of the Colored Church assembled that year at Jackson, Tennessee, it was enacted that colored candidates for the ministry must be able to read before ordination."[2]

It cannot be denied that the pleas of the Southern churchmen were frequently based on appeals to sectional interest, but there can be little doubt that they employed such arguments chiefly for the purpose of keeping down and dispelling prejudice against the education of the blacks. Referring to the position taken by the Churches in Alabama, General Swayne, in his report for 1866, said: "The principal argument was an appeal to sectional and sectarian prejudice, lest, the work being inevitable, the influence which must come from it be realized by others; but it is believed that this was the shield and weapon which men of unselfish principle found necessary at first."[3]

---

[1] *Cf.* Pastoral Address of April 1867, as quoted in *New Orleans Christian Advocate,* May 25, 1867.

[2] *Cf.* Nashville *Christian Advocate,* December 5, 1867.

[3] *Cf.* Fleming, *op. cit.,* p. 642. A strong appeal of such character was made by the *Southern Christian Advocate* in May 1867. Calling attention to the fact that two ministers of the Mobile Conference were teaching in schools established under auspices of this kind, the *Advocate,* in an editorial headed "Reconstruction on the Right Plan", said: "Now this is what is wanted all over the country. It is proper that all classes of the population should be educated, too, by those who belong to the South, not by spies or intermeddlers or hired political emissaries, who are not only not in sympathy with our people, but hostile to them." It declared that an effort was making in the North to create a "Northern party" in the Southern States, for the purpose of holding the South's agricultural interests tributary to Northern manufacturing. Expressing the opinion that this could never be accomplished, even temporarily, if both races in the South could be made to understand the issue, it said: "Educate the colored race—whether it be done by ourselves or others—and they will eventually see it, and their own interests, as Southerners, will outweigh all their gratitude towards those who would use them as partisans to oppose home interests, and to build up another section. Then, they will affiliate with their own people. This state of affairs may, however, be delayed by our permitting

The appeals of the Southern leaders not only served to keep down opposition to Negro education, but also enabled the Bureau to secure a large number of native whites as teachers for its schools. General Swayne reported that the Southern whites were especially willing to do such work after their Church officials had expressed their approval.[1] Indeed, the position assumed by the Methodist Episcopal Church, South, with regard to the education of the freedmen, was in no wise repugnant to the general sentiment of the dominant classes in the South at that time. The old opposition to the educated Negro as a "dangerous Negro" had swiftly vanished under the pressure of circumstances. As has been mentioned, opposition to the instruction of the blacks was expressed in some quarters before the close of 1866. But there is an abundance of evidence to show that, during the years immediately following the War, the controlling elements of society not only looked with favor upon the steps that were being taken but that they felt an urgent necessity for some provision.[2]

Southerners now believed that the discipline of learning must be substituted for that of slavery. Some sort of intellectual training was felt to be essential to the continuation of friendly relations between the two races.[3] Mass meetings of white citizens in many places pledged aid in promoting Negro education. Thus in Alabama the Monroe County Agricultural Association declared it a duty of the whites to teach the blacks, and appointed a com-

---

them for a while, to come under the influence of those who are bent on trying to alienate them from the whites, and to make them feel that the white masses are enemies to the Negro. To save the country from this interval of antagonism, the whites should do what they can toward giving instruction to the colored people; and he ought to be considered a patriot, who with these views will undertake their instruction in letters. The Southern teacher of the humblest Negro school is doing more for his country than many noisy politicians are doing, or can do." Cf. *Southern Christian Advocate*, May 24, 1867.

[1]Cf. Fleming, *op. cit.*, p. 460; cf. *Senate Executive Document*, No. 6, 39th Congress, 2nd Session.

[2]In an article on "The Freedmen's Bureau", in *The Atlantic Monthly* for March 1901, Dr. W. E. Burghardt Du Bois has asserted that the opposition to Negro education was bitter among all classes in the South at that time, but there is varied and abundant evidence to prove that such was not the case. Simkins and Woody, *op. cit.*, p. 422, state that "No longer did anyone favor the prohibition of literary instruction to that race." And Fleming, *op. cit.*, p. 457, asserts that the evidence on this point "is all one way."

[3]Fleming, *op. cit.*, p. 457.

mittee to devise an appropriate plan.[1] Similar action was taken by other such groups in the State. A considerable number of whites of the best antecedents there sought employment in the Bureau schools.[2] When the Bureau Superintendent of Schools had no Northern teacher available for a school in Russell County, he allowed the whites of the community to select one of their own number for the position. A group of prominent men urged the local Methodist preacher to undertake the work, and upon being assured that his family would not suffer socially because of his action, he did so. With the assistence of other members of his family, the classes were conducted for two years in his door-yard, outbuildings, and verandahs, and all were satisfied with the arrangement until political alienation caused the Negroes to demand a Northern teacher or one of their own color.[3] Many of the outstanding political leaders of the old order warmly favored Negro education.[4] It is significant that, as late as 1869, approximately one-half of the four hundred and five native whites teaching in public schools in South Carolina were conducting schools for Negroes.[5]

But forces tending to alienate the races and to cause those who had advocated Negro education to lose interest in, if not actually to look with disfavor upon, schooling for the blacks, were already at work. Such forces now sufficed for a decade or more to destroy almost entirely the influence of the Southern Church among the great majority of the blacks and to render the Methodists in a large measure indifferent to Negro education. As early as March 1867 the venerable Bishop Andrew lamented that the Northern missionaries were encouraging in the Negroes "such a course of conduct as may induce in the mind of the white man a state of feeling which must be eventually prejudicial to the Negro race."[6] Not only were the Negroes alienated for political reasons. To avenge their social treatment, the missionaries, many of whom served as teachers in the Bureau schools, frequently encouraged

---

[1]*Ibid.*, p. 626.
[2]*Ibid.*, p. 463.
[3]*Ibid.*, p. 460.
[4]*Cf. Testimony of Select Committee,* Vols. I-XII, passim.
[5]Simkins and Woody, *op. cit.*, p. 423.
[6]Letter of Bishop Andrew in *New Orleans Christian Advocate,* March 2, 1867.

in the freedmen a behavior that inevitably aroused further the resentment of the whites. They inculcated social theories such as to excite the severest disapprobation among the whites. When the equalitarian teachings of the missionaries caused them to be ostracised by the Southerners, they retaliated by teaching the Negroes objectionable songs and sayings, and by imbuing them with a spirit of social insubordination.[1] As a result, the blacks manifested an insolence towards their former masters which caused it to become a commonly accepted belief that "schooling ruins a Negro."[2]

When political regimentation had rendered the blacks inaccessible to guidance by Southern whites, interest in projects for Negro education ceased to manifest itself in the Church almost entirely. For almost a decade after 1870 the Annual Conferences had practically nothing to say on the subject of the mental culture of the blacks. As has been seen, the social practices of the teachers in the colored schools were considered sufficient grounds for withholding from them all recognition. The profession had been discredited, and the duty of teaching in such schools was no longer pressed upon native whites. The journals of the Connection ceased almost entirely to discuss the question of the education of the blacks. In a report to the General Conference of 1874 on the "Religious Condition of the Colored People," the bishops commended "to the good will of all who would do a great work for the Master's cause" a project which had been set on foot by the Colored Methodist Episcopal Church to establish a training school for its ministerial candidates. But sufficient interest was aroused in neither that nor the succeeding General Conference to result in any material aid being given to the proposed school.[3] The alienation had been general. The Methodists of the South no longer felt charged with responsibility for the religious welfare of the blacks and since many had become indifferent or unfavorable to their schooling, the matter received little consideration in any of the councils of the Church during the greater part of the Seventies.

---

[1]Cf. Simkins and Woody, op. cit., p. 343.
[2]Cf. Fleming, op. cit., p. 627
[3]Journal of General Conference, 1874, pp. 459-460.

But with the passing of Reconstruction, when the freedmen became more accessible to the influence of the former master class, as has been said, a lively sense of responsibility for the religious welfare of the blacks began to reassert itself in the Church. Among the first indications of this reviving interest were a fuller recognition of the work being done by various Northern agencies and a growing sensitiveness to criticism in the Connection with regard to the position of the Southern Church on the matter. More than in any other way it was evidenced by a concern for the educational advancement of the blacks which found practical expression in a movement to provide trained Negro leaders for the race.

As early as June 1877 the Reverend David C. Kelley of Nashville expressed his sympathy for the work to elevate the blacks being done by the Methodist Episcopal Church. At that time he addressed the graduating class of the Central Tennessee College, an institution conducted by the Freedmen's Aid Society. The Reverend John Braden, president of the college, characterized Dr. Kelley's address as one of the first utterances he had heard in the section "which encourage us to hope that the educational work among the colored people will receive the cordial and open endorsement of our brethren of all the Southern Churches." Coming from a Southern minister who had been distinguished for his gallantry as a Confederate officer, his words were regarded as "more than usually important, as expressive of the views of the more intelligent class of Southerners on the education of the colored people." Addressing the blacks as "brethren, friends, fellow-citizens," Kelley claimed for himself and the colored people the "feeling of personal regard and the relations embraced in the names."[1] "Some people," said the *Wesleyan Christian Advocate* in speaking of the Freedmen's Aid Society in 1881, "affect to pooh-pooh this work—this is idiotic. The Methodist Episcopal Church has done and is doing a great work for the Negroes through the Freedmen's Aid Society, as well as in other useful ways."[2]

---

[1] *Cf.* account given in letter of the Reverend John Braden in *Southwestern Christian Advocate,* June 14, 1877.

[2] *Cf. Wesleyan Christian Advocate,* February 19, 1881

In March 1878 the Reverend R. K. Hargrove, who was later a bishop of his Church, discussed in the columns of the New Orleans *Advocate* the work of the Freedman's Aid Society. Pointing out that the Society was conducting "twenty-one schools, supplying instruction to 3,170 students, of all grades and departments," and that these schools were encumbered by a debt of only $15,000, he expressed gratification at these results, asserting that they "must meet the approval and receive the blessing of our heavenly Father." But he deplored the fact that the Reverend R. S. Rust, secretary of the Society, had shown so little of the milk of human kindness when at a recent anniversary celebration he had mocked the Southern Churches with having done almost nothing to contribute to the learning of the blacks. "He ought to know," the writer said, "that these Churches, reduced in finances, have had to struggle for existence; that their institutions have been despoiled of their endowments, and many of them have gone into other hands while all are reduced to the greatest extremities. But notwithstanding our deep poverty, his taunt and declaration are not warranted. Even the Protestant Episcopalians and Presbyterians, whom he especially stigmatizes as not having established a single institution for the education of the colored people, have each a theological school exclusively for their benefit."[1] The laity were now reminded with increasing frequency of the noble work which the Church had done for the Negro in the past, and much gratification was expressed that he was again becoming amenable to its influence.[2]

Presently a group of able and eloquent champions of Negro advancement appeared in the Church. Emphasizing the fact that the freedmen were again accessible to guidance by the whites,

---

[1] Communication of the Reverend R. K. Hargrove in *New Orleans Christian Advocate*, March 14, 1878.

[2] Toward the end of 1877 the Alabama Conference adopted a report on the "Condition of the Colored People", in which it was resolved that *"Whereas, The barriers thrown in our way by others have been to a large extent removed, rendering them more accessible to us than formerly,"* the Conference would "encourage them in their educational interests by rendering them such help in their efforts to secure school houses and otherwise as we may be able." The Conference further resolved to "give them such aid in their Churches by participating in their religious services, as we may have the opportunity." *Cf.* Proceedings of Alabama Conference as reported in *New Orleans Christian Advocate,* February 21, 1878.

they urged that the Church would be recreant to its duty should it fail to resume at once its labors for the blacks. Its obligations to the race, they felt, could best be fulfilled by providing for the Negroes trained leaders of their own color. They implored the Church not to permit the experiences of the past to blind it to its obligations or to the needs of the blacks. They emphasized the fact that to leave the Negro alone would be the worst service it could render him.

In an editorial on "Our Duty to the Negro," Dr. O. P. Fitzgerald, of the Nashville *Christian Advocate,* said in November 1878: "The way of duty is plain before our Churches. We mean in particular the Methodist Episcopal Church, South, and the other Southern Churches, Baptist and Presbyterian, that, under God, have done for the Negro religiously pretty much all that was ever done. We beg leave to suggest a few items evolved from the late election. . . . The Southern States have come out of the canvass all on one side. 'A Solid South' is the alarming result as seen by some, the wished for result as seen by others. . . . What is the meaning of this to our Churches? That we can now do something for the Negro." While urging that the Church now send ministers and educational aid to the blacks, Dr. Fitzgerald asked if some person in the Connection would not endow an institution for the training of Negro preachers.[1] About the same time, Dr. Atticus G. Haygood, then serving as editor of the Wesleyan *Advocate,* reminded the Connection that nothing but prejudice could now hinder the Church from resuming its work among the blacks. He said: "There is but one obstacle of importance in our way, and that we must overcome. We must not allow the follies of such men as Bishop Haven of the Northern Church, and Dr. Fowler of the New York *Christian Advocate* to prejudice us against this eminently opportune and Christian work."[2]

The two editors just quoted were, during their subsequent careers as churchmen, increasingly distinguished as champions of the elevation and advancement of the Negro. Fitzgerald, during

[1]*Cf.* Nashville *Christian Advocate,* November 23, 1878.
[2]*Cf. Wesleyan Christian Advocate,* quoted in Nashville *Christian Advocate,* November 30, 1878.

a decade as editor of the official organ of the Connection and after that as a bishop of his Church, never ceased to urge a recognition of the dignity of the race. It will be seen that the work of Atticus G. Haygood, as editor, as college president, and as a bishop, made him the foremost champion of Negro education in the South. Having shown himself friendly to the instruction of the blacks while editor of the Wesleyan, Dr. Haygood continued his efforts during his presidency of Emory College, Oxford, Georgia, to which position he was elected in 1880. On Thanksgiving Day of that year, before the faculty and student body of the college, he preached a sermon on "The New South," which attracted widespread attention to the educational needs of the freedmen. In this discourse he urged the people of the South to view their own position candidly. Admitting that "the rather Pharisaic attitude that many public men at the North have assumed towards us has greatly embarrassed and arrested our efforts to discover our faults and to amend them," he declared that "all this only furnishes a reason for beginning the sooner and trying the harder." "We think better of ourselves than the facts of our history and our present state of progress justify," he said. "As a people we have not enough felt the heart beat of the world outside of us." Reminding the Southern people of the vast amount of illiteracy, both white and black, among them, he sought to impress upon them the obligation to remove it. With regard to the Negro, he asserted that "there is one great historic fact which should, in my sober judgment, above all things excite everywhere in the South profound gratitude to Almighty God: I mean the abolition of African slavery." "I am not called on," he said, "in order to justify my position, to approve the political unwisdom of suddenly placing the ballot in the hands of nearly a million unqualified men—only that since it is done, this also is history that we of the South should accept and that our fellow-citizens of the North should never disturb." This fact, he pointed out, made it incumbent upon Southerners to aid in educating the freedmen. "By every token," he said, "this whole nation should undertake the problem of their education."[1] This sermon, printed

---

[1]Haygood, Atticus G., *The New South* (pamphlet, Oxford, Georgia, 1880), pp. 9-14.

by unanimous vote of the congregation, was widely discussed in both the secular and religious press throughout the country. Further publicity was given to it when, shortly after its publication, a wealthy Methodist layman of New York City expressed approval of Haygood's advanced position by making a large gift to Emory College, and subsequently, when the Atlanta *Methodist Advocate* excited widespread comment by voicing astonishment that a Northern Methodist should have made such a gift to an institution of the Southern Church, and by implying that both donor and recipient had been inspired by mercenary motives.[1]

In 1881, a year after his Thanksgiving sermon, Dr. Haygood published his views on the education of the Negro in a book, *Our Brother In Black,* of which it has been said that it did more than any other work of the *post-bellum* era "to bring both sections sanity in thinking concerning the Negro problem."[2] Recognizing the colored man as a citizen and voter, the author pressed upon the people of the South the necessity of educating this new power in the social and political system. Though there were difficulties to be encountered, he reminded them that perhaps the chief obstacle to success lay in their own sensitiveness to the Northern criticism which had "greatly hindered the South from coming to a knowledge of her own faults." But there was also need in the South for "schooling in right views on this subject." "We of the South have not been without folly and unbelief and sin in our attitude towards this fact of emancipation. We have been slow to accept its full significance even when we fully and finally accepted the fact." "People who give money to send their sons and daughters to convert heathen overseas should be ashamed" to allow their views on the subject to be governed by race or

---

[1]When Dr. J. M. Buckley, editor of the New York *Christian Advocate*, criticized Dr. Fuller for the implications he had made concerning this gift of George I. Seney, a sharp controversy ensued between the two editors. Fuller showed much acrimony. He interpreted both Seney's action and Buckley's criticism of himself as attacks upon the work of the Northern Church in the South. Referring to the statements made by Fuller, the New York editor said: "Dr. Haygood, the fraternal delegate to our last General Conference, who for a long time has taken advanced grounds in favor of the full recognition and education of the colored man as a citizen and a voter, and in favor of general education in the South, it is insinuated, has changed his sentiments because it would pay." *Cf.* New York *Christian Advocate*, May 26, 1881.

[2]*Cf.* Du Bose, *op. cit.,* p. 128.

sectional prejudice. Though the condition of things which had developed after the War had made it impracticable for a time for Southern whites to continue as teachers in Negro schools, too often "we have accepted our dismissal too readily." Emphasizing the remarkable faculty for changing their outlook which Southerners had already demonstrated, he urged that they now rid themselves of all prejudice on the subject. Distinguishing between the Northern teachers who had labored in all sincerity and those who had sought to inspire the freedmen with incendiary notions, he declared that to the former the people of the South owed deep gratitude. "Suppose these Northern teachers had not come," he said, "and that nobody had taught the Negroes set free and citizens! The South would have been uninhabitable by this time."

Though the Southerners had found it difficult to influence the blacks in the past because of the Negro's "feeling of irritated suspicion," this could no longer serve as an excuse for inaction in the section, for "at this time the Negroes are warming toward the Southern people. Of this there are expressions every day and everywhere. Our preachers are not unwelcome now. In some quarters they are in demand." The continuance of good government in America during the next generation would depend upon the Negro being educated, President Haygood argued. "If the work of educating the Negroes of the South is ever to be carried on satisfactorily." he said, "if ever the best results are to be accomplished, then *Southern white people must take part in teaching Negro schools.*" Emphasizing the strong hold of religion upon the mind of the colored man, he urged the Southern Churches to take advantage of this characteristic in order to contribute more fully to the elevation of the freedmen.

As to the duty of his own Church he was specific. The obligation of the Methodist Episcopal Church, South, could be fulfilled most satisfactorily through the medium of the Colored Methodist Episcopal Church, in the establishment of which it had played so important a part. Thus, the strong separatist instinct manifested by the colored people in their religious affiliations would be recognized, and the results more readily achieved. He advocated that the next General Conference of the Methodist

Robert E. Blackwell, President of Randolph-Macon College

Episcopal Church, South, "should take vigorous action to establish a great 'training school' for this colored daughter" which would equip Negro teachers and preachers who could act as leaders for their race.[1]

Our Brother In Black made Haygood the recognized leader in the South of the movement for the elevation of the Negro. The source of the book helped to give it a nation wide circulation and an extraordinary influence. One who disagreed with his views protested that, being a foremost man in his Church, Haygood's utterances "bear a sort of official stamp, which gives them currency and, with many, almost an *ex cathedra* authority."[2] Some critics believed that the publication of the book would prove a blow to Haygood's denominational career. On the contrary, in 1882, at the age of forty-three, he was elected a bishop of his Church. Instead of accepting this honor as a vindication against criticism, and as perhaps a virtual endorsement of his views, he declined to be ordained, feeling that his work as an educator was not done. His liberal and progressive views soon received high recognition from outside the South as well. Later in that same year, he accepted appointment as an agent for the Slater Fund, a bequest made by a wealthy citizen of Connecticut for the education of the Southern Negro. In that capacity his influence was so extended that he was everywhere regarded as one of the most potent characters in the South.[3]

Encouraged by these developments, the advocates of Negro education made themselves heard in the Southern Church in all directions. The *Wesleyan Christian Advocate,* which since its establishment under Haygood's editorship in 1878 had always urged advanced views with regard to the Negro, continued as the leader of the journalistic forces championing the cause. Early in 1882 the Reverend W. F. Glenn informed the *Wesleyan* that it was putting many persons "on the mourner's bench" with regard to work for the freedmen. The writer acknowledged that he, himself, was "on the anxious seat," and had been there for

---

[1] *Cf.* Haygood, Atticus G., *Our Brother in Black* (New York and Cincinnati, 1881), pp. 1-239.

[2] Letter of "I. E. S." in Nashville *Christian Advocate,* October 13, 1883.

[3] *Cf.* Du Bose, *op. cit.,* p. 128.

fifteen years.[1] By March 1882 the *Memphis Advocate* could announce that "Southern Methodist journals are showing an earnest purpose to urge our Church to renewed and increased efforts for the evangelization of the colored people. . . . In the discussion of this subject the *Wesleyan Christian Advocate* is entitled to the honor of leadership. Others—we do not call to mind an exception—are following with good grace. Not only editors but correspondents are also speaking out plainly and strongly, and on the right side—indeed, we do not hear a dissentient voice."[2]

The interest which had thus been aroused in the denomination found expression when the General Conference of the Church assembled at Memphis in 1882. During the sessions the Colored Methodist Episcopal Church petitioned the Methodist Episcopal Church, South, to aid it in establishing institutions for educating its ministry. The Conference, expressing warm sympathy, appointed a group of commissioners to assist it in founding a training school. During the following summer Bishop George F. Pierce met with the bishop of the Colored Church, and the two men selected Augusta, Georgia, as the seat of the projected institution. They also chose six commissioners, three from the white and three from the colored Church, to execute the plans. Shortly afterwards Bishop Pierce appointed the Reverend James E. Edwards of the Methodist Episcopal Church, South, to act as general agent for the new institution. The cordial interest felt in the undertaking was further evidenced by the pains taken in choosing a president for the school. It was said that "no broken down man," no "second-rate man," nor any man "looking for a place" must be considered for so important a work.[3] The task of appointing a head was greatly simplified when the Reverend Morgan Calloway, declaring that he felt a special call to the work, volunteered to undertake it. The descendant of a distinguished Georgia family, Morgan Calloway had been a slaveholder and an officer in the Confederate army. At the time of his selection he was serving as vice-president of Emory College, one of the oldest

---

[1]Letter of W. F. Glenn in *Wesleyan Christian Advocate,* March 11, 1882.
[2]*Memphis Advocate,* quoted in *Wesleyan Christian Advocate,* March 4, 1882.
[3]*Cf.* communication of Dr. A. G. Haygood in Nashville *Christian Advocate,* December 23, 1882.

educational institutions of the denomination in the far South, where he had for ten years been Professor of the English Language and Literature. Representing the best elements among the former governing classes of the section, his connection with the school did much to combat opposition to Negro education and to commend the institution to the whites.

Described as "a combination Praise-God Barebones and Sir Philip Sidney, with a dash of Hedley Vickars about him,"[1] Dr. Calloway made an eloquent plea for the new school. In a farewell sermon at Oxford, on "Our Man of Macedonia," he urged the men and women of the South to guard against permitting "the sophistry of a former servile relation to impose on our judgment and retard our offices of kindness to the race that cries to us from the depths of a pitiable poverty." Insisting that the Southern people must not forget their responsibility to the Negro, he said: "The Freedmen's Bureau, the many Missionary Societies of the North, a Slater, and other good persons and corporations, have helped nobly; but, notwithstanding their munificence, so gross is the darkness, and so widespread, that it seems that only a few light-houses have been erected where there should be a light burning in every district and every community."[2]

The importance attached to the action of the Methodist Episcopal Church, South, in this matter is suggested in the comments made by *The Methodist Quarterly Review* of the Northern Connection when the Southern Methodist Publishing House issued Calloway's sermon as a pamphlet. It said: "The establishment of this Institute for the education of colored teachers and preachers, the high Christian tone of the discourse itself, and its publication at the Nashville House, are significant of a new chapter in the history of the Church, South. The old purpose of retaining the Negro race in ignorance and pariahism is fairly abandoned. . . . On this high platform, Dr. Calloway places himself; his utterances are free, frank, hearty and profoundly sincere; the work can be safely trusted in his able hands; and every true friend of both races will applaud him in the undertaking, and rejoice in

---

[1] *Idem.*

[2] *Cf.* sermon of Calloway as quoted in *The Methodist Quarterly Review,* Vol. LXV (July, 1883), pp. 597-600.

his success."[1] Just at the time Calloway was chosen to head the new school, the Reverend Moses U. Payne, a minister of the Southern Church residing in Missouri, contributed the first twenty-five thousand dollars of the endowment of the institution, and it was given the name, Payne Institute.[2]

The interest in the development of the blacks reached a high pitch in the Connection in 1883. The agitation of the subject had aroused an opposition both within and outside of the Church, and the hostile criticism which was expressed spurred the leaders of the movement to more vigorous efforts. Its critics appealed to prejudice in many forms. When Haygood's discourse on "The New South" was published and circulated in 1881, a correspondent of the *New Orleans Christian Advocate* charged the college president with "truckling to the North generally," and declared that in order "to build up a new South, we need not spit on the grave of the old." Moreover, the writer saw in the sermon an instance of clerical meddling in politics. He said: "Fully persuaded that his sermon will be profitable for doctrine, for reproof, for correction, for instruction in righteousness to the Southern people, whom he characterizes, in whole or in part, in one place of the sermon or another, directly or indirectly, as croaking, blundering, illiterate, lazy, prodigal, provincial, intolerant, lawless, he has been forced by the conscientiousness which first prompted him to preach it, to print it, and send it at his own expense to us, who sit in the regions of darkness and the habitations of cruelty. . . . I do not like it as a sermon. Its whole make-up and smack are characteristic rather of a political speech made by a dignified, respectful orator, than a gospel sermon, preached in the pulpit of an evangelical Church. The main facts are mostly political and so is their collation."[3]

Dr. J. W. Rush, the editor of the *Alabama Christian Advocate*, put Calloway's idea of a "vision" and a "special call" in the same category with "Yankee fanaticism."[4] The addresses of Atticus

---

[1] *Cf. The Methodist Quarterly Review*, Vol. LXV (July ,1883), pp. 597-598.
[2] Du Bose, *op. cit.*, p. 46.
[3] Letter of "J. W. R." of Prattville, Alabama, in *New Orleans Christian Advocate*, April 7, 1881.
[4] *Cf. Alabama Christian Advocate*, quoted in *Wesleyan Christian Advocate*, February 14, 1883.

G. Haygood were characterized as being "inflammatory" and "essentially levelling." The Reverend W. L. C. Hunnicutt of Mississippi, president of one of the colleges of the denomination, said of Haygood that "Neither his speech-making nor his flag-waving is after the Southern heart, though they seem to please the Northern well. Many of the secular papers in Georgia are very severe in their criticisms of his utterances, and denounce his sentiments as subversive of the peace and welfare of the country. Dr. Haygood's philanthropy seems to have taken the form of negrophilism."[1]

The opposition not infrequently expressed itself in an antago-nism to higher education for the blacks, based upon a claim that the Negro was incapable of assimilating the higher forms of learning. Although he declared that "No body of people on this globe is more solicitous for the proper education and training of the Negro than the Methodist Episcopal Church, South," the Reverend C. W. Miller of Kentucky saw much in the movement that was regretable. He said: "The disposition which has mani-fested itself from the beginning to close men's eyes to the existence of every evil but the illiteracy of the Negro, and the attempt to mitigate this evil by holding up the South to the derision and contempt of the world, tends directly to alienate the real friends of Negro education, or at least to abate their zeal." "The question presses itself upon us, Why does not the Negro provide educational facilities for himself? Doubtless some will be startled by this question. They are accustomed to think of him only as 'the *poor* Negro,' and the bare suggestion that he should build schools and colleges for himself is an amazement to them. The '*poor* Negro' he undoubtedly is, but who is responsible for his poverty?" Declaring that the American Negroes, under the most favorable conditions surrounding any laboring class, had done nothing for their own education and that they could have built schools as readily as churches, the writer asserted that "the cry of colleges for the Negro is a stupendous mistake." "Is there," he asked "nothing in the fact that always and everywhere the hour the Negro is thrown on his own resources they fail him,

---

[1]Letter of "W. L. C. H." in *New Orleans Christian Advocate,* September 13, 1883.

and he begins a retrograde movement which seems to be as inexorable as fate?" He thought that good primary schools rather than colleges would meet the need, for "ordinarily this is as far as they, the Negroes, can go." Declaring that the colored man must inevitably degenerate if left to his own initiative, and that "he is sinking into barbarism right under the shadow of his 103 colleges," he urged that compulsory elementary schools be provided for Negro youths, and that stringent vagrancy laws be enacted to enforce their education.[1]

In another letter to the same journal Dr. Miller declared that "The time has come when the oracular utterances of certain self-constituted champions of the Negro should be tested at least a little." He maintained that Dr. Haygood's claims as to the obligations of the Church growing out of the promises of the bishops and of the General Conference were a wild exaggeration. The Church had already done all that it had pledged itself to do. Referring to Bishop Gilbert Haven of the Northern Church as an ardent advocate of a thorough social mixing of the races, he said: "I have only to say—and in so saying I am sure that I voice the sentiment of the M. E. Church, South—that our Church does not desire any Gilbert Havenism on this Negro question thrust upon her. That ill-starred Bishop carried about with him the ghastly corpse of this Negro question, and thrust it forward on all occasions. He took it into every pulpit he entered, into every *Advocate* and secular paper for which he wrote, lifted up its grinning repulsive face before every convention whose platform he occupied, and upon all occasions, social or otherwise, the corpse was at his right hand. Our Church does not desire that and will not have it, and the time is not far distant when her forbearance at the attempt to thrust this state of things upon her will give place."[2]

While anxious to allay prejudice and disarm opposition, those who most earnestly strove for the elevation of the Negro redoubled their efforts when such antagonism was encountered. Referring to criticisms in the *Alabama Christian Advocate* of Dr. Morgan Calloway and the work at Payne Institute, the Reverend R. G. Porter, an outstanding minister of the denomination in

---

[1]Letter of C. W. Miller in Nashville *Christian Advocate,* October 6, 1883.
[2]Letter of C. W. Miller in Nashville *Christian Advocate,* September 8, 1883.

Mississippi, said in March 1883: "One is slow to believe that any prominent man in the Southern Methodist Church, seated in the editorial chair of the official organ of two of our most influential Conferences, and occupying a prominent and important position, could be found to say a word to hinder this great work." "He, most certainly, 'blows hot and cold in the same breath,' so far as Paine [sic] Institute is concerned. He appears to favor the establishment and maintenance of training schools for the freedmen, and also appears to oppose the general work of teaching Negroes. He does not believe that Dr. Calloway is called of God, in any special sense, to undertake this great work. . . . If the editor of the Alabama *Advocate* utters the sentiments of his readers it will take a man of strong nerve, large back-bone and great personal consecration to Christ to teach a Negro school in the territory where his paper circulates, and such a teacher will, indeed, find small glory, so far as his white brethren are concerned. The editor most earnestly 'cautions our white people against fanaticism in this work,' a caution well put, indeed; and this writer, with equal earnestness, would caution them against 'prejudice' against this work."[1]

Referring to the adverse criticism recently made of some of the addresses of Dr. Haygood, the Reverend David C. Kelley wrote in October 1883: "It is probable that those who think with Dr. Haygood have remained silent because they thought him sufficient for the work—we speak now, lest silence should be construed as giving a majority against his views." Dr. Kelley expressed amazement that men "who had intelligence to write as these men have written" should entertain such views on the subject of the education of the Negro. Declaring of Dr. Haygood that "no man treads Southern soil whose heart is truer to the interests of the white man of the South," the writer asserted that the "interests of the white man and the Negro of the South are one, and both lie along the path of Christian education."[2]

Atticus G. Haygood, himself, as the leading exponent of such views in his Church and in the South, became increasingly outspoken. One who opposed his views at this time complained

---

[1] *Cf.* letter of "Gilderoy" in *New Orleans Christian Advocate*, March 1, 1883.
[2] Communication of the Reverend D. C. Kelley in Nashville *Christian Advocate*, October 20, 1883.

that, although Haygood had been severely criticised, "he manifests a stoical indifference or a 'Byronical' contempt for his critics and reviewers."[1] Speaking before a Summer Assembly held in August 1883 under Methodist patronage at Monteagle, Tennessee, Haygood lamented that the Commissioners for Payne Institute had already labored for seven months with but small success. "It is incredible," he said, "that we should have in the history a case like this; too much conscience to repudiate a duty, but not enough to do it—just enough to use good words." As for the other denominations in the South, he said that they "have small occasion to glory over the Church whose General Conference action I have discussed, for none of them have done anything worthy of special mention; few of them have even gone so far as to talk of doing anything."[2] About the same time, in a communication on "Our Hagar in the Wilderness," which appeared in the journals of his Church, Dr. Haygood gave warning that unless they acted promptly with regard to the education of the blacks, the Southern people would soon be justly arraigned by the Christian sentiment of the world. As to the duty of the Southern Church to aid the educational work of the Colored Methodist Episcopal Church, he asserted that the Methodist Episcopal Church, South, "should help in money or get out of the way" so that the Colored Church might get assistance from other sources. "As the case now stands, we, the Methodist Episcopal Church, South, are in the way. We keep off other help." He reminded the Southern Methodists that it was because of its relation to their own Church that the Colored Methodist Episcopal Church was the only Negro Church in the South not in a position to get financial aid from the North.[3]

The Nashville *Christian Advocate,* as the official organ of the entire Southern Connection, demonstrated its friendliness to the cause by encouraging discussion of the question in its columns. Its editor, Dr. O. P. Fitzgerald, protested against the insinuations as to Haygood's motives, and he predicted that "sooner or later critics and objectors will applaud his wisdom and Christian

---

[1]Letter of "I. E. S." of Dalton, Georgia, in Nashville *Christian Advocate,* October 13, 1883.

[2]*Cf.* Nashville *Christian Advocate,* August 18, 1883.

[3]Communication of Dr. A. G. Haygood in *New Orleans Christian Advocate,* August 16, 1883.

patriotism." He impressed upon his readers the urgent need for competent colored preachers and teachers. "If ignorance is to preach to ignorance from the pulpit, and irreligion is to preside in the school-room," he said, "there can be no rational hope for a happy solution of the grave problems before us." Meanwhile, he warned them, the Church, "like a wagon mired down, with one part of the team making spasmodic and ineffectual jerks, and the other refusing to pull, or holding back," "is making no progress in the work it has undertaken."[1]

Noting that public opinion in many places was still unsettled as to the wisdom of the work and that in some there was direct hostility to it, Bishop Pierce boldly declared: "To the doubtful and reluctant let me say the education of the Negro is not an open question. It is settled by State legislation—by action of the Churches—by individual philanthropy and munificence—by the aspirations and new relations of the colored race, and by the responsibilities of their citizenship. The power of education to elevate humanity, and to eliminate the elements of evil in natural constitution and social life may be overestimated. The extravagant calculations of ardent theorists about the capabilities of the Negro may never be realized. . . . But these facts, as probable possibilities, do not justify either opposition or indifference to a well-directed effort to make the best of an experiment which is being made. . . . As a rule, the common schools, as now managed, are a mockery as to grade and duration. Teachers must be educated, trained and made capable of good work."[2]

Due, in a large measure, perhaps, to the fact that Southern Methodists no longer felt a direct responsibility for the oversight of the blacks, the material contributions of the Methodist Episcopal Church, South, to educational institutions for the Negro were generally meager enough. Yet the patronage which the Church continued to give to Payne Institute, and to Lane Institute, a similar school organized a little later, was of very real benefit to the cause. Southern Methodist ministers continued to serve as presidents and as faculty members in these schools. In 1889 the

---

[1]Nashville *Christian Advocate*, October 20, 1883.
[2]Communication of Bishop Pierce in Nashville *Christian Advocate*, June 16, 1883.

charters of Payne and Lane Institutes were amended so as to make possible the addition of seven members of the Methodist Episcopal Church, South, to the Boards of Trustees of these institutions.[1] By authority of the General Conference of 1890, the bishops that year appointed a minister of the Southern Church to act as a general Commissioner of Education for the schools of the Colored Connection.[2]

Apart from furnishing trained teachers and preachers, the Methodist Episcopal Church, South, continued its efforts to dispel the apathy and prejudice which had developed both in the Church and in society at large with regard to the advancement of the blacks. The spokesmen of the denomination were untiring in their labors to create a sentiment in favor of Negro education. The work done by the Church for the colored people in the past was continually held up as an incentive. In the words of the Tennessee Conference in 1893, "Twenty-eight years have elapsed since the close of that bitter struggle that freed the slaves of the South, and during all those years our eyes have been strangely holden to see not the needs of this race whose wants once called forth our highest activity. . . . it seems manifest that the time has come for the advance movement in the cause not merely of colored education but also of colored evangelization, as the way may open before us. . . . Let us lay the needs of the Negro, and our duty in view of those needs, broadly upon the conscience of the Church, making the Negro one of our mission fields, operating it is true, through our own natural agent, the Colored Methodist Episcopal Church in America, but operating for the Negro of the whole United States." The Conference resolved to advise the next General Conference against "appointing a commissioner to lead a forlorn hope in the gathering of a scant pittance for colored education." Instead it recommended that the whole problem of the elevation of the blacks be remanded to the Board of Missions and Church Extension, thereby "creating the Negro race a mission field of the Methodist Episcopal Church, South, to

---

[1] *Cf.* Nashville *Christian Advocate,* February 8, 1889.
[2] *Cf.* New York *Christian Advocate,* August 7, 1890.

be cultivated through the Colored Methodist Episcopal Church in America, and directly if need be."[1]

The churchmen never ceased emphasizing the dangers to Southern civilization from the presence of a vast mass of illiterate black citizens. In this connection the *Advocates* warmly championed the Blair Educational Bill, a measure discussed at great length in Congress during the Eighties, and which proposed Federal aid for the States for elementary education in proportion to the illiteracy within their borders. The Methodist journals sought particularly to arouse the people of the South to a realization of the importance of the measure as regards its relation to colored education. In April 1884 the *Southern Christian Advocate* said: "We verily believe that our people have more interest than they feel in the bill now pending the action of Congress, known as the *Blair Educational Bill*. . . . If there is and to the extent there is indifference, not to say opposition, to the lower classes in our midst being educated, or, not to put a fine point on it, if there is indifference or opposition to the education of our colored people, let us bear with it for a while with patience, but yield to it *never*—NEVER, at the peril of our civilization, and of our country itself. Here is a problem before us, and one that our children will find more difficult of solution than we do, if not approached at once with courage and wisdom and charity."[2]

"If we would measure the elevation of a people we must begin at the bottom," said Atticus G. Haygood in 1885. "We have already suffered many things from the Negro in our midst; if, as some say we have pressed him down, he has pulled us down. . . . The worst people are teaching him daily in many schools. No fanatics smitten with Negro or other 'phobia,' are so zealous. Daily and hourly the worst people are teaching him the whole curriculum of the grog-shop, the gambling hell, the corrupt ballot, and all the other 'mysteries of iniquity!' These things, at least, the Negro can learn and does learn; he is fast moving to the front ranks in such deadly learning. . . . If we who profess the name of Christ . . . if we who say we believe in Christian education,' for the saving of our own children, 'let the Negro

---

[1]*Journal of Tennessee Conference,* 1893, pp. 30-31.
[2]*Cf. Southern Christian Advocate,* April 5, 1884.

alone,' what will become of us—to say nothing of him?"[1] "He is a dull observer," said the editor of the Nashville *Advocate* that same year, "who does not see that the behavior of the Negroes in these States is largely dependent upon the instruction they receive from their preachers. And he is a dull logician who does not on this account recognize the importance of giving them intelligent and truly Christian teachers, and of supporting every earnest and sensible effort in this direction."[2] The General Conference in 1886 declared that "The attitude of the Negro toward all the institutions of the country is a problem civil and spiritual which becomes hourly more difficult of solution. . . . Twenty-five years have passed since their emancipation, and the experience of this period through the South indicates that the white teacher and white preacher were never more necessary to the elevation and instruction of the Negro than at the present time."[3] It was urged that "Instead of one school like Payne Institute, we should have many in our Southern States, under charge and direction of the Church."[4]

Leaders of the Southern Church gave an increasingly friendly recognition and encouragement to the educational work carried on among the blacks by agencies from the North. By 1885 the head of Fisk University, a Congregational school for Negroes at Nashville, acknowledged that "We have been cheered on our way over and over again by the good words of such Southern men as

---

[1]Communication of Dr. A. G. Haygood in Nashville *Christian Advocate*, January 24, 1885.

[2]Dr. O. P. Fitzgerald in Nashville *Christian Advocate*, January 17, 1885.

[3]*Journal of General Conference*, 1886, p. 18.

[4]*Cf. Minutes of North Georgia Conference*, 1887, p. 15. Reminding the Southern people that their obligations to the Africans in the South were proportionately greater than those to the Negroes in Africa, this Conference lamented that, although "reasons have existed in our obligations to God, and in the nature of our social relations for such a school as Payne Institute, since the close of our civil war," those reasons had not influenced "our conscience and convictions sufficiently to express themselves in a school for colored people until recent years." Asserting that the colored man now held the balance of power in public affairs, the Conference declared that "unless we have the consent of our minds to let this power be applied by bad men to the destruction of our institutions, we must take hold of it with our schools and missionaries, and lift it up."

Dr. Fitzgerald, Dr. Kelley, Bishop McTyeire and Dr. McFerrin."[1]
Teachers in the Negro schools conducted by organizations in the
North were now sometimes invited to address the Conferences of
the Southern Church on the subject of colored education. In 1889
Emory College conferred a degree upon the Reverend Wilbur F.
Thirkield in recognition of his educational services to the Negro
as dean of the Gammon Theological School, an institution maintained by the Methodist Episcopal Church at Atlanta.[2] The
changed attitude towards Northern missionaries and teachers was
further reflected in the words of the editor of the *Richmond
Christian Advocate,* who remarked at that time: "I looked upon
the sweet face of Dr. Thirkield, dean of the theological faculty,
and saw the soul of a Saint John shining with a soft light in his
eyes."[3]

Southern churchmen made eloquent pleas for a sympathetic
understanding of the position and services of the Northern
teachers. Discussing the personnel of the schools supported by
the Slater Fund, and speaking now as a bishop of his Church,
Atticus G. Haygood said in 1891: "Among them I have met
gentlemen and ladies—ordinarily I would write men and women
—with diplomas from such schools as Yale, Wesleyan (Connecticut), Harvard, Brown University, University of Michigan, Smith
College, Mt. Holyoke, Wellesley, and such like. It is *possible*
that some of these teachers are where they are for salary only:
not one have I met who suggested the thought to me." Declaring
that these men and women felt very keenly their isolation from
the people of their own race, he added: "These schools are under
Christian influences, and these old missionaries teach and illustrate old-fashioned religion. In God's name we ought to help
them. If anyone should ask me: 'How help them?' I would
answer: At this time, most of all by Christian recognition and
Christian sympathy."[4]

Another evidence of a changed attitude appeared in the special

---

[1]H. S. Bennet, as reported in Nashville *Christian Advocate,* April 4, 1885.
[2]*Cf. Southwestern Christian Advocate,* August 8, 1889.
[3]*Cf. Richmond Christian Advocate* quoted in *Southwestern Christian Advocate,* July 18, 1889.
[4]Communication of Bishop Atticus G. Haygood in Nashville *Christian
Advocate,* May 9, 1891.

consideration which was shown for the ministers of the Southern
Church who taught in the schools of the Colored Methodist
Episcopal Church. Typical of the spirit manifested towards these
men was that of the North Georgia Conference. In 1887 that
body expressed the warmest sympathy for the work that was being
done by the Reverend George W. Walker as president of the
Payne Institute, and it declared that " our hearts go out to him
as they never did before."[1]

Recognition was accorded, moreover, to individuals of the
Negro race who labored for the elevation of their people. In
1896 the colored educator, Booker T. Washington, founder of
the Tuskegee Institute, delivered an address at Trinity College
(now Duke University), a Methodist institution in North Carolina, at the invitation of its faculty and students.[2] The recognition
accorded Washington on that occasion foreshadowed the stand
which the trustees of this college took seven years later when,
despite a tremendous public furor, they declined to dismiss from
its faculty the historian, John S. Bassett, who had made the
statement that, next to Robert E. Lee, perhaps, Booker T. Washington was the greatest man the South had produced during the
nineteenth century.[3]

The separatist instinct of the Negro in religious affairs and his
hostility to anything that savored of surveillance by the Southern
whites, as well as apathy and prejudice in the white Church,
continued to make direct efforts for the education of the blacks
by that body largely impracticable. It is true also that the action
taken in the councils of the Church was usually hortatory rather
than mandatory. Nevertheless there can be little doubt that the
Methodist Episcopal Church, South, created much sentiment
favorable to Negro education or that its attitude towards the
subject had much to do with making Southern whites willing to
assume the burden of the tax supported common schools, in which
the great majority of the race were destined to receive their
schooling. When Haygood's *Our Brother in Black* was published
in 1881 the *Wesleyan Christian Advocate* emphasized the fact

---

[1]*Minutes of North Georgia Conference,* 1887, p. 15.
[2]*Cf. Southwestern Christian Advocate,* November 5, 1896.
[3]*Cf.* Plyer, Marion Timothy, *Thomas Neal Ivey* (Nashville, 1925), p. 64.

that the author had been brave enough to "think aloud" the "sentiment of the people in proportion as they allow themselves to think."[1] Referring to the utterances in behalf of Negro education which had recently been made by Haygood, George W. Cable, the novelist, and President James H. Carlisle of Wofford College, Dr. E. O. Thayer, president of the Northern Methodist Clarke University at Atlanta, said in 1885: "When three such men as Haygood, Cable, and Carlisle demand from the world recognition of the Negro's claims to education and his constitutional rights it is a sure indication that God reigns and that something is about to happen. Such bold and progressive utterances are valuable from such sources, because they indicate a widespread change in public sentiment which only awaits such leaders to call it forth."[2] Indeed, when Atticus G. Haygood and the Reverend O. P. Fitzgerald were ordained bishops in 1890, the *Christian Register* of Boston interpreted their election both as a token of a great change of sentiment toward the blacks in the Methodist Episcopal Church, South, and as "a very significant indication of the progress that has been made in the South in relation to the Negro question."[3]

By way of summary it may be said that at the close of the Civil War the Methodist Episcopal Church, South, promptly and cheerfully asserted its sense of responsibility for the religious welfare of the blacks in the South. Acknowledging its obligations to the Negro, it at once set about devising means of promoting the spiritual interests of the race. Much attention was given to adjusting the economy and machinery of the Church to its needs. The leaders and representative bodies of the Connection expressed themselves warmly in favor of education as a means of elevating the race, and special consideration was given to projects for Negro schools. It was hoped that the great body of blacks who had been alienated from the fold during the excitements of the War could now be induced to return. But forces of an opposite tendency served to widen further the breach,

---

[1] Cf. *Wesleyan Christian Advocate*, May 28, 1881.

[2] Letter of President E. O. Thayer in New York *Christian Advocate*, March 19, 1885.

[3] Cf. statement of *Christian Register* as reported in Nashville *Christian Advocate*, July 26, 1890.

making the blacks inaccessible to guidance by the Church and causing it gradually to become in a large measure indifferent to the needs of the Africans, many having come to look with disfavor upon schooling for them. By 1870 the Church had definitely abandoned the idea of regaining its colored following, and for a decade or more thereafter it virtually ceased all direct labors for the Negro's spiritual interests and mental culture.

With the passing of Reconstruction, when the blacks became more accessible to the influence of the Southern whites, however, a lively concern for the religious welfare of the Africans manifested itself at once in the Church. This was evidenced primarily by an anxiety for the mental improvement of the race, finding practical expression in a movement to provide trained Negro leaders for the colored people. Apart from furnishing educated teachers and preachers, the Southern Church contributed much to the religious interests of the blacks through the influence it exerted among the Southern people at large in favor of Negro education.

CHAPTER VI

THE ATTITUDE OF SOUTHERN METHODISM TOWARDS NEGRO RIGHTS

THERE remains to be considered in detail the position maintained by the Methodist Episcopal Church, South, with regard to the Southern caste system and the spirit of social injustice and repression towards the blacks which it fostered. The question of the social status of the Negro—of the place to be assigned to the Negro as a man among men in the new order—was inevitably bound up with all discussion of the subject of his mental and religious culture. And involved in this consideration were all the problems having to do with "social equality," miscegenation, amalgamation of the races, and the matter of political dominion, problems growing out of the relations of large numbers of the two races dwelling side by side in the same territory.

No conviction resulting from the experiences of slavery was more generally or firmly held by the Southern whites at the close of the Civil War than that the two people were divided by racial traits that were fundamental and ineradicable. Moreover, it was generally assumed that the whites enjoyed a superiority in all instances in which such differences appeared.[1] While the presence of a large mulatto element bore witness to the mixing of blood that had taken place in the past, it was believed that the whites possessed an instinctive aversion to such a blending of the races, and that this aversion was overcome only by a bestiality that manifested itself in the lower nature of man. Indeed, it was taken for granted that all social intercourse with his darker skinned brother, except upon terms of acknowledged inferiority upon the part of the Negro, would be repulsive to the white. It was generally held that the blacks lacked qualities necessary to the exercise of the privileges of freedom on a plane with the whites.[2] Because they believed the Negro incapable of assimilating the higher forms of learning and civilization, a profound

---

[1]Cf. Simkins and Woody, *op. cit.*, passim.
[2]*Ibid.*, p. 20.

pessimism prevailed with many as to the possibility of a satisfactory existence with the blacks as freedmen.[1] It was felt that
any interference with traditional social relations would lead to
disaster. All the above views were reflected in the various "black
codes" by which the several State governments sought to remand
the freedmen to a position of inferiority shortly after the War.
So tenaciously were such opinions held that to the end of the
century any white who openly disregarded them was liable to lose
caste with his own people.[2]

To understand more fully the attitude maintained by the
Methodist Episcopal Church, South, toward these matters, it will
be necessary to review the position of the Northern Methodist
Church toward them, for the radical stand taken by the Methodist
Episcopal Church continued to force such questions prominently
before the Southern Church. Proclaiming it as their mission "to
teach a better theory concerning the Negro than the South has
heretofore held,"[3] the representatives of the Northern Church
denounced the attempts to retain the Negro in a subordinate social
and political relation as a manifestation of caste spirit of the most
wicked sort. Observing the efforts to preserve the old caste
restrictions in the South, they resolved "to ignore all those arti-
ficial distinctions of society founded on ungenerous prejudices."[4]
The equalitarian sentiments of such men and the eagerness of
their Church to bring the Negro into its fold prompted it to
refuse all recognition of race as a factor in social relations.

In April 1865 the New England Conference urged the Church
to employ colored ministers in its work in the South, and it
deplored the fact that the General Conference had seen fit to
organize two exclusively colored Conferences in 1864. "We must
avoid the danger of recognizing the distinction of color among
a common Church and ministry," the Conference warned.[5] Declaring that the Church for three years had had within its grasp a
vast field for work among the Southern Negroes and had yet done

---

[1] *Idem.*
[2] *Ibid., passim.*
[3] *Cf. Western Christian Advocate,* quoted in Price, *op. cit.,* Vol. V, p. 363.
[4] *Cf.* Simkins and Woody, *op. cit.,* p. 377.
[5] *Cf.* Report on Reconstruction of the Church as given in New York
Christian Advocate, April 27, 1865.

but little to attach them to it, the Reverend Gilbert Haven said in May 1865: *"We have not dared to do right.* We cling to a false and fatal notion, which is paralyzing our arm. . . . We presume to distinguish between His children on account of certain shades of complexion, or sources of distant origin." In organizing them into exclusively colored and dependent missionary Conferences the Church was, he felt, fixing upon the blacks an ignominious badge of inferiority which the State was attempting to remove. As a result the Negroes were standing as a unit against the missionaries, who could offer them only an ignoble place in the Church. He felt that "The only right and successful way is *to entirely ignore the idea of color in the organization of our Churches and Conferences throughout the whole land."*[1]

Again, early in 1866, Dr. Haven asserted that he had frequently been told of the Negro's "agony under this universal scorn and contumely," and demanded to know what the attitude of his Church toward the question of color was going to be. "Shall the Church disregard it, despise it, remove it from her pale, and as fast as she can from society? What else is her mission?" In entering the South "Let her say, 'We do not recognize the only sin that yet divides you. All are brethren. Whatever congregations shall gather about our preachers, they shall never be known as colored and white. Whoever shall attend our schools shall never have this brand of distinction."[2]

---

[1] Communication of the Reverend Gilbert Haven in New York *Christian Advocate,* May 25, 1865.

[2] Letter of the Reverend Gilbert Haven in New York *Christian Advocate,* February 22, 1866. Although admitting that it might be partially true that the blacks preferred to be organized into conferences and congregations exclusively of their own color, the writer maintained that "that even does not prove that they ought to be separated," for this was true only because the whites were unwilling to treat them as equals. He insisted that the Church must show an especial consideration for the feelings of the Negroes with regard to the matter of color. "Let not the word color be once named or conceived," he said. "If only those of this complexion come, it matters not. Treat them as though we never thought of this peculiarity. If Churches are collected of this class, never call them thus; never allow others to thus name them. If some brethren in the ministry can find appointments yet only over Churches composed chiefly of their own hue, let the Bishop regard that as he does the fitness and unfitness of all other brethren, some of whom will have more unpopular peculiarities than complexion, and never publicly record this reason any more than he does others. The Minutes of the Mississippi Conference would be perfect but for the words 'Colored Congregations' attached to them. . . . Are any words too strong to express this dreadful sin and danger?"

By March 1866 Haven predicted that the Church would "undermine and overtop this social sin and sweep it into oblivion." "If we pursue this more excellent way," he argued, "we shall also coöperate with the great statesmen who are struggling to make pure democracy prevail in all the land. . . . The grand statement of national principles by Mr. Sumner must yet be the law of the land. The Church should keep equal step with them. . . . She will thus finally secure the complete unification of the South. The banner of caste will be removed. White and black, one at the polls, will soon be one everywhere. . . . The New England Conference, I doubt not, will go forward. . . . Her faithfulness carried New England across the Hudson, swept the west, and won the victory. So will she this."[1]

Under the inspiration of such leaders as Gilbert Haven, who, early in the Seventies, was sent as a bishop to take charge of the Southern Conferences, the Northern Church strove zealously, as it advanced into the South, to abolish "the color line" in all phases of social intercourse. It organized everywhere "mixed" Conferences, in which the white missionary from the North met his colored brother of the South on terms of cordial intimacy and equality. When the Mississippi Mission Conference was organized at New Orleans in December 1865, "the whole audience, composed of whites and blacks, were affected, some to tears, some to shouts," at the sight of the ordination of three colored ministers with a white one. "There they stood side by side at the same altar, and the same hands which were laid upon the latter, were placed upon the heads of the former." "Was this not the commencement of a new era in the South?" wrote the recording secretary of the Conference.[2] The Church sought persistently to build up mixed congregations of blacks and whites.[3] As has been men-

---

[1]Communication of the Reverend Gilbert Haven in New York *Christian Advocate*, March 1, 1866.

[2]*Journal of Mississippi Mission Conference*, 1865, p. 3.

[3]In its issue of November 8, 1866 the New York *Christian Advocate* said: "Our official action should be distinct and outspoken on this subject; the theory of 'color-blindness' should be clearly enunciated and at once reduced to practice. Colored ministers should be invited to membership in our Annual Conferences, and introduced into our pulpits. Colored families should be welcomed to our Churches, not to sit on separate seats assigned to them as a distinct *caste;* but in free churches to sit where they please, and in pewed churches, in such pews as they may choose to pay for. . . . With this theory and practice our Church

tioned, the missionaries made a special plea to the Negro on the basis of "the equality of relations" in its assemblages. After they had listened to white leaders plead with them to remain in the Southern Church as they sat in the gallery of Trinity Church in Charleston, the colored members of the congregation were addressed by the Reverend T. Willard Lewis of the Northern Church, who rose and said: "Brothers and sisters, there will be no galleries in heaven. Those who are willing to go with a Church which makes no distinctions follow me to the normal school." One who witnessed the scene wrote that "the congregation rose to a man and marched with enthusiasm to the school."[1]

Many of the missionaries expressed sentiments favoring an amalgamation of the races. Some urged measures to legalize intermarriage between the whites and blacks. In 1869 Bishop Haven declared that "The hour is not far off when the white hued husband shall boast of the dusky beauty of his wife, and the Caucasian wife shall admire the sun-kissed countenance of her husband as deeply and as unconscious of the present ruling abhorrence as is his admiration for her lighter tint."[2] Again, writing to one of his Church papers, and referring to the mulatto population of Charleston, the Bishop said in 1873: "I can pardon a little the devil of slavery when I see what fine specimens of humanity it produced. If you want to see the coming race in all its virile perfection, come to this city. Here is amalgamation made perfect. * * * What exquisite tints of delicate brown; what handsome features; what beautiful eyes, what graceful forms. No boorish Hanoverian blood here, but the best Plantaganet. * * * The best old Beacon Street wine of humanity is theirs, and soars to the rich quality that flashes in these eyes and veins and figures. It is an improved breed—the best the country has

---

should go forward with her mission in the South." Admitting that the Church had been remiss in these respects in the North, the editor pointed out that the colored population there had been too small for its action to affect society perceptibly one way or another. "Not so, however, with the South," he said. "There they form too large a proportion of the whole population to allow them to be safely disregarded. They must be elevated or the social level will become greatly depressed."

[1]Cf. Simkins and Woody, op. cit., p. 378.

[2]Letter of Gilbert Haven in Independent, quoted in Richmond Christian Advocate, February 11, 1869.

today. It will be so reckoned in the boudoirs of Newport and the court of Washington ere many years. * * * Let the white man make the less white lady his wife, and let her not degrade herself by any voluntary association of sin."[1] About the same time, in referring to the colored population of Nashville, Bishop Haven expressed the opinion that "these browns and blacks are destined to mingle largely in all future society of this region, as they have done in the past, but in a very different position."[2]

Frequently the representatives of the Northern Church worked for an enforced association of the races in the public schools and elsewhere. The *Southwestern Christian Advocate* at New Orleans was an outspoken advocate of mixed education in the common schools. Its editor, the Reverend J. C. Hartzell, who labored diligently to encourage a social commingling of the races, used his influence as a member of the school board of that city to establish co-racial schools there.[3] Many of the missionaries denounced with the greatest severity the segregation of the races in such places of public entertainment as theaters, restaurants, and hotels and in public conveyances. They constantly rebuked the Southern people for the uncharitable spirit which they felt prompted such practices. They frequently sought openly to ignore the customs of the section in such matters. When behavior of this sort resulted in their being roughly handled, they filled the air with angry denunciation and criminations.

The fact that the Northern Church soon found itself unable to maintain a consistent and uncompromising position toward the caste system of the South had little effect in softening the tone of its criticisms of the Southern organization on that head. The desire to retain a white membership there soon greatly influenced its action where race relations were concerned, thereby causing it much embarrassment. So insistent became the demand for the organization of Conferences exclusively of one color that by 1876 the General Conference authorized the bishops to form from any of the Southern Conferences two new Conferences, whenever "it

[1]Letter of Bishop Gilbert Haven as given in *The Pacific Methodist* and quoted in *New Orleans Christian Advocate*, October 2, 1873.
[2]Letter of Bishop Gilbert Haven in New York *Christian Advocate*, June 19, 1873.
[3]*Cf. New Orleans Christian Advocate*, September 23, 1875.

shall be requested by a majority of the white members, and also a majority of the colored members" of such a Conference.[1] This policy at first met with bitter opposition among the colored communicants and the missionaries. The General Conference was flooded with petitions and memorials from predominantly colored representative bodies protesting against such division. Nevertheless, a "color line" was drawn in practically all of the Southern Conferences before the end of the Eighties. Although in some instances groups in which Negroes were in a majority asked for a division, it was obvious that the change had been inspired by no spontaneous demand upon the part of the blacks. Referring to the segregation of the races which had already taken place, a minister of the Northern Church wrote in 1884: "It is true that a memorial came to the General Conference of 1872 from the colored members of the Georgia Conference, asking for a division of their Conference on the color line, and that there were some colored delegates in the General Conference of 1876 who favored such a policy, but it is also true that all such demonstrations were co-ordinated or antedated by similar movements of white members seeking separation from their colored brethren. It must not be overlooked, in considering the situation, that all manifestations of preference for organic separation on the part of our colored members are made under the pressure of an ostracism which strikes with a death-chill every move or look toward equality in the Church relations of the two races."[2] Sometimes the missionaries themselves bowed before the prejudices of the section when it was necessary to do so in order to expand their influence among

---

[1] *Journal of General Conference*, 1876, p. 331.

[2] Letter of William R. Clark, D. D., of Boston in New York *Christian Advocate*, March 13, 1884. "Let us suppose an analagous case," wrote this minister. "A gentleman invites to his home for an evening's entertainment a company of friends about equally divided between white and black; when assembled, he says to his colored guests, 'A majority of our white friends prefer to spend the evening by themselves, and, thinking you might prefer to be by yourselves also, I have provided another room for you, just as pleasant, just as well furnished as this, and the table which I shall spread for you will be just the same as the one I shall set for my white guests, and if you choose to be by yourselves you can be gratified. I shall drop in occasionally during the evening and have a chat with you, and perhaps you will spend the hour more pleasantly by yourselves. But do not go unless you prefer to do so.' What would be expected of his colored guests under those circumstances, but that they would do just as our colored members of the Southern Conferences did do in going off by themselves?"

the whites. In 1882 a Northern Methodist minister at Birmingham, Alabama, actually inserted a card in the secular papers stating that colored persons were neither invited nor expected to attend the services at his Church.[1]

Despite the fact that the Northern Church had fallen so far short of putting the theories it had advocated into practice, representatives of that Church continued to scourge the Southern Methodists for their treatment of the Negro, and thus constantly forced upon the attention of the Methodist Episcopal Church, South, issues involving a consideration of the welfare of the colored race. "There is but a single issue between the Methodist Episcopal Church and the Methodist Episcopal Church, South, and that relates to the colored people in America," said the *Southwestern Christian Advocate* in 1874 when referring to the action of the Southern Church in forming an independent General Conference for its colored members. "She claims now to have adapted her methods to the changed condition of the descendants of the African race in the midst of us. Which simply means that the Church South has inaugurated means which, if carried out by all will keep the colored people in social and intellectual slavery,

---

[1]Referring to this Birmingham incident, the Reverend I. J. Lansing wrote: "Knowledge of the Ames Church, New Orleans, Marietta street, Atlanta, our Richmond Church as it was, and the many Churches of which these centers are representative, leads us to say that if the Rev. Mr. King acted under the pressing advice of his Birmingham congregation, he acted as he would have been urged to do by representative white Methodist Episcopal congregations in any part of the South. We do not know a congregation, either composed of Southern-born white people or of white people of Northern birth, which does not sympathize with the sentiment, and make itself understood in the community where it is, that colored people are neither invited nor expected to attend their Churches." *Cf.* letter of the Reverend I. J. Lansing in New York *Christian Advocate*, November 23, 1882. For other accounts of this incident see *Methodist Advocate*, November 1, 1882; *ibid.*, December 13, 1882; *Southwestern Christian Advocate*, November 9, 1882; *ibid.*, January 25, 1883; *ibid.*, February 8, 1883; New York *Christian Advocate*, November 23, 1882. This "Alabama leprosy" placed the Church in an awkward position on numerous occasions during the Eighties. On one occasion a teacher in one of the schools conducted by the Church caused a sensation by refusing to shake hands with a colored man to whom he was introduced. At the same time that the color line was being drawn in its Conferences, the Negro caused the Church further embarrassment by demanding the election of a colored bishop as a recognition of the race. Beginning in 1872, many petitions and memorials on this subject were presented to the successive General Conferences. In 1892 Dr. A. E. P. Albert stated that, being ridiculed by Southerners for being "in a 'Nigger Church'," and anxious to show that they had nothing in common with Negroes, the white members of the Northern Church in the South had "out-Heroded

now they are free; just as her policy secured more firmly their bondage before they were free."[1]

Despite all the taunts of the Northern Methodists, the Southern Church continued to show no inclination to revise radically its notions regarding the proper relations between the races in the Church and in society. While still cordially inviting him to remain in his accustomed place until it was seen that he was determined to depart, the Church made no effort to retain the Negro through the inducement of a free mixing in the congregation or by admitting him to a full legislative and administrative capacity. If the blacks were to remain it must be in a subordinate and dependent relation. Social relations were accorded the freedmen only on the basis of an acknowledged inferiority on their part.[2] The attitude taken by the Church was well expressed by the *Southern Christian Advocate* in 1866 when it stated that, since the blacks were unwilling to remain in any organization which did not admit them to the legislative and pastoral capacity, and since "the social relations of the two races preclude the idea of such equality," independent colored organizations would be necessary.[3] "So long as the colored man affects only that position in society which he is able to fill," said the *New Orleans Christian Advocate* in 1867, "he will be cheerfully recognized as worthy of all respect; he will be treated justly, generously and with all the consideration due to his sphere. . . . He is, and must continue to be, the laboring man of the South, because he is not fitted either by talents, education or enterprise, for anything higher. To be placed where the public opinion of the world cannot sympathize with him, but rather revolts at the sight of him, can only contribute to his confusion and final complete overthrow."[4] On another occasion the same journal asserted that "Common

---

Herod," and had become "more proscriptive in their treatment of the colored people and the white teachers and missionaries that labored among them, than the Southern Church." He felt that "in many places the fraternal relation of our white to our colored work is less cordial than that between the Southern Church and our colored work." Cf. Albert, A. E. P., "The Church in the South," *The Methodist Review*, Vol. LXXIV (March, 1892), pp. 237-239.

[1]*Southwestern Christian Advocate*, September 10, 1874.

[2]*Cf*. Simkins and Woody, *op. cit.*, pp. 383-384.

[3]*Cf. Southern Christian Advocate*, June 15, 1866, as quoted in Simkins and Woody, *op. cit.*, p. 387.

[4]*New Orleans Christian Advocate*, September 7, 1867.

sense and the deepest instincts of our nature suggest that it is for the good of both races that the lines of social separateness be kept as distinct as Nature has drawn them. No one but a weak friend, or very decided enemy of the black man, could counsel any other policy."[1]

The determination of the Southern Church to regard the Negro only as an inferior was often further illustrated in its criticism of the position assumed by the representatives of the Methodist Episcopal Church. "Does Dr. Curry's indorsement of his Bishop's Negro-equality tastes and habits receive the approval of his Church?" asked the Nashville *Advocate* when Bishop Haven had dined at the home of some Negro communicants in Atlanta. "It is easy to say, 'No.' We shall see."[2] The *St. Louis Christian Advocate* remarked sarcastically at the time that Southerners should allow Bishop Haven to indulge his proclivities as a matter of taste.[3]

The "Negro-equality" sentiments which prompted the attempt to associate the races in the common schools and in places of public resort were denounced with particular severity. Many saw in such efforts only a design to humiliate the Southern whites. Referring to the activities of the Reverend J. C. Hartzell and the Reverend Lucius C. Matlack, as members of the school board at New Orleans, the editor of the *Advocate* of that city said in 1874: "These partisan directors are bent on mixing up the schools. They are not content that the Negro children shall have separate schools, equal in all respects to those provided for the whites, but they are determined to force upon us this most obnoxious measure, not only of putting the two races in the same rooms, but of putting Negro teachers over white pupils. . . . The purpose to Africanize our schools, and to insult and degrade the white people, is evident. . . . The white people who support the schools are naturally indignant at this state of affairs, and very properly demand a change."[4] Alluding to the criticism which had been made by the Northern Methodist journals of the Glenn Bill, a

---

[1]*Ibid.*, September 7, 1867.
[2]Nashville *Christian Advocate,* July 11, 1867.
[3]*Cf. St. Louis Christian Advocate,* quoted in New York *Christian Advocate,* July 23, 1874.
[4]*New Orleans Christian Advocate,* September 23, 1875.

measure pending before the Georgia legislature to prohibit the attendance of white children at schools established for Negroes, and referring to the recent embarrassment of the Northern Church when the officials of one of its Southern colleges refused to admit colored students to its classes,[1] the *Wesleyan Christian Advocate* said in 1887: "And yet the *Northwestern* and the Northern Methodist Church, and the Freedmen's Aid Society, which claims to have a monopoly of the 'progressive idea for the solution of the race problem,' are not still from their squirming, and writhing and twisting in the hot embers of this problem as raised in Chattanooga University, from which they turned out two Negroes while saying that they wouldn't do it. There the black idea got into the Northern man's skull, and knocked his theories to smithereens, and he had to resort to the Georgian's idea of treating the question as a practical one, with due regard to surrounding circumstances, or else quit the field entirely." The *Wesleyan* asserted that the Northern journals were now abusing Georgians for doing "precisely what they all finally acquiesed in having done at Chattanooga University, viz.: keeping the Negro and white schools separate. . . . The attack of the Northern press is not made exclusively on any particular feature of the Glenn bill; if that had been the case we should probably have kept silence; but it was made upon the State for holding the doctrine of separate schools for whites and Negroes."[2]

When representatives of the Methodist Episcopal Church criticized the Southern Church for its action in setting off its colored membership as a separate organization, the New Orleans *Advocate* retorted that the Northern Methodists could not possibly condemn what had been done "as much as we condemn and abhor their efforts to mix up white men and Negroes, ecclesiastically, politically and socially." It felt that "The plea that all men sprang from Adam, that 'God is no respecter of persons' and that in Christ Jesus there is neither bond nor free, male nor female" could not "soften the wickedness of attempting to break down

---

[1] By their action in refusing to admit these students to the institution' the authorities occasioned a widespread controversy in the Connection. *Cf.* New York *Christian Advocate,* February 10, 1887; *Southwestern Christian Advocate,* December 30, 1886; *ibid.,* June 23, 1887; *ibid..* September 22, 1887.

[2] *Wesleyan Christian Advocate,* August 24, 1887.

that social distinction between the white and black races which Nature, God, and the best interests of mankind have so far preserved."[1]

All suggestions of miscegenation and amalgamation of the races quickly drew forth expressions of disapproval from the Southern journals. When Bishop Haven wrote a series of letters to the papers of his Connection in 1873 and 1874, advocating legal intermarriage between the whites and the blacks, he was bitterly denounced. The New Orleans *Advocate* declared that it had "regarded Bishop Haven's voluminous indecencies on amalgamation and miscegenation, lately appearing in the Northern Methodist papers, as unfit to be quoted or noticed."[2] In an editorial entitled "The Last Feather Breaks the Camel's Back," the Richmond *Advocate* cited Haven's letters as representing the spirit of "the Radicals of the extreme type in the Northern Methodist Church," and said: "The end of such fanaticism must be that it will kill itself. The good sense of the American people cannot stand such an outrage."[3]

Even Bishop Haygood, the foremost advocate of the elevation of the Negro in the Southern Church, did not oppose the drawing of a "color line." In 1895 when much indignation was being expressed in the North because the Negro delegates to an Epworth League Convention at Chattanooga had been assigned to seats in a separate section in the assembly, Bishop Haygood said: "Our Northern Methodist editors, with few exceptions, have so often and during so many years exercised themselves into indignation about the 'color line,' that the exhausted nerves respond feebly to ordinary excitations. . . . The effort to be virtuously indignant, or indignantly virtuous, because a special part of the big tent at Chattanooga at the Epworth League meeting was assigned to the 'brother in black,' is simply ridiculous—perhaps we may add silly. *Doctrinaires* who evolve theories concerning other people, out of

---

[1] *New Orleans Christian Advocate,* July 30, 1870.
[2] *Ibid.,* October 2, 1873.
[3] *Richmond Christian Advocate,* February 11, 1869. In 1889 the Reverend W. M. Leftwich said: "The race problem will never be settled upon the basis of social equality. Equality is impossible without amalgamation, and amalgamation is too revolting to be entertained for a moment." *Cf.* Leftwich, W. M., "The Race Problem in the South", *The Quarterly Review,* Vol. IV (April, 1889), pp. 86-96.

their own consciousness, without regard to facts, will not agree with our view in regard to this tempest in a teapot. . . . When Northern Methodists scourge with bitter tongues the South for its notions and practices in social relations with the colored people, they are absolutely blind to the fact that they have set their Negro members off into separate Conferences. They did it; the Negroes did not. They are, in their brazen inconsistency, like poor Adam and Eve when sin had blinded them—'naked and not ashamed.' "[1]

The *Advocates* of the Southern Connection were frank in expressing their belief that the Negroes in the Southern States must be governed by the whites. Regarding the Africans as deficient in qualities necessary to the highest development, they declared that it "is right and just, and in the interest of civilization and humanity" that the Caucasian should control in the section.[2] In October 1867 the *Richmond Christian Advocate* said: "The white race must rule. All see and feel this, even those who are using the Negro as a mere stepping stone to place and power; and who, when their purpose is served by him, will fling him aside as a worthless thing."[3] "No true friend of the Negro can desire to see him put in authority over white men," declared the New Orleans *Advocate* about the same time.[4] "Not a Negro at the polls," exclaimed the same journal in November 1868. "This is just as it should be. They never should have been there. Let the Negroes now come out of the Legislature, and let us have a white man for lieutenant-governor, and there will be some reasonable prospect that this State will again become a strength and an equal among the United States. . . . Let Negroes and Chinamen and Indians suffer the superior race of white men to whom Providence has given this country, to control it. A good

---

[1]Communication of Bishop Atticus G. Haygood in Nashville *Christian Advocate,* June 25, 1895.

[2]*Cf. New Orleans Christian Advocate,* October 30, 1879. The New Orleans journal expressed satisfaction that the Southern States had not been "remanded to the semi-barbarism of Negro ascendency. These views would meet the approval of nearly all Northern minds not influenced by partisan spirit or fanaticism."

[3]*Richmond Christian Advocate,* October 31, 1867.

[4]*New Orleans Christian Advocate,* September 7, 1867.

government for the white man will be good enough for the Mongolian, the African or the aboriginal American."[1]

Such sentiments were but little modified by the passage of time. When discussing the feelings entertained towards the Negro by the Southern Methodists, the Richmond *Advocate* said in 1889: "Though firmly resolved not to be governed by the Negro race nor to admit them to social equality, they have no malicious or unrighteous feelings toward that race. They are in perfect accord with the President, Benjamin Harrison, a Northern man and Republican leader, if correctly reported as saying recently that he would not like to have a Negro mayor or postmaster at Indianapolis or to practice his profession before a Negro Federal judge or with a Negro United States attorney, and that he would not inflict on the South in his appointments what would be disagreeable to himself."[2] A decade later, in 1898, the Nashville *Advocate* said: "There is no community of Anglo-Saxons on the face of the earth that would submit quietly and permanently to be ruled by a colored race. . . . We have no trace of ill will against our colored fellow-citizens. . . . We are glad to see them get property, acquire knowledge, and advance in every way. But we record it as our sober judgment they will not in a thousand years reach that level of intelligence and that stability of character which will make them equals man for man of the white race. They will never again have a controlling influence in the Southern States. That question is settled. The whole force of the United States government, political and military, brought to bear for a period of ten or fifteen years, utterly failed to bring such a result to pass."[3]

As has been seen, a belief in the fundamental inferiority of the blacks was reflected in the attitude of numerous churchmen

---

[1] *Ibid.,* November 7, 1868. Referring to the Negroes who were then serving as President of the Senate and Speaker of the House in the Louisiana legislature, the New Orleans *Advocate* declared that "Sitting as they do in the presence of a race superior to themselves and to most other races of men," they "know themselves to be out of place, and everybody else knows them to be, that they have no right to represent either the wealth, the intelligence or the industry of the State; and that in a thousand years they could not, by their own force or merit, if freed from every disadvantage of caste prejudice, have attained to such an eminence." Cf. *New Orleans Christian Advocate,* July 4, 1868.

[2] *Richmond Christian Advocate,* July 18, 1889.

[3] *Cf.* Nashville *Christian Advocate,* December 1, 1898.

who would have had themselves regarded as the best friends and, in the truest sense, the benefactors of the Negro. Such men not infrequently expressed concern lest the freedman be "educated out of his place." Thus in 1897 the Reverend Samuel A. Steele of Mississippi, while urging upon the Church the duty of educating the blacks, declared that *"hic, haec, hoc* will be the ruin of the African. He needs sensible, sympathetic, kindly instruction from those of us who know his place and will see that he don't get out of it."[1] When urging that higher education should be the function of the Church rather than of the State, the Reverend Warren A. Candler, later a bishop of the Southern Connection, said in 1898: "Is higher education of this secular and political sort the best for the Negro? Will it not inflame more ambition than can be satisfied? Will it not beget unrest, discontent, and eventually create disorder? The conservatism of the Negro has been largely the result of his religious character. . . . Pious, affectionate, ignorant Uncle Remus was the author of much peace and happiness. Will Remus, Jr., just out of a State College, full of political ambition, emptied of all religious conviction, looking at things from a secular standpoint, through gold-rimmed eyeglasses, be quite as agreeable and useful? What will be his influence in the common school where he will teach?"[2]

If it be true, as the Northern Methodists claimed, that the attitude of the Methodist Episcopal Church, South, was responsible in large measure for the Negro being remanded to a subordinate and inferior place in Southern life, the Southern Church nonetheless exerted a strong influence to make possible for the black man "the best opportunity of becoming all that he is capable of becoming" in that status. The leaders and journals of the Church appealed for a considerate treatment of the race, emphasizing the great obstacles with which the blacks were confronted. "If he be weak and degraded," it was said, "the appeal is the stronger to every *Christian* to give aid in proportion to his weak-

---

[1] *Cf.* editorial entitled "On the Wing", as quoted in Bowen, J. W. E., "An Apology for the Higher Education of the Negro", *The Methodist Review,* Vol. LXXXIX (September, 1897), p. 734.
[2] Letter of W. A. Candler in Nashville *Christian Advocate,* January 6, 1898.

ness and need."[1] The whites were urged to provide economic opportunities for the Negroes, and to encourage in them habits of industry and frugality, that they might attain a dignified existence. The *Advocates* time and again appealed to the white man's sense of magnanimity and fair play in his dealings with the freedmen. They demanded that the Negro be accorded an impartial legal protection in the enjoyment of his rights. They denounced with the utmost vehemence the idea that the Negro could be improved through being repressed, deploring the spirit that would oppress the blacks merely because it could be done with impunity. As has been seen, they strove valiantly to dispel prejudice against colored education. "To educate, to Christianize, and by every means to elevate, are the duties of the present hour, and we heartily honor all, who in a spirit of benevolence, and in the love of God, are doing this work," said the New Orleans *Advocate* in 1881. "The best thing for them, and for the country, is to open for them every path of useful industry, and see to it that they are generously and justly rewarded for their toil. If it were desirable, still it were impossible to get rid of the Negro. We must accept the situation, and do what is possible toward making him a Christian man and intelligent and useful citizen."[2]

None of the *Advocates* gave more earnest consideration to the problem of the advancement of the blacks than the central organ at Nashville. In an editorial on "Our Duty to the Negro," the *Advocate* said in 1895: "There are many features of the Negro problem in regard to which even Christian men may cherish honest differences of opinion. . . . But there are some other points about which there is no room for more than one view. The Negro is a man and a citizen; and as such, he has, in common with the rest of us, the full right to 'life, liberty, and the pursuit of happiness.' The fact that he is ignorant, weak, thriftless furnishes no warrant for denying him the fullest opportunity to make the

---

[1] *Cf.* letter of D. C. Kelley in Nashville *Christian Advocate*, October 20, 1883. "As to whether the Negro is capable of a high stage of civilization", Dr. Kelley said, "only the veritable tyro can afford to give an opinion. No man whose studies have been extensive in this field but knows the *data* insufficient to project a theory, much less yield a demonstration."

[2] *New Orleans Christian Advocate*, March 10, 1881.

most of such abilities, natural and acquired, as he may possess. Over his humble cabin, the impartial law should spread its protecting shield. . . . If there be any persons who, more than others are entitled to considerate care of the powers that be, they are those who are not able to care for themselves. With the utmost definiteness and vigor, therefore, we wish to denounce the spirit that would oppress the colored people simply because it is possible to do so with impunity. . . . Nothing is more unjust than the disposition which is sometimes manifest to look with contempt upon all Negroes on the ground that some of them are guilty of great crimes." Pointing out that the vast majority of the blacks were still confined to menial employments, the editor reminded his readers that "there is a grave danger, where unskilled laborers are plentiful as they are in the South, that employers will come to look upon them as being only machines or beasts of burden, and not as fellow human beings whose natural rights to considerate treatment are to be taken into account." "Will our readers suffer us to remind them that the Bible has special denunciations for those that oppress the hireling in his wages? Injustice in dealing with a dependent class is a great sin."

Emphasizing the fact that, while wages were generally low in the South, living was fortunately cheap, he continued: "It is often possible, also, for a generous employer, without much additional expense to himself, to supplement the income of his 'hands' in many ways. Land is abundant. To every cabin, therefore, a garden should be attached, and the occupants should be not only allowed but also encouraged to cultivate it. A cow is no small addition to the resources of a family, and a couple of pigs in the pen will help out the winter's supply of food amazingly. Any one who helps the colored man to get these is a benefactor." "We know that there are difficulties in carrying out such suggestions," the writer concluded. "But we are not talking to infidels or heathens. Our remarks are addressed to Christian men, who, by the very fact that they are Christians admit that they are in duty bound to be mindful of other people as well as themselves."[1] "Nothing is more absurd," declared this same editor on another

---

[1] *Cf.* editorial by Dr. E. E. Hoss in Nashville *Christian Advocate,* August 15, 1895.

occasion, "than the idea that thrusting back and thrusting down a large class of human beings is the way to improve them as citizens of a free Republic."[1]

While disapproval of the use which was made of the freedmen politically sometimes gave an academic sound to the discussions in the Methodist journals regarding the outrages which were perpetrated upon colored individuals during periods of political excitement, the Church nevertheless stood forth as an outspoken champion of the personal safety of the Negro. Although as late as 1876 the *Methodist Review* of the Northern Connection charged that their condemnation was "so mixed with apologies, and with curses against the Government and the North, that to any Northerner, and to any Ku Klux" it would be apparent that the Southern journals "held the outrages to be about right,"[2] the *Advocates* became increasingly energetic in their denunciation of all deeds of violence against the blacks. When, after the restoration of white dominion, race prejudice led to the lynching of Negroes and to attempts to drive the colored people out of entire sections, the leaders of the Church spoke out boldly against such prejudice and lawlessness. The *Advocates* contained many ringing editorials on the subject. They not only voiced their horror at the inhumanity of the practice, but also deplored the inevitably pernicious effect of such behavior upon the civilization of the section. Foremost among them in this regard, perhaps, were the Nashville *Advocate*, the *Wesleyan*, and the *Holston Methodist*.

Early in 1879 the editor of the Nashville paper urged the civil authorities to strike down every such law-breaker, "whether it be the skulking assassin who murders his victim alone, or the member

---

[1]*Cf.* Nashville *Christian Advocate*, October 12, 1893.

[2]*Cf. Methodist Quarterly Review* as quoted in Nashville *Christian Advocate*, November 25, 1876. The attitude sometimes adopted by editors in the South is well illustrated in the remarks of Dr. Thomas O. Summers, the dogmatic editor of the Nashville *Advocate*, made when the editor of the Northern *Review* had charged that the Southern Church was the protege of the Ku Klux Klan in 1873. Dr. Summers wrote: "We have no doubt that some Southern men, stung by the outrages to which they have been subjected, have sought redress in an unlawful way. We have uniformly denounced all such methods by whomsoever, and under whatsoever provocations, they have been resorted to; and hence we are the more indignant when the insinuation is made that the Methodist Episcopal Church, South, was the *protégé* of the Ku Klux conspirators. We assume not a single Southern Methodist ever belonged to the Clan, whatever it might be." *Cf.* Nashville *Christian Advocate*, February 3, 1873.

of the cowardly gangs who murder in the name of justice."[1]
In 1884 a member of the Alabama Conference, writing to the
Nashville *Advocate,* pleaded eloquently that there must be no
exceptions to the ban on mob violence. Declaring that when
"men are infuriated they are liable to think the case they are
considering is an exceptional one, in which mob violence is ad-
missible," he said: "We must improve our civilization. We
must get beyond the rage for howling men down. We MUST
enthrone calm reason, and put raging passion in chains. We
must, we *must,* we must! And every good man with pen and
voice must help."[2] This plea was warmly commended by Dr.
O. P. Fitzgerald, editor of the *Advocate.* Referring to the recent
lynching of Negroes in the South, and declaring that there could
be no such thing as "lynch law," Atticus G. Haygood said in a
letter to the *Wesleyan Christian Advocate* in 1888: "The government that winks at lynching is vicious; the government that does
not care is foolish; the government that will not put it down is
bad, as well as foolish; the government that cannot is weak."[3]

During the early Nineties when the lynching of Negroes in
the South became alarmingly frequent, the Methodist journals
spoke vehemently in condemnation of such outrages and argued
eloquently for fair play for the Negro. Although inspired with a
special horror of the Negro rapist when his victim was white, the
Advocates insisted that even in such cases punishment must be
meted out according to law. Pointing out that the clashes between whites and blacks were usually the result of the contact of
vicious persons of both races, the *Texas Christian Advocate* urged
that the Negro must not be held to a greater responsibility than
the whites. "Whatever crisis may come upon us," it said, "let
us preserve the spirit of Christ, our Master. Let neither the
persuasions of misguided friends, the threats and arrogance of
foolish Negroes, nor the aggravating and irritating lectures read
to us by those who are utterly ignorant of the factors of the
problem, hurry us into the commission or countenancing of any
wrong act. Remember that the sacred right of self-defense be-

---

[1]Nashville *Christian Advocate,* January 25, 1879.
[2]*Cf.* letter of W. H. Morris of Choctaw Corner, Alabama, in Nashville
Christian Advocate, August 30, 1884.
[3]Letter of Dr. A. G. Haygood in *Wesleyan Christian Advocate,* June 2, 1888.

longs to the Negro as to all, and when in the exercise of that right, he kills a white man, it should arouse no prejudice against him or his race. Remember also that he has a right in all cases to a fair trial before the courts of the Country. Remember, above all, that he is a brother in Christ, with a right to our sympathy, helpfulness and prayers."[1]

In 1892 the editor of the Nashville *Advocate* said: "The recent burning of a Negro man at Texarkana as a penalty for an unnamable offense fills us with a sense of horror. What are we coming to? Are our courts good for nothing? Is law useless? Are we drifting back to barbarism? Awful as is the crime of which the Negro in this case was guilty, there was no excuse for the action of the mob. In a perfectly lawful way he could have been speedily tried and swiftly executed. In the name of civilization, in the name of humanity, in the name of God, we must protest against such things. Our former utterances on this subject have lost us some subscribers. We should not change our course by a hair's breadth if 10,000 names were dropped tomorrow."[2]

In Mississippi Bishop Charles B. Galloway and other leaders of Southern Methodism were foremost in denouncing such lynchings. The Mississippi Annual Conference adopted a resolution in 1897, condemning all lynching and calling upon the "people everywhere to support the officers of the law . . . in preventing a repetition of those acts of lawlessness which have so disgraced and hurt us in the eyes of others, and which are so unworthy a civilized Christian people."[3] The Negro editor of one of the

---

[1] Cf. *Texas Christian Advocate*, quoted in *New Orleans Christian Advocate*, November 14, 1889.

[2] Cf. editorial of Dr. E. E. Hoss in Nashville *Christian Advocate*, March 3, 1892. In an editorial headed "The Barnwell Butchery", and referring to the lynching of a group of Negroes, who were charged with, and generally believed to be guilty of, the murder of three white men in South Carolina, the *Southern Christian Advocate* said in its issue of January 2, 1890: "The *Advocate* has not words strong enough to denounce as it deserves the Barnwell butchery. A more cowardly and brutal violation of the law, human and Divine, has never before disgraced the State. The prisoners were in the hands of the law awaiting trial for the crimes with which they were charged. They were unarmed and defenseless. . . . In the dead of the night they were taken from their place of security and shot down like dogs. Was there ever anything more infamous and cruel in all the history of the State? . . . Is public sentiment so demoralized and corrupt as to make possible such inhuman butcheries? . . . We are sowing to the wind, and sooner or later we shall reap the whirlwind."

[3] *Journal of Mississippi Annual Conference*, 1897, p. 9.

Northern Methodist journals published in the South declared that the Mississippi Conference, "in the adoption of these resolutions, has shown no small degree of moral courage. For while there are thousands of most excellent people all over the South who entertain just such views as are herein expressed, they hesitate for various reasons to speak out in condemnation of mob law. But this the Conference has done and with no uncertain sound."[1] Although, after declining noticeably during the first year of the decade, the number of Negroes lynched in the country rose during the Nineties until in 1900 approximately eighteen per cent more lynchings occurred than in 1890, the number fell off sharply just after the turn of the century and has continued to decline since that time. And there can be little doubt that the clerical condemnation which has been described here had much to do with the formation of the public sentiment which led to this result.[2]

Perhaps the chief influence exerted by the Methodist Episcopal Church, South, on the race problem was the outcome of the efforts exerted by its leaders to convince the Southern people of the possibility of a satisfactory adjustment between the races. The *Advocates* continually exhorted the people to adopt a hopeful view, and, when things looked darkest, they sought earnestly to impress upon them the efficacy of Christianity as an agency for enabling the two people to live together successfully. They frequently emphasized the interdependence of the whites and blacks, and maintained that it was possible for them to live side by side in amity. They deplored the agitation of all schemes for the emigration or colonization of the Negroes, not only on the ground that such schemes were the projects of political demagogues, but also because they served to divert the popular mind from consideration of the real problem, that of making it possible for the two races to dwell together amicably. These journals expressed the belief that the Negro was in the South "by the providence of God" for "some wise and gracious purpose," and that the problem must be solved by the men of the South, as Christians, and not by mere partisans for selfish ends.

---

[1] *Cf. Southwestern Christian Advocate,* January 20, 1898.
[2] *Cf.* Raper, Arthur F., *The Tragedy of Lynching* (Chapel Hill, 1933), pp. 480-481. In 1890 the number of Negroes lynched was ninety; in 1900 it was one hundred and seven. In 1902 the number fell to eighty-six.

As has been mentioned, a large migration of Negroes from the South began shortly before the Seventies. Economic depression, crop failures, and the abuses of an usurious credit system, as well as the violence resulting from political upheavals, kept many restive. Excited by agitators of their own race and by agents of Western railway and land companies, thousands of wretched blacks, ill clad and often without funds, found their way to the banks of the Mississippi, seeking transportation to a new Canaan in the North. Although detained by violence and fraud in some sections where planting interests were fearful of losing their chief labor supply, perhaps twenty or twenty-five thousand persons succeeded in making their way to Kansas, the principal destination, before the movement ended. Thoroughly unprepared for such a trek, some were turned back at Kansas City or St. Louis, and many others were saved after their arrival only by the exertions of Northern emergency relief societies.[1]

Referring to this migration the *Southern Christian Advocate* asserted in May 1879 that "We are clear in the conviction that the Negro had better stay where he is. . . . We are equally clear in the opinion that we need the Negro." Urging the whites to accept the inevitability of the situation, and to make the best possible use of the African, it said: "He has political rights. Let them be respected. It is not sufficient that the great body of our people personally respect those rights, but it is theirs so to create and control public opinion as to make it impossible for the restless and irresponsible *irreconcilables* of any community to disturb them. . . . Let us heartily endorse measures looking to his education. The more generally he is educated, the more intelligent will be his interest in whatever appertains to the public weal. . . . Let us practically identify him with the country. Rent to him at reasonable rates, or sell the unoccupied land that can be well spared from our overgrown farms, and make the payments as easy as possible. . . . Help him to secure the privileges of the gospel, to build houses of worship, and to sustain the operations of the Churches laboring for his benefit."[2]

---

[1]*Cf.* Schlesinger, Arthur Meier, *The Rise of the City* (New York, 1933), pp. 375-376.
[2]*Southern Christian Advocate*, May 3, 1879.

Foremost in encouraging the Southern people to a hopeful view of the situation was the official journal of the Connection. Referring to the large exodus of colored persons then under way, the Nashville paper said in October 1879: "Some say the two races cannot live here together; that we have no successful precedents in history to justify the experiment. They should remember that the experiment was never tried with the Christian conditions which exist in our country. . . . If Christianity shall maintain and intensify its hold upon our people, white and black, they will live peacefully and happily in the same land, and will be of mutual profit to each other. It is not schemes of colonization, but efforts of Christianization we should encourage. Religion will remove passion and violence from white ruffians who would oppress a feeble people, and it will cleanse Negro agitators of those dangerous forms of ambition and insolence which impel some of them to seek the establishment of Negro governments that they may rule over them."[1]

The following year the *Advocate* discussed the race problem on many occasions and at great length. In its issue of January 11, 1890, it said: "In the first place we deprecate the too prevalent disposition to magnify the difficulty of solving this race question. The fears of one class, the prejudices of another, the excitability of yet another, contribute to this result. The assumption that it cannot be successfully managed by those concerned is an impeachment of their common sense, their patriotism, and their religion. It is a confession that the majority cannot see that the welfare of both races is involved in the welfare of each. It is practically a declaration that despite the teachings of Christ and the lessons of history and experience, we are a nation of fools, *minus* conscience, common sense, and even the ordinary instincts of self-preservation. We cannot believe that there is not sense enough and grace enough in this nation for the solution of this

---

[1]Nashville *Christian Advocate*, October 10, 1879. Declaring that if the people of the North would allow the Southerners to settle the problem in their own way, they would find a satisfactory adjustment, the editor of the *Advocate* said in its issue of February 22, 1890: "We will settle our troubles, and we will do it without forcing the colored people to emigrate, or asking the government to assist in colonizing them in Africa. It is true that we are 'hopelessly Southern', as a certain writer recently put it, but we have manhood and statesmanship, and religion. We can solve our problems honorably to all."

problem. We do not believe our people will play the fool in any such gratuitous way. Let us take hold of this matter with a calmness worthy of a great people who believe in God. Let hysterical alarmists be silent. If we cannot put them into strait-jackets, let us at least refuse to listen to them."

After having urged the Southern people to rise above party considerations in forming their judgments on this subject, the *Advocate* continued: "There are prejudices that lie outside of party spirit—prejudices that blind us to the lessons of the past, and to the signs of the future; prejudices that ignore obvious facts, and that cling to exploded fallacies; prejudices that block the path of progress with dead issues and passions that ought to have died with them." Again, in 1890, Atticus G. Haygood, speaking through the columns of the Nashville journal, warned the Southern people that the only reason at all for considering the scheme of salvation through emigration was that it diverted attention from "the real practical work that can be done to help both races do peaceably and prosperously what, so far as present indications show they will have to do in some way for a good long time—live together."[1]

The attitude of Southern Methodism toward Negro rights during the post-war period may be briefly summarized. Although showing little inclination to revise its former notions with regard to the relations of the races in the Church and in society, the Southern Church nonetheless did much to gain a recognition of the dignity and rights of the colored race and to make possible for the African an opportunity for the fullest development. At all times the spokesmen of the denomination appealed for a considerate treatment of the blacks, emphasizing the unpreparedness of the colored man for the situation in which he found himself. The leaders and journals of the Church sought to promote the material welfare of the Negroes, urging the whites to provide economic opportunities for them, and appealing to the white man's sense of magnanimity and fair play in his dealings with his colored brother. The Church moreover stood forth as an outspoken champion of the personal safety of the Africans,

---

[1]Communication of Atticus G. Haygood in Nashville *Christian Advocate,* February 15, 1890.

demanding for them an impartial legal protection in the enjoyment of their rights. It did much, as has been seen, to promote and to dispel prejudice against colored education. The chief contribution of the Southern Church to the advancement of the Negro, perhaps, were its untiring efforts to convince the whites of the possibility of a satisfactory adjustment between the races in the section. The attitude of the Church was undoubtedly an important factor in determining the social policy of the Southern States with regard to the Negro.

CHAPTER VII

CONTRIBUTIONS TO PRIMARY AND SECONDARY EDUCATION

THE post-war interest of Southern Methodism in secular education was not a new thing. From its earliest days American Methodism had been committed to the work of education. Next to the conversion of men's souls, Bishop Asbury had been interested in the promotion of secondary and collegiate learning. And the first schools established by the denomination were in the Southern States. In 1784, under the guidance of Asbury, Cokesbury College, the earliest Methodist institution of higher learning on the continent, was founded at Abingdon, Maryland.[1] About the same time several academies or preparatory schools, destined to be important factors in the educational development of the South for three or four decades, were established. The better known were the Ebenezer Academy in Virginia and the Mount Bethel Academy, which was founded in 1795 in Newberry District, South Carolina.[2]

The auspicious beginning of the denomination in the field of higher education was lost when, in 1795, after its buildings had been destroyed for the second time by fire, Cokesbury College was not set up again. Bishop Asbury, much discouraged by the untoward fate of the venture, was reported to have exclaimed that "The Lord does not want the Methodists to have colleges."[3] Although it is doubtful that he ever spoke these words, it was under the inspiration of this sentiment attributed to Asbury that the work of the denomination in the field of higher education halted for a quarter of a century. Until 1820 the Church contented itself with establishing and conducting academies such as were popular in all parts of the country at that period. And in the field of secondary education the efforts of the Methodists were especially successful. The work expanded until by 1860 the

---

[1] *Cf.* Du Bose, *op. cit.,* p. 474.
[2] *Ibid.,* pp. 474-550. Ebenezer Academy was established in 1796.
[3] *Cf.* statement of W. W. Bennett in *Daily Advocate,* May 3, 1882.

Methodist Episcopal Church, South, was maintaining 106 academies or preparatory schools throughout the South.[1]

But there was in the General Conference of 1820 and that of 1824 a group of men who had conceived the idea of a system of Methodist institutions of higher education, and the Conference of 1820 recommended that "each Annual Conference should establish a seminary of learning under its own regulation and patronage."[2] Under the impetus of this recommendation the Church resumed its labors in the field of higher education, and the next quarter of a century witnessed a remarkable activity among the Methodists in the founding of colleges as well as secondary schools. The first college incorporated after the General Conference's recommendation was projected by the Virginia Conference in 1830. In that year the board of trustees of Randolph-Macon College was organized, and scholastic work began in 1832.[3]

By 1860 the Southern Methodists were operating more than a dozen colleges for men and some forty institutions of higher learning for women, in some of which the work being done compared favorably with that of the best secular schools of the section. In the far South the activity of the Church constituted an especially important contribution to the development of higher education. In some instances the Methodist colleges antedated all others in the State. Thus La Grange College was founded in 1830, two years prior to the establishment of the University of Alabama, and it gave to the commonwealth a goodly number of the first leaders who had been educated within the State.[4]

The patronage of such institutions was by no means confined to Methodist families, and they often showed a liberality towards other denominations remarkable for that day. That some of them sought to avoid being narrowly sectarian is evident from the

[1] *Cf.* statistics given in a "Tabulated Report of the Institutions of the Methodist Episcopal Church, South", in *The Educational Repository* for August, 1860, and cited in article by J. H. Brunner in Nashville *Christian Advocate*, October 3, 1874.

[2] Statement of W. W. Bennett in *Daily Advocate*, May 3, 1882.

[3] *Cf.* Irby, Richard, *History of Randolph-Macon College, Virginia* (Richmond), p. 8.

[4] Posey, Walter Brownlow, *La Grange, Alabama's Earliest College* (Birmingham, 1933), p. 50.

wording of the charter of La Grange College. That document stated that "The institution hereby incorporated shall be purely literary and scientific; and the trustees are hereby prohibited from the adoption of any system of education which shall provide for the inculcation of the peculiar tenets or doctrines of any religious denomination whatsoever." In marked contrast to the custom of most sectarian colleges, no courses were offered in either the Old or the New Testament.[1] As further evidence of the unusual liberality of spirit, La Grange conferred some of its earliest degrees upon ministers of the Presbyterian faith.[2] Equally notable was the fact that during this early period Randolph-Macon College had two men on its faculty who were members of the Roman Catholic Church.[3]

The Methodists of the South were especially advanced in their views with regard to the education of women. In 1833 Dr. Lovick Pierce and a group of other liberal-minded Methodist ministers determined to establish an institution in which women could obtain advantages equal to and receive the same degrees as those men were acquiring in the best colleges of the section. Although the project met with great opposition and ridicule, the movement culminated in the establishment of the Georgia Female College, now Georgia Wesleyan College, which was chartered by the legislature in 1836. On opening its doors in January 1839 the institution immediately attracted students from the best academies in the South, and during the summer of 1840 it conferred upon a class of twelve what are believed to be the first Bachelor's degrees ever granted to women.[4] An observant New England woman who visited Georgia during the Forties bore testimony to the high character of the instruction. Asserting that Georgia must always be honored for having given to the country its first college for women, she expressed the opinion that "in point of literary excellence and all those privileges calculated to raise the standard of female education far above its ordinary level,

---

[1] *Ibid.*, p. 5.
[2] *Ibid.*, p. 17. Its second doctorate in Divinity was awarded to a Presbyterian clergyman of Mobile.
[3] This fact was given to the author in a conversation with Dr. R. E. Blackwell of Randolph-Macon College in January, 1938.
[4] Du Bose, *op. cit.*, pp. 499-500.

Macon Female College stands the highest in our country excepting the Oberlin College in Ohio."[1] The success of the Georgia experiment soon led to the founding of a number of other colleges for women by the denomination.[2]

The Fifties were a period of special exertion upon the part of the denomination in the field of higher education. A great impetus was given to the cause in 1850 when the Reverend Benjamin Wofford, a minister of the Southern Church, bequeathed one hundred thousand dollars for the establishment of a Methodist college in the State of South Carolina, which should provide "literary, classical, and scientific" education. This, the largest single gift for education which had ever been made in the South, spurred the Methodists on to other educational undertakings.[3] During the decade colleges were founded in every Southern State in which no Methodist institution had previously existed.

Moreover, much consideration was given to the idea of a great central Methodist university for the section. Plans were actually projected looking to the establishment of such an institution. In 1858 the State of Tennessee granted a charter for a "Central University of the Methodist Episcopal Church, South," to a group of Methodist communicants in behalf of the Church. The General Conference expressed approval of the steps taken, and urged the Tennessee Conference to assume especial care of the proposed center of learning, for which Nashville had been chosen. The Conference, moreover, suggested that the charter be amended so that the other Annual Conferences, if any might desire to do so, could acquire a voice in its administration and control.[4] Although Central University existed only on paper when the Civil War broke out, the great interest manifested in higher education among Southern Methodists promised an early and successful realization of the enterprise. The whole scheme inevitably collapsed in the general wreck of the fortunes of the Church which took place during the War. Up to that time the schools of the denomination had contributed a large quota to the educated leaders of the section

---

[1]Burke, Emily P., *Reminiscences of Georgia* (Oberlin, Ohio, 1850), pp. 203-204.

[2]*Cf.* Du Bose, *op. cit.*, pp. 474-550.

[3]*Idem.*

[4]Cf. Du Bose, op. cit., pp. 289-290.

and had done much to mold the public mind of the South.[1]
Thus at the close of the *ante bellum* period the Methodist Episcopal Church, South, occupied a position of outstanding importance in both the higher and preparatory fields of the Southern
educational system.[2]

In no other sphere of the Church's activity was there so complete a prostration in 1865 as in that of education. In many
places its efforts along such lines had come to a standstill during
the early days of the struggle. The War had wrought with an
especially disastrous effect upon the preparatory schools of the
denomination. Few of the academies managed to keep their
doors open throughout the period, and an overwhelming number
found it impossible to continue operations after peace came. Of
the one hundred and six preparatory schools conducted by the
denomination in 1860, only fourteen had been set in motion again
by 1870.[3] The poverty which prevailed everywhere in the Connection made the reopening of such schools a very difficult matter.
The condition of Southern education as a whole, at the same time,
seemed to add greatly to the obligations devolving upon the
Methodists.

The school system of the Southern States was indeed chaotic.
For a time it remained an open question as to what system would
replace the academies and privately supported community schools
which had sufficed during the days before the War. The very
magnitude of the problem precluded an early solution. While
taxable property had greatly depreciated in value, four million
illiterates had been added to the school population. Three times
as many children were to be educated on one-third the amount
of money formerly required.[4] The disturbed conditions of the
times added greatly to the difficulties.

---

[1] *Cf.* statistics given in *Educational Repository* for August, 1860, and cited
in article of J. H. Brunner in Nashville *Christian Advocate*, October 3, 1874.
Of the institutions of higher learning the *Repository* classified four as universities; six as male colleges; and forty as female colleges.

[2] *Ibid.* The distribution of Methodist institutions among the States was as
follows: North Carolina, 23; Texas, 16; Virginia, 15; Tennessee, 14; Georgia,
13; Kentucky, 12; Alabama, 11; Mississippi, 11; Louisiana, 10; Arkansas, 5;
Indian Territory, 5; South Carolina, 4; Florida, 2; Kansas, 2; California, 1.
The highest enrollment reported in any institution was 300.

[3] *Ibid.*

[4] Boone, Richard G., *Education in the United States* (New York, 1889),
p. 351.

Although steps had been taken to create a system of common schools in practically all the Southern States prior to the War, the system had never taken deep root. "Literary Funds" had been established and grants made for the education of children who had no other means of acquiring learning. Superintendents of Public Instruction had been provided for. But such legislation had usually been permissive rather than mandatory. Moreover, education of this type, with only rare exceptions, carried with it a social stigma. Although the States of Georgia, North Carolina, Louisiana, Tennessee, Mississippi, Alabama, and Kentucky had each spent annually from a quarter to three-quarters of a million dollars on common schools during the years just preceding the Civil War, there had been no public education in the sense of schools being free and open to all without class distinctions.[1] The tendency towards large plantations naturally operated against the success of common schools. Apart from the establishment of school systems in Baltimore, St. Louis, and Louisville, with beginnings in Charleston and New Orleans, public education had, broadly speaking, proved a failure in the section.[2] Referring to the system in a particular State, *De Bow's Review* declared in 1859: "After ten years trial it has been proved that laws cannot be carried out, that more than half the families in Louisiana will not accept of the mental food the State offers to her children. Some parishes will not accept any of it."[3]

Though the general sentiment of the articulate classes had remained indifferent, if not antagonistic, to free education throughout the *ante-bellum* period, the years immediately following the War saw a creditable beginning toward providing a system of public schools in a number of these States. An unexpected interest was manifested in the subject from 1865 to 1867, with the result that, during the period of presidential reconstruction, considerable legislation was enacted for the improvement and support of common schools. The Arkansas legislature of 1866-1867 took an advanced position in this regard, making provision for tax supported public schools for three months of the year,

[1] *Ibid.*, p. 349.
[2] *Idem.*
[3] *Cf. De Bow's Review*, Vol. XVII, p. 278, quoted in Boone, *op. cit.*, p. 379.

and appointing a State superintendant of schools.[1] The Alabama constitution, adopted in 1865, ordered that laws be enacted for the support and encouragement of public schools. Accordingly, in February 1867, the legislature provided for a system of schools to be open to "every child between the ages of six and twenty years."[2] Similar progress was made in other States. But the favorable sentiment and beneficial effects which resulted from these undertakings were in a large measure destroyed by the inauguration of Congressional reconstruction in 1867.

Although the Carpet-bag governments in every instance enacted educational provisions that were mandatory, and more specific than any previously adopted, the conditions under which the public schools were established made them very unpopular. The constitutions and laws adopted under the new regime provided for uniform methods of taxation for school support, for definitely prescribed school terms, for State and local administrative organization, for courses of study, and for the examination and certification of teachers, but such legislation was often nominal and proved otherwise defective.[3] Moreover, legislative enactments alone could not build up a good school system. The political and social disorders of the times militated against the successful operation of the public schools. For years they were forced to struggle for existence. Extravagance, financial mismanagement, and the misapplication and diversion of school funds constituted some of the greatest obstacles to success.

In Virginia, where the system had the advantage of a conservative native-born white superintendent, funds which had been collected for the support of public education were, largely because of defective legislation, applied to the extinction of the State debt.[4] By 1878 there was a general relaxation of educational endeavor, and during that and the following year many schools were temporarily suspended, while in other instances the term was considerably decreased. Teachers went unpaid, or were given

---

[1]Knight, Edgar W., *Public Education in the South* (Boston and New York, 1922), pp. 313-314.
[2]*Ibid.*, p. 314.
[3]*Cf. ibid.*, pp. 316-317.
[4]*Ibid.*, pp. 341-346.

warrants which they were forced to sell at a large discount.[1] In Georgia, where there had been a similar diversion of appropriations, the superintendent of education reported an "utter lack of school funds" in 1872.[2] Corruption and swindling were especially flagrant in the school system of Mississippi and led to an outright opposition to public schools that sometimes resulted in the destruction of school property and other acts of violence.[3] Radical fraud in other States likewise worked against the success of the system.

The attempt to mix the races in the public schools had a blighting effect upon them. In Louisiana the provision was made that such schools must be open alike to all children of a fixed age without distinction of race or color. The whites generally refused to attend, and, during the time the rule was enforced, were without the advantages of public education.[4] Similar legislation in South Carolina, Mississippi, and other States, even when no attempt was made to give it practical application, aroused a determined opposition to public schools. Further hostility was caused by the agitation of the Civil Rights Bill in Congress and by the appointment of Negroes as county superintendents of education in some of the States.

With the passing of reconstruction the conservative reaction led to practices of rigid economy in public education in all parts of the South.[5] At the same time the partisan spirit which survived the period often subordinated the schools to other interests. Moreover attempts to restore the old systems of private and parochial schools had the effect of reducing materially the patronage of the common schools.[6] For two decades the education of both whites and blacks was greatly neglected by the government, and though the idea of universal public education was slowly gaining acceptance through the influence of such agencies as the

---

[1]*Ibid.*, p. 346.

[2]*Ibid.*, p. 354.

[3]*Cf.* Garner, James Wilford, *Reconstruction in Mississippi* (New York, 1902), p. 361.

[4]Knight, *op. cit.*, pp. 356-357.

[5]*Cf. ibid.*, pp. 417-418.

[6]*Ibid.*, p. 392. In 1873 sixty private schools, all charging high rates of tuition, were in operation in the city of Atlanta.

Peabody Fund, educational facilities in many parts of the South during the Nineties were inferior to what they had been in 1860.[1]

Outside of the cities, school terms continued to be of only a few months' duration, and teachers' salaries were generally low. The average annual salary of teachers in the Southern States decreased from $175 in 1860 to $159 in 1890. The average for the entire United States in 1890 was $310.[2] The examinations for certification were often mere formalities, and outside the cities the teachers were usually inadequately educated and trained. The schools were generally of an elementary grade. Almost no public high-school instruction was furnished outside the urban districts.[3]

Within a short time after the War efforts were being made here and there by the Methodists to set up schools to take the place of the *ante-bellum* establishments. It seemed likely that the Church would essay a role as a practical educator in the lower branches of learning commensurate with its energies and resources. In addition to the inadequate facilities of the secular institutions and the crying need for additional schools, the belief that moral and religious instruction should constitute an important part of all elementary education naturally prompted the Church to create a system of denominational schools. The fact that an agitation was being carried on throughout the country for the exclusion of the Bible from the public schools added greatly to the sentiment in favor of Church schools. By creating a system of parochial schools the Church would be in a position to exercise a profound influence upon educational development in the South and would be able to render an important public service which the State could not at the time perform. It was not likely that the Church would fail to perceive the opportunity thus presented.

Several of the Annual Conferences quickly projected plans for a system of common grade schools. During the fall of 1865 the Louisiana Conference appointed a committee to draft a plan for the establishment of such schools to be conducted under the auspices of the Church, and ordered that the plan be reported to

---

[1] *Cf. ibid.*, pp. 420-421.

[2] *Ibid.*, p. 420. In the same year the teachers in the public schools of North Carolina and Alabama received an average monthly salary of only twenty-four dollars; in Virginia and Mississippi thirty-four dollars.

[3] *Ibid.*, p. 421.

the Conference at its next session.[1] The few Methodists academies which had survived the War served as models for the new schools. Perhaps the best known of these institutions was the Methodist Conference School at Cokesbury, South Carolina.[2] By the early Seventies plans were being matured in several Conferences for a system of Methodist District High Schools which would include elementary departments. Much interest was manifested in these experiments throughout the Church. Citing the fact that the Bible was being excluded from the public schools, Atticus G. Haygood advanced this as an added reason why such schools should be established. Referring to a high school which had recently been started in one of the Georgia Conferences when Vanderbilt University was established, he said: "I rejoice in 'the Vanderbilt University' and I also rejoice in 'the Andrew High School.' One Vanderbilt will do at present; but we need and must have, a great many Methodist high schools. They are exactly adapted to the wants of the mass of our people, and easily adjustable, through our District Conferences, to our Church machinery."[3] In December 1873 Bishop Keener expressed the hope that a plan for conducting such District High Schools would be engrafted upon the economy of the Church at large during the forthcoming General Conference.[4] By 1874 the Holston Conference had developed a complete educational system which provided for a high school for each presiding elder's district. These District High Schools were put under the control of principals chosen by the Conference, and invested with full authority. A fixed course of study was prescribed. Although primary departments were attached, special attention was given to the preparation of students for college. The advanced classes were required to complete the study of "Algebra, Græca Minora and Cæsar."[5]

The success of the Holston system aroused much enthusiasm. In November 1876 the Richmond *Advocate* reported that these schools were flourishing and feeding the colleges. It urged that

---

[1]*Cf. Journal of Louisiana Conference*, 1865, p. 15.

[2]*Cf.* Simkins and Woody, *op. cit.*, p. 419.

[3]Letter of A. G. Haygood in Nashville *Christian Advocate*, July 19, 1873.

[4]*Cf.* letter of Bishop Keener in *New Orleans Christian Advocate*, November 6, 1873.

[5]*Idem.*

the plan be given a fair trial in other sections. "The State Public Instruction does not go far enough, and there is a gap between the Free School and the College," it said. "These High Schools receiving the solid Methodist patronage of each District have been a success among our Holston brethren and supplied a public need for a good Classical School. We are glad to see there is a movement in some parts of the Baltimore Conference in this direction."[1]

In the Episcopal Address of 1874 the bishops announced that they anticipated the development in the near future of a complete denominational system, in which academies and district high schools would constitute a fundamental feature.[2] The General Conference that year, in response to a memorial from the Virginia Conference, praying that it would order the establishment of such district high schools throughout the Connection, recommended "that, as far as practicable, Southern Methodist Schools be established in every district in our work; provided that they are strictly contributory to and in no case conflict with our colleges, male or female, or any other of our institutions of a higher grade."[3] "The cry of our times is education—education," the Conference said. "But it is for the education of the pure intellect, and not of the moral constitution. And, unfortunately, as we think, the tendency and aim of our public and State education are to the development of the intellectual faculties, to the neglect and to the ignoring of the moral and the higher nature. We want an *intelligent* people, it is true, but it is also and especially true, that we want a virtuous people—a people who have and practice and exemplify the cardinal virtues."[4]

The General Conference of 1878 further indorsed the efforts which were being made to build up a system of district high schools. "We heartily approve of the plan of district schools recommended by the last General Conference," it said. "They meet the wants of our people in many localities for the education of their children. . . . We are happy to say that many have been established since the recommendation was made." The Conference commended these schools especially as "reaching all classes

[1] *Richmond Christian Advocate*, November 2, 1876.
[2] *Cf.* Pastoral Address in *Journal of General Conference*, 1874, pp. 385-386.
[3] *Journal of General Conference*, 1874, pp. 507-509.
[4] *Idem.*

and preparing students both for our male and female colleges,"
as well as for being "the only antidote to that godless feature
in the public schools which ignores the Holy Scriptures in the
training of youth."[1]

Although wanting somewhat as to completeness and exact
classification in both instances, the educational statistics reported
in the General Conference of 1878 form an interesting contrast
to those presented in 1874. Of the sixty-one denominational
institutions reported in the earlier Conference, four were listed
as universities, forty-three as colleges, and the remaining fourteen
were designated as either seminaries, institutes, high-schools, or
manual labor schools. Of the ninety-five institutions listed in the
latter year, two were universities, fifty-five were described as
colleges, and the remaining thirty-eight were reported as being
devoted to high-school and preparatory work.[2] The proportionately large increase in the number of high-schools indicated by
these figures reflects the notable interest manifested in building
up adequate preparatory schools.

Although the system of district high-schools was never made a
feature of the connectional system, such schools continued in
operation in many places throughout the South to the end of the
century. As late as 1895 the Alabama Conference, which comprised the southern part of that State and a strip across Northern
Florida, reported that its five District High Schools, located in
the Selma, the Mobile, the Eufaula, and the Marianna districts,
were flourishing and doing good work.[3] The significant relation
of the Methodist academies and district high-schools to the development of preparatory education in the Southern States in
general becomes apparent when one calls to mind the fact that
there were still fewer than one hundred four-year public high-
schools in the entire South in 1900.[4]

Notwithstanding its own aspirations, and despite the fact that
attempts to exclude the Bible from common schools caused some
of its leaders for a time to yield but a grudging support to public

[1]*Journal of General Conference*, 1878, pp. 36-37.
[2]*Cf.* table of official statistics in Nashville *Christian Advocate*, June 15, 1878.
[3]*Cf. Minutes of Alabama Conference*, 1895, p. 44.
[4]*Cf.* Dabney, *op. cit.*, p. 333.

schools,[1] the Church soon manifested a willingness to accept both primary and secondary education as a function of the State. As a result the contribution of the denomination to preparatory education lay perhaps as much in the encouragement given to the development of public schools as in its own endeavors in the field. The press, the pulpit, and the representative bodies of the Church became active champions of free common schools. The *Advocates* sought earnestly to impress on the public mind the advantages of a well equipped system of public schools. They stressed the needs of the schools and the folly of giving them an inadequate support. As early as 1869 the *New Orleans Christian Advocate* expressed the opinion that the "common schools and the Holy Bible are the two stones of the mill that are slowly but surely grinding up the grist of the world." Declar-

---

[1]As late as 1872, Bishop McTyeire said: "I take the ground that the Church has a distinct duty and function to educate. I take this ground because the Church can do it better and cheaper than any other organization, and turn out better work. I have not been hopeful of our public school system. I beg not to be considered an enemy of popular education. The public school may supply the need of mere intellectual training, but omits that higher training—the culture of the moral faculties. It cannot be relied on for this last result. . . . I must liken public schools to soup houses in great cities. The poor are abundant, and as we don't want them to starve to death, we establish soup houses. . . . So with the public schools; for those who want no religious education, for the poor who would have no education but for these public schools, we say go there and learn something. The evil in them we will try to correct by our Sunday-schools, the Church and other means of grace. . . . The Episcopalians established parochial schools, and so do the Presbyterians and Baptists. We will have to do so also. Within fifty years I prophesy that our Church will have a school wherever we preach the word." *Cf.* Address of Bishop H. N. McTyeire at Pacific Methodist College as reported in the *Pacific Methodist* and quoted in *New Orleans Christian Advocate*, November 21, 1872. About the same time, the dogmatic Dr. Thomas O. Summers, editor of the Nashville *Advocate*, said: "We want no British Parliament, no American Congress, no State, no municipality, to take this matter in hand. Let the Church educate her own children, and as many besides as she can honorably get under her control. . . . We hazard nothing in saying that the three great Protestant Communions— Baptist, Methodist, and Presbyterian—are competent to take this matter in hand. They can educate all the children in the South. . . . We are taxed for the public school fund to educate other peoples' children; and we have no control over the education that is given them. We would rather pay our taxes to the Church and let her manage the business. . . . . But suppose the State does take this matter in hand—and does levy a school-tax upon us—what then? Why, pay the tax, and still support your own Church-schools. . . . in every age before the present, the Church has controlled the education of the young, and we shall do all in our power to restore to her the prerogatives which she justly claims . . . If that is treason, make the most of it." *Cf.* Nashville *Christian Advocate*, November 30, 1872.

ing that an attempt to mix the races in the schools would disrupt them, and that Catholic communicants generally would be pleased at such a result, it urged the public not to elect members of that faith to school boards until they should have disavowed the sentiments attributed to them.[1]

It is true that the Church manifested little interest in the public schools during the greater part of the Seventies because of their relation to the political upheavals and corruption of that decade. As has been said, the inefficiency and venality of their management caused them to be looked upon with disfavor by the white population at large during that time. But no sooner had native white rule been restored than the Church made it clear that it would not oppose the development of the public schools, and its attitude toward them became increasingly friendly. In an editorial on "Our Tenets and Practices," referring to the charge made by a Northern minister that the Southern organization was "not the staunchest friend of public schools," the New Orleans *Advocate* said in 1879: "The charge against the Methodist Episcopal Church, South, that we do not advocate public schools, is, so far as we can judge, without foundation. That individuals here and there may have opposed them is possible, but we believe our Southern Methodists, as a body, are heartily in favor of them. . . . there has never been a deliverance by us, as a Church, against them. . . . We do not know a Southern Methodist who is not in favor of them. If there be such, it will be found that their views are based upon other grounds than a desire to keep the masses in ignorance."[2]

The following year the New Orleans paper urged upon the country the necessity of a liberal support for the public schools. It said: "Good schools are among the things that make a country desirable. . . . It is a foolish, short-sighted and ruinous policy, to economize at this point. . . . The support of the public schools appeals to our material interests, our benevolence, and to our love of country."[3] In the Episcopal Address of 1882, the bishops, while declaring that the Church must not give over the higher

---

[1] *New Orleans Christian Advocate,* May 15, 1869.
[2] *Ibid.,* November 27, 1879.
[3] *Ibid.,* May 27, 1880.

education of its children to the State, were careful to explain that "the provision made by civil and municipal governments for lessening the illiteracy of the masses does not interfere with the work the Church proposes to do."[1] The General Conference of that year, although it expressed concern lest all moral instruction be overlooked in the public schools, took occasion to disclaim any unfriendliness toward the system. It said: "A system of primary schools has been generally adopted throughout the country, and maintained by a tax upon the property of all classes of citizens. With this system we have neither the power nor the disposition to interfere."[2] The following year the Nashville *Advocate*, when criticizing certain State policies in higher education, took pains to state that it wished "always to be counted in favor of public schools, and the education of the people."[3]

As has been mentioned, the journals of the Connection warmly espoused the Blair Educational Bill which proposed that federal aid be given to each State for public schools in proportion to the amount of illiteracy within its borders. The *Advocates* vigorously rebuked the prejudice and selfish interests which would defeat the bill. The *Southern Christian Advocate* denounced without reserve the spirit that would oppose the measure because its benefits would be shared alike by black and white. Referring to the support which Senator Wade Hampton had given the bill, its editor said in April 1884: "As a Christian journalist and a citizen of South Carolina, the editor of this paper thanks him for the elevated and conspicuous stand he has taken upon the great measure of relieving the vampire burden of illiteracy, which not only compromises our status as a section of the country, but actually threatens the permanency and integrity of our institutions, as we stand related to the general government."[4] When sectional considerations led Senators John A. Logan and John Sherman to oppose that feature of the bill which provided for distribution in proportion to illiteracy, the New Orleans *Advocate* said: "Taxes are levied for the support of a public school system because illiteracy is dangerous to the body politic. A nation educates

---

[1]*Cf.* Episcopal Address in *Journal of General Conference*, 1882, p. 23.
[2]*Journal of General Conference*, 1882, p. 120.
[3]*Cf.* Nashville *Christian Advocate*, November 17, 1883.
[4]*Southern Christian Advocate*, April 5, 1884.

as a measure of self-preservation. Then it logically follows that there should be the largest facilities where there is the greatest need." The *Advocate* deplored the fact that a partisan spirit should thus retard the development of public schools.[1]

As the decade of the Eighties passed the increasing friendliness to the schools was reflected often in suggestions that were made for better facilities. The *Southern Christian Advocate* and other journals of the Connection frequently stressed the need for improvement as regards teachers' salaries, buildings and equipment, and the length of the school term. In an editorial headed "A Few Words About Our Public Schools," the *Southern* pointed out in March 1885 that conditions in the public schools of South Carolina were bad in many respects, and asked the question: "What are you going to do about it?" "If this article doesn't set our people to thinking," declared the editor, "it is not because it doesn't give them something to think about."[2] During the decade Atticus G. Haygood became one of the outstanding champions of the public schools in the South. He constantly sought to promote their interests through public addresses and writings. In a commencement address delivered at Emory College in 1888, Dr. Haygood stressed the advantages of a well appointed system of public schools and pointed out the folly of half-way measures for their support. Referring to the situation in Georgia, he said: "We must provide better public schools. If Texas has a good public school for nine months and Georgia a poor one for three months, the home-hunter will go to Texas. Our attitude toward the public school is irrational. We do just enough to obstruct private enterprise, but not enough to have good schools. It is penny-wise and pound foolish."[3] The following year Haygood contributed a discerning article to *Harper's Magazine*, in which he emphasized the appalling amount of illiteracy in the Southern States and ably presented the needs of the public schools.[4] The Reverend Warren A. Candler, who succeeded Haygood as presi-

[1] *New Orleans Christian Advocate*, April 3, 1884.

[2] *Southern Christian Advocate*, March 18, 1885.

[3] *Cf. New Orleans Christian Advocate*, July 12, 1888.

[4] *Cf.* Haygood, Atticus G., "The South and the School Problem", *Harper's New Monthly Magazine*, Vol. LXXIX (July, 1889), pp. 225-231.

dent of Emory College, also did much to bring before the people the needs of elementary public education.

What was probably the most notable single influence exerted by Southern Methodism upon the development of the public school system resulted from an agitation carried on in the two Georgia Conferences during the late Eighties and the early Nineties. This movement was led by the *Wesleyan Christian Advocate,* the official organ of the two Conferences. Throughout that time Dr. Weyman H. Potter, the liberal and progressive editor of the *Advocate,* was untiring in his efforts to encourage free popular education. He awakened a profound interest in the need for good public schools in Georgia by constantly forcing upon the attention of the people the very large amount of illiteracy in the State. Upon one occasion he declared that "ignorance in Georgia is not an open sore; it is a bone-felon, which will never be cured until split to the bone, and the bone scraped."[1] The *Wesleyan* emphasized the fact that opposition to the public school system had now come to be tantamount to opposition to all education for the masses. In its issue of March 20, 1889, it said: "For some years after the war it was an open question whether we should try to revive the voluntary neighborhood schools somewhat as they existed before the War in the South, or whether we should adopt the public free school system supported by the State for elementary education. The ground was well fought over and the State system of public schools was adopted. For some years now there has been in Georgia and other States but one practicable way to give the masses an elementary education. . . . For some years past, then, opposition to the State public schools has been practically the equivalent of opposition to the elementary education of the masses."

Dr. Potter stirred up a remarkable activity in the Georgia Conferences when he charged that there was in his own Church a party which opposed education. In March 1889 he said: "Methodism, which from the beginning has been the Church of the people and has stood for uplifting the masses, for the betterment of the condition of the poor, for the enlightenment of the ignorant and for the salvation of all classes has, since the War, in

---

[1]*Cf. Wesleyan Christian Advocate,* March 6, 1889.

these Southern States, found itself water-logged in a sea of ignorance. Any man who attempts to get out of the trough of this muddy sea and steer his Church towards a goodly land finds himself splashed in the face by the raging waves of opposition. It was not so before the War; it is so now." This opposition to education, he explained, had not been "much concerned about whether it is secular or religious. . . . It is opposition to being disturbed on the subject at all, especially in its opposition to paying out money or making any sacrifices for the betterment of mankind of which other peoples' children may get a part. It is in opposition to 'taxing one man,' whether by State law or Christian impulse, 'to educate another man's children.' " "What concerns us most," he said, "is that this opposition is made in the name of Christian religion. They plead the preference for 'piety;' they clamor for 'more religion;' they are intensely in earnest for the salvation of souls." Referring to a correspondent, who had recently expressed a desire for the time "when there shall not be so much said about education and much more about winning souls for Christ," he declared: "The letter perplexes us. What kind of religion does he wish us to write about and preach about. He wants the people to turn their feet to the testimony of the Lord. He certainly knows two facts: There are hundreds of thousands of persons in Georgia that can't read (?). No man can read (or turn his feet to) the testimony of the Lord until he learns to read."[1]

"We never thought of a party opposed to education in any form for everybody," Dr. Potter explained in a subsequent article. "But our editorial concerned education as we have it in Georgia, public school education for all classes, white and black, and college education for such as may acquire it for the good of the Church and State. To this education there is opposition both of the outspoken and the silent, sulky, let-alone sort." "Opposition to a righteous cause struggling for recognition among men is often most effectively expressed by silence."[2] Although acknowledging that the party which opposed education was not a controlling one and that it was declining, Potter asserted that it had

[1]*Ibid.*, March 13, 1889.
[2]*Ibid.*, March 20, 1889.

yet been so potent that no Southern religious journal had dared
"to champion the cause of the education of the masses and stand
persistently to its colors." "Men, leaders among men, newspapers, set for the defense of the truth and pledged to the
advancement of the kingdom have canvassed all social, civil, and
financial conditions to find excuses for this opposition while
making only sporadic efforts to overcome it." "We do not claim
to be exceptions to this statement to any praiseworthy degree," he
said, "but we do claim, as General Hood said at Marietta during
the famous retreat, to have 'felt of the enemy until they thumped
solid.' We are sure the line of battle in the woods we are shelling
in [sic] a dense one."[1]

In an editorial on "Our Educational Platform," in its issue of
March 27, 1889, the *Wesleyan* set forth a full program for the
State. This platform called for "good elementary schools for all
children of school age for nine months in the year (this implies
good school houses) supported by the State, agreeably to the
present constitution of Georgia." It specified "academies for
academic instruction in every eligible community, supported by
the united, voluntary effort of the people of the community or by
county taxation, as in Bibb County, this State." In the field of
higher education it advocated "denominational colleges, male and
female, well endowed by the denominations to which they belong,
and embracing as many industrial, technological and professional
schools as their endowment will permit." And above these there
was to be "a State University with all the name implies." When
the Georgia legislature showed a disposition to improve the school
system of the State, the *Wesleyan* sought in every way to encourage it. The editor urged the adoption of legislation which
would enable the State to pay its teachers at least quarterly. The
paper characterized as "hardly less than iniquitous" the existing
law, under which teachers were forced to suffer a discount on
their salaries.[2]

Largely as a result of the interest awakened by the *Wesleyan*,
the members of the Georgia Conferences became very active in
promoting the development of the public schools. In 1888 both

---

[1] *Ibid.*, March 13, 1889.
[2] *Cf. ibid.*, July 17, 1889; *ibid.*, July 31, 1889.

Conferences formally committed themselves to the cause. Both adopted resolutions petitioning the legislature to lengthen the school term and to levy further taxes for the support of the schools. The significant character of such action upon the part of representative bodies of the Methodist Episcopal Church, South, was revealed in an amusing way in the unconscious irony of the comments of a secular journal. Referring to the resolution favoring increased appropriations for public schools adopted by the North Georgia Conference, the Atlanta *Constitution* said: "The reproach of the Northern Methodist Church—from which the Southern Methodist Church has kept singularly free—is that it is a political as well as a religious body. Let us see that we do not fall into the ways against which we have cried out so long and so lustily. We trust that we shall never again see a Methodist Conference pass a resolution urging the Legislature to take one course or another on a secular issue!"[1]

But the complacency with which the North Georgia Conference reviewed its record the following year made it obvious that Georgia Methodists were no longer content with so passive a rôle. Asserting that the State had arrived at an educational awakening such as it had never before experienced, that body said: "While the ministers of a great Church have hardly time for self congratulations, the members of the North Georgia Conference will not be blamed if they recall with pleasure and self-approval the fact that to their efforts this tremenduous awakening is largely due."[2] And there can be little doubt that the subsequent extension of the school term from three to five months and other improvements made in the Georgia school system at that period came largely as a result of the advanced position of the *Wesleyan Christian Advocate* and the representative bodies of the Methodist Episcopal Church, South.

A similar interest was stirring Methodist Conferences to action in other parts of the South. Characteristic of the attitude taken by these bodies was that expressed by the Louisiana Conference in 1892. Declaring that the common schools were now the accepted

---

[1] *Cf.* Atlanta *Constitution,* quoted in *Wesleyan Christian Advocate,* December 25, 1888.
[2] *Cf. Minutes of North Georgia Conference,* 1891, p. 22.

system, it said: "It behooves us, therefore, to study carefully the system in its practical operation; to seek in every legitimate way to increase its merits and to reduce, and if possible, to eliminate its objectionable features, where such are found. Especially should we, as Christians and upright citizens, watch carefully lest teachers of immoral character, or otherwise unfitted for so responsible a position, be employed in these schools, reporting all such cases to the school authorities of the State."[1]

Apart from the encouragement given in such ways, the denomination did much through its own example to promote the elevation of the standards of preparatory education. The Church sought continually to establish advanced and definite standards for its schools and to furnish thorough and exact instruction in them. To this end a central Board of Education of the Methodist Episcopal Church, South, was created by the General Conference of 1894. Four years later the Conference provided for the appointment of a Commission of Education, to consist of a group of practical educators, whose duty it would be to aid the Board in properly relating the schools of the Connection and in other ways to protect the educational standards of the Church.[2] It will be seen that the men connected with the denomination's institutions of higher learning did much to foster the development of adequate secular preparatory schools in the section.

Thus the Methodist Episcopal Church, South, contributed much to the development of primary and secondary education in the South both through its own endeavors in the field and through the encouragement it gave to secular and public schools. At a time when the State was unable to perform the function the Church rendered an important public service by providing sound instruction for many who would otherwise have been unable to obtain it. The denomination undertook to maintain standards in its schools which inevitably reacted favorably upon those of the other institutions of the section. The spokesmen of the Church sought in many ways to foster the growth of adequate secular and public schools.

---

[1]Cf. *Journal of General Conference*, 1894, pp. 196-198.
[2]*Journal of General Conference*, 1898, pp. 67-68.

CHAPTER VIII

CONTRIBUTIONS TO HIGHER EDUCATION AND LIBERAL THOUGHT

THE achievement of the Southern Methodists in the field of higher education prior to the Civil War has been discussed in connection with the account of their activities in promoting primary and secondary education.

The Methodist institutions of higher learning suffered hardly less from the War than the lower schools. Practically all the colleges for men were forced to close their doors before the return of peace. Wofford College had been able to continue in operation only because its president and faculty had "refused to surrender to want."[1] College buildings had been occupied as Confederate hospitals, appropriated for military purposes by the Federal forces, or allowed to deteriorate while standing abandoned. Others had been accidentally burned, or destroyed at the command of Federal officers. Faculties and student bodies had been disrupted and scattered and their numbers decimated in battle. Endowments, where they had not been entirely swept away, had shrunk to insignificant proportions.

In some instances college properties were now sacrificed at prices far below their original cost and value, to defray debts which had been contracted during the struggle. In Alabama the Church actually gave to the State two colleges which its communicants found themselves unable to support.[2] In other cases economic need forced trustees to rent school buildings for use as hotels and for other purposes. The Georgia Wesleyan College at Macon managed to keep its doors open only by providing board for a number of residents of the city who for reasons of economy and mutual protection had resorted thither.[3] The premises of Ran-

---

[1] Simkins and Woody, op. cit., p. 420.

[2] Rivers, R. H., The Life of Robert Paine, D. D., Bishop of the Methodist Episcopal Church, South (Nashville, 1884), p. 268.

[3] Among these persons were the poet, Sidney Lanier and his father, and sister. Sidney's grandfather, Sterling Lanier, who came of a wealthy Virginian planter family, was an ardent Methodist and a liberal supporter of Methodist institutions. He sent his daughters to be educated at the Wesleyan Female College at Macon and his son, Robert S. Lanier, Sidney's father, was among the

dolph-Macon College were occupied by Federal military authorities for some months after the peace, its main building serving as a headquarters for officials of the Freedmen's Bureau, and its rooms thronged with "wards of the nation."[1]

It was apparent also that the fortunes of many schools had been adversely affected by the changing relation of the population to the seats of such institutions. The destruction of railroads had left some of the colleges in inaccessible positions; Randolph-Macon was now a day's journey from any railroad.[2] Colleges which had been located contiguous to rich planting areas, their sites having been determined by the generosity of the general population, now saw those who had been their patrons and benefactors seeking homes in other regions. Despite the urgent necessity for removal in such instances, local interests generally sought to block all efforts of the kind. In 1868 President Thomas Carter Johnson of Randolph-Macon College declared to its trustees that unless the institution were quickly removed to a more favorable location it would be forced to close its doors again.[3]

As was the case with regard to preparatory training, the condition of Southern education as a whole added greatly to the obligations devolving upon the Methodist institutions of higher learning. The fortunes of the State colleges and universities were at their lowest ebb. They, too, had suffered much from the ravages of war, and, like the Methodist Colleges, most of them had suspended instruction before peace came. Their buildings had been occupied in turn by Confederate and by Union troops, and their equipment badly damaged or destroyed. One institution, the University of Alabama, had been reduced to ashes by the order of General J. H. Wilson of the Federal army in April 1865.[4]

When the Alabama University sought in October 1865 to reopen its doors in make-shift buildings, and with a faculty consisting of its president and two other teachers, only one student pre-

---

earliest graduates of the Methodist Randolph-Macon College in Virginia. Robert Lanier became a Presbyterian subsequent to his marriage to a young woman of that faith. Cf. Starke, Aubrey Harrison, *Sidney Lanier* (Chapel Hill, 1933), *passim*.

[1]Irby, *op. cit.*, p. 160.
[2]Du Bose, *op. cit.*, p. 480.
[3]Irby, *op. cit.*, p. 172.
[4]Clark, Willis G., *History of Education in Alabama* (Washington, 1889), pp. 97-98.

DAVID C. KELLEY

sented himself for matriculation. The institution was not thrown open to students again until April 1869.[1] Only four youths enrolled when the University of Louisiana resumed operations in October 1865, and the maximum attendance for the year was thirty-five. In 1869 the entire institution was destroyed by fire, and conditions necessitated a new location before it could again offer instruction.[2] The change from presidential to Congressional reconstruction in 1867 came before the administration of the State schools was perfected, and resulted in a further reorganization of their executive boards and their faculties. Thus the beginnings which had been made were, in most instances, lost. New men without broad scholarship or recognized administrative abilities were now given the direction of higher learning. Political bias was evinced in everything that was done. State universities were dominated by zealous adherents of a political party which had made itself obnoxious to the great mass of Southern whites. The former friends and supporters of these institutions were alienated and their patronage was withdrawn. Under the administration of a Republican head, attendance at the University of North Carolina at no time exceeded seventy-five.[3] In January 1871 there were only twenty-one students enrolled at the University of Alabama, and the State Superintendent of Public Instruction reported that the school was in a deplorable condition.[4]

Attempts made by the governing boards to introduce Negro students into the universities proved especially disastrous to their recovery. The Carpet-bag legislature of Louisiana withdrew appropriations for the support of the university at Baton Rouge in an effort to coerce that institution into admitting colored students. As a result the school was closed from 1872 to 1877.[5] Attendance at the North Carolina University declined rapidly when Northern men who had previously been connected with schools for Negroes were put on its faculty. All exercises were discontinued in 1870

[1]*Ibid.*, p. 98. In 1874 the enrollment was still only seventy.
[2]Fay, Edwin Whitfield, *The History of Education in Louisiana* (Washington, 1898), pp. 82-83.
[3]Smith, Charles Lee, *The History of Education in North Carolina* (Washington, 1888), p. 85.
[4]Clark, *op. cit.*, p. 101.
[5]Fay, *op. cit.*, p. 83.

and the University remained closed until 1875.[1] When the University of South Carolina was thrown open to the blacks in 1873, the last member of its *ante-bellum* faculty resigned, and white students immediately left. All operations suspended from 1877 to 1880, at which time the institution was reopened and conducted for two years as a College of Agriculture and the Mechanic Arts.[2]

The restoration of native white rule in the South toward the end of the Seventies marked a further reorganization of State educational enterprises, new heads and faculties being chosen in most cases. But the prestige of these institutions had so declined that it was frequently difficult to secure competent men to take charge of them, and their presidencies sometimes went begging. Moreover the general poverty of the times, together with the jealousy of the Church schools, prevented an adequate legislative support of the State institutions, now without their endowments and deficient in library facilities and experimental apparatus. The lowering of academic standards at such centers of learning was greatly aggravated by the fact that most of the old academies had ceased to exist, and, as yet, no adequate system of preparatory schools had risen to take their place. The attempt to remedy the deficiences in the preparation of their students inevitably diverted the colleges from their legitimate functions.

Impressed by the urgent needs in the field of higher education, the Methodist Episcopal Church, South, promptly took action to revive and reinvigorate its institutions of higher learning. One after another its colleges reopened their doors during 1865 and 1866, and heroic efforts were made to impart new life to those which, despite the perilous times, had managed to maintain a precarious existence. In the Pastoral Address delivered in the General Conference of 1866 the bishops asserted the great importance of resuming at once the educational activities of the Connection, and they urged especially that everything "in our power should be done to revive as speedily as possible" its colleges

[1]Smith, *op. cit.*, p. 85.
[2]Meriwether, Colyer, *History of Higher Education in South Carolina* (Washington, 1889), p. 185.

for men.[1] The New Orleans Conference, declaring in response to the Episcopal Address that the advancement of letters had been thrown back a whole generation by the late convulsion, expressed a determination to awaken the entire Connection to a realization of the necessity for the "intellectual cultivation of the rising generation within the range of our influence." Pointing out the unusual demands of a period when the people were entering upon a new era "with conscious life and with quickened energies," it said: "It behooves us, therefore, in the capacity in which we are now assembled, to give them no indistinct utterance of our convictions, and to invoke them to fulfil the errand of the Church, in this department of her usefulness." Declaring that education was second only to the Gospel as a means of elevating men, it asserted that it would be suicidal for any Church to neglect this agency at such a time. "The Church must keep pace with the intellectual movement of society; nay, she must lead the van, or by an inexorable law, the momentum of accelerated current will, in coming years, sweep from her altars myriads of worshippers."

The Conference saw an additional reason for stressing the educational functions of the Church in the growing skepticism of the popular mind. It said: "Free as the Southern people have hitherto been from the infection, we cannot hope to avoid it much longer. . . . And as error has taken the field in the guise of science and literature, the Church must fortify herself with weapons drawn from the same armory." In conclusion, it sought "to discourage the unnecessary multiplication of institutions of learning for the future, and to insist upon the ample support and patronage of such as we already have; persuaded that the cause of sound learning can be better secured by increasing the number of students at given centers, and by more thoroughly endowing schools of every grade."[2]

With the exception of three or four which had been established but a short time before the War, all of the colleges of the Church which had been in operation in 1860 managed to open their doors again before the end of 1866. Despite the loss of their endow-

---

[1] *Cf. Journal of General Conference,* 1866, p. 19.
[2] *Journal of General Conference,* 1866, pp. 131-137.

ments and the destruction of their equipment, and although maintained in the face of grave financial difficulties, the Methodist colleges were, for perhaps a decade, able to furnish the most ample facilities for higher education that could be obtained in a number of the Southern States. Throughout the Reconstruction period they prepared for the States a number of educated leaders who but for their efforts would have been wanting. While the emphasis on religious teachings was too extensive and the curriculum too narrow according to present standards, and while the library and laboratory facilities were often very meager, the faculties brought to their work gifts of personality and a seriousness and conscientiousness of purpose that did much to compensate for such deficiencies, and which enabled them to leave a lasting impression upon the students of that generation.[1]

Throughout the years of political upheaval the Methodist institutions enjoyed a stability which it was impossible for State schools to attain at the time. For one thing, presidents and faculty members, often drawn largely from the ministry, served with a devotion which kept them at their work in the face of hardships and half-pay, even when tempted with more lucrative and less arduous work elsewhere. The spirit manifested by many of these men is suggested in the remarks made by the North Georgia Conference in 1887 with regard to Emory College; "The members of the faculty have for years faithfully and silently done their work. They have attended our District and Annual Conferences, and reported the conditions of the college, as to patronage, etc. Some facts, however, they have not made known. They have not told us that they were living on half-pay, and some years less than half-pay. They have not told us that they were struggling with heavy hearts to do a most important work of the Church without compensation enough to keep them out of debt. . . . Nearly half of the students have been beneficiaries."[2]

The denominational colleges were, moreover, spared the blighting effects of subordination to political control, and of the agitation for the introduction of Negro students. Because of these advantages, the Methodist schools naturally drew a considerable

[1]Cf. Simkins and Woody, op. cit., pp. 420-421.
[2]Minutes of North Georgia Conference, 1887, p. 16.

patronage which under normal conditions would have been enjoyed by the State colleges. During the darkest days, when the State universities in North Carolina, South Carolina, Alabama, and Louisiana were forced to close their doors, Methodist colleges in those States continued in operation, and, in general, reported increasing enrolments. In 1870, some months after the University of North Carolina had been closed, Trinity College boasted of an enrolment of over two hundred students.[1] Referring to Trinity at that time, Atticus G. Haygood declared that it "is deeply enshrined in the hearts, not only of the Methodists, but of the people of this section. Chapel Hill has fallen into the hands of the Phillistines, and they have dealt with it according to their custom. . . . Trinity College is now the leading educational institution of the State. Its managers have deserved well of the Church and of the Country. . . . it has a regular faculty whose salaries are regularly paid, and it is not in debt, and has educated a large number gratuitously."[2]

Similar grounds of vantage were occupied in South Carolina and Georgia by Wofford College and Emory College respectively. As one of the few colleges in the South which continued in operation throughout the entire period of civil war and reconstruction, Wofford became one of the most important educational influences of the day. Having referred to the prostrate condition of the State institution at Columbia, an editor of the *Southern Christian Advocate* said in 1873: "The extremity of the Country is the opportunity of the Church. The Church which can offer the highest bid in the opportunity for liberal culture and the development of character which it can present, is to be the principal agency in educating the mind and molding the character of the coming generation, if not the future generations of the State. I do not think I am blind to the advantages offered by our other colleges when I state with the emphasis inspired by the great certainty of the truth of the opinion, that Wofford College, whether viewed in reference to her present *status*, or in reference to her prestige of accomplished success, occupies the vantage

---

[1] Smith, *History of Education in North Carolina*, pp. 84-85; Raper, Charles Lee, *The Church and Private Schools of North Carolina* (Greensboro, 1889), p. 182.

[2] Letter of A. G. Haygood in Nashville *Christian Advocate*, July 8, 1871.

ground of the educational enterprises of South Carolina."[1] Emory College was able to throw open its doors and exert a wide influence when the legislature of Georgia in 1866 undertook to provide at that institution for the education of youths who had been disabled in the Confederate service.[2]

Inspired by the larger opportunities presented to them, the interest of Southern Methodists in the promotion of higher education grew until it assumed the character and proportions of a renaissance. It soon found expression in an agitation for concentration and systematization in the educational work of the Church. This agitation culminated in a movement for a great central university for Southern Methodism such as had been conceived during the period preceding the War. Inseparably bound up with this movement, and indeed a part of it, was the demand for a more adequately trained ministry for the Church.

As has been mentioned, there had arisen even during *ante-bellum* days a demand for "more culture in the pulpit." Recognizing this need, the bishops, in the Pastoral Address of 1866, had urged upon the Church the propriety and necessity of taking immediate steps to establish a theological institute. "That we should make some proper arrangement for the more thorough training of our young men before they are received into the Conferences and sent forth to minister in the Church of Christ appears to us so obvious as to need no argument to prove it," said the bishops. "It behooves us to take this matter into serious and immediate consideration, and secure to the Church the invaluable advantages the provision we suggest can only supply."[3] The New Orleans Conference, at the same time that it cautioned the Church against a multiplication of its educational work, commended the bishops' suggestion. Referring to their proposal for a Southern Methodist theological school, it said: "To this point, the convictions of preachers and people, with various alternations and conflicts of opinions, have been tending for years. . . . The spectacle constantly presenting itself to us is the disparity between the intellectual acquisition of our young ministers and the people they are sent to serve: a state of things produced by the unequal

---

[1]Letter of Samuel A. Weber in Nashville *Christian Advocate*, July 19, 1873.
[2]Smith, *Life of Pierce*, p. 496.
[3]*Cf.* Pastoral Address in *Journal of General Conference*, 1866, pp. 19-20.

advantages enjoyed by the larger portion of the youth of the country and those who usually offer themselves for the ministry." The Conference however expressed the opinion that the attempt to carry through such an enterprise would be impracticable under existing conditions, and declared itself unwilling to risk the delay which such an attempt might involve. Instead of authorizing the immediate founding of a theological school, therefore, it provided that "Biblical Schools" should be maintained in connection with certain of the colleges of the denomination until it should be deemed feasible to establish such an institution.[1] This decision naturally found favor with a group of thoroughly conservative men in the Church, of which Bishop Pierce generally assumed the leadership. These men feared that a formal theological training might both imperil the itineracy and other essential features of the Methodist economy and deaden the evangelical ardor of the Church. Although evidence of the fact does not appear in the records, it is probable that this sentiment played a not inconsiderable part in determining the action of the Conference in the matter.

But the champions of an adequately equipped theological institute did not accept the decision of the New Orleans Conference as a final defeat of their plans. During the next four years they agitated the question with great persistency and enthusiasm. The matter was kept alive by constant discussions in the columns of the Church papers. An able spokesman for the cause was soon found in the person of the then youthful David C. Kelley, whose progressive views and subsequent career were to make him one of the most interesting figures in the history of Southern Methodism. Although still in his early thirties, Kelley had already impressed himself upon the Connection as being one of its most brilliant and original preachers. During June 1867 he contributed a series of articles to the Nashville *Advocate*, in which he urged upon the Church the value of a trained ministry and insisted that it must develop one which would be "capacitated for accurate thinking."[2]

As the time for the General Conference of 1870 drew near

---

[1] *Journal of General Conference*, 1866, p. 136.
[2] *Cf.* Nashville *Christian Advocate*, June 27, 1867.

those who advocated the establishment of a theological school redoubled their efforts to create a favorable sentiment in the Connection. During the latter part of 1869 Bishop McTyeire, a foremost champion of a thoroughly educated ministry, together with Dr. Thomas O. Summers of the Nashville *Advocate,* prevailed upon Landon Cabell Garland, then a professor at the University of Mississippi, to take up his pen in the cause. Garland, who at that time had already filled the presidency of Randolph-Macon College and that of the University of Alabama, and who, at one time or another during his career as an educator, was offered a chair or the presidency in perhaps as many as a dozen colleges or universities, commanded a wide hearing throughout the South. In a series of six articles published in the Nashville *Advocate,* covering the whole question, he proposed that a central theological institute for Southern Methodism be established at Nashville.

In his first article Dr. Garland emphasized the unwisdom of continuing to build up an ignorant ministry, and pointed out that the changed relation of Methodism to Southern society made it incumbent upon the Church to furnish a ministry of the highest type. He felt that "It was never a sound policy to admit into the ministry men grossly ignorant, upon the plea that there were multitudes of ignorant people to be served, and that unto such they might be sent." The need for an educated ministry was proportionate to the amount of ignorance in the Connection. Moreover, the Church through its educational activities had created a demand for a learned ministry which it would be folly to ignore.[1] In his second paper Garland argued the necessity for enlightened Biblical criticism and for the study of systematic theology. He stressed the fact that an adequate knowledge of the language and authorship of the Scriptures was indispensable to intelligent preaching. Unless the expounder were able to read the text in the original his thoughts must come to him "at the hazard of dilution, or even of perversion, growing out of the preconceived opinions and prejudices of the translator."[2] The third and fourth articles were devoted to an exposition of the

---

[1] *Ibid.,* October 9, 1869.
[2] *Ibid.,* October 16, 1869.

direct and collateral advantages that were to be derived from a specialized theological training.[1]

The last two papers undertook to show the inadequacy of the system of examination by Annual Conferences as a test of previous education, and the insufficiency of the work in the Biblical Schools in the several colleges. After having asserted that the advocates of a formal theological training would by no means make attendance at the proposed Institute a condition of admission to the Annual Conferences, the writer sought to disarm those who feared the effect of a formal training upon the economy and the fervor of the Church. He said: "To some it looks like 'manufacturing' preachers. If by this is meant that we are usurping the functions of the Holy Ghost, and calling men into the ministry, we repel the charge, by receiving such only as openly profess to have received the Spirit's call." The Church would merely be holding back those who were called to make them ready for greater usefulness. Such a training, he argued, would in itself neither make ministers abstract and metaphysical nor formal and cold. "If by *formal,* exactness of statement and regularity of method in discourse be meant, these are qualities we seek to impart. But if stiffness in manner, if the want of ease and grace in public speaking be meant, these are defects we seek to remove."[2]

The progressive forces exerted all their influence to secure a great central theological school for the Church during the General Conference of 1870. A majority of the committee appointed to consider the matter reported strongly in favor of such an institution, stressing the inadequacies of the theological departments in the colleges. Local interests, representing the Biblical Schools, and supported by the most conservative groups in the Church, were nevertheless able to prevent a realization of the project. The minority members presented a report which demonstrated clearly their unfriendliness to the proposed institution. After discussing the expediency of the undertaking, the report declared: "The history of such institutions has little that is favorable to Methodism, and much that is adverse. They have been the

---

[1] *Ibid.,* October 23, 1869; *ibid.,* October 30, 1869.
[2] *Ibid.,* November 6, 1869; *ibid.,* November 13, 1869.

fruitful source of heresies innumerable, of a manner of preaching not generally desirable and rarely effectual among us, and of much of that formalism that never favors experiential religion. Methodism in earnest is the best form of religion, and the best religion, we think. . . . We would deprecate anything that in the least tends to diminish that zeal and spirituality that have done so much toward making the kingdoms of this world the kingdoms of our Lord and his Christ."[1] The report emphasized the poverty of the times and the wants of the colleges already in existence. Under the plea that the undertaking was inexpedient for the time being, and that no action should be taken until the Biblical Schools should have had an opportunity of laying their first fruits before the bishops, the minority succeeded in carrying the General Conference with it.

Although thus balked again in their plans, the advocates of a more thorough theological training did not for a moment falter in their purpose. While desirous of conciliating opposition, they nevertheless moved straight ahead in their course. They took great pains to expose at once the faulty logic of those who argued against the establishment of a theological school and the effects such logic would have upon the Church. Referring to the report which had been drawn up by the minority members, Landon Cabell Garland wrote: "Now the logic of the Report would sweep away the theological schools from the colleges. But this is not what its authors wanted. There are supposed local benefits accruing from them which must be protected from their logic. But how have they sought to protect them?" This had been done, he said, by "asserting or denying, according to the exigencies of the argument, that theology is taught in those college schools." Thus the Church had been tied down to a system which could "never reach a respectable standard." In the Biblical Schools the instruction had generally been given "by persons who have not made theological study a specialty." So long as this continued the Church could "take no prominent part in the great debates between truth and error that are going on upon the literary and scientific arenas of the age." There would be no adequate facilities for research and no high standards of learning would

---

[1] *Cf. Journal of General Conference*, 1870, pp. 242-243.

be possible. "We cannot even sustain a Quarterly. With an exception or two, our press is not furnishing a single production out of the range of local history or biography, which will live in the next generation." And if this did not soon cease to be true the Church must lose "position among our sister Churches, and respectability with the world."[1]

Those who favored a formal theological training now determined to achieve their end independently of the General Conference, and in connection with the movement which had already been inaugurated to provide for Southern Methodism "a great university of the highest grade, and with the most ample endowment."[2] This movement, already referred to, originated within but two or three years after the close of the War. Indeed, the colleges of the denomination had hardly been put in operation again before there were evidences of such a conception taking form in the mind of the Connection. As early as June 1867, one who styled himself "Amicus" contributed a series of articles to the Nashville *Advocate*, in which he proposed that the Church build up a strong centrally located college, which should have numerous "feeders" in a system of grammar schools or academies that would extend to all parts of the Connection.[3] In January 1869 another correspondent of the Nashville journal, writing from Florence, Alabama, expressed the opinion that the Church ought to create "*a great Central University*—all the chairs filled with the ablest men of the Church: an Institution whose diploma would be as much coveted as that of Yale, or Harvard, or the Virginia University." The writer suggested that the friends of Church education in all the Southwestern Conferences combine their resources to make of Florence Wesleyan University such an institution.[4] A condition distinctly favorable to the establishment

---

[1] Communication of Landon Cabell Garland in *Daily Christian Advocate*, May 25, 1870. "If you charge them with teaching theology, a thing they have denounced," he said, "they deny it. In that case they teach Religion and not Theology. If you tell them that in not teaching Theology they are not meeting the expectation of the Church, they will tell you they are meeting it to admiration, that they omit nothing that would be taught in a complete theological school, and that they teach it, without tendencies to heresy, without damage to the style of preaching."

[2] *Cf.* letter of L. C. Garland in Nashville *Christian Advocate*, May 24, 1890.

[3] Letter of "Amicus" in Nashville *Christian Advocate*, June 27, 1867.

[4] Letter of W. B. Wood in Nashville *Christian Advocate*, January 9, 1869.

of such a central denominational university, and which inspired much enthusiasm in the region concerned, was the fact that the War had left a large central territory in Alabama, Mississippi, Louisiana, and Arkansas without a Methodist college.[1]

That the project was taking definite form in the popular mind of the Connection was evidenced by two communications from the pen of one calling himself "Progress," which appeared in Nashville *Advocate* just prior to the General Conference of 1870. Having praised the valiant efforts of the Church colleges already existing, the writer pointed out that these schools were, nevertheless, unable "to concentrate an intellectual force commensurate with our necessities as a great denomination of Christians." He urged the need for specialization on the part of instructors, and of high salaries for experts. Referring to the methods employed in the ordinary institutions of the Connection, he said: "A professorship of 'Natural Science' is simply monstrous, unless the phrase be used in the most elementary sense, in which case it may very properly be employed to denote a useful department in an institution that proposes to teach only the elements. But if it is proposed to go to the bottom and become original thinkers, to take rank with the great schools of Europe and the oldest ones of this country, the department of 'Natural Science' must be divided, and subdivided, into numerous independent chairs, not less than eight in number; and sixteen would be better. Of course, no one of our Methodist colleges, as at present organized, is prepared to assume this high position of leadership in the world's grand progress of scientific discovery and development. We do but take the crumbs that fall from the tables of the learned and great of other climes, and dispense them to our boys in such scant measure as time and means will allow. This, as I have already said, is a useful and necessary service." Nevertheless, the writer thought, if "it is our wish, as a denomination, to advance in influence and power; if we would convert the world to Methodism, which we believe to be 'Christianity in earnest,' we must not depend upon those who oppose and revile us, to educate our sons. We must not be content with mere Conference colleges, in which five or six good men teach a good school, and

---

[1] *Ibid.*

struggle manfully to enlarge their sphere of usefulness and elevate
the standard of learning but struggle against overwhelming odds.
If we are thus content, we may be sure that the more capacious
and aspiring of our youth will leave us for other halls of learning,
and our Church, to this extent, will lose her prestige and
authority."[1]

In his second letter the writer discussed the need for adequate
instruction in the learned professions. He said: "All the candidates for the learned professions, as well as those who wish to
distinguish themselves in the walks of science and literature, must
go abroad. Not a physician can be educated under Methodist
auspices, not a lawyer, nor a theologian, nor a *savant*. The men
who fashion society and govern the State must acquire their
professional lore and skill in places where Methodism is per-
chance a by-word and reproach. Our colleges are too poor to do
so much. . . . The deliverances of such an institution upon subjects
scientific and theological, involving profound thought and erudi-
tion, would possess an authority which would tend greatly to
conserve the stability of our doctrines, and enhance our respectability before the world." He felt that the proposed university
ought to command the "total financial power of the Church."[2]

No sooner had the scheme for founding a theological institute
been defeated in the General Conference of 1870 than those who
had been advocating a formal ministerial training decided to
achieve their purpose by joining forces with the movement for
the founding of a great central university. They now proposed
to secure the incorporation of a theological school as one of
departments of the projected institution. Indeed, as was to have
been expected, a number of the same men had been among the
leading spirits in both movements from the start. The matter
was thoroughly discussed in the Conference and toward the end
of its sessions the atmosphere became "rife with the conception
of a great university, having as one of its departments a thoroughly organized theological school." A group of those most interested
met informally from time to time to discuss the matter. Outstanding among these men were Bishops Holland N. McTyeire

---

[1]Letter of "Progress" in Nashville *Christian Advocate,* April 16, 1870.
[2]Letter of "Progress" in Nashville *Christian Advocate,* April 23, 1870.

and Robert Paine, Dr. A. L. P. Green, Dr. R. A. Young, and Landon Cabell Garland. Finally, before separating, it was agreed that the question should be agitated "throughout the Connection, through the press and by public addresses, and that the Conferences should be invited to send delegates to a convention for the consideration of the matter."[1]

The step which led directly to a realization of these plans was taken presently by Dr. David C. Kelley, who, although not a member of the General Conference of 1870, had for some time been maturing plans of a similar nature. The particular impetus for Dr. Kelley's action was furnished by an editorial and two letters which appeared in the *Western Methodist* of Memphis during September and October 1871. These articles had been written in accordance with the agreement made at the General Conference, and with special regard to the influence they might exert upon the Tennessee Conference then about to convene. Copies of the three issues in which the editorial and letters had appeared, all marked, were sent by the editor, W. C. Johnson, during the sessions of the Conference at Lebanon the latter part of October, to those members whom he believed would be interested. The editorial in question proposed that the Tennessee, the North Alabama, the Memphis, and the North Mississippi Conferences unite in establishing a thoroughly equipped university for the Connection.[2]

Under the immediate inspiration of this editorial, Dr. Kelley secured the adoption by the Tennessee Conference of a resolution calling upon the presiding bishop to appoint a committee which would confer with the Memphis, the North Alabama, the North Mississippi, and "any other conference likely to coöperate with us in reference to the establishment and endowment of a Methodist university of high grade and large endowment."[3] This committee induced nine Annual Conferences to appoint delegates to meet in an educational convention to be held in Memphis in

---

[1]Letter of Landon Cabell Garland in Nashville *Christian Advocate*, May 24, 1890.

[2]*Cf.* letter of W. C. Johnson in Nashville *Christian Advocate*, October 18, 1890; *cf.* letter of L. C. Garland in Nashville *Christian Advocate*, May 24, 1890.

[3]*Cf.* Merriam, *op. cit.*, p. 110.

January 1872. The Memphis Convention was in session for four days, from January 24 to January 28, 1872, and it comprised delegates from the Little Rock, the White River, the Memphis, the Alabama, the North Alabama, the Mississippi, the North Mississippi, the Louisiana, and the Tennessee Conferences, representing the Methodist communicants of Alabama, Mississippi, Louisiana, Arkansas, and of middle and west Tennessee.[1]

Bishops McTyeire and Paine presided over the deliberations of the Convention, and Dr. A. L. P. Green, who had never really relinquished the idea of a great Southern Methodist university, appeared with a copy of the charter of the Central University of 1858. Special care was taken to profit by a study of the weak points of that instrument. The Convention ordered that steps be taken at once "looking to the establishment, as speedily as practicable, of an institution of the highest order and upon the surest basis, where the youth of the Church and country may prosecute theological, literary, scientific, and professional studies to an extent as great and in a manner as thorough as their wants demand."

It was decided that, for the present, the University should consist of a theological school, a literary and scientific school, a normal school, and a law school. A minimum endowment of one million dollars was specified, and it was stipulated that no one of the five departments of the institution should be put into operation until five hundred thousand dollars had been secured. It was decided that a charter should be obtained which would constitute the incorporators a board of trust, having authority to collect and invest funds. Its members, together with a board of supervisors consisting of the bishops, were to be empowered to "elect officers and professors and prescribe the course of study and the plan of government." It was further agreed that the charter should provide for a fair representation in the management of the University to any other Conferences of the Connection which might thereafter coöperate in its maintenance.[2] On August 19, 1872, the chancery court at Nashville granted a

---

[1] *Ibid.*, p. 111.
[2] *Idem.*

charter embodying these provisions to the "Central University of the Methodist Episcopal Church, South."[1]

The Memphis Convention attracted widespread attention both within and outside of the denomination. The interest felt by the public at large was reflected in the comments of *The South,* a secular journal of that day. Declaring that "a tremendous responsibility" would attend the utterances of this body, that paper said a few days before the Convention assembled: "As we see it from a disinterested stand-point, as we have no personal interests at issue, we may speak with cordial frankness. We tell our Methodist friends now is their great, their glorious opportunity. The Church is awake to the pressing need of an institution of the highest possible character. We urge them to venture boldly before their constituents with a scheme that aims at the loftiest results." "Surely," this journal declared, "such a religious body should be able to offer to its young men a school of learning in which they may catch something of the abounding vitality and ardor which animates the Church at large."[2]

Public interest was further aroused by a somewhat caustic controversy which now ensued between Bishop McTyeire and Bishop Pierce with regard to the projected university, which the latter opposed chiefly because of the theological department. This "battle of two giants" was carried on in a series of letters in the Nashville *Christian Advocate* during March, April, and May, following the Memphis Convention. In Bishop Pierce's opposition were reflected the jealousy of the Conference colleges, the antipathy to a formal theological training, and a type of prejudice against higher education in general having its origins in the alarm occasioned by the threats to orthodoxy implied in the teachings of the new science and scholarship.[3]

The Bishop protested that, even though the General Conference had repudiated the idea of a theological school, such an institution was now being "grafted upon our economy, *nolens volens.*" He discounted learned preaching, and held up to ridicule the training of preachers by "tutors, lectures, and library." "The best preach-

---

[1]*Ibid.,* p. 112.
[2]*The South* as quoted in Nashville *Christian Advocate,* January 20, 1872.
[3]*Cf.* Dabney, Virginius, *Liberalism in the South* (Chapel Hill, 1933), pp. 190-191; Merriam, *op. cit.,* p. 113.

ers I ever heard had never been to college at all—hardly to school." To his mind Church schools in every city and on every circuit would be preferable to having a denominational university. He asserted that "It is my opinion that every dollar invested in a theological school will be a damage to Methodism." "Had I a million," he said, "I would not give a dime for such an object."[1]

With such illiberal views Bishop McTyeire would not compromise. He made it clear that the "bane of our educational projects heretofore has been the want of concentration." Admitting that the mission of the Church was primarily one to the masses, he insisted that it was, nevertheless, one to all others as well. As for the need of thorough ministerial training he did not mince words. "When the Bishop refers to our Baptist brethren' for an example of 'a ministry right out of the people,' " he said, "he will please tell us which wing he means, and which side he takes. It is a cardinal tenet with the Hardshells that the Lord will 'call all the educated ministers he wants' and that critics are a great evil; and they all agree that the best preachers are those 'who have never been to college at all—hardly to school.' . . . It is a noteworthy fact that at the division of the Baptists the Hardshells were in the majority . . . but all that makes the Baptist name respectable today is due to what the *other party* has accomplished. This has increased—that decreased. The Hardshells have gone on fighting missions and an educated ministry and organs and choirs until they have fought well nigh out of every city and town and enlightened neighborhood and have consigned themselves where Bishop Pierce wishes the theological scheme—'to the shades of oblivion.' " For himself, Bishop McTyeire declared that he was unwilling to accept any such inferior mission for his Church. "Of course," he said, "there is to be no separation among us. The two forces will exist side by side in Methodism, and the question is: which of them shall control the policy of the Church." Admitting that high culture would probably never become general, he expressed the conviction that it should nevertheless be made as general as possible, since "the higher forms of education nourish and control the lower."[2] The controversy

[1]*Cf.* Nashville *Christian Advocate,* March 9, 1872 to May 18, 1872.
[2]*Idem.*

was finally brought to a close when the College of Bishops, after mature deliberation, unanimously signified its approval of the undertaking by agreeing to locate the University as soon as the sum of five hundred thousand dollars had been secured for the institution.[1]

Despite the recognition thus accorded the enterprise, the stipulation making the acquisition of half a million dollars a condition precedent to the actual founding of the University, together with the impoverished state of Southern society, soon made it appear that an early realization of the project would be impossible. Vigorous attempts to raise the required amount yielded but meager returns. When prospects seemed darkest the necessary funds were supplied from an unexpected source. Mrs. Frank Crawford Vanderbilt, who, prior to her recent marriage to Commodore Cornelius Vanderbilt of New York, had long been a communicant at the St. Francis Street Methodist Church in Mobile, was devoted to the interests of Southern Methodism.[2] Previously the Commodore had expressed the desire to confer some benefit upon the Southern people. Through Mrs. Vanderbilt and her kinsman, Bishop McTyeire, he now became interested in the projected Southern Methodist university. In March 1873, Mr. Vanderbilt

---

[1]The bishops were not averse to conciliating opposition after this action had been taken. Although stating that they felt free to "give our decided approval to the combination of the several Annual Conferences" for the purpose of establishing the University, they took pains to declare that they could enter into no official relations with it which would "discriminate between it and any and every other institution of the Church." Cf. Nashville *Christian Advocate,* May 30, 1872. Bishop McTyeire and Bishop Pierce now issued a joint statement, declaring that the controversy between themselves had been adjusted "with satisfaction to ourselves," and expressing the hope that no injury to the interests of the Church had resulted from their debates. Thereafter Bishop Pierce offered no further opposition to the plan. Cf. communication from Bishops McTyeire and Pierce in Nashville *Christian Advocate,* May 30, 1872. Bishop Keener reported that the action taken by the bishops was "the result of much earnest deliberation and a determination to be wise in maintaining that harmony and unity of sentiment and of policy which heretofore have been the glory and the beauty both of our Episcopal College and of our whole Church. Let all our preachers and our people imitate the example thus set them, and mentally assent to views which represent the united wisdom both of the best policy on education and that next to the best." Cf. letter of Bishop Keener as quoted in *New Orleans Christian Advocate,* May 30, 1872.

[2]Mrs. Vanderbilt was the daughter of Robert L. Crawford, a Virginian, whose father the Reverend William Crawford had been ordained a minister of the Protestant Episcopal Church by the Reverend James Madison, the first Bishop of that church in the Diocese of Virginia. Cf. letter of February 15, 1934 to the author from Mrs. Janie McTyeire Baskervill of Bristol, Virginia.

suddenly proffered the sum of five hundred thousand dollars to "the Central University of the Methodist Episcopal Church, South," making it a condition of the gift that Bishop McTyeire be chosen president of the Board of Trust of the institution, and that the Bishop be given a broad veto power over its actions.[1] In accepting this gift the Board of Trust, obtaining an amendment of the charter, changed the name of the school to Vanderbilt University.[2]

Under the wise direction of Bishop McTyeire, Vanderbilt University, opening its doors in 1875, became almost at once one of the most potent forces in liberal higher education in the South. At McTyeire's suggestion, Landon Cabell Garland, who had already proven himself "one of the few survivors of a past regime, who were fitted to the new order," was made the first chancellor of the new institution. In this capacity he was destined to serve for almost twenty years. Although in the middle sixties when elected to this post, Garland was receptive to new ideas until he died two decades later, and at the time of his death he was acclaimed the 'grand old man' of Southern education.[3] Further gifts, chiefly from Cornelius Vanderbilt and members of his family, increased the wealth of the institution until, in 1890, it stood at a million and a half. Of this amount nine hundred thousand dollars were reserved as a productive endowment.[4] The revenues derived in this way gave to Vanderbilt a financial independence enjoyed by no other Southern university.

The new University was soon able "to rise so clearly out of the low levels around it that it really became a sort of evangel with its large endowment, its ample buildings and surroundings."[5] It was presently able to pursue fixed and high educational aims in a way that no other institution in the South then could do. Adequately trained and productive scholars were brought to its

---

[1]The donor at first urged the Bishop to resign his Episcopal office and devote his entire time to the interests of the University, at a salary to be fixed at ten thousand dollars. *Cf.* Merriam, *op. cit.,* p. 116.

[2]*Idem.*

[3]Dabney, *op. cit.,* p. 185.

[4]Merriam, *op. cit.,* p. 144.

[5]Commencement address of Professor Henry N. Snyder of Wofford College at Vanderbilt University, June 13, 1898, as reported in Nashville *Christian Advocate,* June 23, 1898.

faculty. Definite and fixed requirements for admission and graduation were maintained. In doing these things Vanderbilt exercised a profound influence upon the whole educational system of the Southern States. "The best contribution that we have made to the educational interests of the South," said Dr. J. H. Kirkland at his inauguration as chancellor of the University in 1893, "is the development of a college of high grade and broad scope of instruction, under whose protecting shadow academies and training schools could spring up, and which should stimulate by a generous rivalry other colleges to better work and a more advanced standard."[1]

It should be mentioned at this point that the general poverty of the Southern institutions of higher learning during the decades immediately following the War not only made it impossible for them to acquire adequate buildings and equipment or to pay ample salaries, but also affected adversely the character of .the work done by them. In many instances it forced them to lower entrance requirements and academic standards generally in order to secure revenue from student tuition fees. This tendency was naturally aggravated by the very large number of institutions, many of them improperly classified, which were then competing in the field of higher education in the section. It was pointed out in 1884 that, while there were but seventeen colleges for men in the six New England States, six of the Southern States were at that time supporting sixty-seven.[2] A rivalry for numbers developed which led many of the Southern colleges not only to disregard their printed requirements for admission and to accept a lower grade of work, but actually to enter into competition with whatever preparatory schools had managed to continue in existence. This policy of the colleges naturally reacted disastrously upon the lower schools. Left with nothing to do, they either ceased to exist, were reduced to furnishing a more elementary type of instruction, or were forced to change their names and masquerade as colleges or universities. By 1884 it was estimated that there was a gap of one or two years between the colleges

---

[1] *Cf. Southern Christian Advocate,* October 5, 1893.
[2] *Cf.* Smith, Charles Forster, "Southern Schools and Colleges", *The Atlantic Monthly,* Vol. LIV (October, 1884), p. 544.

and the few public high schools that existed.[1] The whole situation contributed to the lowering of the standards of instruction in institutions of every grade.

From the beginning the influence of Vanderbilt University was directed to the improvement of these conditions. Although Chancellor Garland declared that it would have been necessary to reject fully two-thirds of those who presented themselves for matriculation during the first year had the institution stood firmly by its rules, and while it was deemed necessary at first to conduct preparatory classes, the standards were quickly and consistently raised. The preparatory department was soon cut off and a rigid system of entrance examinations was instituted. In the meantime the founding of good preparatory schools was fostered and their work encouraged. A definite standard was set for them. In 1879 the University began printing in its regular catalogue specimens of the entrance examinations in Latin, Greek, English, and mathematics. No other institution in the South had undertaken to do this.[2] Students were urged not to enter the University without adequate training. Dr. Charles Forster Smith of the Vanderbilt faculty was recognized as a sort of apostle to the "fitting schools." During the middle Eighties Dr. Smith contributed two articles to *The Atlantic Monthly* which exerted a potent influence in awakening the Southern people to a realization of the educational needs of their section.

While acknowledging that a wholesome interest in public schools was beginning to manifest itself, the writer of these articles emphasized the fact that "in the field of higher education our policy or rather tendency has always been wrong." "The greatest evil in Southern education" lay in the fact that there were "three times as many colleges and universities as the country can support." He pointed out the baneful effect of this situation upon the whole educational system. "There is a large number of so-called higher institutions which give neither preparation for college nor college training. By their low entrance standards they prevent a boy from getting a thorough preparation elsewhere.

---

[1] *Ibid.*, p. 543.
[2] *Cf.* address of Professor Henry N. Snyder in Nashville *Christian Advocate,* June 23, 1898.

And, once entered, he is neither able to take, nor they to give, real college instruction." He felt that it was hard to view this state of affairs "otherwise than as a crime against the youth of the country." He mentioned the fact that while there had been in the State of Tennessee in 1880 twenty-one colleges and universities for men and sixteen colleges and seminaries for women, there were but sixty-three secondary schools, four public high schools, and only two distinctly preparatory schools, although nineteen of the colleges maintained preparatory departments. The writer insisted that a cure for these evils could be had only through the maintenance of higher standards in the Southern colleges. The University of Virginia had, since the War, "held aloft, as ever, her high standard of graduation, although it cost her professors money to do so," and had become "the one model for all our institutions that aspired to do high and good work." "But what might she not have done for . . . higher education, if, while selling her degrees and certificates so dearly, she had been as strict as Harvard in admitting students." Dr. Smith gave it as his considered opinion that "in the United States culture is generally in the inverse ratio to the *number* of colleges."[1] Drawing their inspiration from centers in Germany, Smith and his colleagues, W. M. Baskerville and J. H. Kirkland, jealously guarded the standards of their university.

The standards that were now set at this central institution of Southern Methodism exerted a wide influence on educational policies throughout the South, and especially within the Methodist Connection. Other colleges were stimulated to a healthy emulation. It was at the instigation and largely due to the influence of Vanderbilt that an Association of Colleges and Preparatory Schools of the Southern States, having as its purpose the general elevation of educational standards, was organized in 1895.[2]

The developments at Nashville accelerated the trend toward concentration and centralization in the educational work of the Connection that had led to the founding of the University itself. The multiplication of colleges was constantly discouraged. After

---

[1]*Cf.* Smith, Charles Forster, "Southern Colleges and Schools", *The Atlantic Monthly*, Vol. LIV (October, 1884), pp. 542-557.
[2]*Cf.* Nashville *Christian Advocate*, December 3, 1896.

much agitation of the matter in the General Conferences of 1886 and 1890, as has been said, a central Board of Education of the Methodist Episcopal Church, South was created in 1894. It was provided that the fifteen members of this board, who were to be elected quadrennially, should "seek to increase endowments and otherwise to strengthen our existing institutions in harmony with the general educational policy of the Church, to correlate and systematize the work now being done, and to organize new institutions where they can be judiciously established and maintained."[1] The sentiment which had inspired the adoption of this new feature of Church economy was well expressed by W. W. Smith, who spoke as the chairman of the Board in 1898. He said: "We will not allow our people to be cheated by a name and have their children nominally prepared, to find disappointment confronting them when they come to find that they are not accepted as A. B. graduates, but are compelled to take a grade below. We must do this work of education thoroughly and honestly. The reproach of our country is that we have been over-naming everything and not doing our educational work perfectly, especially in the South; and it is certainly the province of our Church, which so largely represents Southern people, to stand for honest and worthy education."[2]

Shortly after its organization, the Board of Education issued a declaration of "aims and policy." Conspicuous among the items set forth was the determination to "repress the tendency to multiply institutions with inadequate prospects of support," and "to promote the endowment of existing colleges which have the elements of success and the necessary conditions of usefulness." The establishment of adequate academies was to be encouraged as a matter of prime importance, and the whole educational system was to be completed "by correlating as rapidly as possible our Conference colleges with the graduate and professional departments of Vanderbilt University." In order to achieve these purposes, the Board proposed to bring the educational boards of the Annual Conferences into coöperation with itself, and it was urged that each Conference appoint a Secretary of Education and

[1]Cf. *Journal of General Conference*, 1894, pp. 196-198.
[2]Cf. letter of W. W. Smith in *Daily Christian Advocate*, May 16, 1898.

make regular assessments for the work within its bounds. The Board also sought to stimulate local initiative by offering financial aid for educational projects upon terms similar to those stipulated by the Peabody Fund.[1]

Further consolidation was given to the educational system of Southern Methodism when the Educational Commission was created in 1898. It was made the duty of the Commissioners to "classify all the institutions of our Church, and to designate each as university, college, or academy (or secondary school) according to the relation of the work done" to standards that were to be fixed by themselves. They were instructed to publish this classification in all official lists of the educational institutions of the Church. The commissioners were ordered to prescribe fixed minimum requirements for the baccalaurate degree and for admission to the freshman class, to be applied in all Methodist colleges. They were likewise instructed to provide definite standards for the secondary schools of the denomination.[2]

The General Conference of 1898 sought to give stability to all educational enterprises of the Connection by authorizing the Board of Education to begin that year a canvass to raise a million and a half dollars for their support.[3] At the same time, Vanderbilt University was made in law, what it had already become in fact, the central feature of the Southern Methodist educational system. For several years prior to that time the Board of Trust had advocated that the University be given an official relation to the entire Connection. Declaring that the University was "naturally and properly the center of our educational system, to which all our schools and colleges should be correlated," the bishops suggested to the Conference that some action be taken to make it thoroughly connectional. It had been proposed that such a relationship be established by having future members of the Board of Trust selected from the Church at large, without regard to geographical limitation, their election to be confirmed by the General Conference, rather than by the several Annual Conferences which had hitherto exercised that function. The

[1] Cf. Du Bose, op. cit., pp. 111-112.
[2] Journal of General Conference, 1898, pp. 67-68.
[3] Ibid., pp. 218-219.

General Conference now signified its willingness to accept the proposed relationship, and, since the Annual Conferences concerned quickly consented to the arrangement, Vanderbilt was formally and officially recognized as the capstone of the educational system of the Church.[1]

It cannot be denied that there appeared in the Connection before the end of the century evidences of an illiberality with regard to the control of Vanderbilt University, which, together with other forces that were at work, ultimately led the General Conference to sever all connection with the institution. There were at the same time, however, outstanding leaders of the Church who vigilantly combatted this trend. Such men as Bishop R. K. Hargrove, Bishop Charles B. Galloway, and Bishop E. R. Hendrix fought valiantly against the adoption of any policy of narrow denominational control.[2]

But the development of liberal concepts of higher learning in Southern Methodism was by no means restricted to the movement for concentration in which Vanderbilt University had its origins. There were in the smaller denominational institutions a number of men who evolved progressive and constructive educational theories and sought to give them practical application. The spirit which animated these men is reflected in the remarks of President R. E. Blackwell of Randolph-Macon College, who, when discussing the system of higher education in Virginia, said in 1893: "Our Superintendent of Education was boasting, some years ago, that there were proportionately more Virginians pursuing the higher education than any other nationality, not excluding Prussians. This nonsense was repeated all over our State and even in the United States Senate. As long as our people think that a Virginia College is as good as the University of Berlin, why should they be concerned about their educational system?"[3]

It was as a member of the faculty of Randolph-Macon College that Thomas R. Price, who is commonly acknowledged to have

---

[1] *Ibid.*, pp. 196-197.

[2] *Cf.* Dabney, *op. cit.*, p. 353. In this connection it is not irrelevant to note that Emory University, which today stands in much the same relation to Southern Methodism as Vanderbilt then stood, has, since its establishment in 1915, occupied a place among the most liberal of all Southern educational institutions. *Cf. ibid.*, p. 339.

[3] Smith, Charles Forster, *op. cit.*, p. 544.

been the first American educator to recognize the importance of a thorough and systematic study of the English language, first evolved and put into practice his theories with regard to the necessity for exact instruction in the mother tongue. Price conceived the idea of placing the study of English on the curriculum alongside that of Latin and Greek, both in time and importance. "I have felt for twenty-odd years—ever since I began to teach, or to think of teaching—the supreme importance of teaching English to English-speaking children," he declared shortly after beginning his work at Randolph-Macon. "I have felt it more strongly than I ever felt any other truth, that for every human being the most important, the most profitable, the most far-reaching in power upon mind and character, is the study of his mother-tongue. For every man, as for every nation, the culture of that mother-tongue into power and beauty is the needful condition of all high culture, of all great intellectual achievements."[1] Price emphasized the fact that teachers of Latin and Greek everywhere were seeking to give a knowledge of the ancient languages "to boys and young men that knew not enough of their own language to receive it or apply it."[2] He was fortunate in winning immediately to the support of his plans the Reverend James A. Duncan, president of the college, one of the most eloquent men of his day, a man whom Price years later pronounced to have been "the most far-sighted friend of collegiate education" he had ever known.[3] The progressive Duncan, who had previously surrounded himself with an able faculty irrespective of denominational ties,[4] now induced the trustees to create a chair of English in the college and made Price its first incumbent. Thus was begun a School of English which was to have a far-reaching influence in liberalizing the curricula of the colleges in the South.

---

[1] *Cf.* lecture of W. M. Baskerville at Culleoka Academy, as given in Nashville *Christian Advocate,* April 18, 1885. Price subsequently exerted an important influence at the University of Virginia and at Columbia University, in which latter institution he taught for many years.

[2] *Cf.* letter of Price to Captain Richard Irby, as quoted in Irby, *op. cit.,* pp. 208-209.

[3] *Ibid.,* p. 210.

[4] When the youthful Robert E. Blackwell matriculated as a student in 1868 there was in addition to the president only one member of the faculty of Randolph-Macon who was a Methodist. *Cf.* statement made to the author in a conversation with President Blackwell in January, 1938.

As professor of both English and Greek, Price developed his courses in the two subjects, side by side on a four-year basis, constantly recognizing their relation to one another, and balancing evenly the literary and the historical study of the English language.[1] The Randolph-Macon movement soon spread to colleges in all directions. Other Methodist colleges especially, since many of them drew to their faculties men who had been trained at the Virginia institution, became centers from which the new gospel of the study of English was carried forward. "It is very curious to trace the various ramifications of mutual influences, and to see them acting and interacting, crossing and recrossing," declared a writer in the *Sewanee Review*, when referring to the growing interest in the study of the language of the country. "Three main lines may be detected." These, he said, stretched forth from Randolph-Macon, from the University of Virginia, and from Washington and Lee, both of the latter having derived their inspiration directly from the Methodist institution.[2] A number of the students trained under Price at Randolph-Macon proceeded to Leipzig for their doctorates in English and subsequently came home to fill the chairs of English which were now being established in many of the leading Southern institutions. Robert E. Blackwell returned from Germany to fill Price's place at his alma mater.[3]

Outstanding among the disciples of Price was William M. Baskervill, who came back from Leipzig to become the apostle of a thorough and exact study of English, first at Wofford College, and later at Vanderbilt University.[4] At the former institution he at once met with a sympathetic circle. The president, Dr. James H. Carlisle, himself a careful student of the history and meaning of words and always interested in English work, gave him warm

---

[1]Henneman, J. B., "The Study of English in the South", *The Sewanee Review*, Vol. II (February, 1894), pp. 180-197.

[2]*Idem.*

[3]*Cf.* Irby, *op. cit.*, p. 214.

[4]W. M. Baskervill was the son of Dr. John Tabb Baskervill, a Virginian, who was educated as a physician in Baltimore early in the nineteenth century. He practiced his profession in Virginia for a number of years with marked success. The elder Baskervill was an Episcopalian until "converted" at a Methodist meeting. He straightway "paid his gambling debts," joined the Methodist Church and shortly afterwards entered the Methodist ministry. He then removed from Virginia to Western Tennessee where he became one of the

encouragement. There, too, Charles Forster Smith was Baskervill's fellow-instructor, and James H. Kirkland, at first a receptive student, afterwards became his colleague. These three scholars, after Smith and Kirkland had taken degrees at Leipzig, were again associated at Vanderbilt which Baskervill now made an important center for the study of English. Though Kirkland now served as professor of Latin and Smith was professor of Greek their own interest in the subject and their close sympathies with Baskervill made them give a warm encouragement and support to his work. Thus through such fortunate circumstances Baskervill could give an unusual and steady emphasis to the study of the English language and letters. The potent character of the influence exerted upon the colleges and universities of the South by the Randolph-Macon movement is revealed by the fact that a number of them imitated outright the courses and methods developed there, in some instances actually uniting the Greek and English departments.[1] Thus Robert Sharp on his return from Leipzig was soon made Professor of Greek and English at Tulane University.[2] The success of the leaders of this movement in extending their influence in the South is suggested by the executive and administrative positions they were later called upon to fill. Robert Sharp was made president of Tulane University, J. H. Kirkland was chosen as Chancellor of Vanderbilt University, Frank C. Woodward was elected to the presidency of the University of South Carolina, R. E. Blackwell was placed at the head of Randolph-Macon College and John Bell Henneman became dean of the Episcopalian University of the South and editor of the *Sewanee Review*.

A contribution to the cause of liberal higher education of a somewhat different nature is well illustrated in the career of James H. Carlisle, who, beginning in 1875, served as president of Wofford College for more than a quarter of a century. Dr. Carlisle, who was broad and tolerant, and always eager for the truth, possessed a personality so vital that it was frequently

---

most liberal supporters of Methodism. At his home a room under separate cover was reserved for the religious instruction of his slaves. *Cf.* letter of January 22, 1938 to the author from Mrs. Janie McTyeire Baskerville of Bristol, Virginia.

[1]Henneman, *loc. cit.*, pp. 193-197.

[2]This information was given the author in a conversation with Dr. R. E. Blackwell of Randolph-Macon College in January 1938.

asserted that "merely to be associated with him was in itself a liberal education."[1] He was commonly acclaimed the "first citizen" of South Carolina.[2] Carlisle believed profoundly in the importance of personal contact between teacher and student, and the value of his services to the cause of higher education lay to a great extent in the notably intimate relationship which existed between himself and those whom he taught.[3] His readiness to accept new ideas has been suggested in the mention which was made of the support and encouragement given by him to the young instructors who sought to give to the study of English a place of prominence in the curriculum at Wofford. Although called repeatedly to a chair or the presidency of his State university, Carlisle, to the end of his life, chose to devote his services to the educational work of his Church. And in that capacity, it has been asserted, he was able to "put the stamp of his great personality upon the educational life" of South Carolina as no other man had ever been able to do. It was the combination of progressive and far-sighted views with commanding personalities in men like James H. Carlisle, Holland N. McTyeire, Landon Cabell Garland, and James A. Duncan that made it possible for Southern Methodism to exert what was probably the most potent and liberal influence in the field of higher education in the South during the years from 1865 to 1900.

In one particular the attitude of the Church served in some measure to restrict the fullest opportunities for higher education. This was true in that the Church entertained views which were opposed to the acceptance of a theory looking to the advanced education of the masses by the State which was fast gaining popular recognition during the latter part of the nineteenth century. This was the theory that it is the function of the State to provide, without cost to the individual, a higher education for every young man who is not lacking in intelligence. There were, in the main, two reasons for such an attitude. In the first place many persons felt that secular learning should be accompanied at all stages by positive moral and religious instruction; that it

---

[1] *Cf.* Dabney, *op. cit.*, p. 188.
[2] *Cf.* Duncan, Watson Boone, ed., *Carlisle Memorial Volume* (Nashville, 1916), *passim.*
[3] *Cf.* Dabney, *op. cit.*, p. 187.

was the function of the college to conserve and strengthen the religious element in man's character at the same time that it imparted worldly wisdom. A knowledge of the difficulties which a State institution in a modern democracy would encounter in the performance of a function of this sort convinced such persons that no effective instruction of the kind could be given. This belief led them to oppose the patronizing of State colleges. The opinion was frequently expressed that the acquisition of mental culture entirely apart from all religious influences was an undertaking "fraught with the greatest peril to character."[1] The fundamental distrust of State institutions was reflected in the remarks of the *Southern Christian Advocate* when it complained in 1886 that such schools took cognizance of morals only when delinquencies had occurred. It said: "The student is in a state of law and not of grace, and becomes liable to ethical discipline, not by virtue of his ignorance, inexperience and need, but only when some gross violation of law or morals brings him before the authorities, who are competent to administer penalties, but powerless to exercise preventative influence in any telling measure. State institutions are essentially unmoral. Their relation to conduct is general and indirect, not formative but only corrective."[2]

It was felt moreover that the student, left without religious guidance in an atmosphere of intellectual ferment, would be particularly susceptible to the dangers of atheism and false teachings. In the Pastoral Address of 1886 the bishops said: "The cost of education is seriously weighed as against Church schools. . . . We look to the consciences of our people that they guard sacredly the training of their sons and daughters at the generous, susceptible, fiery period of life when the heart, if ever, is to be shaped for Christ; when the mind is full of inquiry and naturally disposed to admire all metaphysical speculation as some new truth; when the scholar is ready to accept at the mouth of the teacher his faith as well as his science. Hard by the Church is the school house. We must not suffer the one to neutralize the other."[3] That same year the Nashville *Advocate* reminded its

---

[1]*Cf.* Nashville *Christian Advocate*, November 6, 1886.

[2]*Southern Christian Advocate*, September 2, 1886.

[3]*Cf.* Pastoral Address as given in Nashville *Christian Advocate*, May 15, 1886.

readers that it was a well known fact that in the past one of the
Southern State universities had "for years sowed seeds of infidelity
which sprang up and choked, almost, if not quite, to extinction,
the religious and ethical principles of many of the most notable
families of a certain commonwealth which shall be nameless
here."[1] "The father who cares for his son's religion can't send
to the State school," wrote Dr. A. G. Haygood about the same
time. "Thousands have wrecked their children for both worlds
by sending them to institutions that make religion subordinate
or taboo it altogether."[2]

The second reason for the opposition to the promotion of
higher education by the State was the fact that, during the
Eighties, a number of State institutions had undertaken to provide
free tuition. It was feared that the denominational colleges
could no longer meet their competition and would be forced out
of existence. To the extent that such uneasiness prevailed efforts
were made to secure the abolition of free tuition in the State
schools and opposition to higher education by the State in general
was engendered. During the period of greatest concern it was
even suggested that the time for the "disestablishment" of State
universities and colleges had arrived. In a communication to the
Nashville *Advocate* in February 1885, with special reference to
the situation in South Carolina, where free tuition had been
granted in several State institutions, Bishop McTyeire raised the
question: "Is it right for a State University to offer free tuition?"
The Bishop declared that the Methodist and other Christian
bodies of the State could not "look with indifference upon a
legislation which arrays itself against them," and he expressed
the opinion that "as things are drifting, every Church College in
South Carolina, Virginia, Georgia, Alabama, Mississippi, and
Texas must sooner or later go to the wall." "Methodist or
Baptist people cannot compete with themselves as citizens—
working in the latter character by taxation, with all the taxable
population super-added, and in the former, as a fractional part
of the population, by voluntary contribution." He suggested the

---

[1]Nashville *Christian Advocate*, November 6, 1886.
[2]*Cf.* communication of A. G. Haygood in *Southern Christian Advocate,*
July 8, 1886.

argument that it was "bad political economy for the State to charge itself with doing that, which, if let alone, religious zeal and private munificence can and will do as well and even better." If there were those who were unwilling to send their sons to denominational schools, they should provide institutions of their own. "It is asking too much of a Christian people to do this for them." However, should the State determine to furnish higher education, let it charge for tuition. The Bishop declared that he had as yet heard of no Methodist organizations proffering complaints "against this destructive legislation." "I greatly mistake if this tone and attitude will not have to be altered before relief comes," he said. "The Methodists, Baptists, and Presbyterians, and others, citizens all, who are pledged to higher education under positive religious auspices, when they wake up to this matter can, irrespective of political parties, force the State institutions within proper lines; and their champions should beware lest, when this work is begun, it may go further than that."[1]

The matter being thus brought prominently before the attention of the Church, similar sentiments were soon expressed in other quarters.[2] Enjoying the support of the journals of several of the other large religious groups in South Carolina, the *Southern Christian Advocate* assumed the leadership in the fight against the continuation of free tuition in State institutions. A few weeks after the publication of McTyeire's letter, the *Southern* announced that the advocates of free tuition had insisted upon "risking the

---

[1] *Cf.* letter of Bishop McTyeire in Nashville *Christian Advocate,* quoted in *New Orleans Christian Advocate,* February 19, 1885.

[2] The Reverend John E. Edwards of Virginia, a corresponding editor of the *Southern Christian Advocate* wrote: "The citizens of any State who are taxed to support public schools, ought to enter a stern and positive remonstrance against annuities from the State Treasury with the condition that tuition be free to any boy in the State. Annuities to State universities in sufficient amounts to aid them, with reasonable tuition fees, to pay expenses, may all be right and proper; but to make such yearly grants from the State Treasury as to enable these institutions to open their doors free of tuition to all the boys of the commonwealth, is an act of unmitigated injustice to the denominational colleges, and strikes a blow at the root of the morals and religious education of our young men. . . . The very life of our denominational Colleges is imperiled, in all those instances where there is no endowment, or at best a very limited endowment fund. . . . The time has come when the Christian people of the State should lift up their voices against free tuition in the University unless it be guarded by such restrictions and limitations as to work no harm to the unendowed denominational colleges of the State." *Cf.* "Our Virginia Letter" in *Southern Christian Advocate,* February 25, 1885.

O. P. FITZGERALD, BISHOP OF THE METHODIST EPISCOPAL CHURCH, SOUTH

usefulness and even the life of the South Carolina College on the cast of this die." It warned those interested that if they "will 'cry Havoc, and let slip the dogs of war,' they shall find that those whom they force into an unwilling contest will not be the first to cry 'Hold, enough!' Let it be clearly understood, that such a conflict is neither challenged nor desired by us; but if unbending obstinacy will force this question to the extreme of a life and death struggle between the State and the denominational colleges, there shall not be wanting tongues and pens to defend, brains to direct and ballots to decide the issue."[1] After a petition to the trustees of the State College from the Methodist, Baptist, Lutheran, and Associate Reformed Presbyterian organizations in the State had remained unanswered, the *Southern* said: "There is but one recourse left, and that is the ballot box! The Legislature of South Carolina and the trustees of the State College are not the masters, but the servants, of the people. We are yet freemen, and in the exercise of our rights and privileges as such, the present Board of Trustees of the State College must go, and the unrighteous discrimination against the denominational colleges must be numbered among the things of the past!" "We have always deprecated making a political issue of this free tuition matter, but the course of the trustees and the Legislature left us no other recourse."[2] "So let the candidates be interrogated," advised the *Advocate* on another occasion. "Let them be made to understand that the sovereign people mean to take this question in hand and settle it most effectually."[3] Thus the *Southern* kept the matter alive until it was made a test question in the State elections during the autumn of 1886, and free tuition, except to really needy students, was abolished.[4]

In 1887 the Nashville *Advocate* announced that the time for disestablishment was at hand. In an editorial entitled "A Vicious and Oppressive Policy," it asserted that, since the poor were unable to avail themselves of the advantages of State colleges, even when free tuition was offered, such tuition was "the luxury of the rich provided by the taxation of the poor. It is robbing

---

[1]Cf. *Southern Christian Advocate*, March 11, 1886.
[2]*Ibid.*, August 12, 1886.
[3]*Ibid.*, June 17, 1886.
[4]Cf. *ibid.*, January 13, 1887.

the poor to give advantages to the rich. It is unrepublican in every part. . . . Whatever be the right and duty of the State in the matter of elementary education, it requiries no argument to prove that it has no more right to establish colleges and universities than it has to establish religion. It is quite time to begin a movement for disestablishment. The people have condemned the policy as unworthy of their patronage, and the people are right. It is a vicious and oppressive policy."[1] Speaking in a more conciliatory tone, the *Advocate* explained in its succeeding issue that, although certain that the growth of popular intelligence and courage would compel the abandonment of higher education by the State, it was of the opinion that the "schools now known as State schools will not be destroyed, but will be sustained and improved (as has been the case with Harvard) by private benevolence when misplaced public charity has been withdrawn."[2]

But as it came to be realized that the real solution of the problem of the denominational schools lay in the acquisition of adequate endowments rather than in limiting the opportunities of the State institutions, such unfriendliness towards the State colleges and universities declined. From the beginning of the agitation some of the journals of the Connection had deprecated all attempts to bolster up the denominational institutions by depriving the State schools of financial support and had pointed out that the true policy of the Methodists was to meet the competition of State education by adequately endowing their own colleges.

As early as February 1885, referring to the letter which Bishop McTyeire had published with regard to the situation in South Carolina, the *New Orleans Christian Advocate* cautioned the Church against being led into a false position. Stating that, under "the plea of fostering a sanctified education, the Romish Church is the avowed enemy of our entire public school system," it urged that Methodists be not driven into a like antagonism through a "passionate, illogical advocacy of denominational schools." It pointed out that while the Bishop had accepted and defended the principle of State education, one or two others, catching inspira-

---

[1] Nashville *Christian Advocate*, June 4, 1887.
[2] *Ibid.*, June 11, 1887.

tion from his letter, had gone to the extreme of denouncing the whole system. It emphasized the fact that for the Church "To sever all connections with State colleges would be to surrender positions of vast influence and opportunities of the greatest value." "But if we antagonize *their existence,*" it said, "in all fairness and consistency, we must withdraw from any share in their emoluments and administration." "Into that attitude," the *Advocate* asserted, "the Church is not ready to be led."[1]

"Two facts may be regarded as settled, said the *Alabama Christian Advocate* the following year. "First our people intend to educate their children as best they can. Second, they wish to get their tuition as low as possible. The lower the cost the larger the number, that will go to college. These facts in connection with free tuition in State colleges, will make it next to impossible for Church colleges to live without handsome endowments. Those whose convictions on this subject are strong and clear will have to prove their love of denominational schools by giving their money to sustain them; there will be no other alternative.

"Perhaps it is best that this is so. When it is seen that Church schools will be utterly squelched, men who hitherto have been utterly indifferent or have hesitated, will say that it shall not be done. Their love of Christ will express itself in taking care of the necessary institutions of the Church. They will rally and pour out their money, and the Church schools will live and flourish."[2]

That a much friendlier feeling with regard to the State colleges had come to prevail in the denomination by 1889 was indicated in the changed attitude of the *Wesleyan Christian Advocate,* which a few years before had been hostile.[3] Referring to the

---

[1] *Cf. New Orleans Christian Advocate,* February 26, 1885.

[2] *Cf. Alabama Christian Advocate,* quoted in Nashville *Christian Advocate,* April 3, 1886.

[3] When commenting upon Bishop McTyeire's letter about free tuition, the *Wesleyan* had said in February 1885: "Christian denominations in Georgia, and in the South, are very reluctant to make an issue with the State. That reluctance, however, is merely prudential, and cannot be counted on to stand the strain of a continued wrong. The free tuition system which the Legislature was induced to adopt for Athens, in order to revive the constantly-waning patronage of its university, has succeeded to so very small an extent as not to awaken much thought about it one way or another. The competition has not yet been felt by Mercer or Emory College, or Pio Nono, to any noteworthy degree. The Bishop intimates that the issue will have to be joined. So it

efforts which were then being made to secure increased appropriations for the University of Georgia, the *Wesleyan* said in July
1889: "As to any permanent harm befalling Church colleges
by undue appropriations to State schools, we have no fears whatever. . . . To do her work well Emory College needs half a
million dollars endowment and that need" is affected "scarcely
at all by the propositions now pending before the Georgia
Legislature. If the State fails to do anything for education then
the Church must come to the rescue of the people as she has
heretofore done and with a more liberal hand; if the State makes
large appropriations to build up her university then the Church
ought to be encouraged by it to do her work with a more hopeful
heart." "Let us all pull together until the common schools,
academies, colleges, and the university are up to the times in
which we live and worthy of our great commonwealth."[1]

From that time forth illiberal sentiments with regard to the
State institutions of higher learning were rarely to find expression
in the denomination. Moreover, whatever effect the opposition
of the churchmen to State colleges may have had in restricting
opportunities for higher education was largely compensated for
by their own activities in the field. It should be borne in mind
that to the extent that the Methodists opposed the influence of
the State in the realm of higher learning, they likewise undertook
to increase their own facilities in order that patronage of the State
institutions would be unnecessary.

With its communicants constituting so large a proportion of
the population of the South, and occupying, as it did, so important
a place in the educational system of the section, the Methodist
Episcopal Church, South, inevitably exerted a profound influence
in determining the character of popular thought along all lines

---

may, and if it should be, the policy of free tuition at the State University will
have short shrift at the ballot-box. The Methodists, Baptists, and Roman
Catholics, and their adherents, who by the assistance of a few friends outside
the State have had to provide mainly for the education of their sons, and
entirely for the education of their daughters, will sweep the State like a
cyclone. And when this question is once raised at the ballot-box, the electors,
who are mostly farmers and citizens, will want to know whether the proceeds
of the Land Script Fund is used for the improvement of the agriculture of the
State, as the Government intended, or to furnish a cheap sort of university
education." Cf. *Wesleyan Christian Advocate*, quoted in Nashville *Christian
Advocate*, February 28, 1885.
[1]*Wesleyan Christian Advocate*, July 31, 1889.

there. Liberality in thinking among a people so susceptible to the appeals of religion as were the Southerners would necessarily depend largely upon the receptivity to new ideas in such an institution. This was especially true of the second half of the nineteenth century when the rapid development and diffusion of new and startling theories in the fields of science, theology, and scholarship seemed to threaten the power of the Church, and to challenge the authority of its very foundations.

In view of this fact, it is significant that the migration of students from Randolph-Macon, Wofford, and other Southern Methodist institutions to Leipzig, the very center of the new learning, was, in no unreal sense, the beginning of the remarkable post-war procession of Southern students to German universities.[1] Moreover, as has been seen, a majority of the earliest of these European trained scholars were called to Southern Methodist Colleges, where, supported by men like Carlisle, Duncan, and Garland, they exerted an important influence. Close connections were likewise established with the new Johns Hopkins University, which but a short time after its founding in 1876 rivaled the German universities in attracting to itself many of the best minds of the South. The young men who returned with their doctorates from Leipzig and Johns Hopkins embodied in their teachings in the Southern Methodist colleges all the findings of modern scientific and scholarly investigation, and they encountered little opposition to their work or disposition to heresy hunting.

The latitude allowed these scholars in their work is indicated in the remarks of one who feared the influence of their teaching. Referring to the subject of the study of the Bible at Wofford College, one, who called himself "Amandale," said in a communication to the *New Orleans Christian Advocate* in 1887: "It may be that since the introduction of new professors (Ph. D's) from Germany, the home of materialism and rationalism, that this most praise-worthy course has been voted down in the faculty. There are colleges in our Methodism which not only do not study the Bible in their course, but absolutely have materialists, skeptics, rationalists, and sometimes infidels among their faculty."[2] When

---

[1] *Cf.* Henneman, *loc. cit.,* p. 190.
[2] *Cf.* letter of "Amandale" in *New Orleans Christian Advocate,* July 7, 1887.

a young faculty member at Vanderbilt University protested indignantly to Chancellor Garland that the Darwinian theory of evolution was being taught by certain professors in that institution, that venerable man replied: "Men never amount to much until they outgrow their fathers' notions, sir."[1] The victory which Bishop McTyeire and Dr. Garland won for a systematic theological training and the critical study of the Bible has been mentioned in connection with the founding of Vanderbilt University.

McTyeire's friendliness to liberal learning was made evident at that time. "A commission has been organized for revising our English Bible—a work in which all Protestant Churches are interested, and ought to be represented," he said. "British Methodism has two or three men on that commission; Northern Methodism one—considering their strength, as compared with the denominations about them who have Andover and Princeton and other old theological schools, they ought to have more. In each case these Methodists have supplied their representatives *from their theological schools.* Southern Methodism has no representative in that commission. Perhaps the old prejudice against the slave region had something to do with this. But suppose we should complain, standing on the platform Bishop Pierce offers us? The commissioners could reply: 'Gentlemen, you have some eloquent preachers and fervent evangelists—but *critics* are wanted for this work—scholars deeply learned in Biblical lore—and by your own confession you do not produce the article. Confine yourself to your mission among the masses, and take such a book as we make up for you.' " As for himself, the Bishop hoped to be pardoned "for declaring that I am not resigned to that condition, either for myself or for my brethren."[2] The arguments of the saintly Pierce gave way before the progressive ideas of McTyeire and Garland.

Although at the outset a "call to preach the gospel" was deemed an all-sufficient requisite for entering the biblical department at Vanderbilt University, McTyeire was able to effect a reorganization of that department a decade later and the entrance require-

---

[1] *Cf.* Dabney, *op. cit.*, p. 184.
[2] *Cf.* letter of Bishop McTyeire in Nashville *Christian Advocate*, quoted in *New Orleans Christian Advocate*, April 18, 1872.

ments were made to conform to those of the other departments.[1] While on an occasion which subsequently arose he failed to show himself as staunch a defender of academic freedom as many could have desired, Bishop McTyeire illustrated the liberality of viewpoint that characterized many of the educational leaders of Southern Methodism when in 1875 he brought to Vanderbilt as a special lecturer on Zoölogy and Historical and Dynamic Geology the able scientist, Alexander Winchell. Under a special arrangement Winchell was to lecture for twelve weeks at the University during the year. Winchell had already done much by his writings to awaken interest in the Darwinian theory. It was four years later, in a new work, that he expressed a belief in the pre-Admaic origin of man. The Bishop had brought the scientist as an especial attraction to give prestige to and to act as a drawing card for the new university. But it now became apparent that his advanced views were becoming so pronounced as to cause adverse criticism, and that his presence was having the opposite effect. Nevertheless, in view of his usual tolerant attitude and progressive outlook, it seemed strange that McTyeire should have allowed himself to be governed in the situation by considerations of executive expediency rather than those of academic freedom. However that may be, he now joined with the Board of Trust in asking the scientist to decline a reappointment to the special three months lectureship held by him, declaring that "Our people are of the opinion that such views are contrary to the plan of redemption."[2] When Winchell refused to do so the Board abolished the lectureship. In fairness to the Bishop it should be said that liberal members of the faculty sympathized with him in the situation, believing that he was motivated solely by a concern for the welfare of the infant university and that his action was in no wise inspired by opposition to the teachings of science.[3]

If, in taking the stand that he did, Bishop McTyeire acted

---

[1] Cf. Dabney, op. cit., p. 192.

[2] Cf. account of Winchell Affair in Nashville Christian Advocate, July 13, 1878.

[3] Andrew D. White, whose account of this affair most other writers on the subject have followed, interpreted it solely as a conflict between science and religion. In his A History of the Warfare of Science and Theology in Christen-

only as a business executive,[1] he had, nevertheless, allowed himself to be forced into a position liable to misconstruction. It is certain that his action was not interpreted in such a light by a number of those who came to his support, and the incident served as an occasion for the voicing of much of that illiberal sentiment in the Church against which he had so long striven. A number of the Church journals expressed with satisfaction the opinion that the Bishop and the Board had undertaken to strike a body blow at "insidious errors creeping in under cover of science." The editor of the Nashville *Advocate* was willing that the struggle over evolution should go on among scientists, but felt that it was "a very different matter when a teacher or professor before his classes and among students inculcates, or is known to favor, certain novelties and mischievous speculations." He commended the prompt stand that had been taken by the Board.[2]

The *Southern Christian Advocate*, referring to the incident, said: "They are in conflict of opinion on an ethnological question on which the Bible is the earliest and best authority. . . . Let us go so far as to suppose that the Trustees are simply in doubt as to the peculiar teachings of Dr. Winchell. It seems to us an easy question, which should have the benefit of the doubt, the Church or the Doctor? Conservatism is not likely to be a fatal mistake in this fast age. The Trustees are not infallible. Suppose they have erred; they have erred on the safe side. It is better to be behind the times than a great way ahead of them. Evolution, to say the least of it, is an open question. We can wait. So far from being offended at Vanderbilt's conduct in this matter, we are thankful to God that the munificent benefaction of the old Commodore is

---

dom, White treats the issue exclusively as one of academic freedom and makes no mention of the fact that Winchell had other academic connections at the time. Throughout the period during which he was a special visiting lecturer at Vanderbilt Winchell had a formal connection with Syracuse University, where he was professor of Geology. White, who obviously relied on biased sources, regarded McTyeire's action only as a persecution of Winchell.

[1] The writer has learned from conversations with Chancellor J. H. Kirkland and Dean Wilbur F. Tillett of Vanderbilt that this is the light in which they regard McTyeire's action. They state that liberal members of the faculty sympathized with the Bishop, when, seeking to protect the infant university from the hurtful situation which had developed, he was forced into a position open to misconstruction. They believe he was in no wise inspired by opposition to the teachings of science.

[2] *Cf.* Nashville *Christian Advocate*, August 17, 1878.

in such safe hands."[1] The *Wesleyan Christian Advocate* thought it no disparagment to those in control of the institution that they had seen fit to close relations with an instructor "whose teachings, in their judgment . . . antagonize the Scriptures."[2] It felt that "one professor seeking reputation in the exciting field of material philosophy is quite sufficient to keep a whole College of young men in a state of intellectual fever."[3]

The Tennessee Conference, one of the number invested with a voice in the control of the University, expressed the livliest gratification at the action which had been taken. During its annual gathering in October 1878, that body declared: "This is the age in which scientific atheism, having divested itself of the habiliments that most adorn and dignify humanity, walks abroad in shameless denudation. The arrogant and impertinent claims of this science, falsely so called, have been so boistrous and persistent that the unthinking masses have been sadly deluded. But our University alone has had the courage to lay its young, but vigorous, hand upon the mane of untamed speculation, and say we will have no more of this science. We want: no crude and undigested theories for the sons of our patrons. Science we must have, science we intend to have, but we want only science clearly demonstrated, and we have great cause to rejoice in this step, for it deals a blow, the force of which scientific atheism will find it exceedingly difficult to break."[4]

Despite the illiberal utterances occasioned by the Winchell incident, little tendency to heresy hunting was manifested among the Southern Methodists during the remainder of the century, and the Methodist Episcopal Church, South, notwithstanding the large element of untutored folk among its communicants, has never as a body entered the Fundamentalist fold, as did the Southern Baptist Church through the action of the Southern Baptist Convention in 1926.[5] Although a number of Southern Methodist

---

[1]*Southern Christian Advocate*, August 6, 1878.

[2]*Wesleyan Christian Advocate*, July 6, 1878.

[3]*Ibid.*, October 5, 1878.

[4]*Cf. Journal of Tennessee Conference*, 1878, p. 334.

[5]This body declared that "this Convention accepts Genesis as teaching that man was a special creation of God, and rejects every theory, evolutionary or other, which teaches that man originated or came by way of lower animal

ministers openly proclaimed their adherence to the evolutionary theory and although the doctrine was frequently expounded by instructors in the colleges of the denomination, no formal charges were at any time preferred against these men. One who feared the effects of such teaching declared in 1890 that there were instructors in Methodist colleges "whose skeptical ideas are not only proclaimed any and everywhere, but found also in print."[1] The lack of constraint with which a Methodist minister might speak on the subject is evidenced by an article on "Evolution as a Method of Creation," which appeared in *The Quarterly Review* of the Southern Church in 1894, and which was written by the Reverend M. B. Chapman, who at that time was serving as editor of the *St. Louis Christian Advocate*. The writer not only expressed a belief in the Darwinian theory, but declared that "the notion of instantaneous creation is crude," and that "it is suggested by a simple, untutored, unexpended [sic] stage of intellectual life." Moreover, it was "not God's method in anything else." He felt it "unwise and unsafe to denounce any scientific theory because it seems to come in conflict with a traditional interpretation of Scripture." The mere fact that extremists had gone into atheism and materialism was no argument for discarding "what is at least valuable as a working hypothesis." "Do not let us commit the old error of condemning unheard and unexamined what we imagine comes in conflict with the Scriptures," he urged. "Let us see whether it really comes in conflict with the Scriptures, or with our unauthorized interpretation of them. We cannot afford to ignore questions which are challenging the thought and investigation of the world. No system of secrecy, or proscription will avail, for nothing is gained by dodging a difficulty, and certainly nothing is gained by concealing that we have found one." In concluding the writer emphasized the fact that "there is a

---

ancestry." This statement was adopted a few months later by the Southern Baptist Education Board. No action relative to evolution was taken by the General Conference of the Methodist Episcopal Church, South, either in 1922, 1926, or 1930, during which time the agitation on the subject in the South reached a climax. Moreover, the Educational Board of the Church recorded its belief in 1927 that "legislation which would interfere with the proper teaching of science in American schools and colleges is futile and can serve no good." *Cf.* Dabney, *op. cit.*, p. 292.

[1] *Cf.* letter of T. J. Simmons in Nashville *Christian Advocate*, March 29, 1890.

theory of evolution that is reverent and devout, and which no more obscures faith in God's existence than does gravitation. The term represents a process, not a power; . . . it represents the method of the divine operation in the work of creation."[1]

The liberal views which prevailed in the Vanderbilt school of theology under the direction of the Reverend Wilbur F. Tillett, who was made its dean in 1885, have been set forth in his *The Paths That Lead To God* and other writings of today.[2] He earnestly urged upon the Church that there was of necessity no conflict between science and religion. During 1886 when Southern Presbyterians were seeking to suppress the teachings of Dr. James Woodrow as a "Christian Evolutionist," Dean Tillett discussed the matter in a communication to the Nashville *Christian Advocate,* and asserted that "so large a proportion of the Christian theologians and scientists of the present day reject the literal interpretation of the six days of creation as twenty-four hours that it is unpardonably narrow in an author to call such men not merely unchristian but 'infidels.' " "Unless our interpretation of the Bible is complete and perfect," he said, "it must change if ultimate truth is to be reached; the same is true of our interpretation of nature. Hence there may be, and in this sense must be, advance both in theology and science. When both theology and science have become perfect in their interpretation of the Bible and of nature, then, and not until then, can there be perfect and permanent agreement between the two." While, therefore, science and theology might be in conflict at points where the two touched, such conflicts should be rare "for the Bible was not written to teach science." Moreover, if this conflict should ever be drawn, "God is on the side of *truth,* and truth is going to come out triumphant in the end."[3]

Such liberality of attitude was perhaps best exemplified in the Connection by the views of Dr. David C. Kelley, who, as one of the prominent officials of the Church, insisted in 1883 that "all

[1]Chapman, M. B., "Evolution as a Method of Creation," *The Quarterly Review,* Vol. XIII (September-October, 1894), pp. 224-231.

[2]It is the testimony of this progressive theologian, given in a conversation with the present writer in November 1933, that the same liberal views set forth in this work were expounded at Vanderbilt during the time that it was a Methodist-controlled institution.

[3]Communication of the Reverend W. F. Tillett in Nashville *Christian Advocate,* February 27, 1886.

that is human" in the standards of the Church must be subject to investigation, and, if need be, to improvement. "Any other position," he said, must be one "of palpable blindness to the best interests of our Methodism."[1] Very different, it is true, was the attitude of the venerable Dr. John B. McFerrin, of Kelley's own State, who declared that the Church needed no "new theological revelations by science or philosophy." "How fearful," he said, was Dr. Kelley's statement that theology would go on adding "new and more exact forms of truth while time endures."[2] When McFerrin urged Kelley to stick to his work as Missionary Secretary, and to cease "tampering with science and philosophy among us home-folks," the latter said: "Everybody interested in such matters in this region knows well that the Doctor for the last twenty years has taken spells of *whipping* the writer, after his usual manner; that in all these contests he has been *victorious*— that the writer has laughed and applauded with the merriest the Doctor's signal triumphs. We both know that, after the exercise is over and the dust settled, the truth contended for by the writer has made more rapid way than ever before. With this state of facts, the writer has grown fond of the old Doctor's drubbings, and has generally forborne to reply."[3]

Referring to the spirit which had animated Dr. McFerrin, Kelley said on another occasion: "About thirty years ago Dr. McFerrin was at the head of a movement which *he* called *Old Methodism,* which, in its spirit of repressing narrowness and ostracism, is the antagonism of the grand spirit of Wesley and the men of humble, earnest scholarship and piety which laid deep the foundations of Methodism. The writer had but a short acquaintance with Bishop Soule and Dr. Summers before he became aware that much of this spirit and a number of these methods were as unlike the Methodism of the East as they were unlike the Methodism of Wesley. It required some nerve to attack the barnacles on the ship. More than one man gave warning of the direful effect of the wrath of Achilles. No *man* was attacked. The form of thought and action, born of a period when the West

---

[1]*Cf.* letter D. C. Kelley in Nashville *Christian Advocate,* February 24, 1883.
[2]*Cf.* letter of J. B. McFerrin in Nashville *Christian Advocate,* March 3, 1883.
[3]*Cf.* letter of D. C. Kelley in Nashville *Christian Advocate,* March 10, 1883.

was compelled to give her energies to pioneer work, valuable for pioneer purposes, which had given a new and different type to Methodism, were recognized at their true value; but declared to be neither the original Methodism, nor of necessity the Methodism of the future. Among them the writer had been born; all of them were dear to him by association; but to hold by them, to run in these narrow ruts, it was believed would be death to the Church, dearer to him than life. This is the head and front of his offending."[1]

When illiberal views were expressed in the Connection from time to time with regard to the freedom of inquiry and other such matters, they were certain to draw forth protest and dissent from advanced thinkers. The readiness with which such men spoke in defense of liberal principles is illustrated by "A Protest" which the Reverend W. T. Poynter of Kentucky published in the Nashville *Advocate* with regard to the impression created by some of the delegates of his Church at the Ecumenical Conference of Methodism at Washington in 1891. The writer deplored the fact that two bishops of the Church had virtually put Southern Methodism "down on the same plane with Elder Jasper of 'the sun-do-move fame,' " through the attitude they had assumed toward evolution and higher criticism. "There are in the ranks

---

[1]*Cf.* letter of D. C. Kelley in Nashville *Christian Advocate*, March 24, 1883. As to the charge of desiring to add to the gospel, Kelley replied that Mc-Ferrin's argument "would seem to make our creed, the gospel of Christ, revelation and theology synonymous." "Only in this way," he said, "could the reader be brought to the conclusion you desire, *i. e.,* to regard me as wishing to do the fearful thing of adding to the Gospel. But, Doctor, when you remember how persistently you fought to prevent the word 'theological' from attaching to the school for young preachers in Vanderbilt University—how you insisted on the difference between the *revealed Word* and *theology*—it is plain at least that you knew when you wrote these sentences that the words do not represent the same ideas. For truth's sake I must withstand you here, my venerable father. To say that theology will add new and more exact forms of truth is *not* to deny, as you know perfectly well, that 'the revelation is full, the plan complete.' You knew perfectly well when you wrote that sentence that I did not propose to add to or take from the Gospel of Christ; you knew perfectly well the difference between the Gospel of Christ and theology. Why, then, did you say 'how fearful this sentence.'? Can there be any other purpose but to impose upon the ignorant and the unlearned? . . . there is nothing fearful in the matter save the narrowness that would expect no new forms or larger development of truth. Such narrowness would, indeed, be enough to bring pallor to the cheek of every Methodist hoping and praying for the grand future of the Church." *Cf.* letter of D. C. Kelley in Nashville *Christian Advocate*, March 10, 1883.

of Southern Methodism," he said, "a goodly company who hold
to evolution as the method of creation, and who are following the
devout seekers of truth along all lines, with the single aim of
possessing the truth. These men do not believe that all truth has
been put into the Articles of the Southern Methodist Church, nor
even into the books of the Southern Methodist Publishing House,
and they dare read wherever they choose, and to think for themselves, and the effort of those in authority to suppress thought
must utterly fail." "Are we as preachers competent to say to
scientific men that they know nothing about science," he asked,
"and that because some of their conclusions may not suit our
views of what we had supposed to be the teachings of the Bible,
that therefore these men are ignorant blunderers, and should be
driven from the pales of the Church? Who has said that a man
must reject evolution in order to be a Christian? or that if a man
should subject the Bible to rational criticism as to its authorship
or its claims that such a man must have no place with us."[1]
Early in 1899 the Reverend E. B. Chappell, a member of the
Tennessee Conference which in 1878 had expressed its gratification at the checking of "untamed speculation," deplored all
ecclesiastical interference with free inquiry. In an article on
"Scientific Preaching" in *The Methodist Review,* Dr. Chappell
expressed the opinion that "Our interference in such matters in
the past has not been creditable to us or helpful to our cause."
"It does seem," he said, "as if we of this generation ought to be
more discreet, in view of the humiliating experiences of those who
have preceded us."[2]

The following year the *New Orleans Christian Advocate* said:
"A certain class of professing Christians evidently entertain the
notion that all 'higher criticism' of the Bible is of the devil, and
that to admit any of the conclusions of the higher critics which
involve a departure from the traditional view regarding the age
and authorship of certain portions of the Scriptures is to undermine the very foundations of Christianity." Such a view was
unfortunate, the *Advocate* said, because it not only forbade inquiry

---

[1]*Cf.* communication of the Reverend W. T. Poynter in Nashville *Christian
Advocate,* December 5, 1891.

[2]*Cf.* Chappell, E. B., "Scientific Preaching", *The Methodist Review,* Vol. VI
(January-February, 1899), pp. 22-26.

but also led many to feel that the Bible could not stand the light of investigation. It was an injustice to such critics to "imagine that they are engaged in a disreputable or an unimportant work." The *Advocate* emphasized the fact that as a result of their labors "the views of most theologians have undergone a radical change as regards the manner of inspiration." The higher critics had also "reached well-defined and well-supported conclusions" concerning "the date and authorship of certain portions of the Bible." Moreover the "truth unadulterated by tradition or supposition is what we ought to desire above all things."[1]

Aside from the fact that Southern Methodism continued to entertain a traditional Protestant hostility to the "fatal errors" of Catholicism which encouraged a spirit of intolerance and bigotry where that faith was concerned,[2] the absence of particularistic doctrines and exclusive pretensions served to make its adherents tolerant of other creeds. Moreover, their active co-operation with other denominations inclined them to liberality in doctrinal matters, making them the more ready to examine critically their own creed.

---

[1] *Cf. New Orleans Christian Advocate*, October 11, 1900.

[2] The Catholic Church was denounced by officials and representative bodies of the Connection, not only because of the "fatal errors" of its doctrine, but also because of its supposed disloyalty to the American Government, and hostility to republican institutions in general. Characteristic of the light in which the Roman doctrines were viewed was the attitude expressed by the Reverend Linus Parker, editor of the New Orleans *Advocate*. When a correspondent of a secular paper rebuked Parker for his uncharitable attitude toward the communicants of that faith in 1871, asking if it were true that the editor and the Catholics worshipped the same God, and "by what right, Christian or other, he dare scoff at those who, however the forms of their faith may differ," looked to the same means of salvation, he replied: "As to worshipping the same God, we are not clear that the Romanists worship God at all, 'since God is a Spirit and they that worship him must worship in spirit and in truth.' We can by no means be classed with those who bow down to a wafer, and who pray to Mary and the other saints." *Cf. New Orleans Christian Advocate*, July 6, 1871. "We must yet earnestly contend for the faith, and no maudlin sentimentality should prevent us," wrote the reactionary Dr. W. L. C. Hunnicutt in 1887. "It is quite too late for Protestants to apologize for protesting against the errors of Romanism. This is the calling and work of Protestants, as such. . . . If any think our opposition to Romanism unnecessary, we reply that the world is in greatest danger from those evils which are compounded with good." "Nothing is so harmful as a false religion, unless it be one which is partly false." *Cf.* letter of "W. L. C. H." in *New Orleans Christian Advocate*, July 7, 1887. The New Orleans *Advocate*, issuing from the very stronghold of Catholicism in the Southern States, assumed the leadership in opposing the supposed political aggression of the Roman Church. Typical of the attitude maintained by that journal were its comments upon an occasion when it was reported that the notably liberal Archbishop Gibbons of Baltimore had stated

Thus there was among the leaders and communicants of the Methodist Episcopal Church, South, an important group of men who were not only willing to subject the standards of their Church to critical tests when occasion arose, but were likewise content to follow the seekers of truth in all fields of thought. The tolerant views of these men contributed much to the advancement of liberal thinking both in the Methodist Connection and among the Southern people at large.

---

at a banquet in Rome that the Catholics of this country were "American in voice, but Roman in heart." The *Advocate* declared that the Archbishop's words "have of course, one meaning, and that confirmatory of Protestant opinion everywhere expressed concerning the Romish priesthood. . . . We have become accustomed to emphatic denials of what is now so positively affirmed. When charged with adherence to their peculiar tenents and methods, for which they would sacrifice the interests and integrity of the State, they have loudly protested and declared unalterable devotion to the country. Their patriotism is above suspicion, their republicanism beyond question. But a great primate of the Church in America now boldly avows his superior and more sacred allegiance to a system antagonistic to our institutions. . . . Alas! for this country if the Archbishop's followers should become sufficiently numerous to be a dominant power. Then, with such a shibboleth upon their lips, we might expect the bloody days of Alva to return again. . . . So, then, a Romish priest is not a sincere friend of our broad, free republican institutions. . . . We deprecate any ecclesiastical test of a man's fitness for public office, but the facts are as stated. The American people are too well versed in Romish History—they know too thoroughly its story of persecution and carnage, its crowning and uncrowning of kings—ever to imperil their liberties in Roman hands." *Cf. New Orleans Christian Advocate*, October 23, 1884. The parochial schools were especially feared as an agency of Roman aggression.

CHAPTER IX

TEMPERANCE

AS has been seen, the tendency to moral laxity which manifested itself during the post-war years caused the Churches of the South to fear for their moral integrity. Everywhere an inordinate craving for pleasure revealed itself. It was felt that the pathway of the Christian was beset with unusual and manifold pitfalls. Since Methodist theology recognized the possibility of "falling from grace," the need for reform measures was urgently felt in the Methodist Episcopal Church, South, during that time. Because conversion could not be taken as a sufficient guarantee that one would live as a follower of Christ should, the Church constantly sought to impress upon its members the necessity for mending their ways and for keeping themselves "unspotted from the world." Moral accountability was made to extend to every act which might be conducive to evil, and the communicant was held to a high degree of individual responsibility. The General Rules forbade all pleasures which could not be "taken in the name of the Lord Jesus."

Moral suasion was constantly employed to induce men to keep themselves free of immoralities and worldliness. The sins of individuals and of groups were exposed with startling frankness. Such efforts were reinforced by the whole authority of the Church. A careful watch was kept over transgressors with a view to disciplining them or to expelling those who were guilty of glaring or persistent misconduct.[1] Moreover it was gradually realized that spiritual salvation must be assured through efforts to "redeem the total life of man." Men were awakening to the fact that religious welfare was dependent upon social conditions and temperal well-being. As it came to be recognized that men could not be disassociated from their social surroundings, and that Methodists were "resolved to be like other people," the Church exerted itself increasingly to make the world a safer place for the Christian to dwell in. As the important relation of humanitarian to moral

---

[1] Cf. Simkins and Woody, op. cit., p. 406.

reform was understood, the Methodists advanced humanitarian arguments more and more in support of measures of moral uplift, and their interest in humanitarian reforms as ends in themselves increased proportionately. This new interest did much to destroy the old ideas with regard to "fanaticism" in such matters. It made the Church willing not only to lend its endorsement and support to various organized reform movements of the day, but also to encourage the enactment of prohibitory State legislation for moral and humanitarian elevation.

The most vigorous efforts of Southern Methodism for enforcing personal and social morality were those directed against the drink evil. The recent War had given what appeared to be a body blow to the temperance cause in the South. The temperance societies which had flourished in the section during *ante-bellum* days had virtually ceased to exist.[1] It was soon obvious that the drink habit had been greatly fostered by the War.[2] Social drinking and tippling were everywhere prevalent, and drunkenness appeared to be increasing rapidly. Intemperance was aggravated by such developments as the wider distribution of ready cash, the rise of the commercial village and the growth of the country store.[3] It was further stimulated by the despondency with which the future was regarded. An English observer reported in 1877 that many Southerners had been "driven to drink by their misfortunes," and that drunkenness had become "deplorably prevalent."[4] It was feared that young men everywhere, brooding over their blighted prospects, would take to their cups. Southern villages were the scenes of the wildest confusion on Saturday afternoons when no woman or child ventured upon the streets.[5] In 1885 a prosecuting officer in South Carolina expressed the belief that nine-tenths of the crimes of violence committed since the War had been caused by drunkenness.[6]

Confronted by this state of affairs the Methodist Episcopal

---

[1]Scomp, H. A., *King Alcohol in the Realm of King Cotton* (Emory College, 1887), p. 577.

[2]Colvin, D. Leigh, *Prohibition in the United States* (New York, 1926), p. 58.

[3]*Cf.* Simkins and Woody, *op. cit.*, p. 322.

[4]*Idem.*

[5]*Idem.*

[6]Scomp, *op. cit.*, p. 218.

Church, South, soon began to exert itself vigorously to banish the use of strong drink. Intemperance was fought as "the great crime of the century." In following this course the Church met considerable difficulty. To begin with, it had not always in the past borne a consistent or unequivocal testimony against drinking. The General Rules, as adopted by the organizing Conference in 1784, had, indeed, required that members abstain from doing harm "by avoiding evil of every kind, especially that which is most generally practiced, such as drunkenness, buying or selling spirituous liquors, or drinking them unless in cases of extreme necessity."[1] But drinking and trafficking in ardent spirits were well-nigh universal at the time, and the Church soon receded from its well defined position. In 1790 the prohibition against "buying and selling" was stricken out of the Rule, and the inhibition was then against "drunkenness, or drinking spirituous liquors, unless in cases of extreme necessity." The law at that time merely provided that "If any member of our society retail or give spirituous liquors, and anything disorderly be transacted under his roof on this account, the preacher who has oversight of the circuit shall proceed against him, as in the case of other immoralities, and the person accused shall be cleared, censured, suspended, or excluded, according to his conduct, as on other charges of immorality."[2]

When the Reverend James Axley sought to induce the General Conference of 1812 to provide for the incorporation of a new section in the *Discipline* which would forbid preachers to distill or sell spirituous liquors, that body instead adopted a resolution which only served to indicate the extent to which the Methodists had yielded to the pressure of universal practice. This resolution declared: "It is with real regret that we have seen the use of ardent spirits, dram-drinking, etc., so common among the Methodists. We have endeavored to suppress the practice by our example, but it is necessary that we add precept to example. And we really think it is not consistent with the character of a Christian to be immersed in the practice of distilling or retailing an article so destructive to the morals of society; and we do most earnestly

---

[1] *Ibid.*, p. 219.
[2] *Ibid.*, p. 220.

recommend the Annual Conferences and our people to join with us in making a firm and constant stand against the evil which has ruined thousands, both in time and in eternity."[1]

Although the Reverend Axley was successful in securing the adoption of a rule forbidding preachers to retail spirituous or malt liquors in 1816, an attempt to have the General Conference of 1820 make the distilling of spirits a cause for the forfeiture of Church standing failed.[2] While efforts for strengthening the position of the denomination with regard to drink were made from time to time, the rising agitation of the slavery question soon so absorbed the attention of reformers that little was accomplished, and the original rule had not been restored when the great division of the Church took place in 1844.

In 1848 Wesley's rule was again placed in the *Discipline* of the Northern Church. Although trafficking in intoxicating liquors by members was frequently dealt with as an immorality in .the Southern Church from the time of its formation,[3] the specific rule making "buying and selling" punishable on such grounds had not been restored to the Southern *Discipline* at the beginning of the post-war era. So far from specifically condemning the manufacture and sale of strong drink as an immorality, that instrument during the early years after the War contained a section declaring that "if any shall engage in such manufacture or sale, let the discipline be administered as in the case of imprudent or improper conduct."[4] Despite the fact that the Church, relying upon the spirit and intent of its Rules as a sufficient warrant for proceeding against offenders, still frequently resorted to admonition and expulsion when members engaged in such traffic, the manufacture and sale of ardent spirits continued to be widely prevalent in the Connection. The degree to which the moral sense of the Church had been allowed to slumber where

---

[1]*Idem.*

[2]*Idem.*

[3]In 1846 Bishop Capers advised the Georgia Conference with regard to instances of such traffic, first, to "use private admonition, then admonish in presence and with the aid, of one or two more, remonstrating to the offending brother of his doing harm, and not walking charitably and inoffensively as one of Christ's flock; and *lastly*, there being no help left, let him be brought to trial, and if still incorrigible, let him be cut off." Cf. Scomp, *op. cit.*, p. 521.

[4]Cf. Scomp, *op. cit.*, p. 738.

the liquor business was concerned was indicated by the fact that during 1867 three different firms were permitted to advertise whiskey in the columns of the *New Orleans Christian Advocate* over a period of six months. Upon having his attention called to the matter by a subscriber, the editor said: "The advertisement was in for six months before *we* saw it, and therefore, we cannot complain against an old friend for not complaining of it sooner. But it got in, and was paid for, and had rights of occupation, and could not be ejected before the legal expiration of its time."[1] In an attempt to account for the extent to which the Church had winked at such practices among its members, the *Western Methodist* said in 1874: "Unfortunately the traffic in intoxicating liquors in this country has been almost universally associated with the grocery business, and on this account Methodists, as well as members of other Churches, have been led into this great evil, appeasoning [sic] conscience by reasoning which is sophistical and altogether unsatisfactory to the enlightened understanding. Thus men who in all other respects are meritorious and even exemplary are today engaged in a traffic which is ruinous to their souls, and to the souls as well as the bodies and estates of their fellow-men, and which brings shame and reproach on the Church."[2]

The record as regards the use of intoxicants in the Connection was hardly less embarrassing. Habitual drinking and drunkenness were found everywhere. "Whiskey drinking in the Church is, in my opinion, one of the greatest hindrances to the Church and the enjoyment of religion with which our societies are cursed," wrote a correspondent of the New Orleans *Advocate* in 1870. "Ministers of the Gospel drink it—and to drunkenness. Official members of the Church drink it, and it is becoming quite common to see them drink."[3] The following year the South Carolina Conference reported that the Church at large was "deeply afflicted and embarrassed" by the drink evil.[4] As late as 1885 a Methodist minister in Louisiana could say that "There is a great

---

[1] *Cf. New Orleans Christian Advocate*, June 1, 1867.
[2] *Cf. The Western Methodist*, quoted in *New Orleans Christian Advocate*, July 2, 1874.
[3] *Cf.* letter of "J. T. C." in *New Orleans Christian Advocate*, December 10, 1870.
[4] *Minutes of South Carolina Conference*, 1871, p. 15.

multitude of professors of religion who are secret if not open friends of whiskey and the liquor traffic; and friends because they like it. . . . A member of my charge told me a few days ago that it was the exception when a member of the Church refused to take social drinks, especially in private and during political excitements."[1]

Communicants of the Church were subject to "strange chronic ailments" for which they habitually took "bitters."[2] The New Orleans *Advocate* in 1870 characterized the age as one of *"bitters* as well as *chivalry,"* and deplored the prevalent use of such "poisoned cups of intoxication" in the denomination.[3] Brandy and whiskey were declared to be "the great panaceas for all the ills and aches that frail humanity is subject to in the Church, as well as out of it."[4]

When leaders of the Connection, appalled now by the increasing evidences of dissipation, argued that the Church must bear a more definite witness against the drink evil, the suggestion met with opposition on various grounds. It was contended by many that law enough could already be found in the *Discipline* to warrant the trial and expulsion of the makers and venders of spirituous liquors. Further legislation on the subject, it was felt, was not only unnecessary, but would imply that the traffic had not been condemned in the past, thus casting a reproach upon the Church. It was urged that there was no Scriptural authority for taking an absolute position on the subject, and that such action would be tantamount to making a new moral law.[5] Some ob-

---

[1] *Cf.* letter of the Reverend Jas. J. Billingsly in *New Orleans Christian Advocate,* June 4, 1885.

[2] *Cf.* Simkins and Woody, *op. cit.,* p. 405.

[3] *New Orleans Christian Advocate,* June 25, 1870.

[4] Letter of "J. T. C." in *New Orleans Christian Advocate,* December 10, 1870.

[5] When the General Conference of 1874 submitted to the Annual Conferences a proposal for a change in the General Rules touching this subject, Dr. Lovick Pierce wrote: "The whole underlying element in this move, is to conform this condition of membership to the temperance idea of the times. No one would ever have thought of conforming our General Rules to this idea on the subject of liquor, but for this temperance enthusiasm—we mean to say total abstinence enthusiasm. For no one of safe mind will say that total abstinence from anything that may be temperately used, ever was, or ever can be, a moral obligation *per se.* Mr. Wesley, like a wise man, made temperance one of his fundamental conditions of Methodist fellowship. But this he did—not upon the basis of total abstinence, but upon the basis of a useless use of liquor." *Cf.* letter of Dr. Lovick Pierce in Nashville *Christian Advocate,* August 29,

jected to the Church committing itself definitely upon the subject because of its relation to the political issues of the day. As will be seen, the temperance movement in the United States during that period entered upon a phase in which the reformers gradually ceased to rely primarily upon moral suasion, and sought to achieve their ends chiefly through legislation. Many persons felt that for the Church to commit itself under the circumstances would constitute political interference. Such arguments were reinforced by appeals to the distaste for "fanaticism" which had long prevailed in the Connection. In the Annual Conferences it was objected that the creation of temperance committees would be an "entering wedge of isms," and that they would result in too great a concentration on particular vices.[1]

Despite all such arguments, and although the tendency to imbibe continued strong among many of its communicants, the Methodist Episcopal Church, South, became increasingly energetic in attacking the drink evil. A remarkable interest soon manifested itself in the subject, an interest greatly stimulated by the fact that local chapters of temperance orders, designed to promote total abstinence and prohibitive legislation, were again being established everywhere. The Church was contributing a large quota to the membership of the Sons of Temperance, the Good Templars, and other such organizations, and in turn was receiving from them much inspiration for its war on the "demon rum."

A persistent fight was carried on to rid the Church of all complicity with the liquor evil. A stricter enforcement of the rules against strong drinks was constantly urged, and a vigorous movement began for a more definite condemnation of the traffic. It was hoped to banish all use of intoxicants from the Church. Annual Conferences began regularly to appoint special temperance committees and to instruct the presiding elders and pastors to bring the subject frequently before their congregations. Some of

---

1874. A correspondent of the New Orleans *Advocate* protested that the proposed change was inspired by "the Constitution and By-Laws of the Sons of Temperance" rather than by anything in the Scriptures. He declared that the "total abstinence law is not in the Scriptures, neither directly set forth nor from any law found therein." *Cf.* letter of "S." in *New Orleans Christian Advocate,* July 30, 1874.

[1] For an account of such objections made in the Annual Conferences see communication of "J. P." in *New Orleans Christian Advocate,* February 8, 1877.

the Conferences provided that a temperance sermon should be delivered at each appointment during the year.[1] Ministers were encouraged to prepare suitable articles on the subject for the journals of the Connection. The propriety of total abstinence upon the part of Church members was continually stressed, and moral suasion was employed to that end upon all occasions. "As a Church we are too lax upon this evil of habitual drinking, and the greater evil of selling whiskey," exhorted the New Orleans *Advocate* in characteristic fashion in 1869. "We have had such a detestation of 'fanaticism' that we have furnished an occasion to the Enemy that he has not failed to improve. . . . Let us now begin to preach against it; let us banish the mildest forms of this evil from our side-boards and tables, that we may rescue our friends and our families from a consuming fire. . . . we will by *personal* example and associated effort do what we may to stay this widening stream of sorrow."[2]

Abortive efforts were made in 1870 and 1874 to have the trafficking in liquor declared an immorality. In the former year a motion to have the General Conference define specifically the meaning of the General Rule on the subject was lost.[3] A resolution calling upon the bishops to explain definitely what was meant by the rule and a memorial from the Virginia Conference asking that a specific rule with regard to the traffic be inserted in the *Discipline* met a like fate.[4] The discussion of these measures nevertheless aroused a deep interest in the question and those who were anxious for the Church to assume an unequivocal stand on the subject agitated the matter widely during the months preceding the General Conference of 1874. The issue was debated at length in the Annual Conferences and in the *Advocates*. Those who were anxious for a specific condemnation of the liquor traffic as an immorality were careful to point out that past custom would not warrant an interpretation of the General Rules which would allow for expulsion on such grounds. "I know that it is

---

[1] The Louisville Conference made such a provision as early as 1867. *Cf.* Nashville *Christian Advocate*, October 17, 1867.

[2] *New Orleans Christian Advocate*, June 12, 1869.

[3] *Cf. Daily Christian Advocate*, May 6, 1870.

[4] *Cf. Proceedings* of General Conference as given in *New Orleans Christian Advocate*, May 21, 1870.

held that the *usage* of the Church has established the *law* against it," wrote a correspondent of the New Orleans *Advocate* in 1873. "I protest that this is a debatable question. Where and when has the custom of the Church established such a law? To have made it a law it must have been a universal custom. But it has been in communities here and there, that is all. To my certain knowledge there is not nor has there been such a custom in the Alabama Conference, in many years past; and judging from statements made in our *Advocate*, I conclude not anywhere. There is plenty of law in the discipline to expel a man for it; and so I claim; but it is manifestly a forced construction of the law." The writer declared that although the Annual Conferences had gone on adopting resolutions condemning the liquor traffic, such measures, lacking real authority, had been forgotten or ignored. He emphasized his argument by citing an instance in which a member of the Church had defended his action in selling intoxicants while holding the *Discipline* in his hand.[1] Although the General Conference of 1874 approved a proposed amendment to the General Rules which would make the buying and selling of ardent spirits punishable as an immorality, the measure failed of ratification when sent to the Annual Conferences for their action.[2]

By 1882 the advocates of a rule which would definitely stigmatize the traffic had marshaled their forces for another drive. The General Conference of that year was flooded with "divers papers" asking for a restoration of Wesley's original rule. Instead of complying with this demand, however, that body provided for the incorporation of a section in the *Discipline* which directed "our preachers and members" to "abstain from the manufacture or sale of intoxicating liquors to be used as a beverage," and stipulated that "if any shall engage in such manufacture or sale," they should be proceeded against "as in cases of imprudent or improper conduct."[3]

The fact that the buying and selling of liquor had been characterized by the General Conference merely as imprudent or improper conduct caused those who desired an absolute condem-

---

[1] *Cf.* letter of W. H. P. Connelly in *New Orleans Christian Advocate*, August 21, 1873.
[2] *Cf. Daily Advocate*, May 22, 1874.
[3] *Journal of General Conference*, 1882, p. 170.

nation to redouble their activity. At last their efforts were crowned with success when the General Conference of 1886, after warm debate, made the manufacture and sale of intoxicating beverages punishable as an immorality.[1] At its next sessions the Conference recommended the use of unfermented wines in the observance of the Sacrament.[2] Four years later an even more advanced position was taken. The General Conference of 1894 provided that the renting of property for the purpose of selling, the signing of petitions for licenses to sell, and "becoming bondsmen for any person as a condition for obtaining a license to sell" intoxicants should be punished as immoralities.[3] The General Rules no longer prevented the Church from bearing an unequivocal testimony against strong drink.

At the same time that the Methodist Episcopal Church, South, had been proceeding along these lines, it had been employing more direct methods for the promotion of temperance reform among the people at large. Methodist journals and representative bodies everywhere pledged themselves to aid in ridding society of the "monster iniquity." As early as 1867 the Louisville Conference declared that it would discountenance in every proper way the habits of dram drinking and of treating others with spirits.[4] The Mississippi Conference promised in 1869 to "use our best endeavors to banish from the social circle and the festive board all use, as a beverage, of every sort of intoxicating liquors."[5] The South Carolina Conference resolved to use its influence both privately and publicly to "abate this evil." "Into what legislative body, into what civil or political gathering, into what social party, or even religious assembly, can you go without having your sensibilities shocked by the noxious fumes of intoxicating drinks?" exclaimed that body in 1872. It felt that the necessity for immediate action was imperative.[6]

---

[1] *Journal of General Conference,* 1886, p. 198.
[2] *Cf.* account of the Reverend J. D. Walsh in New York *Christian Advocate,* June 19, 1890.
[3] *Journal of General Conference,* 1894, pp. 143-144.
[4] *Cf. Proceedings* of Louisville Conference as given in Nashville *Christian Advocate,* October 17, 1867.
[5] *Cf. Proceedings* of Mississippi Conference as given in New Orleans *Christian Advocate,* December 18, 1869.
[6] *Cf. Minutes of South Carolina Conference,* 1872, pp. 11-12.

Efforts were constantly made to stigmatize drinking of all kinds and under all circumstances, and to brand the liquor traffic as a crime against society.[1] The degrading effects of the drink habit were dwelt upon continually. The public was reminded that no Methodist could take a single dram while in the enjoyment of health without drawing upon himself the censure of his Church, and that no Christian could drink to intoxication without forfeiting his title to heaven. The North Georgia Conference rejoiced in 1889 to know that moral sentiment had been awakened to the extent that "attaches disgrace to intoxication in any degree."[2] The Louisiana Conference but echoed sentiments which had been heard in its sister Conferences when it exclaimed in 1891: "Rum, rape, and rebellion—the three disgraces—are responsible for the ruin of more men and empires born for greatness, and for more 'howling wildernesses' on the map of the world's civilization, than any baleful combination of cause and effect than were ever born out of Satan's quiver-full, or selected by him as tested weapons from the magazine of death."[3]

The Conferences were active in promoting popular education on the subject of temperance. They regularly adopted long reports depicting the evil effects of drink upon both body and mind. They instructed their preachers to bring the subject "frequently and forcibly" before the public through lectures and special sermons. The North Georgia Conference directed its members to "keep the waters troubled," urging that "Every moral influence and effort should be brought to bear upon the young that a generation may be raised up knowing nothing of the power of this evil. Parents must be convinced that children can be raised without it. Young people must be made to feel that it is more

---

[1] As early as 1873 the Reverend D. C. Kelley addressed a sermon to the members of the Tennessee legislature in which he depicted the vicious and sinister character of the whiskey traffic. He stated that through careful investigation he had discovered that five-eights of the crimes of the State were attributable to strong drink. He appealed to the legislators, "in the name of the ruined homes, and the tears of wives and children; in the name of the whole country and their own State, and in the name of the Heavenly Father, to make liquor dealers responsible for the legitimate results of their iniquitous trade." *Cf.* sermon as reported in Nashville *Banner,* and quoted in Nashville *Christian Advocate,* January 25, 1873.

[2] *Minutes of North Georgia Conference,* 1889, p. 15.

[3] *Minutes of Louisiana Conference,* 1891, p. 25.

manly to decline than to accept an invitation to drink."[1] The
Conference journals strove continually to impress upon the public
"the harmful nature of intoxicants, and the dreadful evils resulting from their use." "Let the work of educating the people
upon the subject go on unceasingly," said the New Orleans
Advocate. "There must be given 'line upon line and precept
upon precept; here a little, there a little.' Let the pulpit continue
to thunder against the saloon and the drink habit, and depict the
blessings of total abstinence and prohibition. Voting out whiskey
will do but little good if interest in the matter be allowed to die
down. . . . Nothing short of constant vigilance and a perpetual
campaign of temperance education will insure victory over this
monster iniquity."[2] The churchmen came to urge temperance
reform no less on humanitarian than on moral grounds. The
Tennessee Conference argued that the destruction of the saloon
would "remove the greatest obstruction to the path of human
progress and happiness ever known."[3]

Representative bodies of the Church used their influence to
have "scientific instruction" on the use of alcohol furnished in
the common schools of the section. In 1885 the Mississippi
Conference urged the legislature of that State to "engraft upon
our public school system compulsory instructions touching the subject of Temperance and its relation to Hygiene and Physiology."[4]
Two years later the Louisiana Conference resolved that "scientific
instruction on the Temperance question is the need of the day,
and to this end we approve any movement looking to petitioning
the Legislature, at its next session, to provide for such instruction
in the public schools of this State."[5] In 1892 the North Georgia
Conference memorialized the Georgia legislature, requesting it
"to provide for having 'scientific temperance' taught in all the
public schools of the State."[6]

The Church did much to advance the cause of reform through
the hearty coöperation which it accorded such temperance organi-

---

[1]*Minutes of North Georgia Conference,* 1889, p. 15.
[2]*New Orleans Christian Advocate,* March 26, 1896.
[3]*Journal of Tennessee Conference,* 1891, pp. 31-32.
[4]*Journal of Mississippi Conference,* 1885, p. 17.
[5]*Journal of Louisiana Conference,* 1887, p. 11.
[6]*Minutes of the North Georgia Conference,* 1892, p. 30.

zations as the Sons of Temperance, the Social Circle, and the Friends of Temperance. The *Advocates* and the Annual Conferences warmly commended the work of these orders and pledged their suport to them. Individuals were urged to join them. Methodist houses of worship were frequently thrown open for their use. Representatives of the temperance societies addressed large audiences and organized local chapters in the churches. Ministers read the temperance pledges to their congregations. Much cordiality was shown to the recently organized Woman's Christian Temperance Union.[1]

The organized reform forces concentrated their energies more and more upon efforts to drive out strong drink through restrictive laws and absolute prohibition.[2] As a result many Methodists feared that participation in the battles for reform by the Church would constitute clerical interference in politics. Even those most sensitive with regard to the position of the denomination on the drink evil were half apologetic at first about urging such a course. Discussing the changed aspects of the temperance crusade the committee appointed to report on the matter in the Mississippi Conference said in 1881: "But the important inquiry for us to consider is the attitude the Church should assume at this juncture and to this new phase of the subject. The relation between Church and State is a delicate question awakening the jealousy of each. While it is not the province of the Church to exercise civil functions or control in civil matters, by her moral power and positive teaching and aggressive agencies she may create a demand for legislative reform, and largely aid the State in its police administration."[3] Asserting that while the ballot would necessarily be an essential factor in securing prohibition, the work would nevertheless have to be accomplished in the main by the Church, the Louisiana Conference said that same year: "Neither do we think it necessary to become alarmed about becoming a political Church. . . . the professed Christian, whether he belongs to a political party or not, should advocate temperance measures and the nomination of temperance men for office, and then vote

---

[1]*Cf.* Scomp, *op. cit.,* pp. 577-683.
[2]*Cf.* Colvin, *op. cit.,* pp. 355-379.
[3]*Cf. Proceedings* of Mississippi Conference as given in *New Orleans Christian Advocate,* December 29, 1881.

for them. . . . Why should the Church hesitate to use the ballot-box as a means of arresting one of the mightiest evils of the land when the advocates of the drink system look to it as almost the exclusive means of their success?"[1]

It soon became apparent that the old fear of political contamination would not suffice to prevent the representative bodies and official organs of the Connection from committing themselves in favor of measures for the legal suppression of the liquor evil. The Memphis Conference, less apologetic than its sister organizations, declared as early as 1881 that it would do all in its power, "by voice and vote and influence, to drive the use of alcoholic beverages from the Methodist Church and from the country, and to secure the election to office of sound Temperance men, and to obtain such legislation as may be necessary to exterminate the whole traffic."[2] The *Texas Christian Advocate* had already expressed itself in favor of the enactment of local option laws in 1879,[3] and in 1881 the New Orleans *Advocate* and the *Wesleyan* pledged their support to all legal measures designed to suppress strong drink. The New Orleans journal declared that it was "in favor of prohibition, of local option, of any and all legislation that assumes and asserts the right to prohibit, and that stamps the liquor traffic as a crime against society."[4] The *Wesleyan* urged adequate prohibition laws upon the Georgia legislature, asserting that the least that the legislators *"can decently think of is a general local option law that gives to communities as incorporated towns or counties, the right to forbid the traffic upon the vote of the majority."*[5] The New Orleans *Advocate* warned the Church in 1886 that the effort to keep the temperance movement separate from politics would, if successful, fasten the saloons upon the country more securely than ever. It declared that the liquor power had found its stronghold in politics, and that the Church, if it would conquer the saloon, must follow it to all of its hiding-

---

[1] *Cf. Proceedings* of Louisiana Conference as given in *New Orleans Christian Advocate*, January 20, 1881.
[2] *Journal of Memphis Conference*, 1881, p. 25.
[3] *Cf.* Nashville *Christian Advocate*, July 12, 1879.
[4] *Cf.* New Orleans *Christian Advocate*, February 24, 1881.
[5] *Cf. Wesleyan Christian Advocate*, July 30, 1881.

places.[1] One after another the *Advocates* and Annual Conferences became outspoken during the Eighties in advocating the legal suppression of the evil.

By 1887 the Florida Conference announced with great satisfaction that "Our Church . . . leads the van in creating adverse sentiment, in restricting, and in prohibiting the use and traffic in this powerful agency in the hands of the devil to retard the progress of Christianity. . . . It affords us pleasure to report that our Church almost as a unit was true to our faith in the recent crusades against King Alcohol within the bounds of our beloved State."[2] "Time and again," explained the Alabama Conference the following year, "this and other Conferences have declined to unite with sister Churches in memorializing legislatures on sabbath desecration and other important subjects, because of our antipathy to what might appear a Methodist faction in politics; but we are glad to know that as a Church organization, no less than as patriotic citizens, and by influencing legislation, no less than by molding private opinion, we have done our full share of what has been accomplished in temperance work."[3]

About the same time the Tennessee Conference acknowledged that it had received new light upon the subject. "Our fathers walked in the light they had," it said: "We propose no censure on them when we say that in dealing with the liquor traffic in the past many of its infamies have been winked at, but now God by the light of today commands in unmistakable terms all men everywhere to repent." While expressing its recognition of the lines of distinction between the legitimate spheres of Church and State, it declared that it could not for a moment "forget that in the field of morals covered by the second great commandment there is a common ground which has ever been and must forever be occupied by both." For the Church to "hesitate to prosecute with all her power a great moral evil like the whiskey traffic, because it has contrived to protect itself under the forms of law, would be not only recreant to her commission, but a denial of the

---

[1] *Cf. New Orleans Christian Advocate,* September 9, 1886.
[2] *Journal of Florida Conference,* 1887, p. 35.
[3] *Cf.* Report of Committee on Temperance in *Minutes of Alabama Conference,* 1888.

Master who gave up his life rather than compromise with sin."[1] By the end of the Eighties representative bodies everywhere in the Connection vied with one another in taking action which placed them in precisely the same position that their Northern brethren had occupied during the slavery controversy forty years before.

Rejoiced at having committed itself so unqualifiedly in 1886, the General Conference when it met at St. Louis in 1890 expressed its willingness to assume an even more forward position. It said: "We are convinced that if any more advanced position is possible for any Church (any position, we mean, that comes within the province of a Church) than the one which the Methodist Episcopal Church, South, occupies today upon the question of temperance and prohibition, our membership is ready at once to take it. We are emphatically a prohibition Church. . . . We offer no compromise to and seek no terms for a sin of this heinous quality. We are opposed to all forms of license of this iniquity, whether the same be 'high' or 'low.' It cannot be so high that the prayers of God's people for its suppression will not rise above it, nor so 'low,' though it makes its bed in hell, that the shrieks of the souls lost through its accursed agency will not descend beneath it."[2]

In the actual contests waged for local option and prohibition during the Eighties and Nineties the Methodists were a potent force. In the first place the Church furnished a number of experienced and resourceful leaders. Such outstanding churchmen as Bishop Charles B. Galloway and Atticus Haygood and Dr. David C. Kelley participated personally in campaigns in the various States, bringing tongue and pen to the support of the cause. They exerted a powerful influence on the formation of public opinion, often speaking daily before large audiences.[3]

---

[1] *Journal of Tennessee Conference*, 1889, p. 89.

[2] *Journal of General Conference*, 1890, p. 151.

[3] The extraordinary personal popularity of Bishop Galloway made him an ideal leader for the prohibition forces in Mississippi. The adoption of State-wide local option and the ultimate success of prohibition were probably due more to his untiring efforts and his eloquence than to any other single factor. *Cf.* Candler, *op. cit., passim.* Haygood rendered a very conspicuous service during the campaign for State-wide prohibition in Texas in 1887. He addressed large gatherings daily during the latter stages of the struggle. *Cf.* Nashville *Christian Advocate*, August 6, 1887.

Many of the pastors in charge served as leaders of the reform groups in their local communities.[1]

The Quarterly, District, and Annual Conferences attempted to influence the outcome of elections which involved temperance issues. They urged that candidates favoring the legal suppression of the liquor traffic be chosen for office. They adopted long reports and resolutions expressing approval of proposed constitutional changes which would make prohibition possible. Pressure was brought to bear upon State officials and legislatures to affect their political action. Petitions were circulated which called upon law-making bodies to submit proposed constitutional amendments for popular action. Memorials were drawn up urging the passage of local option and prohibition measures pending before the State legislatures.[2] When such petitions were ignored the Conferences pledged themselves to aid in electing members who "will give the people their inalienable rights."[3]

---

[1] The colorful David C. Kelley imparted a dramatic interest to the prohibition movement in Tennessee which added much to its strength. While filling a pastorate at Lebanon in 1890 he became the candidate of the Prohibition party for governor, entering upon the contest with great enthusiasm, and denouncing unsparingly the position of the two major parties on the temperance issue. Although he had secured the Reverend W. G. Dorris as a supply for his appointment, the Tennessee Conference promptly suspended Kelley temporarily from the performance of the functions of the ministry on the ground that he had "left his charge" without being canonically excused. This action was taken despite the fact that his presiding elder had preferred no charges against him. The episode aroused a storm of protest. It was averred that there had been flagrant technical irregularities in the trial of the case, and that the action had in reality been a persecution of Kelley due to the stand that he had taken for prohibition. It was said to have been inspired by Bishop Hargrove who presided in the Conference, and who was not only known to disapprove of such ministerial participation in public affairs, but was also alleged to be opposed to prohibition. Although not made governor, Kelley received the largest vote ever polled by the Prohibition party in Tennessee. His trial aroused much interest throughout the Connection. An appeal from the verdict of the Annual Conference, charging Bishop Hargrove with maladministration, was taken to the General Conference of 1894. It is interesting to note that that body, although finding the Bishop "guilty of no intentional wrong," gave a verdict in favor of Dr. Kelley, reversing the action of the Tennessee Conference. *Cf.* letter of the Reverend B. F. Haynes in Nashville *Christian Advocate,* November 22, 1890; Du Bose, *op. cit.,* pp. 124-125.

[2] When not specifically endorsing bills of this kind the Conferences usually made general declarations in favor of the legal suppression of the traffic at the time such measures were being debated. For examples of the advocacy of particular measures see: *Minutes of South Carolina Conference,* 1891, pp. 15-16; *Minutes of North Georgia Conference,* 1892, p. 30.

[3] *Cf. Journal of Tennessee Conference,* 1897, pp. 32-33.

The *Advocates* entered wholeheartedly into the campaigns for local option and prohibition. They undertook at all times to keep the public adequately informed of the issues at stake. The sinister influence of the organized liquor traffic was constantly dwelt upon. The activities of the liquor lobbyists were exposed with great effect. In an "Open Letter" to the legislature of Tennessee, already referred to, the editor of the Nashville *Advocate* said in 1898: "In previous years the presence of these lobbyists has been so open and notorious as to be the occasion for jokes and merriment in the public press. At one time the king and leader of them all occupied a seat in the Senate Chamber as regularly as if he had been elected to it by a lawful constituency, and his presence was tolerated without rebuke, and apparently without sense of shame. If such a thing should ever happen again, we promise to make it too hot for the gentlemen in question and for the Senators who debase themselves by allowing so brazen a performance."[1]

The attempts of the major political parties to prevent the agitation of reform issues were boldly denounced. When they sought to straddle such questions Democrats, Republicans, and Populists alike were called upon to commit themselves definitely on specific measures. When public men refused to pledge their coöperation the fact was widely advertised, and active opposition to reform legislation was censured in the strongest terms. In some instances a record of the individual ballots on particular measures was published. None of the journals was more watchful and outspoken than the official Church paper at Nashville. During a spirited contest in Tennessee in 1895 this *Advocate* said: "We have always thought, and still think, that the issues involved are such as can be best adjusted without reference to political parties. But we hereby serve notice upon the Democrats and the Republicans and the Populists that they will be called upon in their next State Conventions to pledge themselves to the passage of an efficient Local Option Law. No tricks and no evasions will be tolerated. We propose also, when the present Legislature has adjourned, to publish a full history of all attempted legislation for the restriction of the liquor traffic, with a showing as to how the different members of the Senate and House voted in every case.

---

[1]Nashville *Christian Advocate*, November 17, 1898.

Such a publication may be of service in the future."[1] The following year the *Advocate* reverted to the subject: "The editor of this paper, representing the non-partisan temperance movement in the State of Tennessee, appeared before the Democratic Convention on the 7th inst., and asked it to insert in its platform the promise of a general option law for the incorporated towns and cities of the State. A very courteous hearing was given him, but the matter of his request was simply referred to the Committee on Resolutions and was not further noticed. This was bad policy. A party which is forever talking about local self-government can ill afford to fasten the saloon on every incorporated community in the State, and absolutely refuse to grant any relief. The fear of losing the influence of saloon keepers is an ignoble motive. The Republican Convention will also be asked to take definite action on this subject. . . . At present we have nothing more to say except to advise the enemies of the saloon to take an active part in securing the nomination of men for the two branches of the Legislature, and especially for the Senate, who will pledge themselves to vote for the very moderate measure of relief that is asked."[2]

The Methodist journals, moreover, lent a moral support which was of inestimable value to all who were striving for temperance reform. When the outlook appeared darkest they were ever ready with words of encouragement. When temporary reverses were met the *Advocates* were careful to explain their true character, and they cheered the forces on to renewed efforts with the assurance that theirs was a righteous cause which must ultimately prevail. Shortly after the attempt to secure a prohibition amendment in Texas had failed in 1887, the editor of the Nashville *Advocate* said with regard to a similar campaign then under way in Tennessee: "The liquor men can now withdraw from Texas whatever is left of their corruption fund and concentrate all their forces on Tennessee. They come weakened by the drafts made upon their strength there, though flushed with their temporary success. Let us close up our ranks and go foward to meet them with a calmly-directed and well-sustained onset, and we can

---

[1]Nashville *Christian Advocate*, May 9, 1895.
[2]*Ibid.*, May 14, 1896.

overcome them. Let local organizations be perfected, and the name, residence, and sentiment of every voter in every precinct in the State be ascertained. Let tracts, papers, pamphlets, and literature of every sort bearing on the subject be placed in the hands of the voters. Cover every phase of the question. Explain every detail. Arrange for rallies at convenient points. Secure the best speakers who can be had. See to it that in the selection of the election managers enough prohibitionists are chosen to secure a fair count; the law of the land guarantees this privilege; demand it under the law. In a word get a full ballot and a fair count, and our cause is safe beyond a peradventure."[1] When the attempt to curb the traffic in Tennessee had likewise proved unsuccessful, the *Advocate* assured the temperance people that "the election of the 29th of September was a moral triumph for prohibition." It declared that the liquor men realized that they had only gotten a respite, and that they had emerged from the contest with the knowledge that "the intelligence and moral sense of the State are largely against them."[2] The *Advocates* constantly reminded the Church and the public of the necessity for vigilance in guarding the ground which had been "wrested from the enemy."

By 1890 temperance sentiment had made great progress in the South. Local option laws had been adopted in every one of the Southern States, and local prohibition existed to some extent in all of them.[3] Encouraged by the successes which had been achieved, the reformers during the remainder of the century directed their efforts chiefly toward securing State-wide prohibition laws. Having committed themselves fully to the cause, the Methodists of the South carried on the struggle with enthusiasm. It was due in no small measure to the aggressive leadership and moral encouragement afforded by the Methodist Episcopal Church, South, that the ground which had been won could be retained and the way prepared for the ultimate acceptance of State-wide and national prohibition.

---

[1] *Ibid.*, August 20, 1887.
[2] *Ibid.*, August 20, 1887.
[3] Between 1855 and 1875 Alabama, Georgia, North Carolina, and Arkansas obtained a considerable measure of local prohibition through local laws. State local option laws were enacted as follows: Texas, 1876; South Carolina, 1882; Georgia, 1885; Florida, 1885; Virginia, 1886. Tennessee adopted local prohibition measures in 1877 and 1887. *Cf.* Colvin, *op. cit.*, pp. 355-379.

CHAPTER X

OTHER MORAL AND HUMANITARIAN REFORMS

IN general it may be said that the Methodist Episcopal Church, South, maintained traditional views with regard to the position of women in society. As the feminist movement steadily gained ground, eloquent pleas were made to induce women to remain upon the lofty plane on which Southern chivalry had placed her. The authority of the Scriptures was invoked to support that of tradition and custom. The influence of the franchise upon the sex was especially feared. With but one notable exception, the *Advocates* either openly denounced Woman's Suffrage or treated the whole subject in a cavalier fashion.[1] Typical of the discussions of these journals was an appeal made by the *Alabama Christian Advocate* in 1888. "Now a word of serious, sober counsel to our Southern women," it said. "You stand at the head of the list, and present to the world the sublimest spectacle of Christian womanhood. You are loved, honored and trusted by your husbands, fathers and brothers to the fullest extent. You are the lights of ten thousand happy homes as well as the secret source of that heroic spirit which has inspired the loftiest deeds of daring and self-sacrifice in redeeming the South from the devastations of war. Besides all this, it is in your pure hearts that Christianity is to find its last stronghold. Therefore in view of your queenly character, proud history, and unstained record, we beseech you to be 'wise as serpents and harmless as doves.' The trend of many of the female organizations is towards this Woman's Rights Crusade, and all such should receive at your hands merited condemnation. You can find work enough in the Church and in the various charities of the day to consume all the time you can spare, and enough to satisfy all

---

[1] During the Eighties the *Wesleyan* took the position that Woman's Suffrage was a political question, and therefore not one having "any of those elements of morality or religion which would make it a matter of conscience or religion with Christian people to take sides." Cf. *Wesleyan Christian Advocate,* February 9, 1887.

your rightful ambition for publicity."[1] It was feared that the suffrage would not only rob women of their feminine charm but would also convert them into "wrangling ward politicians."[2]

Despite the persistence of such views among many of the leaders of the denomination, evidences were not lacking of a willingness to grant woman a more dignified position in the Church and to concede to her a broader sphere of activity in society at large. Customs which had limited the action and privileges of women in the congregation were allowed to die out. The old habit of men and women sitting apart was virtually abandoned.[3] Women began to speak out in Church gatherings in a fashion that would have been shocking at a former time. By 1898 the Reverend R. G. Porter of Mississippi could express amazement that the editor of the New Orleans *Advocate* had not undertaken to correct the views of a correspondent who had cited the Apostle Paul as an authority against women speaking in public and especially in the Church.[4] The formal recognition of the Woman's Missionary Society by the General Conference of 1878

---

[1]*Cf. Alabama Christian Advocate,* quoted in Nashville *Christian Advocate,* April 21, 1888. "Let no one try to reverse the Divine order," urged the *Southern Christian Advocate* in its issue of March 3, 1887. "Woman is now Queen,—queen of hearts and queen of homes. But whenever she steps down from her high vantage ground and takes her place besides the sterner, yet ruder, sex, she may still be recognized as queen, but it will be a queen shorn of her glory and her power—a queen without subjects and without an empire." "We do not favor any movement which would unsex the women without making them men," said the Nashville *Advocate* in its issue of February 24, 1872. "Like the ball of abolitionism, it has been set in motion, and it may not be possible to stop it until it has run its rabid and ruinous course; but we shall not accelerate its course."

[2]When the Woman's Christian Temperance Union indorsed the struggle which was being waged to secure the ballot for women, the *Southern Christian Advocate* said: "Well may we stand amazed, well nigh dumfounded, at the menaces of the W. C. T. U. seeking to destroy this home and throw upon the hustings and converting into wrangling ward politicians the glorious women of the South. The South may survive the deadly saloon, she may recuperate from wasting famine and decimating pestilence, and come forth a mighty, unsubdued giant from a contest of blood with the civilized world, but she will succumb to this deadly blow, this enemy, this blight; this death will dig her grave and bury her splendid womanhood in dishonor." *Cf.* "Georgia Notes" in *Southern Christian Advocate,* April 27, 1893.

[3]Promiscuous seating had become so generally the rule by 1888 that the editor of the New Orleans *Advocate* observed with some surprise at that time that the old custom seemed still to be observed at Starksville, Mississippi. *Cf. New Orleans Christian Advocate,* December 20, 1888.

[4]*Cf.* letter of "Gilderoy" in *New Orleans Christian Advocate,* April 14, 1898.

was the confirmation of a new conception of woman's role in the Church. The following year a well known North Carolina minister assured his daughter that membership in the organization would be "no compromise of female modesty and refinement."[1] In 1890 the Mississippi Conference went so far as to memorialize the General Conference "to formulate a plan for employing godly women as deaconesses in the Church."[2]

The great emphasis which the Church placed upon the education of women during the post-war period naturally served to give it a broader conception of the place of woman in society. Throughout the period the Methodists sought to elevate the standards of female education. The disparity between what had been done for the sexes in the past was constantly stressed.[3] The danger to be apprehended from giving one sex a higher intellectual cultivation than the other was frequently pointed out. "If in our homes there are to be hereafter cultured men and comparatively ignorant women," said the Nashville *Advocate*, "the happy equilibrium of home life will be fatally disturbed, women will sink to a lower relative plane and our civilization will surely sink with her."[4] It was said that such a difference in the education of the sexes would "so divide them in intelligence and sympathy as to imperil our domestic and social institutions which depend for their stability on their united effort."[5]

The importance which the Church attached to intellectual development of women is indicated by the fact that of the sixty-nine institutions of higher learning maintained by the denomination in 1885, thirty-three were schools for women and of the

---

[1]Plyler, A. W., *The Iron Duke of the Methodist Itinerancy* (Nashville, 1925), p. 166.

[2]*Cf. Journal of General Conference*, 1890, p. 144.

[3]In 1884 the Nashville *Advocate* said: "The enormous disparity between the expenditure for the education of the different sexes is astonishing. If you will stop to think of it, your surprise will grow as you ponder the facts. . . . There has been one Vassar in the North and none in the South. Even the women benefactors of education as a rule give nothing for their own sex— thinking, perhaps, that the other is in more need of the refining influence of liberal culture; or what is more probable, not thinking at all about the matter. . . . But it is time for both the men and women to do some thinking on this subject." *Cf.* Nashville *Christian Advocate*, November 1, 1884.

[4]*Ibid.*, November 1, 1884.

[5]*Ibid.*, June 11, 1887.

remainder twenty-two were co-educational.[1] It was urged that
the Church must establish a center of higher learning for women
which would be "in every respect equal to Vanderbilt University."
Plans for such an institution were brought forward from time to
time, and a few years before his death in 1895 Bishop Haygood
set on foot a movement for the establishment of a central Southern
University for women, to be located at Sheffield, Alabama. Much
interest was shown in the project. That the undertaking was never
realized was no doubt due very largely to the fact that Vanderbilt
opened its classes to women during the Nineties and that the
Educational Commission in 1898 recommended that the Methodists of each State concentrate their energies on a single institution
of higher learning, which would be co-educational.[2] The significance of the Methodist contribution to the cause of higher
education for women becomes apparent when it is recalled that
the State at that time had done almost nothing towards providing
higher mental culture for females. It was an easy transition from
the advocacy of the fullest privileges for women in the field of
education to a recognition of their claims along other lines.

That an increasing number of persons in the Church were
coming to favor the fullest enfranchisement of women was
evidenced by the protest which the Reverend W. T. Poynter made
with regard to the impression created by the representatives of
the Church at the Ecumenical Conference in 1895.[3] Declaring
that they had conveyed the idea that Southern Methodists as a
unit were opposed to the political enfranchisement of women, he
said: "Will you say for one—and he represents many—that he
favors the largest liberty for woman in Church work and elsewhere. He finds nothing in the Bible nor in the reason of the
case why a woman should not do any work she is competent to
do, and he asks in all seriousness 'Who gave man the right to say

---

[1] Cf. *Journal of General Conference*, 1886, p. 119.

[2] When a motion was offered in the General Conference of 1898 proposing
that the Church establish such an institution, that body, while pointing out the
unwisdom of founding new schools until those already established were adequately endowed, agreed to direct the undertaking whenever those who objected
to co-education should furnish the funds, and it expressed "the keenest sympathy
with the spirit that prompts this call for ampler facilities for the education of
our daughters." Cf. *Journal of General Conference*, 1898, pp. 218-219.

[3] Dr. Poynter served as the head of the famous Science Hill school for
women in Kentucky.

that woman has no rights?' All the twaddle about honoring woman, and at the same time putting her in the position of a servant to man, is worthy of heathendom. The voice of Christianity is: 'In Christ Jesus there is neither male nor female, for ye are all one in him.' "[1]

In the rapidly increasing divorce rate in American society the Church saw an alarming indication of moral disintegration. In 1867 there were only 9,937 divorces in the entire country. But the number rose steadily to 16,089 in 1878, an increase of over sixty per cent.[2] In 1888 and 1898 respectively the number of marriages terminated in the courts were approximately 29,000 and 48,000. The proportion of divorces was higher in the United States than in any of the foreign countries except Japan. Many felt that the sanctity of the marriage tie would be destroyed, and in 1881 a National Divorce Reform League was formed. Seeing in the lax standards of the law regarding marriage and divorce in many of the States a condition responsible for the great majority of divorces, this organization directed its chief efforts toward the abolition of the diversity of State legislation on such matters. Legislative changes tending to greater strictness were made in a number of States after 1878.[3]

Apart from the fact that an increasing number of divorces were being granted on unscriptural grounds, the Methodists saw in the custom a fearful portent of the disruption of the family and the destruction of the very foundations of society. "The law of God is perfectly clear and profoundly emphatic on the subject," said the *Wesleyan Christian Advocate* in 1885, "but we believe that public opinion in large sections of this country is rapidly

---

[1]*Cf.* communication of W. T. Poynter in Nashville *Christian Advocate*, December 5, 1895. Dr. Weyman Potter, editor of the *Wesleyan* spoke out no less boldly on the subject. Declaring that "It is not a sin in a woman to believe that she ought to be allowed to vote, for which she ought to be consigned to the pains and penalties of everlasting death, or even the scorn of her editorial judges," he said: "We have . . . advocated plainly, the right of women to teach the gospel, even to preach the gospel, as laymen do, to be presidents of colleges and trustees of colleges, especially of their own sex, to be Sunday-school superintendents and stewards in the Church, and to have an equal chance with men in all such industries as they are able to engage in . . ." *Cf. Wesleyan Christian Advocate,* quoted in Nashville *Christian Advocate,* March 19, 1887.

[2]*Cf.* Nevins, Allen, *The Emergence of Modern America* (New York, 1932), pp. 215-216.

[3]*Cf.* Schlesinger, Arthur Meier, *The Rise of the City,* pp. 154-156.

drifting away from the divine standard of principle in this matter.
What this means is evident to every man. It means licentiousness
in its lowest and most aggravated form. It means unbridled
debauchery. Marriage is the greatest and divinest of all checks
on the natural lusts and passions of man-kind, the bulwark of
Omnipotence against the worst and most iniquitous of social sins,
that one terrific monster, which modern civilization has agreed
to designate 'the evil of society.' . . . God help us, when we are
so far gone in beastly stupidity and wickedness as to forget that
this anchor is the one security of Providence against our drifting
into the fate of Sodom and Gomorrah. Legislation did not create
marriage. Almighty God created it. And society is a traitor to
God and is making ready to cut its own throat when it becomes
lax in its opinions and sentiments on this holy and conservative
institution."[1]

The Church sought to preserve the sanctity of the marriage tie
by advocating stricter legislation upon the subject and by stigmatizing all divorce not based on the ground of adultery as immoral.
It urged that the hardship imposed in individual cases by rigid
laws was not to be considered as against the great damage society
would suffer from lax standards. Even desertion was regarded
as an insufficient ground for dissolving the bonds of matrimony.
Moreover it was argued that whatever hardships were suffered
were almost invariably the result of the "looseness, lightness, or
wickedness of the contracting parties, in assuming carelessly bonds
that should be regarded as solemnly and perpetually binding."[2]
The psychological effect of an incompatible union was but imperfectly understood and received little attention. Those who had
made hard beds must be willing to lie upon them. "Neither
Church, nor society, nor State can or should seek to mitigate the
just punishments that fall upon foolish or wicked people, who
have used marriage as the procuress of lust or greed, find themselves incommoded by its righteous restrictions, and cry out to the
guardians of national life and domestic purity for release from
the sacred obligation they have dishonored," said the Nashville

---

[1]Cf. *Wesleyan Christian Advocate,* quoted in Nashville *Christian Advocate,*
July 25, 1885.
[2]Cf. Nashville *Christian Advocate,* July 17, 1886.

Advocate in 1886. It warned the public that "Every deference to the divorce-seeking class, every point yielded to their selfish demands, is a menace to social purity and an invitation to licentiousness."[1] In 1890 the General Conference declared that it would "rejoice when by concurrent action of the several States the laws of divorce shall be based only upon the Word of Christ, and with the limitations which that word involves."[2]

The Church did much to attach disgrace to divorce of all kinds in the popular mind. Much was said and written of the immorality of persons who remarried after having been divorced. In 1886 the General Conference ordered that "no minister of the Methodist Episcopal Church, South, knowingly upon due inquiry, shall solemnize the marriage of any person who has a divorced wife or husband still living; *provided* this inhibition shall not apply to the innocent party to a divorce granted for scriptural cause, or to parties once divorced seeking remarriage."[3] Typical of the attitude maintained towards all unscriptural divorce were the comments of the *New Orleans Christian Advocate* in 1895 when an English nobleman sought to obtain a release from his marriage vows upon the grounds of his wife's insanity: "The telegrams from London announced last week that Lord Durham's suit for divorce on the grounds of insanity of his wife, was dismissed leaving him to pay the cost. A righteous decision. But the heartlessness of such a case deserves universal execration. It is enough to shame the brutality of a Zulu chief. His lordship is at heart a Mormon and his place is among the latter day saints."[4] While the rapid growth of the divorce rate in American society was in general an accompaniment of urban growth, there can be little doubt that the unbending attitude of the Methodist Episcopal Church, South, toward the institution was in large measure responsible for the fact that disrupted marriages continued to be less common in the South than in other sections of the country.[5]

As has been mentioned, a new interest in humanitarian reform

[1]*Idem.*
[2]*Journal of General Conference,* 1890, p. 203.
[3]*Journal of General Conference,* 1886, p. 233.
[4]*New Orleans Christian Advocate,* March 19, 1895.
[5]*Cf.* Schlesinger, *The Rise of the City,* pp. 154-156.

where no immediate moral issues were involved began in many instances to manifest itself in the Church. It was urged with increasing emphasis that the Church must cease abdicating to outside organizations the function of ameliorating the conditions of man's existence. A growing sensitiveness to criticism on the subject was manifested in the denomination.[1] "The taunt is flung in the face of the Church that it concerns itself only about the life to come, and does nothing to help suffering humanity in the present life," said the Nashville *Advocate* in 1884. "Unjust as this is, the accusation has been invited by the failure of the Church to dispense its own benefactions in the name of the Lord Jesus Christ."[2] Although still inclined to see in the Golden Rule the only effective remedy for alleviating human misery, and still prone to believe that it "is not hunger, lack of clothes, lack of houses, lack of government; it is sin that makes man unhappy," the Church became increasingly interested in humanitarian uplift.

This new interest was evidenced especially by a growing concern for the welfare of the poor and downtrodden. Despite the rapid growth of Methodism in the cities of the South, the success of the Salvation Army and the work undertaken by certain organized philanthropic groups made it obvious that in many instances the Methodists were not reaching the poorest elements of the city population. Realization of this fact and the fear that the destitute would be completely alienated from the Church increased the solicitude on this head. "The very poor—those who wear rags and know not where tomorrow's meals will come from—are conspicuous by their absence from our Church services," warned

---

[1] With reference to charges which had been made against the religious bodies of the day by *Light*, a journal devoted to "alleviating the sufferings of dumb creation," the New Orleans *Advocate* said in 1892: "While we do not wish to appear as condoning the derelictions of Christians, yet we ask, Is it true 'that Christians, and the organizations to which they belong, have not seemed to fully understand Christ and his mission to the world' as humane societies? If so, then let us close our Churches and organize ourselves into one great humane society, that we might the more 'fully understand Christ and his mission to the world.' . . . The humane society is born of Christianity. Christianity is far more than its foster-mother. The Church was not intended by God to do everything by direct, but many things by indirect means. How would the editor of *Light* like to see his great and influential Church of the Bluff City appearing every morning, or at irregular times, before the police courts, prosecuting violators of our humane laws? How long would she hold her influence at home and abroad?" Cf. *New Orleans Christian Advocate*, June 30, 1892.

[2] Cf. Nashville *Christian Advocate*, January 5, 1884.

the New Orleans *Advocate*.[1] Thus the Church was inclined to a broader view of its duties to the poor, and it began to create new philanthropic agencies and eleemosynary institutions for their benefit. In addition to its educational work, the Church established Orphans' Homes and Widows' Homes and maintained "poor lists."[2]

The inequalities between capital and labor were not so apparent in the South as in the more industrialized North, nor was the conflict between them so well defined. The strong individualism of the age, moreover, inclined churchmen there as elsewhere to condone the miseries and injustices borne by the oppressed.[3] There were evidences in the Church, nevertheless, of an awakening interest in the laboring people as a class. Although understanding but imperfectly the great odds against the wage-earners in their struggles to secure an adequate living wage and looking upon the strike with growing disapproval because of the violence which often manifested itself during labor disputes, the Methodist journals frequently charged that the laboring classes were being wronged. Pulpit and press inveighed against corporate

---

[1]*Cf. New Orleans Christian Advocate*, April 9, 1896.

[2]"The Methodists have made a beginning in this line of things," said the Nashville *Advocate* in its issue of January 5, 1884. "In Georgia they have an Orphans' Home, which is developing healthfully. In Kentucky they have a Widows' and Orphans' Home, which is assuming the proportions of a noble Christian charity." In 1891 the editor of the New Orleans *Advocate* urged that the Church substitute for the "poor lists" some system "by which the needs of our poor may be supplied in such a way that they will see the opportunity and seize it of supplying their own necessities." *Cf. New Orleans Christian Advocate*, April 23, 1891.

[3]In an editorial article, signed by "A," in the issue of the New Orleans *Advocate* of August 29, 1895, the writer said: "The pulpit as a rule sides with the weak. Thus it champions the cause of the oppressed, the poor—the laborer included. . . . But the true laborer asks not for sympathy. He spurns it. He is a nobleman. Able to pay as he goes. Submits to the Admaic curse of eating his bread in the sweat of his brow. Knows nothing of the harassing cares of the employer. He is aware, as Carlyle says, 'Labor, wide as earth, has its summit in heaven.' Work becomes a pleasure. . . . The intelligent laborer is aware that many in affluence work harder than himself, though not for bodily subsistence. Frequently the toil of the employer more onerous than the employee. . . .

"Hence the pulpit's championship of the so-called laboring man's cause may prove iniquitous." In an issue of April 1886, the *Wesleyan* declared that it had no faith in the power of "any legislative enactments or police regulations" to stop labor conflicts. *Cf. Wesleyan Christian Advocate*, quoted in Nashville *Christian Advocate*, April 24, 1886.

wealth for denying labor a living wage.[1] They pointed out that
the legislation designed for an agricultural society no longer
served to protect the working man in our industrialized life.
"That labor in the United States is suffering wrongs that ought
to be righted no fair man familiar with the question can doubt,"
said the Nashville *Advocate* in 1887.[2] The following year the
same journal declared: "Nearly all of the necessaries of life are
now controlled by 'the trusts,' even to the medicine for the healing
of the sick, the oil that feeds the light of the anxious watcher by
the bed of the dying, and the coffin in which the loved one is
finally laid to sleep. Nothing escapes the extortion of these worst
publicans the world ever saw. . . . It is within the province of
legislation to protect the weak against the aggression of the strong,
and these aggressions should be checked when made by the
power of money as well as when made by brute force. The fact
is we are still trying to control in many departments of our
complex civilization modern evils with ancient expedients. . . .
Our laws must say to men so lost to humanity that they are
willing the poor should go hungry and naked that they may
make millions: 'You shall not do this thing: or if you do you
shall learn better morals in the penitentiary.'"[3]

During the closing years of the century the interest of the
Church in the laboring classes increased perceptibly. In 1899
the Reverend Henry Parker Gibbs of the North Mississippi Conference published a series of articles on "The Factory and Its
People" in *The Headlight,* a secular magazine. The articles, an
outgrowth of a study of the conditions in the local mills at Water
Valley, were submitted after they had received the endorsement
of his presiding elder and other Methodist ministers of the
vicinity. They attempted to give an account of "the poverty,
wretchedness, and morals of these poor people with a view to
the amelioration of their condition." Shortly after the publication
of these articles, the minister who had written them was brutally

[1]As early as 1877, when great railroad strikes were troubling the country,
the New Orleans paper declared that "From all we can learn the railroad
employees have been wronged by the wealthy corporations in reducing their
wages below a living rate." Cf. *New Orleans Christian Advocate,* August 2,
1877.
[2]Nashville *Christian Advocate,* September 10, 1887.
[3]*Ibid.,* September 1, 1888.

assaulted by the secretary of the mills and subsequently died, presumably as a result of the attack made upon him. The comments of the *New Orleans Christian Advocate* at the time indicated that such journals had advanced to a new position with regard to matters of this kind. After reprobating the murder of the minister in the strongest terms, the *Advocate* pointed out that the great secular dailies had not discussed the issues involved. "Why this silence?" it asked. "It would seem that conscienceless capital in some instances has power, not only to oppress the poor, and to strike down a minister of the Gospel who lifts his voice to protest against that oppression, but even to muzzle the press."[1] That same year, in calling attention to the evils of the sweating system, the editor of the *Quarterly Review* emphasized the fact that the "workingman bears the burden of it all." "Is it not time that the religious public was awakened to the Heaven-defying iniquities perpetrated in the trading world?" he asked. "How long can this high-pressure' system endure?"[2]

The post-war tendency to moral laxity revealed itself noticeably in a rapidly increasing desecration of the Sabbath. Although less so in the agricultural South than in other sections of the country, the old-fashioned American Lord's Day, devoted to religious observance and rest, was everywhere giving way before a more liberal conception of the Sabbath. A variety of factors were contributing to the secularization of the day. The example of German and Irish immigrant groups who spent their Sundays in beer gardens or congregated for musical concerts was making its influence felt in society at large. Observing Saturday as their holy day, such groups as the Jews and the Seventh Day Adventists felt no obligation to keep the traditional American Sabbath. The popular craving for diversion expressed itself more and more in demands for Sunday amusements. The pressure of life in urban centers, moreover, turned the laboring classes to thoughts of recreation on their one day of leisure.[3] To provide for their pleasure it was necessary that thousands of persons should be engaged in operating trains and street cars and in furnishing means of entertainment.

---

[1] *New Orleans Christian Advocate*, May 11, 1899.
[2] *Cf. The Quarterly Review*, January 1899, pp. 410-414.
[3] Schlesinger, *A Critical Period in American Religion*, p. 13.

It is true that there were Sabbath laws in nearly every State of the Union, prohibiting all but necessary and charitable labors, and, in many cases, forbidding travel and almost every type of amusement.[1] But public sentiment had become notably indifferent to the lax enforcement of such laws in the urban districts. During the Eighties some of the strongly urban States relaxed or repealed their Sunday blue laws. It was observed that the Sabbath had become a day "for labor meetings, for excursions, for saloons, beer-gardens, base-ball games and carousals."[2]

This trend of affairs led to a vigorous movement to restore the sanctity of the Lord's Day. Religious organizations in all parts of the country conducted militant campaigns to check Sabbath desecration. By the middle Eighties several secular organizations, formed especially for the purpose, were crusading for a proper observance of the Sabbath. Among these were the International Sabbath Association, the Sunday League of America, and the American Sabbath Union. In 1884 the Woman's Christian Temperance Union added a department of Sabbath observance to its other activities. But it is a notable fact that such organizations based their plea primarily upon a rational regard for a secular day of rest rather than upon Scriptural injunction. The arguments advanced were chiefly humanitarian.[3]

The Methodists of the South saw an ominous portent in the growing desecration of the Sabbath. They felt that continued encroachments upon the sanctity of the day would undermine the very foundations of social order and private virtue.[4] It was believed that the Continental Sunday would bring in its train a whole succession of disasters. The Tennessee Conference saw in the disrespect to the claims of the Sabbath "an entering wedge

---

[1] *Ibid.,* pp. 13-14.

[2] *Cf.* Schlesinger, *A Critical Period in American Religion,* p. 13. In 1877 it was reported that Sunday in New Orleans "is the day for target shooting, for baseball, for excursions, for horse-races, and for all manner of godless diversions." *Cf. New Orleans Christian Advocate,* November 22, 1877.

[3] *Cf.* Schlesinger, *A Critical Period in American Religion,* pp. 13-14.

[4] The Tennessee Conference declared in 1884 that all violations of the Sabbath were calculated to "undermine the foundations of sound morals and good order." *Cf. Journal of Tennessee Conference,* 1884, p. 11. Let the observance of the Sabbath be ignored, said the *Episcopal Methodist,* and "the very foundations of public morality and private virtue will be undermined." *Cf. Episcopal Methodist,* quoted in *New Orleans Christian Advocate,* April 29, 1880.

designed by infidels and skeptics to destroy the influence of the
Christian religion, and an open door for the exercise of the
unrestrained passions of the human heart."[1] "The men who are
battling to maintain the Christian Sabbath in these United States,"
said the Nashville *Advocate* in 1884, "are battling for its civil
institutions as well as its moral and religious welfare. The
Continental Sunday will give us anarchy or despotism—or both
in their natural order of succession."[2]

Alarmed at the increasing inroads upon the traditional Sabbath,
the Methodist Episcopal Church, South, exerted its whole influence to guard the sanctity of the day. Movements were under
way to secure national laws and stricter State legislation upon the
subject. Although unwilling at first to commit itself in favor of
the enactment of laws to enforce Sabbath observance, the Church
began early in the Eighties to pledge its support to organizations
sponsoring such legislation, and within a few years the *Advocates*
and Conferences advocated the passage of blue laws without
reserve.[3] Representative bodies in all parts of the Connection
memorialized legislatures upon the subject, and circulated petitions
calling for new enactments and the stricter enforcement of
existing ones.[4] Moreover, the Church urged Sabbath observance
no less upon humanitarian grounds than as a religious duty.
Sabbath breaking was represented as a sin against man and beast
as well as against God. The fact was stressed that the institution

---

[1] *Journal of Tennessee Conference*, 1884, p. 11.

[2] Nashville *Christian Advocate*, September 20, 1884.

[3] During the period immediately following the War the Church sought to
preserve the Sabbath chiefly through emphasizing its "divine institution," and
through securing the strictest observance upon the part of its communicants.
"Should there be a legislative prohibition on these things?" asked the New
Orleans *Advocate* in its issue of June 29, 1867. "Christianity cannot be legis-
lated into the world. It must enter through the lives and testimony of Christian
men. It is this agency that we invoke—a more careful and conscientious
observance upon the part of our religious people. . . . We know of nothing
that will go further to impress the truth upon the world, and to deepen the
piety and power of the Church."

[4] The Kentucky Conference called upon the Constitutional Convention which
convened in that State in 1890 to provide "such enactment as may give just
and full recognition to the institution, rights, and privileges of the Christian
Sabbath." Cf. *Minutes of Kentucky Conference*, 1890, p. 20. In 1895 the
Louisiana Conference resolved to "use our best efforts" to "engage all our
people, in common with all those who love the honor of our State, to secure

afforded "manifold benefits to men in all relations."[1]   "All classes are entitled to one day of rest during the week, and society has a right to demand it," said the New Orleans *Advocate* when commending a Sunday law pending before the legislature of Louisiana in 1880. "Will our legislators prove themselves in this matter the friends of the poor and good order and virtue? We shall see."[2]

The churchmen directed their chief exertions against the running of passenger trains and the opening of places of public amusement on Sundays. State and national legislatures were memorialized upon the subject of Sunday travel. Petitions calling for the cessation of dispensable Sunday labor in inter-State commerce and in the postal service were circulated. The aggressive attitude adopted by the Methodists was well illustrated by the General Conference in 1882. In response to an overture from the General Assembly of the Southern Presbyterian Church inquiring as to its willingness to unite in a general effort "to abate, if not entirely suspend, these public evils," and asking its cooperation in petitioning Congress against the running of trains and the delivering of mails on the Sabbath, that body said: "We cordially approve the great objects in view. . . . We are prepared to join you in a respectful and earnest appeal to Congress to discontinue the making up, delivery, and transportation of mailmatter on Sunday. This point gained, a great step in advance, we can turn our attention to the police regulations of States and

---

the election of such senators and representatives, only, as will pledge themselves to diligence in maintaining the present statute or passing one better suited to secure the Sunday rest which is the right of all our people." *Cf. Journal of Louisiana Conference*, 1895, p. 19.

[1] *Cf. Proceedings* of Louisiana Conference in *New Orleans Christian Advocate*, January 19, 1882.

[2] *Cf. New Orleans Christian Advocate*, March 4, 1880. This rational regard for a day of rest did not extend to a recognition of the need for diverting recreations. The Sabbath was to remain a day for religious observance and rest. "The violation of the Sabbath is not required to give rest or recreation to the working people," said the Nashville *Advocate* when a game of Sunday baseball had been played in that city in 1887. "It is a libel upon them to say the demand for such outrages upon our Christian civilization comes from them. It is the demand of idlers, gamblers and their followers." *Cf.* Nashville *Christian Advocate*, April 30, 1887. In its issue of July 16, 1887, the same journal said with regard to a Sunday concert which had been given there: "Of course these things will be defended by appeals in behalf of the poor working man. This is barefaced demagoguery. The working people do not ask for these diversions, and they do not patronize them."

municipal corporations, to correct such abuses as may be reached by proper authority."[1] "If, as it has been suggested," said the Mississippi Conference in 1884, "our legislatures possess the legal and constitutional authority to enact statutes which shall prohibit trains from passing through their territories on the Sabbath, then ought we not in our quarterly and Annual Conferences, as Methodists, petition and persistently petition our legislative bodies to stop this running of trains on the Sabbath day and worship God in the beauty of holiness."[2] Such resolutions and petitions were adopted annually, although each succeeding year saw an increasing number of trains on the tracks.[3]

All attempts to introduce popular amusements or to relax the laws in favor of Sunday recreations were vigorously opposed by the Methodists. The Conferences entered "solemn protest" against "base ball plays and other worldly amusements such as secular concerts, etc., that are calculated to destroy the sanctity of the holy Sabbath" and "bring disrepute upon the Christian religion."[4] A close watch was kept and the *Advocates* were quick to report every attempt to open places of public amusement on Sunday.[5] Officers of the law who offered no obstruction to Sunday baseball games and other forms of entertainment were severely arraigned before the bar of public opinion. When great expositions were held in New Orleans, in Chicago, and at Nashville during this period, the Methodists vigorously opposed every suggestion for the opening of their gates on the Sabbath. Their Managing Boards were memorialized "to respect the Christian conscience of

---

[1] *Journal of General Conference,* 1882, p. 75.
[2] *Journal of Mississippi Conference,* 1884, p. 15.
[3] *Cf.* Schlesinger, *A Critical Period in American Religion,* p. 14.
[4] *Cf. Journal of Tennessee Conference,* 1884, p. 11.
[5] When an attempt was made to introduce Sunday concerts at Nashville, the *Advocate* of that city exclaimed: "Let our people, rich and poor, high and low, who value orderliness and good government tell these gentlemen firmly and promptly, that we will have none of these things, that we want no Chicago indecencies and Continental profanities. We must settle this question right now, once for all, or these people will overthrow our inistitutions and make the South as undesirable for residence as the wretched Sabbathless countries of the Old World or crime cursed regions of the Northwest. Let us put these things down, now *and forever. Cf.* Nashville *Christian Advocate,* July 16, 1887. When a Sunday game of baseball was played in Nashville in 1887, the *Advocate* denounced the affair as "a sin and a shame which the young fellows composing the 'Southern League' are not going to be allowed to carry on in the South." It was in no small measure due to its influence that such games were banned in the future. *Cf. ibid.,* April 30, 1887; *ibid.,* January 28, 1888.

the common country" by closing their exhibits.[1] Congressmen were urged to see that public appropriations for such undertakings were made conditional upon their gates being closed on the Sabbath.[2]

Despite the fact that the sabbatarians lost ground year after year with regard to Sunday travel, and, in a lesser degree, with regard to public amusements, the traditional Lord's Day was preserved to a greater extent in the South than in any other section. And there can be little doubt that the aggressive policy of the Methodist Episcopal Church, South, in guarding the sanctity of the day was largely responsible for that result.

A major portion of the Southern Methodist efforts at reform was directed against the participation in those "worldly amusements" which, although not specifically condemned by the Scriptures, were yet believed to be conducive to immorality. It was the phenomenal craving for such diversions as the Church felt could not "be used in the name of the Lord Jesus" rather than evidences of real vice and infidelity which caused the gravest concern.[3] The allurements of such amusements were felt to constitute the most subtle of all the pitfalls in the pathway of the Christian. The tendency to conform to the ways of the world in such matters was a source of constant anxiety to the leaders of the denomination.[4] "Some of the grosser immoralities and

---

[1]*Cf. Proceedings* of North Mississippi Conference in *New Orleans Christian Advocate,* December 17, 1891. The management of the World's Fair at Chicago vacillated, finally offering incomplete exhibits on Sunday, but attendance was so poor that the doors were soon closed again. Methodist Conferences in all parts of the South expressed their disapproval of its action in showing the exhibits.

[2]The Louisiana Conference resolved that "as representatives of a religious body in Louisiana, numbering more than twenty thousand members, we respectfully and most earnestly request our members in Congress to oppose any efforts on the part of the management of the Columbian Exposition to have Congress rescind their action by which the donation to the Exposition was made conditional upon closing the gates of the Exposition on Sunday . . ." *Cf. Journal of Louisiana Conference,* 1892, p. 15.

[3]"The most serious peril which threatens the Church does not come from infidelity," said the New Orleans *Advocate* in its issue of June 17, 1880. "Ingersollism, materialism, and all forms of atheism do not touch the heart of the Church. . . . The worst enemy of the Church is worldliness, and it is doing more to destroy its spirituality and power than all the forces of infidelity and vice put together. . . . While we are aiming at Ingersollism and fighting vice, this worldliness in sapping the very foundations, and robbing the Church of its purity and power."

[4]"It requires no little carefulness on the part of religious people to keep

vices connected with certain popular diversions may be evident to every considerate and fair-minded person," said the New Orleans *Advocate* in 1873, "but how many of them are fatal to spirituality, or tend to overthrow piety, can be fully understood by those alone with whom religion is a matter of personal experience."[1] Declaring that acts of worldliness to which the Church half a century back had been a stranger were now regarded by many Christian men and women without alarm, the bishops said in 1886: "It is not merely that such things are done, but that the doing shocks the spiritual sensibility of the membership so little."[2] Time and again the bishops gave warning that "vain and demoralizing amusements" were adulterating the purity of the Church and breaking down its authority.[3]

Alarmed at the eager rush of society after amusement, and fearful lest its members be corrupted by the popular craze for

---

clear of all complicity in some of the vices and sins prevailing in the world," said the editor of the New Orleans *Advocate* in 1874. "The sanctions of custom, public opinion and legislation are apt to be regarded as an adequate justification, while the precepts of religion receive an interpretation which is shaped by the popular practice. Then, again, 'fellowship' is regarded as a shade less responsible, and somewhat less criminal than to be leaders and organizers in doubtful undertakings. The amusements of the world and many of its prominent forms of evil are already existing. To have fellowship with them in some degree seems almost a social necessity. While the Christian conscience would protest against their introduction, and would perhaps wish them done away, it may be perverted so as to tolerate and accept them as things it is useless to oppose. The danger lies in this tolerance of wrong, and in this fellowship with the established and customary forms of sin." *Cf. New Orleans Christian Advocate*, January 15, 1874.

[1]*New Orleans Christian Advocate*, August 21, 1875.

[2]*Cf.* Pastoral Address as given in Nashville *Christian Advocate*, May 15, 1886.

[3]As early as 1870 the bishops called the attention of the Church to the fact that an eager pursuit of "amusements of one kind or another, is one of the startling signs of the times." They felt that "Nothing less than a genuine godliness, in the power of its regenerating influence," could "arrest this current, or counteract its tendency to ruinous social degredation." *Cf.* Pastoral Address in *Journal of General Conference*, 1870, pp. 334-336. Four years later the bishops pointed out that "the multiplied and insiduous forms of popular amusement" had become "a source of perpetual temptation and damage." They said: "Among our young people everywhere, especially in the towns and cities, there is a tendency to worldliness—to vain and demoralizing amusements, which demands a corrective. . . . The toleration of these things by loose notions of Christian liberty, the fact that many Elis among us do not restrain their children, the loose admission of members, the incapacity of the unconverted for spiritual discernment, the long suffrance of evil in the Church, adulterate her purity and break down her authority." *Cf.* Pastoral Address in *Journal of General Conference*, 1874, pp. 386-387.

such diversions as dancing, theater-going, card-playing, and horse-racing, the Methodist Episcopal Church, South, strove unceasingly to banish these pastimes. This it sought to do not only by admonishing and disciplining its own members, but also by stigmatizing such diversions as so potential with evil that no Christian could consistently participate in or encourage them. It is true the General Rules did not condemn these things in terms, and that attempts to alter the *Discipline* in order to specify them were successfully opposed on the ground that they were sufficiently covered by the rule forbidding all diversions which could not "be used in the name of the Lord Jesus." The pulpit and press, nevertheless, at all times thundered forth denunciations of dancing, card-playing, and other particular pastimes as pleasures that were interdicted. Moreover the bishops and the general Conference from time to time enumerated such diversions as being comprehended by the rule. What was more to the point, the participation in amusements of this kind was regularly acted upon by the Church as a justifiable ground for judicial action. Members who partook of "worldly pleasures" were admonished, and, when they persisted in such "revelling," were expelled from the Church.

The debasing effects of participation in the fashionable amusements of the day were constantly dwelt upon.[1] The moral disintegration of those who gave themselves up to the enjoyment of worldly entertainment was vividly pictured. The incompatibility of such pleasure-taking with a consecrated life was continually stressed. Organized groups as well as individuals were held to a strict accountability for any complicity with dancing, card-playing and the like.[2] Those who indulged in these things

---

[1] "We are against this bear-bating," said the Nashville *Advocate* when discussing the popular amusements of the time, "because it pleases the spectators, and pleasing them debases them." Cf. Nashville *Christian Advocate*, March 26, 1887.

[2] The Church did not spare the rod where other religious bodies were concerned. The Catholics and Episcopalians were frequently censured for their laxity with regard to such things. In 1866 the editor of the New Orleans *Advocate*, when discussing the conduct of the Catholic inhabitants of that city, said: "A member of the Catholic Church can swear, attend theaters, gamble, be drunken, attend the race course, violate the sanctity of the Sabbath at will, mix with masqueraders, and dance to the verge of hell, and yet be a good Catholic; if *per contra*, he will recount his prayers, observe lent, attend high mass, and comply with sundry financial prescriptions of his ghostly preceptor. . . . Whenever Methodism shall so conform to the world that her voice dies

were often publicly rebuked. Transgressors in high places were named. As has been seen, the revival was utilized as an agency specially adapted to combatting the influence of the "worldly" diversions of the day. The boldness with which the Church spoke out on such matters is suggested by the remarks of the Nashville *Advocate* with regard to these things in 1886. It said: "It has seemed to us that there has been a wholesome tendency among us in the direction of plainness of speech in our pulpits. Not only have the people been reminded of their sinfulness, but their own particular sins have been uncovered to their sight. The ministers of Christ have been specific in their indictments of transgressors. Thus genuine convictions have followed their preaching. Awakenings have been real. . . . The pulpit has been clothed with greater power as it has shown more boldness and directness in dealing with popular sins and sinners of high degree. It has come to close quarters and pressed this fight. The line of separation between the Church and the world has been defined more clearly, and the Church's spiritual power has been increased in proportion to its non-complicity in evil."[1]

But the arts of persuasion were not less relied upon. To all those who craved such diversions as the Church frowned upon, the necessity for self denial upon the part of the Christian was constantly reiterated. "What are people to do for amusements,

---

away amid the sound of the viol, and she moves to the time and tramp of the earth, the mission of Methodism will have ceased." Cf. *New Orleans Christian Advocate*, August 25, 1866. When a "benefit" was given for a charitable institution of the Protestant Episcopal Church at New Orleans by several corporations which provided public entertainment, the *Advocate* said: "The Children's Home of the Protestant Episcopal Church is receiving this week a somewhat remarkable 'benefit.' Every evening 'refreshments' and a 'dance' at the Varieties Theater, including a 'full dramatic representation on Saturday night; and on Friday afternoon, at the Metaire Course, 'races,' 'refreshments' and a 'dance.' . . . In addition we see that the Committee have applied for and obtained a benefit 'from the academy of music.' . . . if it be necessary to tacitly endorse theaters, race courses, and gambling 'hells' in order to support orphans, we question if even the great excellence of the end will repay the community for the weighty sanction which is thus given to the most active agencies now at work for corrupting the morals and youth of our city. . . . Though we doubt not the Committee will avail itself of the ready anti-'Puritanical' response, we beg leave to suggest that there is a wide margin between Puritanism and such an utter letting go of the proprieties of the Christian profession. We do not expect more of the Episcopal Church than any other, but certainly as much; and we cannot see her representatively trail the cause of God in the dirt and

[1]Nashville *Christian Advocate*, April 24, 1886.

and what especially are young people to do?" asked the New
Orleans *Advocate* when stressing the close association of certain
popular pastimes with sin. "Clearly they are not to do those
things which are at war with public morals, as well as incompatible with personal piety. If these exhaust the catalogue of
all recreations and amusements, then they are to have none. Here,
perhaps, is a chance to meet and exercise the self-denial which
has to come in somewhere in our Christian discipleship. But
there can be social gatherings without the card-table or the dance,
and there are surely many pleasures of sense and taste, as well
as of thought and devotion, in which there is no tendency to
vice."[1] "We do not advocate a gloomy austerity in the Christian
household," said the Richmond *Advocate,* "but insist upon the
utmost prudence in association with an ungodly world. Self-
denial in the matter of pleasure is one of the first lessons to be
learned at the foot of the cross. It should never be forgotten
that—

> 'The world can never give
> The bliss for which we sigh.' "[2]

None of the popular diversions troubled the Church more than
dancing. The appeal of this "fascinating art" made itself felt
in all parts of the Connection, and especially among the "fashionable" Methodists. Throughout the period the Church found it
necessary to "reprove, rebuke, exhort with all long suffering and
doctrine" as well as to discipline its members with regard to
dancing. Its difficulties were due in part to the fact that not only
was there no specific condemnation of the diversion among its
rules but an original section of the *Discipline* which named

---

mire without uttering a protest." *Cf. New Orleans Christian Advocate,* May 8,
1869. Secular institutions fared little better. Referring to recent commencement festivities at the University of Georgia, the *Wesleyan* said in 1896:
". . . it does seem to us that there is a determination on the part of many to
supplant our University by converting it into a dancing and match-game club,
a club for dissipation rather than education. And against this we protest. . .
We do not know that any of the University authorities are responsible for the
inaugural of these revelries, but we do know that they are responsible for
allowing them to go on. They could at least prohibit the use of the University
and its classes and societies in connection with these frivolous things, and they
could forbid the boys attending them and wasting time that ought to be
devoted to higher ends." *Cf. Wesleyan Christian Advocate,* June 17, 1896.
[1] *New Orleans Christian Advocate,* August 21, 1873.
[2] *Richmond Christian Advocate,* June 12, 1884.

dancing among things interdicted had been expunged from the book. The removal of this section was interpreted by many as a relaxation of law amounting to license.[1] The necessity for explaining its position on the subject as well as infractions of its rules led to a constant agitation against the dance.

At all times the Church sought to expose the real character and tendency of the amusement. Dancing was declared to be the "favored amusement of the licentious and profane," and the *"very highest expression of the world's worldliness."* It was represented as not only destructive of a growth in grace but as tending only to dissipation and immorality.[2] A typical ministerial description of the dance was the following: "To reduce dancing to a mere physical exercise, an innocent hilarity of action, is to misconceive its true character. It is to be looked at not in its physical aspects merely, but as emotional action, the expression of emotion by rhythmic, choric movement. It is employed also to give vigor to emotions and to swell their excitement. . . . Irreligious people know the pleasures of the emotions, and the excitements of the dance, and they put no confidence in the religion of the person who is captivated by the involution, the passions and the performance of a scene which is regarded as the *very highest expression of the world's worldliness.*

"It is here that many a fair maiden and noble youth have betrayed the Saviour, and for one sip of sensual pleasure have

---

[1] *Cf. Journal of General Conference,* 1874, pp. 386-387.

[2] A correspondent of the New Orleans *Advocate* wrote in 1870: "The advocates and devotees of social and promiscuous dancing are not the exemplary and pious members of the Church. They are not the devoted laborers in the cause of Christ.—They are not the supporters of religious literature. . . . Dancing is one of the most seductive weapons used by the devil to lead unwary souls from Christ and heaven. . . . Hence all Christians . . . fly from the atmosphere of the ball room as from the breath of a plague." *Cf.* letter of "Watchman" in *New Orleans Christian Advocate,* August 6, 1870. "There will be no fascination in the dance to those who love God and enjoy the comforts of religion . . .," said the New Orleans *Advocate* in its issue of June 25, 1874. The Mobile Conference in 1866 strongly denounced "promiscuous dances at balls and other gatherings of the sort, as tending to dissipation and immorality." It explained that "while the Church takes no cognizance of the inartificial dances of children, sacred dances, and those in which the sexes dance apart," it would discountenance "all those social dances in which the sexes unite, as they may readily run into improprieties and result in scandal." *Cf. Proceedings* of Mobile Conference in *New Orleans Christian Advocate,* December 22, 1866.

sold a birthright."[1] "Let the sexes promiscuously indulge in this fascinating art," said a South Carolina minister, "and see at once the tendency to dissipation and lasciviousness."[2]

While the diversion appears to have been winked at in some places at times, complaints were usually lodged against those who danced. The readiness with which the Church disciplined anyone who engaged in or sanctioned dancing is well illustrated by its action in 1882 when it was discovered that one of the outstanding laymen of the Connection had "openly and before the world violated the spirit of the General Rules of the Church by permitting dancing in his house." He was threatened with the loss of his seat as a delegate in the General Conference until it was ascertained that the law of the Church had been fully vindicated. Although he escaped further penalties, the Conference characterized the conduct of this delegate as "scandalous and fraught with immense mischief to the good order of the Church."[3]

Nor was the Church less forward in rebuking non-Methodists who danced or countenanced the amusement. When a "Bal Poudre" was given at the chapel of Trinity Church in Vicksburg in 1887, the New Orleans *Advocate* said: "In the name of Heaven, is God's Church to be converted into a house of revelry? Is the trysting place of the soul to be profaned by the silly trip of 'the light fantastic toe?' . . . This is written with no purpose to caricature or offend any body of Christians, but for the honor or purity of Christ's cause. But if our friends of the Protestant Episcopal Church are really serious in wanting a union of the evangelical Churches, they must purge themselves of such affairs as the above, and disclaim responsibility therefor."[4]

The theater was regarded as so thoroughly conducive to dis-

---

[1] *Cf. New Orleans Christian Advocate,* September 8, 1866.
[2] *Cf.* Simkins and Woody, *op. cit.,* p. 405.
[3] *Cf. Journal of General Conference,* 1882, p. 62.
[4] *Cf. New Orleans Christian Advocate,* February 3, 1887. When dancing was made a part of the commencement festivities at the University of the South at Sewanee, Tennessee, in 1887, a correspondent of the New Orleans *Advocate* said: "But the presence of Bishop and clergy did not prevent the scandal of a 'hop' at the close of a Church school. We may have no right to criticize such affairs at State institutions; but Church colleges, where the Christian religion is supposed to be taught, are expected to send young men home with prayers and benedictions on their heads and in their hearts, rather than with memories of 'hops', and 'carpet dances', and like abominations. The idea of a Christian university encouraging, condoning or permitting 'the dance of death.'

sipation and immorality that the Church opposed all attendance upon dramatic performances. The play-house was believed to be "one of the ante-chambers of hell," where persons drank in sounds which ministered to their passions, and were under "the tutelage of Olympic performers and dancers, who easily pass from the boards to the bagnio."[1] It was asserted that the institution was not susceptible to reform in any real sense. The profession was one which inevitably damaged the characters of those who were engaged in it. To patronize such an institution amounted to "moral cannibalism." Amateur performances were hardly less frowned upon.[2] The Church would make no compromise with the theater.[3] A characteristic Methodist view of the drama was the following: "The passion of love, exhibited in either comic or tragic situation, is the stock in trade of the stage. When this— the most sacred impulse of human nature, the instinct which should be held in loftiest reserve—is represented for a sport, and

---

"The Episcopal Church is largely responsible for the modern dance and its attendant evils. Who are the chaperones of the ball-room belles in our communities? And who are the 'accomplished dancers' that find complimentary mention in the society columns of the newspapers? With conspicuous exceptions, their ecclesiastical whereabouts are known and read of all men. In the name of our holy Christianity, such things ought not to be so." Cf. communication signed "* * *" in *New Orleans Christian Advocate*, August 18, 1887. Public officials who sanctioned "inaugural balls" and dancing at State educational institutions were severely criticized.

[1]Cf. *New Orleans Christian Advocate*, February 1, 1868.

[2]The South Carolina Conference asserted that "an attendance upon the theater, or circus or any professional or amateur impersonating exhibition, is inconsistent with the obligations of a Christian profession to '*renounce the world, the flesh, and the devil.*'" Cf. *Journal of South Carolina Conference*, 1887, p. 37. When it was announced in 1899 that the elocution class at the University of Mississippi would give a representation of "As You Like It", with Stark Young playing the rôle of "Oliver", a correspondent of the New Orleans *Advocate* said: "We should like to have a statement from the University authorities as to the significance of this announcement. Does it mean that Methodists, Baptists and Presbyterians of Mississippi are being taxed to pay an elocution teacher whose appointed task is to make actors and actresses out of our boys and girls? We were not aware before that the university had such a department—a department for equipping our young people for the stage. The Christian constituency of the institution would like to know what all this means." Cf. letter of "A Mississippian" in *New Orleans Christian Advocate*, June 29, 1899.

[3]"We cannot sufficiently characterize the folly and sin of indorsing this Sabbath-desecrating, all-engulfing, comprehensive evil," said the New Orleans *Advocate* in its issue of February 1, 1868. "Many do this by going only to see 'tragedies, dramas, and great actors.' The endorsement is complete, and the descent easy." In 1880 the Reverend Warren A. Candler urged that "it now be printed in bold type that the habit of certain of our colleges (especially our

the exhibition gives pleasure to the audience, the ax is laid to
the root of the tree of domestic and social purity. It is sometimes
said that the theater should be reformed. This is baldest nonsense.
The theater is rotten to the core. The evil lies in the immorality
of making a sport out of the material which the stage is forced
to use in order to exist at all."[1] "It is no sufficient defense of the
theater to say that all plays and all actors are not immoral," said
the *Southern Christian Advocate*. "This may be readily granted,
and yet there is abundant reason why the Church should continue
her opposition to the drama. It fosters the spirit of worldliness,
it is corrupting to taste, it is destructive of spirituality and
heavenly-mindedness. It educates downwards, not upwards. The
love of the play-house and of the sanctuary will not flourish in
the same bosom. . . . The Church will be recreant to her duty if
she does not at least warn, entreat and protest."[2]

In 1887 an episode occurred at Nashville which stimulated the
opposition to theatrical performances throughout the Connection,
and caused the officials of the Church to undertake a stricter enforcement of the *Discipline* during the remainder of the century,
and especially in the cities, where theater-going had sometimes
been winked at. At the close of a sermon at McKendree Chapel,

---

female colleges) introducing amateur theatricals in the programme of their
commencement exercises is inexcusably wrong. . . . For no consideration can
we agree to have Methodist girls encouraged and helped to do in college what
at any other time or place would be an offense against the 'General Rules.'
    "The preachers in charge of city Churches will remember upon reflection
that most of those abominations of fairs, concerts, etc., often gotten up in
cities for Church purposes, originated with ladies who contracted the habit at
college. . . . It is time to turn our attention to the source of the evil. Most of
our colleges will stop the practice as soon as the attention of the college
authorities is called to its evil. If any refuse to do so it will be lamentable,
for a Methodist public will be compelled to kill those institutions, and we
have none to spare." Cf. letter of W. A. Candler in Nashville *Christian
Advocate*, September 18, 1880.
    [1]Cf. Nashville *Christian Advocate*, August 18, 1887.
    [2]*Southern Christian Advocate*, October 27, 1887. The circus was opposed
upon the same grounds as the theater. In 1876 the Richmond *Advocate* said:
"Old John Robinson's circus will soon appear in this State. In one of his
flaming hand-bills in a shop window in this city he pronounces it a 'strictly
moral circus.'
    "The idea of a circus being moral!—Now reader we beg of you do not be
seen in this or any other circus. . . . We are told that many Church-members
go to circuses as they pass through the country, and we are pained to believe it.
How can any Christian go to such places? . . . It is a school of vanity and
vice. You may get harm but certainly no good at such a place." Cf. *Richmond
Christian Advocate*, August 31, 1876.

in which the Reverend W. A. Candler had condemned the stage unqualifiedly, Emma Abbot, an actress then appearing in opera in the city, arose in the extreme rear of the congregation to dispute what had been said in the discourse.[1] The dramatic situation created a sensation in the Church and throughout the city. Two days later an unsigned communication from one described as an "Eminent Divine," which deplored the extreme position taken by the preacher and defended the action of the actress, appeared in one of the secular dailies.[2] When Candler, resenting certain personal allusions in this letter, demanded the name of the writer, Dr. David C. Kelley, "the petted idol of the fashionable Methodists at Nashville," acknowledged himself to be its author.

The attention of the entire Connection was now centered on the happenings in Tennessee, for, in the words of a Mississippi minister, "what they do at McKendree Church, in Nashville, is felt to a greater or less extent to the borders of Southern Methodism."[3] The Church had not long to wait. The official Board at McKendree promptly adopted a series of resolutions endorsing the position of the Reverend Candler and voicing its indignation at "the violation of propriety and the law of the land" by the actress.[4]

Dr. Kelley now felt it incumbent upon himself to explain his position further. In a note to Candler and in a card to the public he asserted that he had acted only to strike at the extreme position of the sermon which he regarded as hurtful to the Church. While he had taken exception to the statement that attendance at the

---

[1]See account of this affair as given in Nashville *Daily American*, October 10, 1887. For days the secular press of the city talked of little else.

[2]*Cf.* Nashville *Daily American*, October 12, 1887, as quoted in Nashville *Christian Advocate*, October 22, 1887. The writer deplored the wholesale condemnation of the theater and held up to ridicule the logic of the pastor's argument. He declared that, if the affair had been correctly reported, he was of the opinion that there were "few refined, Christian people, who would not have chosen the attitude of Miss Abbot on that Sunday to the preacher's—her discriminating applause of the noble in the profession to his uncharitable, universal denunciation." He felt that "The histrionic talent is as surely God-given and for noble purposes as the preacher's gifts or the power of song and poetry." He believed that "A pure theater will help to usher in the milliennium and form doubtless an element in its duration." Moreover he said, "Miss Abbot, as an untarnished Christian, had the right of defense, and used it in the right time and place."

[3]*Cf.* letter of "Gilderoy" (R. G. Porter) in *Richmond Christian Advocate*, October 22, 1887.

[4]*Cf.* Nashville *Christian Advocate*, October 14, 1887.

theater upon the part of Church members amounted to perjury, he would uphold "the correction of this evil by public and private admonition, and by a patient and kind, but firm," administration of the *Discipline*. He withdrew his commendation of the conduct of the actress at the time of the occurrence.[1]

But the Church at large had become thoroughly aroused and was determined to crush out theater-going, and Dr. Kelley did not escape without further censure. The journals of the Connection greeted the action of the McKendree Board with a round of applause.[2] Communications on the subject flooded the *Advocates*. The Nashville *Advocate* characterized these missives as "all for the Church and against the theater, with an emphasis that is refreshing, and that gives assurance that our people, so generally right in theory, will henceforth be more nearly right in practice."[3] One after another the Annual Conferences in all parts of the South took the matter under consideration. With one accord they called for and pledged themselves to a stricter enforcement of the *Discipline* with regard to theater-going.

---

[1] *Cf. Wesleyan Christian Advocate*, November 16, 1887; Nashville *Christian Advocate*, October 22, 1887; *ibid.*, December 3, 1887.

[2] The Richmond *Advocate* said: "A female actor rose and contradicted the preacher, and orated in favor of theaters. It is strange that a policeman didn't take the woman in charge. Churches are not built as a place for any termagant actress to scream and void her viciousness when her trade is in danger." *Cf. Richmond Christian Advocate*, quoted in Nashville *Christian Advocate*, October 29, 1887. "What if Jenny Lind was charitable, and what if in the 'Bohemian Girl' there are pathetic passages?" said the *Wesleyan*. "After her so-called 'defense of her character' she hurried off on a Sunday train to meet an engagement the next night in Chattanooga." *Cf. Wesleyan Christian Advocate*, quoted in Nashville *Christian Advocate*, October 29, 1887. For all those who were attempting "to put the stage on higher ground than the pulpit," the Alabama *Advocate* expressed "an unrestrained contempt mingled with a degree of pity such as moral idiocy always excites." Moreover, it believed that Miss Abbot was the exception in her profession. *Cf. Alabama Christian Advocate*, quoted in Nashville *Christian Advocate*, October 29, 1887. "Who believes that Miss Abbot acts in the name of the Lord Jesus?" was the sarcastic observation of the *Arkansas Methodist*. "We close by expressing our delight at the action of the McKendree Board and our unequivocal condemnation of this vain actress." *Cf. Arkansas Methodist*, quoted in Nashville *Christian Advocate*, October 29, 1887. Declaring that "the theater has come into the Church and thrown down the gauntlet," the Nashville *Advocate* said: "The fight had to be made. It seems to us it comes providentially as to time, place and attendant circumstances. This is the Church's opportunity to reaffirm with unmistakable emphasis its position on this question, and to take a fresh departure in the direction of making its practical administration conform more fully to its avowed principles." *Cf.* Nashville *Christian Advocate*, October 22, 1887.

[3] *Cf.* Nashville *Christian Advocate*, November 12, 1887.

Notwithstanding the disavowals he had made, persons in various quarters asserted that Dr. Kelley had impaired his usefulness as Missionary Treasurer of the Connection and urged that he be rebuked by the Church at large. They declared that he had so crippled himself for his work that further measures would be necessary to restore his power for service. The North Texas Conference resolved that "with deep regret, and mortification, we feel it our bounden duty to the Church for whose purity and integrity we are in part responsible to express the sense . . . that Dr. D. C. Kelley should tender his resignation of the office of Missionary Treasurer."[1] And, indeed, resolutions pending before the Board of Missions, expressing disapprobation of the conduct of its Treasurer, were withdrawn only after Dr. Kelley had presented to the Board a signed paper for publication, in which he defined more explicitly his real position on the subject.[2]

That the determination which manifested itself at the time of the Candler-Abbot affair was no mere flurry of popular excitement was evidenced when the General Conference assembled three years later. The Conference straightway adopted a series of resolutions, obviously inspired by the Nashville incident, calling for a rigid enforcement of the *Discipline* with regard to "theater-going, dancing, card-playing, and the like." The resolutions deplored the laxity with which the rules of the Church had been observed where such matters were concerned, and the ministers were urged "to give all diligence in warning against worldliness" and to "execute with love and fidelity the requirements of the Discipline in such cases." The Conference stated explicity that "we regard the impression made on the minds of some of our young people by the use of such expressions as 'reformed theater,' 'legitimate drama,' and the like, as misleading and dangerous, and the more so if they emanate from a preacher of the gospel, and we heartily condemn the use of these expressions by our preachers as hurtful to the cause of Christ."[3] Looking to the future the Conference

---

[1] *Cf. Minutes of North Texas Conference,* 1887, p. 16.

[2] *Cf.* Nashville *Christian Advocate,* December 3, 1887. Dr. Kelley subsequently declared that he would not have signed this statement had he known that any action was contemplated on these resolutions which had been offered by the Reverend W. D. Kirkland of South Carolina and the Reverend P. A. Peterson of Virginia.

[3] *Cf. Journal of General Conference,* 1890, p. 51.

created a special Committee of Fifteen on the Spiritual State of the Church, and ordered that this body formulate a deliverance on worldliness to be inserted as an appendix to the *Discipline*.[1]

With the rise of organized and professional sports during the period following the Civil War, the Church came to look with growing disapprobation upon a number of the popular athletic diversions of the time. Many believed that football, baseball, boxing and wrestling matches exerted both a demoralizing and a brutalizing influence. The Church greatly feared the effects of these amusements upon the rising generation. Because of the frequency with which persons indulged in such diversions on the Sabbath and because of the conviviality of the crowds which patronized them, the churchmen inevitably associated these sports with wrong-doing. The disfavor with which the Methodists looked upon these pastimes is well illustrated by the attitude which the *Raleigh Christian Advocate* expressed towards baseball in 1884: "If it be true, then, that the game, as now carried to excess, promotes intemperance and gambling, is a financial tax upon the people, paralyzes business, is injurious to health, and threatens the country with indelicate exposures of our young women, is it not an evil, to say the least of it? And if it is an evil, ought good men to encourage it with their means and presence? We know that this view of the matter will brook public sentiment, and be objected to by very many, but that makes it the more important that men who have convictions should utter them. Let our boys have these games occasionally as matters of recreation if they want them, but our grown men, both white and colored, ought to be in better employment."[2]

The Church feared especially the influence of professional prize-fights and that of intercollegiate matches. The brutality of the ring-side was frequently emphasized. The Church journals denounced in the strongest terms every suggestion for holding a championship fight in a Southern city.[3] The *Advocates* felt it

---

[1] *Cf. Daily Christian Advocate*, May 21, 1890.

[2] *Cf. Raleigh Christian Advocate*, quoted in Nashville *Christian Advocate*, October 4, 1884.

[3] The *Wesleyan Christian Advocate* was scandalized when it was proposed that a championship fight should take place in Atlanta in 1894. In an editorial headed "Shame! Shame!" it said: "Poor Atlanta has had many indignities heaped upon her but, aside from nefarious whiskey traffic, she has had none so

humiliating that "such a thing could take place in broad daylight, and at 'this point of the world's history."[1] They urged that organized efforts be made to keep such exhibitions out of the Southern cities.[2]

The churchmen feared that the colleges of the day would make "educated sluggers" of the young men who attended them. Apart from the supposed demoralizing and brutalizing tendencies of the intercollegiate football and baseball games of the time, Methodist leaders felt that "these sports cannot in any proper sense comport with higher intellectual education."[3] Some of the Methodist colleges prohibited all intercollegiate games.[4] A number of the

---

calculated to bow her head so low with shame as the mere proposition to have the Corbett-Mitchell prize-fight in her walls. Of course the fight will not take place here; there is both law and self-respect enough to prevent that, but the bare suggestion, as made in the *Constitution* of last Monday, is enough to blight the town for years to come, and make every good citizen blush with shame." Cf. *Wesleyan Christian Advocate,* January 3, 1894.

[1]Despite the fact that the governors of Louisiana and Mississippi had issued proclamations prohibiting the encounter within their respective borders, the mighty John L. Sullivan matched his prowess against an opponent in Mississippi in 1889. The Nashville *Advocate* announced that "The civilization of the United States has been disgraced and the soil of Mississippi has been polluted recently by a 'mill' between two brutal ruffians, one hailing from Boston and the other from Baltimore." Cf. Nashville *Christian Advocate,* July 18, 1889.

[2]"We ought to be up and doing to put an end to this brutality," said the New Orleans *Advocate* in its issue of November 16, 1893. "We verily believe that the decent, civilized element in this city is sufficiently strong to accomplish this end by proper organized effort. But it will take effort—vigorous, persistent, organized effort. Should we not be willing to make the effort?"

[3]Cf. *Wesleyan Christian Advocate,* December 11, 1895.

[4]Emory College, which had never permitted intercollegiate football games, in 1896 adopted a regulation prohibiting match games between the classes, and students were warned that "every element of brutality must be eliminated from the game or it should not be played at all." Cf. *Wesleyan Christian Advocate,* November 17, 1897. At a meeting of the Board of Trust of Vanderbilt University in 1897 Bishop John C. Keener introduced a resolution declaring that "Intercollegiate gymnastic contests have come to a plane of influence highly mischievous to the moral, social and educational well-being of the youth of the country," and providing that Vanderbilt should "withdraw from all such fields of contest." The resolution further stipulated that "any professor or student who shall directly or indirectly violate the letter or spirit of this order" should be "discontinued from all connection with this institution." Although this resolution failed of adoption by one vote, it was referred to a committee which was instructed to report on the subject at the next meeting of the Board. "If Bishop Keener's resolutions had been adopted," lamented the New Orleans *Advocate* when this measure met defeat, "the Church would have been in the lead on this question. . . . The Church is put in a pitiable attitude when she follows instead of leading public opinion in a matter of this sort." Cf. *New Orleans Christian Advocate,* February 3, 1893.

Advocates opposed all participation in the game of football, even to the extent of advocating its legal suppression.[1]

Because of their relation to gambling and other vices, the Church opposed all diversions in which wagers were laid or stakes played for. Card games, billiard playing, and horse racing were hardly less frowned upon than professional gambling. Typical of the light in which such amusements were viewed were the comments of a correspondent of the New Orleans *Advocate,* who said in 1866: "I have all my days had a card playing community open to my observation, and I am yet able to be made to believe that a game which is the universal resort of the starved in soul and intellect, which has never in any way linked itself with tender, elevating or beautiful associations, the tendency of which is to unduly absorb the attention from more weighty matters, can recommend itself to the favor of Christ's disciples. The use of culture and genius may embellish, but can never dignify it. I have at this moment ringing in my ears the dying injunction of my father's friend: 'Keep your sons from cards; over them I've murdered time and lost heaven.'"[2] It was said that "deep down in the conscience of every one who indulges, even in a social game, is a feeling that it is wrong—that it in no wise commends one to the favor of Heaven."[3] The Church sought constantly to place all such diversions beyond the pale of respectability.

---

[1]The *Wesleyan* waged open warfare on football in Georgia. Referring to the recent death of a student who had been injured in a game in that State, it said in 1897: "Intercollegiate games of every kind are detrimental to all right education, demoralizing in their results; but the foot-ball business is so brutal as to make it unworthy of any consideration, except to be condemned. . . . Now is the time for our legislature to act. The weal of our commonwealth demands it." *Cf. Wesleyan Christian Advocate,* November 10, 1897. A short time later the legislature of Georgia enacted a law prohibiting all football games in the State. When the governor vetoed this measure, declaring it to be "governmental paternalism of the most vicious type," the *Wesleyan* said: "It does not meet the case to say that this species of lunacy is a voluntary imposition. Society has the right to protect itself even against itself, whatever be the spirit that gives rise to the necessity. . . . The football game is so barbarous, so entirely brutal, as to put it at once outside of the pales of civilized society; and if the sentiment of the people is not sufficient to put it beyond the possibility of doing harm, then the State ought to come in and give relief." *Cf. Wesleyan Christian Advocate,* November 15, 1897. In an editorial headed "Football Must Go", in its issue of November 11, 1897, the New Orleans *Advocate* declared that "it is high time for the game to be put under the ban everywhere. . . . We would be glad to see it prohibited by law."
[2]*Cf. New Orleans Christian Advocate,* August 25, 1866.
[3]*Ibid.,* March 6, 1884.

While not a cause of open scandal, and therefore occupying the attention of the Church to a lesser degree, the reading of novels was frowned upon for much the same reasons as theater-going. Many regarded indulgence in this pastime as "one aspect of that worldliness which overshadows the soul, and drives away the conviction of eternal things," and believed it to be one of the most powerful "causes of the present demoralization of American society." They frequently dwelt upon the habit-forming and debasing effects of the diversion. The New Orleans *Advocate* declared that the practice became "an overmastering passion—a species of mental infatuation." "The lady who is given to intemperate novel reading," it said, "exhibits the fact in her whole deportment, conversation, tone of voice, and in the lines of the face. . . . Novel reading has kept thousands from coming to Christ."[1] The journals warned parents to guard carefully the reading of their children, and urged that, if allowed at all, the novels read should be "as pure as angels, and like angels' visits, few and far between."[2]

It cannot be doubted that the influence which the Methodist

---

[1] Cf. New Orleans Christian Advocate, March 29, 1877. In its issue of January 25, 1872 the *Advocate* warned that unless a careful discrimination and moderate indulgence were exercised, "mental imbecility, moral relaxation, and utter frivolity are certain to follow." Evidently the novels of Augusta Evans Wilson, widely read in the South throughout this period, were considered above reproach for no condemnation of them appeared in the Church papers. This erudite lady was well known in the Connection as a devoted member of the fashionable St. Francis Street Church in Mobile in which she served as organist and where she formed a close friendship with Frank Armstrong Crawford, who as the wife of Commodore Vanderbilt was later distinguished for her liberality to the Methodists of the South. *Cf.* letter of January 22, 1938 to the author from Mrs. Janie McTyeire Baskervill of Bristol, Virginia.

[2] *Cf. New Orleans Christian Advocate,* March 29, 1877. The Nashville *Advocate* warned the communicants of the Church that their libraries must be expurgated. It urged that "All bad books should be put out of their homes—not only the very bad, but all bad books. The poison of some is slow, that of others is quick; but it is death in all." *Cf.* Nashville *Christian Advocate,* April 16, 1887. "The literature furnished to our children should be most carefully inspected," said the New Orleans *Advocate* in its issue of January 25, 1872. "Your boys are at home of nights, but they might possibly be in better company abroad. The pure and virtuous influences of home depend much upon what they are reading. Your girls are housed and their associations guarded; but that volume, bound in green and gold, over which they are poring may be Reade's 'Terrible Temptation', or something worse. A taste for vicious and sensational reading is an evil of fearful magnitude, and a life long calamity. . . . The reading of youth must be more carefully watched than all their other associations."

Episcopal Church, South, exerted in inducing men to eschew the pleasures of the world did much to impart a Puritanic flavor to Southern society during the post-war period. The extent to which it could affect the everyday lives of practical men of the world is well illustrated in the attitude of Walter B. Hill of Georgia, who was in many respects one of the most liberal-minded Southerners of his day, and who served with distinction as a justice of the Supreme Court, as head of the Georgia Bar Association, and as Chancellor of the University of Georgia. On an occasion in 1896 when expressing a fear that "a monotony of 'don'ts' " upon the part of the Church might lead to the idea of the false alternative, that a Christian could take no pleasure in society, Hill implored that his position be not misunderstood, and he made it clear that he was personally true to the rules of the Church with regard to interdicted diversions. "It is not within my comprehension, for instance," he said, "how people with moral sensibilities can enjoy games played with the instruments of gambling. The association of ideas is too frightfully unpleasant. I could as soon enjoy a game of ten pins where the balls were dead men's skulls and the pins were skeletons. Upon the same footing is the moral callousness and indifference to consequences implied in the act of the host or hostess who mingles with the feast the poison of intoxication."[1]

It should not, nevertheless, be inferred from what has been said here that the Methodists of the South led gloomy, austere lives, renouncing altogether the pleasures of the world. Traditions of open-handed hospitality operated against such a re pressive narrowness. The denomination, moreover, did not officially condemn certain forms of conviviality. It was reported that many ministers were notorious for their fondness for "good roast beef and lamb and lemonade, if not disguised brandy smashers," and for their "strength and health, extended girth and rubicund faces."[2] Of one South Carolina pastor it was said: "His face is as fat as his body. He eats!—yes, eats more heartily than other men—not ambrosia, but simple hog and hominy. He drinks,

---

[1] *Cf.* letter of Walter B. Hill in *Wesleyan Christian Advocate,* March 11, 1896.

[2] *Cf.* Simkins and Woody, *op. cit.,* p. 407.

aye, freely—but it is not sack and brandy; but simple water, tea and coffee. He sleeps and that so soundly and sonorously that he generally monopolizes all of that blessed commodity which happens to be in the house at the time."[1] Even ministers enjoyed the delights of tobacco with an abandon that was a scandal to their Northern brethren.[2] When referring to a "treatise upon this wonderful weed" by "the Rev. Dr. Walker," which appeared in its columns, the New Orleans *Advocate* said in 1868: "Fortunate it is that he does not belong to the North Ohio Conference. He would have to make many confessions, promises of amendment, besides eating an enormous quantity of cod-fish, if those brethren had the handling of the case."[3] Attempts to have the Church express official disapproval of the tobacco habit failed miserably.

Church gatherings, in which social interests frequently took precedence over religious ones, offered a welcome escape from rural isolation. These gatherings often partook of a carnival character such as one usually associates with the church life of less puritanical denominations. No special obligation to go within doors was imposed upon the numerous persons who collected about rural churches on Sundays. Upon such occasions as Quarterly Meetings friends not infrequently spent the mornings chatting and waiting for the "savory viands" which were served upon the long tables that were spread under the trees near the building. It was notorious that the spiritual purposes of "protracted meetings" were often subordinated to feasting, the display of new finery, and animated discussions of secular topics.[4]

Gambling was a source of much anxiety to the Methodists throughout the period. Legalized and professional gambling flourished under various guises. The professional gambler was looked upon as one of the most sinister figures in society. Lotteries and public gambling houses were among the most successful

---

[1]*Idem.*

[2]When the question of organic unity was being discussed in 1896 the Nashville *Advocate* remarked sarcastically: "Dr. Schell of the Epworth League says that there can never be any organic union of the two Methodisms until the Southern preachers quit using tobacco. This is a new test." *Cf.* Nashville *Christian Advocate*, April 23, 1896.

[3]*New Orleans Christian Advocate*, January 4, 1868.

[4]Simkins and Woody, *op. cit.*, pp. 406-409, gives a good account of these phases of church life.

ventures of the day. The Louisiana State Lottery, chartered by a carpet-bag legislature in 1867, assumed the proportions of a national institution, drawing patronage from all parts of the union. To the Methodists such an organization appeared a "monster iniquity."[1]

The Church not only sought to place all gambling and those diversions usually associated with the practice beyond the pale of respectability, but also used its influence to secure the legal suppression of "gambling hells" and all forms of licensed gambling.[2] Its efforts in this direction were exerted chiefly for the overthrow of the Louisiana Lottery as the most notorious of the offenders. When it became apparent several years prior to the expiration of its charter in 1890 that this corporation would do all in its power to secure an amendment to the constitution of the State which would make possible an extension of its privileges, the Church resolved to leave no stone unturned to accomplish its final des-

---

[1] When the legislature of Alabama chartered a lottery in 1866, stipulating that a part of its proceeds should be devoted to the rebuilding of the State university, Bishop McTyeire said: "This in Alabama, among a Christian people and in the latter half of the Nineteenth Century! . . . The gambler is not respectable. . . . But this lottery is made respectable 'by authority.' . . . It comes to us under the patronage of education—of adorning and refitting and refurnishing the University of Alabama. . . . Better its walls should never rise from their ashes; better its foundations were sowed with salt and plowed up, than that by such means, it should be helped. . . . it becomes us to exhaust every legitimate means by which it may be abated, limited, checked, protested, condemned, exposed or wiped out. Let pulpit, and press and people bear a vigorous and faithful testimony till this is done." *Cf.* sermon of Bishop McTyeire as reported in *Montgomery Advertiser* and quoted in *New Orleans Christian Advocate,* September 15, 1866. When two popular ex-Confederate generals lent the prestige of their names to the support of the Louisiana Lottery, they were unsparingly criticized in the Methodist press. "We have heretofore called attention to the fact that the names of two once distinguished, but now notorious Confederate generals have been associated with this gambling contrivance. Five thousand dollars a year is a tempting price, but it is a pity that such men as Beauregard and Early should have accepted it." *Cf. New Orleans Christian Advocate,* December 12, 1878.

[2] "So long as men hide their vicious practices from the gaze of their fellows, they in so far evidence some sense of virtue," said the New Orleans *Advocate* in its issue of March 20, 1869. "But when they are encouraged by the highest authority of the State to overstep all moral restraint, to defy the opinion of the good, to abandon all shame and, in open day, assume the desperate fortunes and character of a gambler, it would seem as if the mouth of hell had been opened by law." In its issue of May 8, 1869 the same journal said: "By looking into the public gambling saloons of St. Charles street one may see the tail of the dragon of which the present government of Louisiana is the head. These 'hells', where the last barrier between virtue and vice is passed, are the monstrous but natural progeny of legislative corruption."

truction.[1] The *Advocates* and Annual Conferences in all parts of the South pledged themselves to aid in striking it down. The General Conference expressed a "profound sympathy" for those who were conducting the fight in Louisiana, and declared that it would, "by all proper means within its power aid them in their effort to forever rid themselves" of this "national disgrace."[2]

Thus encouraged by the Church at large, the Louisiana Methodists conducted a militant campaign to oust the Lottery from their State. The Annual Conference pledged itself in 1889 that, "as citizens, we will never knowingly cast a vote for the election of any man to any State office, or to membership in the Legislature, who is in any wise in sympathy with or under the influence of the Louisiana State Lottery." It called upon the legislators of the State to exert their whole influence to destroy the institution.[3] Shortly before the proposed constitutional amendment was to be voted upon in 1890, the New Orleans *Advocate* carried in its columns the form of a memorial to the State legislature protesting against the change. It urged that such petitions be circulated, and, when a sufficient number of signatures had been appended, that they be returned to the *Advocate* office to be forwarded to the capital.[4]

When the supporters of the Lottery succeeded in having such an amendment adopted, the Church merely redoubled its efforts. The New Orleans *Advocate* promptly published a roll of honor, on which it listed the names of the twenty-four members of the legislature who had voted against amending the constitution.[5] At its forthcoming session the Louisiana Conference memorialized the representatives of the State in Congress to "secure the amendment of the Constitution of the United States, so as to prohibit

---

[1] The State constitution provided that all lottery charters should expire on January 1, 1895, "from which time all lotteries are prohibited in the State." Cf. *New Orleans Christian Advocate*, April 24, 1890.

[2] Cf. *Journal of General Conference*, 1890, pp. 69-70.

[3] *Journal of Louisiana Conference*, 1889, p. 14.

[4] "There is still left us the inalienable right of freemen—the right of petition," said the *Advocate* in its issue of March 6, 1890. "The Legislature cannot, and will not ignore the prayer of thousands of the best citizens in the land. Let petitions be gotten up everywhere and signed by the people, to spare our fair State the shame and humiliation and reproach of another regime of lottery by turning a deaf ear to any and every request of this public robber and plunderer."

[5] Cf. *New Orleans Christian Advocate*, July 3, 1890.

the charter of lotteries by any State in the Union."[1]   Due largely
no doubt to the aggressive leadership furnished by the Methodist
Episcopal Church, South, the Legislature of Louisiana, after a
desperate struggle, overthrew the Lottery before the close of 1890
by refusing to grant it a new charter. Congress assured the fruits
of this victory in 1894 when it enacted laws prohibiting the importation of lottery tickets into the country and their transportation
by railway and express companies.[2]

The shocking insecurity of human life in many parts of the
Southern States during the post-war period awakened the strongest
humanitarian impulse in the Church. It sought earnestly to arouse
the public to the cheapness with which life was held and to create
a public sentiment which would insure an adequate punishment
of murder and other crimes of violence. The pulpit and press
denounced with great vehemence the chivalric code of the section
which required that certain insults be avenged with blood and
that a man should jeopardize his life in defense of his character
by whomsoever assailed.[3] The *Advocates* inveighed against the
vitiated public sentiment which rendered possible the notoriously
lax enforcement of the law in cases where the murderer was
possessed of money and influence, and they constantly urged that
heavier penalties be imposed. They demanded that pressure be
brought to bear upon police officers and jurors to see that the
law was administered conscientiously and without favor. "Hang-

---

[1]*Journal of Louisiana Conference,* 1890, pp. 13-14.
[2]*Cf.* Woodbridge, S. Homer, *Anti-Lottery Campaign* (Washington, 1921),
pp. 1-16.
[3]"It is not courage but cowardice that prompts a man to risk his life in
what the world calls a defence of his honor," said the *Southern* in 1879.
"He goes to the field to kill or be killed, to atone for some indignity offered or
received. Suppose he is killed; well, we have only to drop a tear of sorrow
over the grave of a suicide. Suppose he kills his adversary; then he walks the
earth a miserable, unhung murderer, *his brother's blood crying from the ground
against him.* Suppose he neither kills or is killed; then his honor is avenged
and his character is made. He is a brave man. No. He is an arrant coward.
To be afraid of public opinion when you conscientiously feel that you are right,
is cowardice, and nothing else. A true man, a man of genuine moral courage,
will acknowledge a fault or error when he is unfortunately guilty; and will
vindicate his character when it is maliciously assailed by the facts in the
case. . . . What right has a man—a man, whose estate will not pay his debts, a
man accountable for the well-being of society; a man immortal and responsible,
we repeat it, what right has such a man deliberately to threaten the life of
another and thoughtlessly to blast the interest and peace of others." *Cf. Southern Christian Advocate,* August 2, 1879.

ing is a dreadful thing," declared the New Orleans *Advocate* in 1880. . . . "it is humiliating to our human nature to strangle a man or break his neck for crime. And yet we believe that it would be better for society if ten times more hanging were done. . . . Hanging is a miserable and horrifying spectacle, and a most deplorable fate to overtake a human creature, but murder is still more horrible, and it is the right of society to protect itself against those who are blood thirsty, or who have no regard for the lives of their fellow beings."[1] In 1895 the *Southern Christian Advocate* called upon the Constitutional Convention held in South Carolina that year to provide for the disenfranchisement of future homicides, and urged that this be a permanent disability and not removeable by the pardoning power.[2] As has been seen, the Church denounced with special emphasis the impunity with which the lives of defenceless Negroes were taken, and called for a stringent execution of justice in such cases. It cannot be doubted that the outspoken denunciation of lynching by the journals and leaders of the denomination did much to check such violence in the South.

---

[1]*New Orleans Christian Advocate,* September 16, 1880.
[2]*Southern Christian Advocate,* November 14, 1895.

CHAPTER XI

CONCLUSION

EMERGING from the Civil War with shattered fortunes and uncertain of its future, the Methodist Episcopal Church, South, was yet able, through force of circumstance and because of its abounding zeal, to exert a profound influence upon social relations of every kind in the South during the remainder of the nineteenth century. The emphasis upon matters of this kind in the denomination shifted noticeably at intervals during that time. The decade immediately following the War was for the Church primarily a period of rehabilitation and readjustment in which it was forced to combat an active policy of "disintegration and absorption" on the part of its sister Church of the North.

Warmly supported in this situation by the sympathies of the Southern people, the Church urgently appealed to the popular dislike of any Northern interference in Southern affairs. Antagonized constantly by their co-religionists of the North, the leaders of the denomination adopted an unbending attitude towards every suggestion of reform emamating from that quarter, and especially when measures were advocated as the outgrowth of "Northern" ideas. Although with the adjustment of the relations between the two Methodisms in 1876 and with the passing of Reconstruction this attitude became less pronounced, it persisted in some measure to the end of the century. By thus contributing to the prolongation of sectional animosities, the Church affected materially the course of social reform in the Southern States. For the reasons stated and because of a traditional dislike of "fanaticism" in matters pertaining to social relations as well as on account of its deep-seated aversion to ecclesiastical interference in politics, the Church confined its attempts to influence social relations during this first decade very largely to matters of an essentially moral nature. The leaders of the denomination saw in the rapid growth of such vices as drunkenness and in the unusual craving for "worldly" diversions an alarming portent of moral disintegration which caused them to fear for the integrity of the Church. Its chief energies were spent in combatting this trend. A "perfect blaze of revivals" swept over the Connection during these years.

As the necessity for a defensive policy decreased, however, the Church developed a new conception of its powers. After the Cape May settlement of 1876 and as it came to be increasingly recognized that men's spiritual welfare was largely dependent upon their social surroundings, the traditional dislike of fanaticism and the old fear of political corruption gave way before the need for social reform. More and more the denomination sought to influence matters of a civic and social character. With increasing frequency the Church advanced humanitarian arguments in support of measures of moral reform and urged humanitarian reforms as ends in themselves. The journals and representative bodies of the Connection came to express themselves on matters of public policy in precisely the fashion their Northern brethren had done in *ante-bellum* times.

One of the first problems to attract the attention of the denomination at the close of the War was the plight of the freedmen. The Methodists of the South promptly and cheerfully acknowledged their sense of responsibility for the religious welfare of colored population of the section. It was hoped that the great mass of the blacks who had been alienated from the Church during the excitements of the struggle could be induced to return to its fold. Much attention was given to adjusting the economy and machinery of the Church to the needs of the freedmen. The spokesmen of the denomination expressed themselves warmly in favor of education as a means of elevating the race, and much interest was displayed in projects for Negro schools.

But forces of an opposite tendency widened further the breach. To begin with, the Methodist Episcopal Church, South, in common with the other large denominations of the section, found it difficult to comprehend fully the significance of emancipation as regards its religious implications. The Church showed little inclination to revise radically its conception of the proper place of the Negro in the Connection and in society. While cordially inviting him to remain in his accustomed place in the Church, the leaders of the denomination expected that the African would continue in an inferior and subordinate relation. They manifested no disposition to grant him any real voice in the control of the affairs of the Church or to admit him to an unrestricted pastoral or legislative capacity. The blacks, on the other hand, felt that they had a right to freedom and equality in religious matters. Furthermore the Negroes at that time regarded it as a token of one's freedom to have new religious affiliations. But perhaps the chief reason for the failure of the Southern Church to regain its following of colored communicants was the interference of the Methodist Episcopal Church. Against all efforts of Southern Methodists to work among the blacks the Northern Church opposed an untiring resistence. In following this course it was greatly facilitated by the political regimentation of the freedmen which its own missionaries did so much to bring about. By 1870 the Southern Church had definitely abandoned the idea of recovering its colored following. Finding the blacks no longer accessible to its guidance, the Church for almost a decade thereafter gave little attention to the spiritual or temporal needs of the Africans.

As the blacks became amenable to the influence of Southern whites with the passing of Reconstruction however, a lively interest in the religious welfare of the Negroes manifested itself at once in the Connection and continued strong to the end of the century. This was evidenced primarily by a concern for the mental improvement of the Africans which found practical expression in a movement to provide trained Negro leaders for the race. By 1883 this interest reached a high pitch. Apart from furnishing trained Negro teachers and preachers, the Methodist Episcopal Church, South, did much to dispel the apathy and prejudice which had developed in the South with regard to the mental and spiritual elevation of the blacks and to create a sentiment favorable to Negro education. Its spokesmen were especially active in developing a favorable attitude toward the tax-supported public schools in which the great majority of the blacks were destined to receive their education.

Although unwilling to revise its notions with regard to the social relations between the races, the Church proved itself a foremost champion of Negro rights. It did much to gain a recognition of the dignity of the race and to make possible for the African an opportunity for the fullest development. The spokesmen of the Church at all times appealed for a considerate treatment of the blacks, emphasizing the great obstacles which the Negro had to overcome. The leaders and journals of the denomination sought earnestly to promote the material welfare of the Negroes, constantly urging the whites to provide economic opportunities for them and appealing to the white man's sense of magnanimity and fair play in his dealings with the colored man. The Church stood forth as an outspoken champion of the personal safety of the blacks, demanding for them an impartial protection of the law in the enjoyment of their rights. While disapproval of the political use made of the freedmen sometimes gave an academic tone to the discussion of outrages against Negroes in the Methodist journals during the earlier part of the period, the Church became increasingly outspoken in denouncing all violence against the blacks. The *Advocates* deplored all schemes to solve the Negro problem through emigration and colonization. The Church did much to convince the people of the South of the possibility of a satisfactory adjustment between the races in the section.

Through its function as an educator the Methodist Episcopal Church, South, was able to exert a strong influence upon social policies. Throughout the period from the Civil War to the end of the century, and especially during Reconstruction when the States were unable to perform the function, the schools of the denomination rendered an important public service by providing sound instruction for many who would otherwise have been unable to obtain it. The Church undertook to maintain standards in its schools which inevitably reacted favorably upon those of the other schools in the section. A system of district schools was organized in various parts of the Connection during the Seventies. Notwithstanding its own aspirations, and despite the fact that attempts to exclude the Bible from common schools caused some Methodists leaders for a time to yield but a grudging support to public schools, the Church manifested a willingness, as soon as Reconstruction was over, to accept both primary and secondary education as a function of the State. The contribution of the denomination to elementary education lay perhaps as much in the encouragement given to the development of public schools as in its own endeavors in the field. The representative bodies, the press, and the pulpit of the Connection became active champions of free common schools.

Despite the loss of their endowments and the destruction of their equipment, and although maintained in the face of grave financial difficulties, the Methodist colleges were, for perhaps a decade, able to provide the most adequate facilities for higher education that could be obtained in a number of the Southern States. Throughout the Reconstruction period they prepared for the States a number of educated leaders who but for the activity of the Church would have been wanting. Inspired by the larger opportunities presented to them, the interest of Southern Methodists in the promotion of higher education grew until it assumed the character and proportions of a renaissance. It found expression in a movement for concentration and systematization in the educational work of the Church which culminated in the founding of a great central university for Southern Methodism, having as one of its departments a theological school for the training of the ministerial candidates of the Connection. This institution, Vanderbilt University, founded in 1875, was soon able to establish and maintain high and fixed educational standards in a way that no other institution in the Southern States then could do. The standards set at this central institution of Southern Methodism exerted a wide influence on educational policies throughout the South and especially in the Methodist Connection. The men who controlled the other institutions of the denomination contributed much to the development of liberal concepts of higher learning in the South. The combination of progressive and far-sighted views with commanding personalities in such men as James H. Carlisle, Holland N. McTyeire, Landon Cabell Garland, and James A. Duncan enabled the Methodist Episcopal Church, South, to exert what was probably the most potent and liberal influence in the field of higher education in the South during the years from 1865 to 1900.

With its membership constituting so large a proportion of the population of the section, and occupying, as it did, so important a place in the educational system of the region, the Church inevitably exerted a profound influence upon the character of popular thought along all lines in the South. The denomination proved itself to a surprising degree friendly to liberal thought and free inquiry. The remarkable post-war procession of Southern students to the liberal universities of Germany had its origins in a very real sense in the migration of young men from Randolph-Macon and other Southern Methodist institutions to Leipzig. A large proportion of these first European trained scholars returned to teach in Methodist colleges in the South where they were allowed a wide scope in their teachings. But little tendency to heresy hunting manifested itself in the Connection during the period. Among the leaders and communicants of the Church there was a group of men who were not only willing to subject the standards of their denomination to critical tests when occasion arose, but were likewise content to follow the seekers of truth in all fields of thought. The tolerant views of these men contributed much to the advancement of liberal thinking in the South.

The most vigorous, and perhaps the most successful, efforts of Southern Methodism for enforcing personal and social morality were those directed against the drink evil. Alarmed at the increasing drunkenness in Southern society during the decade immediately following the War and feeling the need of bearing a more definite witness against strong drink, the Church a few years after the War undertook to rid itself of all complicity with the evil and to banish the use of intoxicants from society. Forgetting their old fears of political contamination the journals and representative bodies of the Connection exerted their whole influence in support of measures for the legal restriction or absolute prohibition of the liquor traffic. The leaders of the denomination employed moral suasion at all times to check intemperance. The Church did much to stigmatize drinking of every kind and to brand the liquor traffic as a crime against society. It was in no small measure due to the aggressive leadership and moral encouragement afforded by the Church that local prohibition was secured to some extent in all the Southern States by 1890, and that the ground which had been won could be held until the way was prepared for the ultimate acceptance of State-wide and national prohibition.

In general the Church maintained traditional views with regard to the position of women in society. The influence of the franchise upon the sex was greatly feared. Eloquent pleas were made to induce woman to remain upon the exalted plane upon which Southern chivalry had placed her. There were, nevertheless, evidences of a willingness to grant to woman a place of greater dignity in the Church and to concede to her a broader sphere of activity in society at large. Many of the customs which had limited the action of women in the congregation were allowed to die out. The formal recognition of the Woman's Missionary Society by the General Conference in 1878 was the confirmation of a new conception of woman's role in the Church. The denomination placed an emphasis upon the intellectual development of women which inevitably led to a recognition of their claims along other lines.

The Methodists saw an alarming sign of moral disintegration in the rapidly increasing divorce rate in American society. The Church sought to preserve the sanctity of the marriage tie by advocating stricter marriage and divorce laws and by stigmatizing all divorce not based on adultry as immoral. It did much to attach disgrace to divorce of all kinds in the popular mind. Its unbending attitude toward the institution was in a large measure responsible for the fact that disrupted marriages continued to be less common in the South than in other parts of the country.

The Southern Church saw another ominous portent in the increasing desecration of the Sabbath everywhere in American society. Believing that continued encroachments upon the sanctity of the day would undermine the very foundations of social order and private virtue, it exerted its whole influence to secure a proper observance of the day. Although unwilling at first to commit itself in favor of the enactment of laws to enforce Sabbath observance, it began early in the Eighties to pledge its support to organizations sponsoring such legislation. Within a few years the journals and representative bodies of the Connection advocated the passage of blue laws without reserve, bringing pressure to bear upon State and national legislatures for that purpose. Its chief efforts along this line were directed against the running of passenger trains and the opening of places of public amusement on Sunday. Though the sabbatarians lost ground year after year where these matters were concerned, it was due in no small measure to the aggressive policy of the Methodist Episcopal Church, South, that the traditional Lord's Day was preserved to a greater extent in the South than in any other section of the country.

A major portion of the Southern Methodist efforts at reform were directed against the participation in those "worldly" amusements which, though not specifically condemned by the Scriptures, were yet believed to be conducive to immorality. Fearful that its members would be corrupted by the eager rush of society after such diversions as dancing, card-playing, theater-going, and some of the organized and professional sports, the Church sought to banish these pastimes. This it undertook to do by disciplining its own members and by stigmatizing such diversions as so potential with evil that no Christian could participate in or encourage them. The influence which the Methodist Episcopal Church, South, exerted in inducing men to eschew the pleasures of the world undoubtedly did much to impart a Puritanical flavor to Southern society during the period.

The Church sought to place all gambling beyond the pale of respectability and used its influence to secure the suppression of "gambling hells" and all forms of licensed gambling. It conducted a militant campaign against the Louisiana Lottery as the most notorious of the offenders, contributing greatly to the overthrow of that "monster iniquity" in 1890.

Against crime of a graver sort the Church bore a powerful witness. It sought earnestly to awaken the public to the cheapness with which human life was held in many parts of the South and to arouse a public sentiment which would insure an adequate punishment of murder and other crimes of violence. The pulpit and press of the denomination denounced with great vehemence the chivalric code of the section which required that certain insults be avenged with blood and that a man should jeopardize his life in defense of his honor whenever and by whomsoever assailed. The *Advocates* inveighed against the vitiated public opinion which rendered possible a lax enforcement of the law in cases where criminals were possessed of money and influence, and they constantly urged that heavier penalties for such crimes be imposed.

Although still inclined to see in the Golden Rule the only effective remedy for alleviating human misery, the Church gained a new interest in humanitarian uplift toward the close of the century. Alarmed at the fact that it was not reaching the poorest elements of the city population, it was inclined to a broader view of its duties and began to create new philanthropic agencies and eleemosynary institutions for their benefit. Although understanding but imperfectly the great odds against the working classes in their struggles to secure an adequate living wage, the Church evidenced an awakening interest in the laboring people as a class. During the Eighties pulpit and press frequently inveighed against corporate wealth for denying to labor a living wage. During the last years of the century the interest of the denomination in the laboring classes increased perceptibly.

Notwithstanding the social aspects of the church gatherings of the Connection in the more rural sections of the South and despite the quickened interest of the denomination in the unfortunate and down-trodden classes, the church still remained primarily and essentially a house of worship. The day had not yet arrived when the Church would seek to conserve its power and extend its influence through the development of "institutional" features. It was not regarded as a function of the Church to provide recreation and amusement. Not until after the beginning of the new century were serious efforts made to establish social clubs among the poor and the unchurched. As yet houses of worship were not designed to include the kitchens, the gymnasiums, the reading rooms or social halls that were to be introduced early in the twentieth century. The Church still made no attempt to influence various aspects of the social and economic order such as child labor, the conditions of tenement life, or the plight of the newly arrived immigrant. The period was nevertheless one in which religion played a profound part in the lives of the great majority of the Southern people and the Methodist Episcopal Church, South, was able to exert a far-reaching influence upon social relations throughout the years from Appomattox to the close of the century.

BIBLIOGRAPHY

PRIMARY SOURCES

1. *Works on the Methodist Episcopal Church, South*

Alabama Conference, *Journal,* 1870-1900.

Baltimore Conference, *Journal,* 1866-1900.

Caldwell, John H., "Relations of the Colored People to the Methodist Episcopal Church, South", *Quarterly Review,* vol. xlviii (July, 1866), pp. 418-443.

Chapman, M. B., "Evolution as a Method of Creation", *The Quarterly Review,* vol. xiii (September-October, 1894), pp. 224-231.

Chappell, E. B., "Scientific Preaching", *The Methodist Review,* vol. xi (January-February, 1899), pp. 22-26.

Cotter, William Jasper, *My Autobiography.* Charles O. Jones, ed.

Daily Christian Advocate, 1866-1900. Published at various places.

Deems, Charles Force, *Autobiography of Charles Force Deems.* Edward H. Deems and Francis M. Deems, eds. New York, 1897.

Dodd, T. J., "Methodism and Advanced Thought", *The Quarterly Review,* vol. ix (October, 1890), pp. 54 ff.

Du Bose, H. M., "Bishop Haygood as a Philosopher and Reformer", *The Methodist Review,* vol. lxxviii (July-August, 1896), pp. 587-598.

Finney, Thos. M., *Life and Labors of Enoch Mather Marvin.* St. Louis, 1880.

Fitzgerald, O. P. and Galloway, C. B., *Eminent Methodists.* Nashville, 1897.

Fitzgerald, O. P., *Judge Longstreet.* Nashville, 1891.

Fitzgerald, O. P., *Sunset Views.* Nashville, 1900.

Florida Conference, *Journal,* 1865-1900.

Galloway, Chas. B., *The Editor-Bishop: Linus Parker, His Life and Writings.* Nashville, 1886.

General Conference of the Methodist Episcopal Church, South, *Journal,* 1866-1900. Published at Nashville.

Georgia Conference, *Minutes,* 1865-1900.

Green, Wm. M., *Life and Papers of A. L. P. Green, D. D.* Thomas O. Summers, ed. Nashville, 1877.

Haygood, Atticus G., ed., *Bishop Pierce's Sermons and Addresses with a Few Special Discourses by Dr. Pierce.* Nashville, 1896.

Holston Conference, *Journal,* 1873-1900.

Irby, Richard, *History of Randolph-Macon College, Virginia.* Richmond.

Leftwich, W. M., "The Race Problem in the South", *The Quarterly Review,* vol. vi (April, 1889), pp. 86-96.

Louisiana Conference, *Journal,* 1865-1900.

Louisville Conference, *Journal,* 1866-1900.

M'Anally, David Rice, *The Life and Labors of Rev. E. M. Marvin.* St. Louis, 1888.

Marvin, Enoch Mather, *The Life of Rev. William Goff Caples.* St. Louis, 1871.

Mathews, John, *Peeps Into Life, Autobiography of Rev. John Mathews, D. D.* Roanoke, Va. n. d.

McLean, John H., *Reminiscences of Rev. Jno. McLean, A. M., D. D.* Nashville. n. d.

Mellen, T. L., ed., *In Memoriam: Life and Labors of The Rev. William Hamilton Watkins.* Nashville, 1886.

Memphis Conference, *Journal,* 1866-1900.

Mississippi Conference, *Journal,* 1865-1900.

Mobile Conference, *Journal,* 1865-1869.

New Orleans Christian Advocate, 1866-1900. New Orleans, Louisiana.

North Georgia Conference, *Minutes,* 1867-1900.

North Texas Conference, *Journal,* 1865-1900.

Pell, Edward Leigh, *A Hundred Years of Richmond Methodism.* Richmond. n. d.

Redford, A. H., *Life and Times of H. H. Kavanaugh, D. D., One of the Bishops of the Methodist Episcopal Church, South.* Nashville, 1884.

Richardson, Simon Peter, *The Lights and Shadows of Itinerant Life: An Autobiography.* Nashville, 1901.

Richmond Christian Advocate, 1866-1900. Richmond, Virginia.

Rivers, R. H., *The Life of Robert Paine, D. D., Bishop of the Methodist Episcopal Church, South.* Nashville, 1884.

Smith, George G., *The Life and Letters of James Osgood Andrew, Bishop of the Methodist Episcopal Church, South.* Nashville, 1883.

South Carolina Conference, *Journal,* 1865-1900.

Southern Christian Advocate, 1865-1900. Macon, Georgia and Charleston, South Carolina.

Sullins, D., *Recollections of an Old Man.* Bristol. n. d.

The Christian Advocate, 1866-1900. Nashville, Tennessee.

Thrall, Homer S., *A Brief History of Methodism in Texas.* Nashville, 1899.

Tennessee Conference, *Journal,* 1865-1900.

Texas Conference, *Journal,* 1865-1900.

Tigert, John J., ed., *Passing through the Gates and Other Sermons by the Late Rev. Holland Nimmons McTyeire, D. D., Senior, Bishop of the Methodist Episcopal Church, South.* Nashville, 1889.

Virginia Conference, *Journal,* 1865-1900.

Wesleyan Christian Advocate, 1878-1900. Macon and Atlanta, Georgia.

West, Anson, *A History of Methodism in Alabama.* Nashville, 1893.

2. *Works on the Methodist Episcopal Church*

Alabama Conference, *Journal,* 1866-1900.

Albert, A. E. P., "The Church in the South", *The Methodist Review*, vol. lxxiv (March, 1892), pp. 237-239.

Baltimore Conference, *Journal*, 1865-1900.

Bowen, J. W. E., "An Apology for the Higher Education of the Negro", *The Methodist Review*, vol. lxxix (September-October, 1897), pp. 723-742.

Central Alabama Conference, *Journal*, 1885-1900.

Central Ohio Conference, *Minutes*, 1865-1875.

Christian Advocate, 1865-1900. New York, N. Y.

Crooks, George R., *The Life of Bishop Matthew Simpson of the Methodist Episcopal Church.* New York, 1891.

Curtiss, George L., *Manual of Methodist Episcopal Church History, Showing the Evolution of Methodism in the United States of America.* New York, 1893.

Fox, Henry J., "Our Work at the South", *Methodist Quarterly Review*, vol. lviii (January, 1874), pp. 29-44.

Fuller, Erasmus Q., *An Appeal to the Records: A Vindication of the Methodist Episcopal Church, in Its Policy and Proceedings toward the South.* New York, 1876.

Fuller, E. Q., "Our Southern Field", *Methodist Quarterly Review*, vol. lx (April, 1878), pp. 219-238.

Freedmen's Aid Society of the Methodist Episcopal Church, *Reports*, 1866-1900. Published at Cincinnati.

General Conference of the Methodist Episcopal Church, *Journal*, 1800-1900.

Georgia Conference, *Journal*, 1866-1900.

Holston Conference, *Journal*, 1866-1900.

Little Rock Conference, *Journal*, 1885-1900.

Louisiana Conference, *Journal*, 1866-1900.

Matlack, L. C., "The Methodist Episcopal Church in the Southern States", *Methodist Quarterly Review*, vol. liv (January, 1872), pp. 103-126.

Mississippi Mission Conference, *Journal*, 1865.

Mississippi Conference, *Journal*, 1867-1900.

New England Conference, *Journal*, 1864-1900.

Pearne, Thomas Hall, *Sixty-One Years of Itinerant Christian Life in Church and State.* New York, 1899.

Porter, James, "General Conference of 1844", *Methodist Quarterly Review*, vol. liii (April, 1871), pp. 234-250.

Ridgaway, Henry B., *The Life of Edmund S. Janes, D. D., LL. D., Late Senior Bishop of the Methodist Episcopal Church.* New York, 1882.

Savannah Conference, *Journal*, 1880-1900.

South Carolina Conference, *Journal*, 1866-1900.

Southwestern Christian Advocate, 1873-1900. New Orleans, Louisiana.

Stevenson, Daniel, "The Methodist Episcopal Church in the South", *The Methodist Review*, vol. lxxviii (May-June, 1896), pp. 384-396.

The Methodist, 1865-1873. New York, N. Y.

The Methodist Advocate, 1868-1882. Atlanta, Georgia.

Thompson, Edward, *Life of Edward Thompson, D. D., LL. D., Late a Bishop of the Methodist Episcopal Church.* Cincinnati, 1885.

Walsh, J. D., "Educational Work of the Methodist Episcopal Church in the South", *The Methodist Review*, vol. lxviii (May, 1886), pp. 329-347.

——, "The Methodist Episcopal Church in the South", *The Methodist Review*, vol. lxx (March, 1888), pp. 245-265.

——, "The Methodist Episcopal Church in the South", *The Methodist Review*, vol. lxxii (January-February, 1890), pp. 35-52.

Wilson, W. W. W., "The Methodist Episcopal Church in Her Relations to the Negro in the South", *The Methodist Review*, vol. lxxv (September-October, 1894), pp. 713-723.

Zion's Herald, 1865-1900. Boston, Massachusetts.

3. *Other Works Pertaining to American Methodism*

Cobleigh, E. N., "Southern Reconstruction", *Methodist Quarterly Review*, vol. lii (July, 1870), pp. 379-397.
——, "Church Property Questions in the South", *Methodist Quarterly Review*, vol. liii (October, 1871), pp. 614-641.

Curry, D., "The Afro-American", *Methodist Quarterly Review*, vol. 1 (April, 1868), pp. 229-252.

De Puy, W. H., ed., *The Methodist Centennial Year-Book for 1884, the One Hundredth Year of the Separate Organization of American Methodism.* New York, 1884.

Drinkhouse, Edward J., *History of Methodist Reform . . . with Special and Comprehensive Reference to Its Most Salient Exhibition in the History of the Methodist Protestant Church.* 2 v. Baltimore, 1899.

Elliot, Charles, *South-Western Methodism.* LeRoy M. Vernon, ed. Cincinnati, 1868.

Foster, R. S., *Union of Episcopal Methodism.* New York, 1892.

Gaines, Wesley J., *African Methodism in the South, or Twenty-Five Years of Freedom.* Atlanta, 1890.

Goss, C. C., *Statistical History of the First Century of American Methodism: With a Summary of the Origin and Present Operations of Other Denominations.* New York, 1866.

Jewell, Horace, *History of Methodism in Arkansas.* Little Rock, 1892.

Lewis, W. H., *The History of Methodism in Missouri for a Decade of Years from 1860 to 1870.* 3 v. Nashville, 1890.

Matlack, Lucius C., "The Disruption of Methodism", *Methodist Quarterly Review*, vol. lviii (April, 1876), pp. 292-308.

McTyeire, Holland N., *History of Methodism.* Nashville, 1884.

Merrill, S. M., *The Organic Union of American Methodism.* New York, 1892.

Mitchell, James, *The Life and Times of Levi Scott, D. D.* New York, 1885.

Myers, Edward H., *The Disruption of the Methodist Episcopal Church, 1844-1846: Comprising a Thirty Years' History of the Relations of the Two Methodisms.* Macon, 1875.

Payne, Daniel A., *African Methodist Episcopal Church.* Nashville, 1891.

Pearne, Thomas H., "The Freedmen", *Methodist Quarterly Review,* vol. lix (January, 1877), pp. 462 ff.

Shipp, Albert M., *The History of Methodism in South Carolina.* Nashville, 1884.

Simpson, Matthew, *A Hundred Years of Methodism.* New York, 1876.

Smith, Geo. G., Jr., *The History of Methodism in Georgia and Florida, from 1785 to 1865.* Macon, 1877.

The Methodist Almanac, 1864-1870. Published at New York.

Woodward, W. S., *Annals of Methodism in Missouri.* Columbia, Missouri, 1893.

4. *Miscellaneous Works*

Arnold, S. C., "Education Among the Freedmen", *Methodist Quarterly Review,* vol. lx (January, 1878), pp. 43-67.

Burke, Emily P., *Reminiscences of Georgia.* Oberlin, Ohio, 1850.

De Bow, J. D. B., *Statistical View . . . embracing a Compendium of the Seventh Census.* Washington, 1854.

Dorchester, Daniel, *Christianity in the United States, from the First Settlement Down to the Present Time.* New York, 1888.

Fox, Henry J., "The Negro", *Methodist Quarterly Review,* vol. lvii (January, 1875), pp. 79-97.

Hartzell, J. C., "The Negro Exodus", *Methodist Quarterly Review,* vol. lxi (October, 1879), pp. 722-747.

——, "The Problem of Education in the Southern States", *The Methodist Review,* vol. lxxiv (January-February, 1892), pp. 39-50.

Haygood, Atticus G., *Our Brother in Black.* New York, 1881.

——, "The South and the School Problem", *Harper's New Monthly Magazine,* vol. lxxix (July, 1889), pp. 225-231.

——, *The New South.* Pamphlet. Published at Oxford, Georgia, 1880.

Henneman, J. B., "The Study of English in the South", *The Sewanee Review,* vol. ii (February, 1894), pp. 180-197.

Leftwich, W. M., *Martyrdom in Missouri, A History of Religious Proscription, the Seizure of Churches, and the Persecution of Ministers of the Gospel, in the State of Missouri during the Late Civil War and under the "Test Oath" of the New Constitution.* 2 v. St. Louis, 1870.

McPherson, Edward, *The Political History of the United States of America, during the Great Rebellion, including . . . a Chapter on the Church and the Rebellion. . . .* Washington, 1865.

Niles' Register, 1840-1845. Baltimore, Maryland.

Pearne, Thomas H., "The Race Question—The Situation", *The Methodist Review,* vol. lxxii (September-October, 1890), pp. 690-705.

Report on . . . the Tenth Census, vol. vii. Washington, 1884.

Scomp, H. A., *King Alcohol in the Realm of King Cotton.* Emory College, 1888.

Senate Executive Document, No. 6, 39th Congress, 2nd. Session.

Smith, Charles Forster, "Southern Schools and Colleges", *The Atlantic Monthly,* vol. liv (October, 1884), pp. 542-557.

Statistics . . . of the Ninth Census, vol. i. Washington, 1874.

Statistics . . . of the Eleventh Census, vol. xvi. Washington, 1894.

Stevens, Abel, "The Problem of Our African Population", *Methodist Quarterly Review,* vol. lxvi (January, 1884), pp. 108-126.

Testimony Taken by the Joint Select Committee to Inquire into the Condition of Affairs in the Late Insurrectionary States. 13 v. Washington, 1872.

War of the Rebellion: A Compilation of the Official Records of the Union and Confederate Armies. 129 v. Washington, 1880-1900.

Wilmer, Richard Hooker, *The Recent Past from a Southern Standpoint.* New York, 1887.

SECONDARY SOURCES

1. *Works Relating to Methodism*

Alexander, Gross, *History of the Methodist Episcopal Church, South (American Church History Series,* vol. xi). New York, 1894.

Andrews, W. T., ed. and comp., *Memorial Sketches of the Lives and Labors of the Deceased Ministers of the North Alabama Conference, Methodist Episcopal Church, South (1870-1912).* Nashville, 1912.

Boswell, John W., *A Short History of Methodism.* Nashville, 1905.

Bowden, Haygood S., *History of Savannah Methodism.* Macon, Georgia, 1929.

Bowen, William A., *Why Two Episcopal Methodist Churches in the United States.* Nashville, 1901.

Buckley, James M., *A History of Methodism in the United States (American Church History Series,* vol. v). New York, 1898.

Candler, Warren A., *Bishop Charles Betts Galloway, A Prince of Preachers and a Christian Statesman.* Nashville, 1927.

Chappell, E. B., *Recent Development of Religious Education in the Methodist Episcopal Church, South, An Interpretation.* Nashville, 1935.

Gross, Robert Allen, *The History of Southern Methodism in New Orleans.* New Orleans, 1931.

Culbreth, J. M., *Studies in Methodist History.* Nashville, 1924.

Denny, Collins, ed., *A Manual of the Discipline of the Methodist Episcopal Church, South, Including the Decisions of the College of Bishops.* Originally prepared by Holland N. McTyeire. Nashville, 1931.

Du Bose, Horace M., *A History of Methodism, being a Volume Supplemental to "A History of Methodism" by Holland N. McTyeire, D. D., Late One of the Bishops of the Methodist Episcopal Church, South.* Nashville, 1916.

Du Bose, Horace M., *Life of Joshua Soule.* Nashville, 1916.

——, *Life and Memories of Rev. J. D. Barbee.* Nashville, 1906.

Duncan, Watson Boone, ed., *Carlisle Memorial Volume.* Nashville, 1926.

——, *Studies in Methodist Literature.* Nashville, 1914.

Hamil, H. M., ed., *Manual of Southern Methodism including Church History, Doctrine, Polity, and Missions.* Nashville, 1914.

Hawkins, H. G., and Caine, G. B., *Historic Sites of Mississippi Methodism.* Vicksburg, 1934.

Hudson, Hilary T., *The Methodist Armor: or A Popular Exposition of the Doctrines, Peculiar Usages, and Ecclesiastical Machinery of the Methodist Episcopal Church, South.* Nashville, 1924.

Hurst, John Fletcher, *The History of Methodism.* New York, 1903.

Jarrell, Charles C. and others, *Methodism on the March.* Nashville, 1924.

Luccock, Halford E., and Hutchinson, Paul, *The Story of Methodism.* New York, 1926.

Neely, Thomas B., *American Methodism, Its Division and Unification.* New York, 1915.

Neely, Thomas B., *The Bishops and the Supervisional System of the Methodist Episcopal Church.* Cincinnati, 1912.

Norwood, John Nelson, *The Schism in the Methodist Episcopal Church, 1844.* Alfred, N. Y., 1923.

Plyler, A. W., *The Iron Duke of the Methodist Itinerancy.* Nashville, 1925.

Plyer, Marion Timothy, *Thomas Neal Ivey.* Nashville, 1925.

Price, R. N., *Holston Methodism,* 5 v. Nashville, 1906-1914.

Rankin, G. C., *The Story of My Life.* Nashville, 1912.

Steel, S. A., *Eminent Men I Met along the Sunny Road.* Nashville.

Sweet, William Warren, "Methodist Church Influence in Southern Politics", *The Mississippi Valley Historical Review,* vol. i (March, 1915), pp. 548 ff.

——, *The Methodist Episcopal Church and the Civil War.* Cincinnati, 1912.

Tigert, Jno. J., *A Constitutional History of American Episcopal Methodism.* Nashville, 1916.

Vincent, Leon H., *John Heyl Vincent, A Biographical Sketch.* New York, 1925.

Wade, John Donald, *Augustus Baldwin Longstreet, A Study of the Development of Culture in the South.* New York, 1924.

2. *Miscellaneous*

Boone, Richard G., *Education in the United States, Its History from the Earliest Settlements.* New York, 1889.

Brown, William Garrot, *The Lower South in American History.* New York, 1902.

Carroll, H. K., *The Religious Forces in the United States . . . Census of 1890 (American Church History Series,* vol. i). New York, 1893.

Clark, Willis G., *History of Education in Alabama.* Washington, 1889.

Raper, Arthur F., *The Tragedy of Lynching.* Chapel Hill, 1933.

Raper, Charles Lee, *The Church and Private Schools of North Carolina*. Greensboro, 1889.

Roland, Dunbar, *History of Mississippi, the Heart of the South*. 2 v. Chicago-Jackson, 1925.

Schlesinger, Arthur Meier, *A Critical Period in American Religion*. Boston, 1933.

——, *The Rise of the City, 1878-1898* (History of American Life, vol. x). New York, 1933.

Simkins, Francis Butler and Woody, Robert Hilliard, *South Carolina During Reconstruction*. Chapel Hill, 1932.

Smith, Charles Lee, *The History of Education in North Carolina*. Washington, 1888.

Smith, Charles Forster, *Reminiscences and Sketches*. Nashville, 1908.

Tillett, Wilbur Fisk, *The Paths that Lead to God, A New Survey of the Grounds of Theistic and Christian Belief*. Nashville, 1926.

Sweet, William Warren, *The Story of Religions in America*. New York, 1930.

Vander Velde, Lewis G., *The Presbyterian Churches and the Federal Union, 1861-1869*. Cambridge, 1932.

White, Andrew Dickson, *A History of the Warfare of Science with Theology in Christendom*. 2 v. New York, 1896.

Woodbridge, S. Homer, *Anti-Lottery Campaign*. Washington, 1921.

Woodson, Carter G., *The History of the Negro Church*. Washington, 1921.

APPENDIX A

VALUE OF CHURCH PROPERTY OF MORE IMPORTANT RELIGIOUS GROUPS IN INDIVIDUAL SOUTHERN STATES IN 1890[1]

	Methodist	Baptist	Presbyterian	Roman Catholic	Protestant Episcopal	Christian
Alabama	$2,278,988	$2,110,362	$ 819,225	$ 602,750	$ 655,752	$ 5,626
Arkansas	1,200,842	1,066,104	357,685	219,750	196,122	1,600
Delaware	1,116,125	184,300	709,800	201,500	388,000	———
Florida	829,551	375,936	484,650	225,100	390,561	———
Georgia	2,783,267	3,109,390	776,025	485,123	492,300	———
Kentucky	2,718,518	3,020,742	748,375	1,800,550	758,800	500
Louisiana	1,134,992	988,967	8,000	1,573,200	387,950	5,605
Maryland	5,347,527	831,275	1,752,424	2,108,670	2,427,406	———
Mississippi	1,625,269	1,431,032	530,290	321,525	322,960	———
Missouri	4,232,428	2,980,316	2,789,652	4,070,370	977,600	12,791
North Carolina	2,418,984	2,556,147	818,745	90,262	545,010	97,705
South Carolina	1,658,182	1,606,385	896,635	384,500	590,234	———
Tennessee	3,491,360	2,561,873	2,002,605	434,200	575,900	———
Texas	2,677,391	2,119,096	1,241,485	1,018,800	624,900	———
Virginia	2,910,835	3,152,582	1,234,501	458,800	1,035,978	66,100
District of Columbia	1,543,000	914,450	950,000	1,015,800	790,500	———
Total	$38,167,259	$29,008,657	$16,120,097	$15,010,250	$12,159,973	$189,926

[1]Compiled from *Statistics of The . . . Eleventh Census*, vol. xvi, pp. 32-38.

APPENDIX A—*Continued*

NUMBER OF COMMUNICANTS OF MORE IMPORTANT RELIGIOUS GROUPS IN INDIVIDUAL SOUTHERN STATES IN 1890[1]

	Methodist	Baptist	Presbyterian	Roman Catholic	Protestant Episcopal	Christian
Alabama	242,624	258,405	21,502	13,230	6,085	687
Arkansas	123,316	128,724	18,022	3,845	2,381	181
Delaware	25,786	2,006	4,622	11,776	2,858	
Florida	70,458	41,647	4,574	16,867	4,225	97
Georgia	275,784	357,241	14,538	11,228	5,225	
Kentucky	141,521	229,525	40,880	92,504	7,161	2,146
Louisiana	65,693	98,552	5,864	211,863	5,167	
Maryland	123,618	16,238	12,483	141,410	24,223	
Mississippi	164,589	224,612	18,250	11,348	3,560	
Missouri	162,514	159,371	53,510	162,864	8,953	1,627
North Carolina	276,336	310,920	36,102	2,640	8,186	12,736
South Carolina	251,477	203,959	26,118	5,360	7,465	
Tennessee	223,116	185,189	66,573	17,950	5,671	
Texas	218,890	248,523	37,811	99,691	7,097	118
Virginia	154,693	303,134	27,746	12,356	20,420	5,770
District of Columbia	16,369	19,372	5,128	37,539	7,476	
Total	2,536,784	2,777,317	393,723	812,471	116,148	12,362

[1]Compiled from *Statistics of The . . . Eleventh Census*, vol. xvi, pp. 38-43.

APPENDIX A—*Continued*

SEATING CAPACITY OF CHURCH EDIFICES OF METHODIST, BAPTIST, AND OF ALL OTHER DENOMINATIONS IN SOUTHERN STATES IN 1890[1]

	Methodist	Baptist	All Other Denominations
Alabama	620,970	906,734	174,183
Arkansas	375,622	518,813	146,565
Delaware	65,940	6,332	38,900
Florida	180,142	151,843	59,147
Georgia	735,033	1,237,431	136,102
Kentucky	391,635	662,455	450,646
Louisiana	182,525	321,455	113,294
Maryland	353,235	37,659	327,565
Mississippi	466,026	732,285	152,231
Missouri	518,301	536,240	808,058
North Carolina	739,557	1,096,084	245,194
South Carolina	497,837	521,009	181,062
Tennessee	689,466	719,815	402,681
Texas	570,328	667,120	330,297
Virginia	410,335	689,609	390,731
District of Columbia	274,891	126,320	401,211
Total	7,199,749	8,959,675	4,405,482

[1]Compiled from *Statistics of The . . . Eleventh Census*, vol. xvi, pp. 38-43.

APPENDIX B

CHURCH ACCOMMODATIONS OF MORE IMPORTANT RELIGIOUS GROUPS IN INDIVIDUAL SLAVEHOULDING STATES IN 1860[1]

	Methodist	Baptist	Presbyterian	Roman Catholic	Protestant Episcopal	Christian
Alabama	212,555	238,055	64,124	8,000	13,840	6,330
Arkansas	102,000	60,503	34,885	2,750	1,615	6,450
Delaware	37,695	3,480	12,210	2,770	8,780	—
Florida	30,360	20,325	9,580	4,350	3,175	—
Georgia	309,079	376,686	50,097	4,300	8,675	2,750
Kentucky	228,100	267,860	98,775	44,820	9,940	104,980
Louisiana	52,181	47,785	17,350	57,600	16,525	950
Maryland	165,191	31,775	24,525	43,487	58,344	875
Mississippi	168,705	172,703	75,002	5,528	8,175	7,020
Missouri	150,160	141,515	77,855	38,826	8,755	54,000
North Carolina	328,497	280,341	83,577	3,250	26,695	12,795
South Carolina	149,812	170,130	70,525	8,705	30,109	1,200
Tennessee	288,460	214,381	159,800	4,305	6,940	35,100
Texas	103,799	77,435	38,417	12,772	8,480	15,905
Virginia	483,244	317,504	117,304	16,650	68,498	24,085
District of Columbia	17,500	3,340	8,650	8,200	9,000	—
Total	2,788,338	2,413,818	728,988	942,676	266,313	273,900

[1]This chart was compiled from figures given in the *Statistics . . . of the Eighth Census*, Miscellaneous volume, pp. 352-501.

APPENDIX B—Continued

VALUE OF CHURCH PROPERTY OF MORE IMPORTANT RELIGIOUS GROUPS IN INDIVIDUAL SLAVEHOLDING STATES IN 1860[1]

	Methodist	Baptist	Presbyterian	Roman Catholic	Protestant Episcopal	Christian
Alabama	$ 606,270	$ 495,599	$ 368,500	$ 230,450	$ 196,050	$ 11,680
Arkansas	185,483	107,595	107,200	23,300	11,000	12,625
Delaware	282,000	47,150	254,100	51,300	154,900	
Florida	111,325	47,915	49,450	31,200	44,000	
Georgia	796,138	787,198	445,005	148,500	211,250	7,050
Kentucky	808,305	888,530	719,885	695,850	199,100	449,810
Louisiana	336,815	231,945	306,600	1,744,700	334,000	13,550
Maryland	1,233,850	143,450	518,050	1,611,500	1,339,400	11,000
Mississippi	575,770	408,499	334,951	117,050	136,900	34,100
Missouri	959,125	573,260	855,325	1,391,632	261,100	203,800
North Carolina	628,859	481,099	389,670	41,300	313,230	22,295
South Carolina	632,948	699,528	718,885	304,300	818,130	6,660
Tennessee	763,655	497,210	785,780	208,400	165,000	94,720
Texas	319,934	228,030	167,980	189,900	111,250	27,395
Virginia	1,619,010	1,244,115	901,020	329,300	873,120	72,500
District of Columbia	190,250	46,000	8,650	269,300	183,400	
Total	$10,050,139	$ 7,227,123	$ 6,930,991	$ 7,387,582	$ 5,151,830	$967,185

[1] *Ibid.* Where some denominations, like the Roman Catholic, owned large properties not used primarily for the purpose of worship, these figures do not afford an accurate comparison of denominational strength.

INDEX